The Penn State Series in German Literature

THE PENN STATE SERIES IN GERMAN LITERATURE

General Editor
Joseph P. Strelka, The Pennsylvania State University

Editorial Board

German Baroque Poetry 1618–1723, by Robert M. Browning

War, Weimar, and Literature: The Story of the Neue Merkur, *1914–1925*,
by Guy Stern

War, Weimar, and Literature

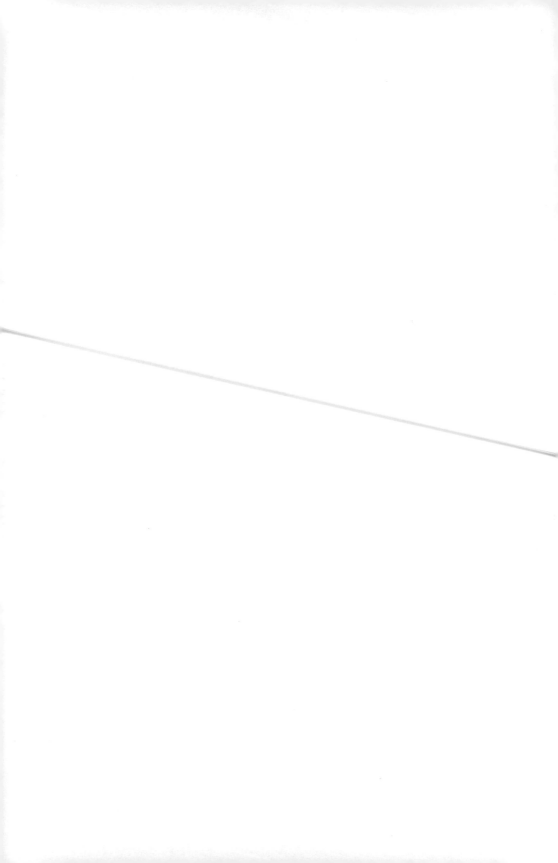

Efraim Frisch

*Portrait by Suzanne Cavallo-Schulein exhibited at
the Leo Baeck Institute, New York. Used by permission
of the artist and the Leo Baeck Institute.*

War, Weimar, and Literature

The Story of the *Neue Merkur*

1914-1925

Guy Stern

The Pennsylvania State University Press

University Park and London

ISBN: 0–271–01147–5
Library of Congress Catalog Card No. 71–136960
Copyright © 1971 by The Pennsylvania State University Press
All rights reserved
Printed in the United States of America
Designed by Glenn Ruby

Published with the help of the Leo Baeck
Institute, Inc., New York, and the Charles
Phelps Taft Memorial Fund of the University
of Cincinnati.

to my wife Margith and my friend Max Kreutzberger

Foreword

When, in 1945—the Year Zero for Germany politically (though not spiritually)—I planned to bring into being a "German periodical for European thought," the compelling memory of one of the most outstanding journals of the second and third decade of the century—the "Neue Merkur" helped me to my title. Readers of both magazines cannot fail to notice that much of the tradition of the older journal has been preserved and continued in the *Merkur*. Important authors of the *Neue Merkur*, ranging from Ferdinand Lion to Rudolf Kassner, frequently had a voice in my magazine during its first decade. Furthermore, the two publications suffered in a similar way from the vicissitudes of fate. Readers of the following study will easily discover parallels not only in respect to a situation of permanent crisis, but also in terms of continual resurrection, in spite of crisis.

This study transmits a true-to-life image of a cultural journal for an intellectual elite, whose threatened situation can be traced, step by step, in every interval of a period now more than a generation behind us. It is not too much to say that all of us who aspire to be successors, in the best sense of the word, to this intellectual achievement, which was wrested from crisis, continue to be nourished by it.

I am familiar with the author's previous writings about the *Neue Merkur*: they are informative chronicles filled with suspense even for an expert on the subject. Again, this volume recreates the age of the *Neue Merkur*; the collaboration and friendship which bound Efraim Frisch and Wilhelm Hausenstein seems to us now a symptomatic instance of German-Jewish symbiosis.

That each good history of a journal is likewise a history of the times is once again demonstrated in this study. If I had any choice in the matter, I should hope that my own journal might attract an equally committed chronicler, when in the distant future its history comes to be written.

HANS PAESCHKE

* Hans Paeschke is co-founder and editor of *Merkur*, one of the most distinguished literary magazines of the German-speaking countries.

Acknowledgments

I would like to express sincere thanks to the Leo Baeck Institute of New York and to the Taft Committee of the University of Cincinnati for grants towards publication of this monograph; also to the Fulbright Commission, the Bollingen Foundation, and the Joint Claims Conference, whose grants made possible archival research and complementary interviews in Germany, Austria, Switzerland, and the United States. For letting me use unpublished material I am greatly indebted to Mrs. Fega Frisch and Dr. Bella Schlesinger, the literary executors of Efraim Frisch, Messrs. Ludwig Hollweg and Richard Lemp, the directors, respectively, of the Monacensia and the Handschriftenabteilung of the Stadtbibliothek München, Dr. Heinz Starkulla of the Zeitungswissenschaftliche Institute of the Universität München, and Dr. Max Kreutzberger of the Leo Baeck Institute. All gave most generously of their time and helped with numerous research problems.

An earlier version of the introduction and parts of Chapter 1 have appeared in the *Yearbook of the Leo Baeck Institute* and brief passages of other chapters in the *German Quarterly*, *Publizistik*, and in my introductions to *Efraim Frisch: Zum Verständnis des Geistigen* (Heidelberg: Lambert Schneider) and *Konstellationen* (Stuttgart: Deutsche Verlags-Anstalt). I thank their publishers for permission to reprint.

The aid of the many relatives, friends, and acquaintances of Efraim Frisch and Wilhelm Hausenstein and of past contributors to their magazine who made documents available to me or granted me interviews cannot be acknowledged here individually. In several instances thanks appear at appropriate places in the text, but my gratitude goes equally to those I could not mention.

I am grateful to my colleagues Fritz Schlawe and Hugh Staples, who gave my manuscript a close and critical reading; also to Dr. Ernest Hamburger, Max Kreutzberger, Heinz Starkulla, and Walter F. Sokel, all of whom read and commented on one or more chapters of this book. For valuable help in editing the manuscript I should like to thank Klaus Uwe Kuchler, Mrs. Erna Bernstein, Mrs. Karin Clark, and Mrs. Virginia Mueller. My wife helped me in my many interviews; she, Dr. Max Kreutzberger, and his colleagues at the Leo Baeck Institute, especially Dr. Margaret Muehsam, Arnold Schoenenberg, and Dr. Fred Grubel, all greatly encouraged me during the years I relived, *kat exochen*, the adventures of the *Neue Merkur*.

Contents

Introduction

The publishing history of leading literary and intellectual magazines has been a favorite and traditional research topic both in Europe and the United States. Some of them, like Lina Morino's history of *La Nouvelle Revue Française*, Thomas W. Beach's of the *Spectator*, Wilmont Haacke's of the *Deutsche Rundschau*, Nicholas Joost's of *The Dial*, and, on a more popular level, Dale Kramer's of the *New Yorker*, have become records not only of the journal itself, but also of its time and environment.[1] The *Neue Merkur*, a German belletristic and political journal, which appeared from 1914 to 1916 and from 1919 to 1925, never enjoyed the wide popularity of these rivals and, compared with some of them, may be said to have died in its infancy. Yet, judging from the magazine itself, its editorial correspondence, contemporary reviews, and from statements of surviving contributors and subscribers, the depth and endurance of its effect compensated for its short life-span.

Considering the times and the magazine's precarious finances, it is surprising it lasted as long as it did. In the course of its short and troubled history the *Neue Merkur* never had more than 1,500 subscribers, an average sale of 200 by bookshops in Berlin, and even less in most of the other large cities of Germany. At best its sales sufficed to pay minimum rates to its contributors, and its recurring financial troubles twice forced a suspension, and finally the cessation of publication.

World and local events added to its difficulties. The magazine—or its beleaguered staff –had to weather one world war, an inflation, a deflation, a local (and temporarily successful) Communist revolution, a short-lived fascist government, Hitler's Beer Hall Putsch, together with such minor annoyances as a printers' strike, censorship, a "deserter" among the business staff, and the suicide of one of its most able and regular contributors.[2]

Yet from the very beginnings the *Neue Merkur*, despite its multiple troubles, was able to gather around itself a sparkling group of steady contributors ("all of the specialist collaborators are leaders in their specialties," said the *Literaria Almanach* of 1921) and to draw frequently on Europe's most prominent writers and thinkers (among them Thomas Mann, Heinrich Mann, Bertolt Brecht, Jakob Wassermann, Alfred Döblin, Max Picard, André Gide, Alfred Weber, Martin Buber, and George Bernard Shaw). It also became an outlet for young and hitherto unknown, often avant-garde authors whom it helped to gain and policies that emerge from its pages, from its editorial correspondence and from subsequent interviews. Together with the expected controversies about fashions, fads, and factions in the arts, music, and philosophy, one also finds some highly unexpected commentaries on current political events and personalities. Walther Rathenau, for example, did not become a hero to the liberal staff of the *Neue Merkur* until after his assassination, while Ludwig Klages, despite his anti-Semitism, never became their villain. World War I, a particularly fascinating period as seen through the perspective of the *Neue Merkur*, brought forth such paradoxes as a pacifist arguing for war and an Austrian advocating Austria's annexation by Germany.[9]

Beyond opinions and facts, the magazine also reveals the fears and hopes of its makers. Many of the articles and letters indulged in prognoses. It is easy, in retrospect, to smile at the utopian delusions, the faith in a speedy German victory and a post-bellum United Europe, which would give birth to social equality and a triumphant and lasting democratic form of government; it is equally easy to deplore the all but complete myopia vis-à-vis Hitler and the rise of National Socialism. But despite errors in pre-judgment (some of which may yet be redeemed by a more euphoric future), there also appeared some amazing examples of clairvoyance, such as the startling prediction of 1915 that the war would catapult Hindenburg from relative obscurity to political prominence.[10] Also, Frisch's rejection notes to some of Germany's most highly reputed political observers reflect extraordinary prescience: More often than not subsequent events confounded the experts and upheld the editor.[11]

Similarly the literary contributions to the *Neue Merkur*, if read in conjunction with the correspondence, provides us with a view of history of literature in the making, a glimpse upon the literary market place. For that reason the literature of the *Neue Merkur* is examined here as one unit and, in the main, in chronological order. Also since works of literature invariably appear in the *Merkur* together with timely essays, today's reader can discern what, beyond their intrinsic strengths and shortcomings, made them topical. Frequently the poems and works of fiction convey the spirit of their times as well or better than the essays. Conversely the essays often are literature.

In looking at the literature of the *Neue Merkur* as a unit, one is struck by the fact that the magazine championed the concept "world literature" both in theory, often through the inspired pen of its "discovery," Ernst Robert Curtius, and in practice. The *Neue Merkur* introduced German readers to Pirandello and Isaak Babel, to D. H. Lawrence and the early works of Flaubert unpublished in his lifetime. There was scarcely an issue that did not include both German and foreign authors. As recently as

1968 Hans Paeschke, the editor of the present-day magazine *Merkur*, had reason to recall the dedication to "European thought" that linked his magazine to its predecessor, the *Neue Merkur*.[12] The accolade is well deserved.

Finally, the *Neue Merkur* represented one of the last examples of a mutually beneficial co-operation between German Jews and German Christians in the editorship of various journals. It was a tradition which had begun with the collaboration of Lessing and Moses Mendelssohn on the *Briefe die neueste Literatur betreffend*, and had continued, in the nineteenth century, with such ventures as Friedrich Schlegel and Dorothea Mendelssohn-Schlegel's *Europa* and, in the twentieth, with Carl von Ossietzki and Kurt Tucholsky's *Weltbühne*; Hugo von Hofmannsthal, Rudolf Alexander Schröder, and Rudolf Borchardt's *Hesperus,* and Michael Georg Conrad, Karl Bleibtreu, Ludwig Jacobowski, and Conrad Alberti's (Sittenfeld) *Gesellschaft*—to name a few among many.

In the *Neue Merkur* Efraim Frisch, a German-speaking Jew from Austrian Galicia, and Wilhelm Hausenstein from Hornberg in the Black Forest (later ambassador of the Federal Republic of Germany to France) joined hands as co-contributors and, briefly, as co-editors. By their close collaboration they not only enriched each other's patrimony, but created, without discarding their own, a new though lamentably short-lived legacy.[13]

Frisch, the *spiritus rector* of the magazine, was superbly qualified for his part in this symbiosis. He was born in 1873 in Stryj in Galicia. His parents, Manasse and Amalie Frisch, rather well-to-do merchants of the town, sent their son to the "K.K. Rudolf-Gymnasium" at Brody (in Eastern Galicia), but at the same time saw to it that his Jewish education, begun in their orthodox household, was not neglected. Many of Frisch's most successful short stories, at all stages of his career as a writer, are testimony to the duality of his education; they evoke the borderland in which the traditions of Western culture and Eastern Jewry peaceably interlink or interlock in conflict. In one of his earliest works, "Die Kantine," he tells the story of a Jewish couple who manage the canteen in an Austrian garrison, their success in business, the seduction of the wife by an Austrian officer, and her ultimate suicide. And in his posthumously published character sketch "Gedalje" he portrays a resourceful Jew who is sent to Siberia during World War I "as a hostage for Franz Josef, our Emperor."

Frisch wrote of both worlds with equal facility. His knowledge of Western culture, acquired at the Rudolf-Gymnasium and the Universities of Vienna, Berlin, and Kiel, was as broad and profound as his understanding of the *Talmud*, Hasidic lore, and cabalistic mysticism which he had gained at his local *cheder*. In fact, his "Four Lectures About Judaism," held at Ascona, Switzerland, in 1938, reveal a close familiarity with Jewish tradition.

The world in which Efraim Frisch moved after his university years also included the same spheres. In 1902, he married Fega Lifschitz, whose background and interests ran parallel with his. Born in Grodno as the daughter of an orthodox, middle-class merchant family, she had pursued her studies of natural sciences and philosophy at the Universities of Berlin and Zürich but also shared her husband's aesthetic appreciation of the arts and literature. She was, in fact, to become a much sought-after translator of Russian and Polish literature into German. When Efraim Frisch, in 1908, joined the Deutsche Theater of Max Reinhardt as dramaturgist, the circle of friends which gathered around the young couple was indicative of the Frisches' abiding interest in both German and Jewish culture. Among their close acquaintances were Christian Morgenstern and Micha Joseph Berdyczewski, Joseph Ponten and Martin Buber, Eduard Stucken and Moritz Heimann, Heinrich Mann and Jakob Wassermann. When Frisch subsequently accepted the offer of the Georg Müller Verlag to become a reader and, later, the editor of the *Neue Merkur*, most of his Berlin friends were among the first "recruits" for his newly founded magazine. This impressive reservoir of talent helped sustain the magazine during its infancy. And many of these first contributors were still present when the magazine, in the words of Harry Pross, had become known for "exquisite humanistic essays of great quality" and for "literature of high standards and transcending all directions."[14]

War, Weimar, and Literature

1   *Mercury and Mars*

1914-1916

The *Neue Merkur* was born under the constellation of Mars. Four months after the appearance of the first issue the shots at Sarajevo foredoomed its initial phase, its publication under the aegis of the Georg Müller Verlag. Within a year and a half most of its staff, including its editor-in-chief, were serving in the armies of Germany or Austria. Despite the efforts of Fega Frisch, the editor's wife, Arthur Kauffmann, the temporary editor, the frequent assistance of August Mayer,[1] and Frisch's continued guidance by mail, the *Neue Merkur* joined, in 1916, many other German publications in war-induced quiescence.[2]

In fact it is likely, if Efraim Frisch and the Georg Müller Verlag had been blessed with prescience, that the *Neue Merkur* would never have seen the light of day. But few German publishers were more perspicacious than German politicians. Thus in the first month of 1914, at the very brink of World War I, three German publishers, emulating numerous competitors, decided to sponsor magazines as an adjunct to their book publishing. Cotta began with the *Greif*, Stackmann followed with the *Turmhahn*, and Georg Müller with the *Neue Merkur: Monatsschrift für geistiges Leben*. Of the three the last one was by far the most ambitious and, a rare public tribute to excellence, the one that survived longest.

From its inception the *Neue Merkur* reflected the thoughts, attitudes, and occasionally the prejudices of Efraim Frisch, its editor. Ever since he had joined the publishing house in 1911 as reader and editor of its publicity journal, he had urged upon Georg Müller the launching of a magazine. With characteristic frankness he told the Georg Müller Verlag that he held a firmly fixed image of the proposed magazine and that he would not lightly deviate from his plans.[3]

It is to the credit of Georg Müller that he consented to Efraim Frisch's terms and, in fact, went to inordinate lengths to keep faith with his editor. While it was one thing to defer all editorial matters to Frisch before his induction in early June 1915 (as Müller did, for example, in a letter of 7 January of that year), it was a completely different matter to leave decisions to Frisch while he was already on active service! Thus Müller wrote Kurt Hiller on 26 June, 1915: Since Frisch now had a permanent address, the decision about the acceptance of contributions would mainly rest with him. Müller's steadfastness always bred delays and often chaos. Thus Kurt Hiller, responding one day later to Müller's letter, could muster nothing but sarcasm for such a "time-wasting" arrangement: he pointed out that the editor was tremendously occupied by military duties, also that the postal connections between Munich and Hungary left something to be desired. And suppose Frisch were ordered to the Turkish theater of war or suppose he should become a Russian prisoner-of-war? He could hardly edit the *Merkur* long-distance from Siberia. Hiller asked to be excused for his sarcasm, but pointed out that he was speaking out in Müller's interest as well. These and similar remonstrances did not avail with the publisher. It might not have been an efficient way of editing a magazine, but this attempt, in the midst of a world conflagration, to combine the arts of Mars and Mercury (in whom Frisch primarily saw the protector of the Muses) appear today singularly appealing.

Of course Müller's compliance with his editor's wishes was also based on shared convictions. When he founded his firm in 1903, Müller had argued that a publishing house must not be doctrinaire: "To be creative, in the spirit of Goethe, means not swearing allegiance to any one direction."[4] Both Müller and Frisch extended this policy to the *Neue Merkur*; as Willy Wolfradt, the distinguished art critic and former editor of the Rowohlt publishing house, put it in an interview of 22 August, 1962: "That is precisely what I liked about the *Neue Merkur*, that it gave a hearing to the entire compass of opinions." Frisch and Müller clung to their announced purposes not only against outright and considerable pressure but also against the small but never absent annoyances of life in pre-war and wartime Germany.

One of the tangible pressures was censorship. While it is not possible to identify the articles snipped by the censors' scissors—even correspondence *about* censorship seems to have been avoided—their handiwork in the *Merkur* was observed by a contemporary reviewer: "With its pacifistic leanings . . . [the *Neue Merkur*] seems to suffer a bit, currently, from censorship, although this does not diminish its quality."[5] Also articles likely to invite censorship troubles were occasionally rejected outright. In a letter of 12 October, 1915 to Professor Friedrich Hirth, Müller, acting for Frisch, rejected Hirth's article on Italian foreign policy. He based his rejection, in part, on his fear that difficulties with the censor would probably ensue.

Except for this concession to the inevitable, Frisch did not compromise his editorial policies. He spelled them out, both in theory and by precept, in the very first issue. According to a reviewer of the times, this issue betrayed "an inner singularity of purpose, apparent to the more sensitive observer, which expresses the program of the editor almost more clearly than the lead editorial of the magazine."[6] Despite its demanding compactness, this lead editorial is actually quite clear and deserves to be summarized at some length as a guide to Frisch's publishing policy.

Frisch begins his disquisition with a survey of the German scene. We are confronted today, he argues, by a chaos of conflicting intellectual endeavors; we have come to accept all of them undiscriminatingly, using their temporary success as sole yardstick. Our young people, out of an intense desire to give shape to inner needs, often attack not merely the current emptiness of certain artistic forms but the form itself; they do not realize that an exuberant advocacy or formulation of new directions is by no means equivalent to the creation of something new.

The artist at the turn of the nineteenth century, he continues, had it easier than our present generation; a materialistic interpretation of history and a strong social consciousness gave most of his works, automatically, a living substance. Our present generation, however, in attempting to return to more traditional art forms, has for the most part descended to platitudes or to a formalism which is divorced from the realities of our time. Others have launched on fads and experiments, or excursions into primitivism, which are just as alien to a true renewal of the artistic spirit. As a result we have become unsure in our intellectual judgments—or so doctrinaire that we condemn as decadent all artistic aims and directions except our own.

What then, Frisch asks, is the role of the *Neue Merkur*? It must seek out intrinsically valuable works, created out of inner necessity, no matter from what literary camp; it must look beneath the false labels and beyond mechanical form for the truth of the contents. "The way of the future does not lie between tradition and break with tradition; but each one must seek and find new directions of his own."

In a "house-ad," obviously written by Frisch as well, he adds a few pronouncements. The *Neue Merkur* will attempt to bring clarity into the present confusion and to serve those who crusade for a renewal of the spirit in an age of technology. In political and social questions it will open its pages only to those who, from a position above the petty day-by-day altercations of the various parties, have a wide perspective and feel responsible toward the future. It will take seriously the concept of world literature and therefore publish outstanding works of foreign as well as German authors. In short, the *Neue Merkur* is meant for all those who seek authentic intellectual growth and a refinement of aesthetic judgment.[7]

It would have been surprising if the *Neue Merkur* had lived up to the expectations of its editor. When Frisch modestly began his editorial with the concession that the realization of his goals was dependent on others, he hit upon the main determinant of the success and failures of the magazine. Had Frisch succeeded in engaging all the creative writers he discriminatingly solicited, he would indeed have assembled under the banner of one journal most of the creative talents, established and potential, of Germany, England, France, Italy and Russia—from Proust to Pirandello, from Gerhart Hauptmann to Ricarda Huch, from Giraudoux to Gundolf. As it was, at first he received refusals—often lengthy and literary documents in themselves—more often than acceptances. To the extent that Frisch failed in gaining contributions from, say, Rilke[8] and Stefan George, Hugo von Hofmannsthal and Arthur Schnitzler, fiction (in addition to essays) from Thomas Mann and André Gide, he also failed in making his magazine completely representative. Gauged by the program of its editor, the *Neue Merkur* must be called a qualified failure; in retrospect and by any standard of literary excellence it was an unqualified success.

Frisch's rejection notes testify to his wish, of course not always realized, of making excellence the sole criterion for acceptance. Even established authors and regular contributors to the *Merkur* received tactful rejection slips if their proffered creations did not reach the usual standard of their work. A rejection sent to Klaus Mann on 16 January, 1925, is typical: The author's fairy tale was charming and successful in many respects, yet the editor didn't consider it quite suitable as Mann's introduction to *Merkur* readers. He preferred to wait for something more rounded and weighty.

With such rigorous standards, the *Neue Merkur* was often embarrassed for material; upon several occasions it had to postpone publication until the arrival of more suitable manuscripts. In a personal letter to Erich von Kahler of 4 October, 1919, Frisch admitted this recurring difficulty: once again he requested regular collaboration on the *Merkur*. The publishers had been forced to skip the August and September issues for the time being and to publish at once the October number. They had explained to the general public that technical difficulties had prevented normal publication: technical difficulties were responsible in great measure, but there was also an embarrassing shortage of material. The number of authors who merited consideration for the *Neue Merkur* and who could really shape its physiognomy in such a way that it would become Germany's best magazine was very small. The editor recognized each day anew how small it was. Frisch, it is clear, preferred no magazine at all to a mediocre one.

Frisch's nonpartisanship in his selection of belletristic contributions becomes, of course, evident from a perusal of the magazine. Far from being merely an organ of the early Expressionistic movement, as the *Grosse Brockhaus* of 1932 erroneously labelled it, the *Neue Merkur* gathered authors from all the major movements of German literature (like all great artists, many defied classification) and such foreign authors as Shaw, Flaubert, Remisov, Croce, Alexei Tolstoy, Paul Claudel, Miguel de Unamuno, to give a fair sampling. More important still, its surveys of European literature, its judgments on writers and books, most of them defensible even from a present-day perspective, were refreshingly free from literary bias.

For a new magazine there was remarkably little groping. The belletristic contributions to the first year of publication (April 1914—March 1915) set the standard of excellence (though not of inclusiveness) for the seven which were to follow. In fact, the first work which Frisch acquired for serialization prior to book publication constituted a major coup. It was destined to become an all-time best-seller, to be translated into all major languages, and, by its author's own testimony, to establish him as a popularly accepted writer in Germany.[9] Efraim Frisch, while a reader at the S. Fischer Verlag, had met Jakob Wassermann and, on the strength of this acquaintance, persuaded him to entrust his novel *Gänsemännchen* (Little Gooseman) to the fledgling periodical.[10]

In addition to the continuations of the *Gänsemännchen*, the first year also brought, among many other works, important new short stories by Alfred Döblin, Max Dauthendey, and Hermann Stehr, poems by Klabund, and posthumously, one by Christian Morgenstern, a close personal friend of the Frisches,[11] several poems by Walt Whitman in translation, a tragedy by Paul Claudel, and letters and diary excerpts from Flaubert and Strindberg, respectively. While these stand out through the prominence of their authors, the other literary contributions are scarcely less meritorious. It will demonstrate Frisch's characteristic acumen to point out that all but four (Hetta Mayr, Andreas Schreiber, F. Mader, Leo Perutz) of the German poets, novelists, story writers, and dramatists who appeared during the first year of publication were ultimately included in Soergel's *Dichtung und Dichter der Gegenwart*, one of the standard histories of modern German literature, and that furthermore Leo Perutz, not mentioned by Soergel, is having a belated vogue in present-day Germany.

The ingenuousness with which the *Neue Merkur* judged submitted literature did not extend to social and political essays. The *Neue Merkur*

wore distinct colors in the political arena, which it changed only under
the emotionalism of World War I. Its attitude was precisely stated by
Wilhelm Hausenstein in a letter to the historian Willy Andreas of 23 October, 1919: "Naturally—and you will not take this confession amiss—we
must test whether your essay would fit into the uniform picture which the
Merkur, despite its liberality, wants to present. Please understand me correctly; we have no party program but besides adhering to a principle of
highest quality, to which your works would quite certainly conform, our
policies take us, by and large, very much to the left of center."

The first year of publication clearly reflects these policies and they are
still recognizable in the distorting mirror of the second, war-time volume.
The principal traits which gave the *Neue Merkur* its distinct features were
advocacy of democracy and social reform in domestic matters, cosmopolitanism in foreign affairs, a predilection for experiments in the arts
and education, and a modified Bergsonianism in philosophy. If the specific reforms advocated seem sometimes mild or even pusillanimous for
an avowed left-of-center magazine, our present-day perspective is probably to be blamed for such a reading.

Judging from some of the letters buried in the editorial files, many a
reader turned apoplectic at the daring and pugnacity of the journal. For
example, two articles, by Lucia Dora Frost and Oscar A. H. Schmitz respectively,[12] which examined the role of women in a modern world, seem
reactionary today, but enraged the conservatives of yesterday. Miss Frost,
then one of the few free-lance women writers in Germany, had argued
that the generation after the suffragettes would like to withdraw into con-
servatism as a protest against their mothers who had enjoyed the head-
lines of the struggle, but left the practical problems to their daughters.
Yet she ultimately rejected this response: "Radicalism has become a necessity." Oscar A. W. Schmitz, even more conservative by today's standards, encumbered and almost vitiated his advocated reforms by propos-
ing innumerable safeguards. After advocating that all self-employed oc-
cupations and the lower and intermediate civil-service positions be opened
to women and that women colleges and universities be founded, he tempered his reformer's zeal by conceding that women, even where they were
the peers of their male colleagues, should "naturally" never be their su-
pervisors. Also they should not be allowed to vote, hold high civil service
posts, or be entrusted with political office. And, at the universities, "all
examinations would, of course, be administered by male examiners." Finally, he warned male readers to protect their wives and sweethearts from
excessive sexual enlightenment. "Aufklärung," he felt, led to the undoing
of all decent women.

Another article, almost equally restrained from a present-day point of view, championed a reform of the Catholic church.[13] The author amassed a wealth of historical data to show the growth of bureaucracy and autocracy within the Church. In the main he held the Roman hierarchy responsible for this development and warned that its continuation would lead to complete secularization. He concluded: "Always, when religions turn political, they do so at the moment of decline. This is now the case, and it is Rome's fault." He advocated, by implication, a return to true religiosity as the only way to save Catholicism. "The eternal treasures and the spiritual nourishment of the doctrine and the sacraments rest with the few true believers." Such views would scarcely be considered heretical today, but at that time the writer must have considered anonymity the better part of valor. In fact he preserved this anonymity so jealously, that it became one of only two instances in the *Merkur* that defied all my attempts at lifting it.

Another proposed reform, however, was by no means modest and has waited long for its realization. In 1914, Theodor Elsner deplored the simultaneous growth of arrogance and servility in the army and demanded more democracy, a bridging of the gulf between officers and enlisted men, and a remodeling of the army as a school for responsible civic service.[14] As late as 1960, Col. Wolf von Baudissin made substantially the same proposals for the new German army.

The call for social reform resounded in numerous articles, often where least expected. An article about Lloyd George's attempted land reforms contained a pointed comparison. "We, as Germans, are also interested in the gigantic accusation . . . against the ruling classes. Our sufferings and complaints also grow from the same root."[15] In the midst of an article on Monte Carlo, the habits and the psychology of its gamblers, appears a comparison between the idle rich at the gaming tables and the oppressed working people of Monte Carlo.[16]

Alfons Paquet argued for cosmopolitanism. He visualized a United Europe, a federation of states under the leadership of a qualified emperor, preferably under Wilhelm II. He also prophesied that continued disunity would result in a world war, in an ever more virulent imperialistic race, and rebellion in the colonies. He foresaw a re-awakening of China and an either-or solution for Germany: "One thing is certain: The emergence of a united Europe will come about either through Germany's leadership or its destruction."[17] A few decades later both alternatives were to be tried.

Three months before World War I, Emil Ludwig foresaw an end to chauvinism through the growth of the competition of individual against individual rather than nation against nation. The main part of his argument, however, attempted to explain and defend the new generation in terms of Bergson's *élan vital*. Our young people, he said, do not lack idealism, but theirs is directed towards the achievement of individual, feasible goals, not towards the attainment of vague, unattainable ideologies.[18] Frisch's postscriptum to this article amounted to a repudiation. Physical effort, he maintained, is meaningless without a metaphysical evaluation; achievement for the sake of achievement is a return to the very mechanization which the author condemns. Frisch enjoined his readers to read Martin Buber's essay "Leistung und Dasein" (Achievement and Existence) by way of comparison.

Frisch could have pointed to three articles besides Buber's which by accident or design attack Ludwig's mechanistic interpretation of Bergson. Buber coined the term "illegitimate achievement" to pillory those who live only to produce and thus poison their lives and their productions. It is "contemporary superstition that achievement is the criterion of the growth of the individual (*Menschwerdung*)"; in art and in literature, in all aesthetic evaluation, we must return to the principle of *dulce et utile*.[19] Kurt Hiller continued the argument: "Art is not an end in itself . . . words must lead to action," he expostulated.[20] He entitled his article "Aktivistische Erziehung"; by coincidence he had reason to recall this article in a letter to the editor of the *Vorwärts* in 1960, forty-five years later.[21] Elsewhere he applied his premise to philosophy: "We set a false value on reasoning for its own sake and on a high level of reasoning; we savour the journey and forget the destination."[22]

In aesthetics, August Halm, a music teacher at Gustav Wyneken's famous progressive school, reasoned, it is not enough to understand art and to teach its understanding. The aesthetician must be more than observer; he must be guide, even leader and commander. He must champion a cultural ideal and be the "organized intelligence" behind its realization.[23] Finally, Bruno Altmann condemned the cult of practical achievement in business and industry. Too many today "submerge themselves in their work,"[24] in the literal sense of the phrase. Through the mechanization and Americanization of our lives we are reduced to the illogicality that machine masters man, that the machine poisons our *élan vital*. That was written in 1914!

The *Neue Merkur* was, in short, an accurate radar screen for all intellectual flights in Europe. Given the "style" of the magazine, this sensitivity was scarcely surprising. In the advertisement of the first issue, Frisch had envisioned the *Neue Merkur* as "vital, individualistic, and constantly in touch with our times." This program imposed on his contributors the need to show the practical and immediate applicability of their ideas or, at least, to include references to current events. His insistence on this approach gave character and uniformity to the magazine and kept it abreast of the times.

Hence, while Altmann's article was the only one to refer to Bergson's fashionable philosophy directly, many of the above rely on Bergsonism, much as today's intellectual journals are borne in part by Existentialism, its pessimistic antithesis. Or, in an essay on modern education, John Dewey's new ideas, if not his name, are registered on its pages.[25] Likewise, disquisitions on Richard Strauss, dismissing his latest works as epigonic of Wagner, reflected the avant-garde movement in music; an article on Julius Meier-Graefe that in the fine arts. The one held that Hans Pfitzner and Max Reger, rather than Strauss stood in the van in music. As an estimate, written at a time when Berg, Schoenberg, and von Webern were composing, it appears less than clairvoyant from today's perspective. The other article, more astute, berated Julius Meier-Graefe for not being attuned to the latest developments in painting. René Beeh, a Munich art critic, argued with much justice that the well-known art historian, after having successfully espoused the Impressionists, was not mustering a like appreciation for the latest, i.e., Expressionistic generation of painters.[26]

In its concern for the future the *Neue Merkur*, as might be expected, addressed itself in several early articles to the situation of Germany's Jews. Beyond the general timeliness of the subject, Frisch may have been drawn to it by the anti-Semitic attacks that followed the birth of his magazine. The *Allgemeine Flugblätter deutscher Nation* of 1914 greeted its appearance with the following epithets:

> Two new magazines have appeared in Munich (*Der Neue Merkur*, *Das Forum*). Both editors (E. Frisch and W. Herzog) are Jews and, according to advance notices, so are most of the contributors. It is not a question of the merit or demerit of the literature itself which will be transmitted via such an unsafe and dangerous route. But matters have now developed to the point that the majority of all German periodicals are published, edited, and written by Jews. Is this to be accepted as a matter of course? Is this insignificant? Is there still any mutton-head left anywhere who would approve of this state of affairs or a crooked [i.e., Jewish] horsetrader who would dare justify it?

Theodor Haecker, a philosopher and critic of some consequence (and, later, a vigorous opponent of Hitler) echoed the sentiments, if not the gutter language, of the *Flugblätter*. He accused the *Neue Merkur* of contributing to the pollution and "Jewification" (*Verjudung*) of the German publishing world and, by implication, of serving as an instrument of Jewish propaganda.[27]

As if to refute the charge of propaganda, Frisch allowed remarks critical of the Jews to stand. "The Jews were one of the most stubborn and despotic of all small peoples" and other such passages would probably have been suppressed by an editor bent on propaganda. More important, the articles on Judaism in the first two volumes were models of objectivity and scholarship.

By far the most weighty article, a lucid and perceptive survey of the prevailing state of Judaic studies, was contributed by Willy Staerk, Professor of Theology at Jena and a widely-read scholar.[28] Complying with the style of the *Neue Merkur*, he chose a current event, the publication of a controversial book, Friedrich Naumann's *Mitteleuropa* (Berlin, 1916), as his point of departure. In advocating social, economic, and political reforms within a Central European hegemony, Naumann had also touched upon the attacks by German anti-Semites upon the Jewish leaders of Austria in business and finance: "After the war we must put an end to provocatory acts from both sides, for behind us lies the shared [experience] of the trenches. Politically that should weigh as much as baptism." Staerk strongly agreed, but argued that not only political morality but also reason itself compelled the implementation of Naumann's demands and that understanding of the Jews and Judaism had grown into a major scientific assignment.

In a historical survey Staerk showed that at least in Germany a scientific approach to Jewish history had come relatively late, only about a life-span before 1915. He lauded and detailed the work of such early scholars as Leopold Zunz, Heinrich Graetz, and Ismar Elbogen, but deplored the lack of public appreciation for the achievements of the new science. Staerk was particularly disappointed about the lethargy of the German universities. While England and the United States had established several chairs for Jewish studies, Germany had contented herself with a single appointment. After the war, he urged, several chairs for Judaism must be established. Staerk concluded with a few pregnant sentences which can stand even today as an objective canon for all Judaic studies:

> As the writing of all intellectual history the study of Judaism must be an end in itself. It is not meant to serve political or religious parties or perform polemic or apologetic functions, but to further objective scientific enquiry. Historical reality is the only goal for which it must strive, even if reality runs counter to the personal

preferences and favorite opinions of the researcher. If beyond
that the science of Judaism succeeds in contributing to an allevi-
ation of the inner tensions which will continue to burden our internal politics even in the future—perhaps for a while even more
than hitherto—then it will render an immeasurable service in raising the cultural level of our politics.

Several other articles, not specifically concerned with Jews and Juda-
ism, are individual mosaics in the *Neue Merkur*'s depiction of German
Jewry. Writing in 1914, Lucia Dora Frost realized the importance of the
Jews to Germany's intellectual life: "We must not overlook that the new
German spirit has a strong Jewish infusion, that, in fact, the Jews have
assumed the leadership of this intellectual upsurge."[29] Albrecht Mendelssohn-Bartholdy praised the author of *Schimpf und Ernst*, Johannes
Pauli, "who was born as a poor Upper-Alsatian Jewish boy," but became
one of the great molders of the German language. Ferdinand Lion discussed the Jewish emancipation, its results, and its benefits for Europe:
"It is interesting, by the way, how a bit of the Orient, living in the midst
of Europe and apparently rigidified in its Talmudic code and its ghetto,
became assimilated by Europe. Once liberated, they became overly flexible. Heine out-voltaired Voltaire. What leaps into the past and the future
were they able to make! What ambivalences! What self-annulment [*Sich-
selbstaufheben*]! Europe listened to a divine parody on itself. Heine became a European event."[30] Finally, Alfons Paquet allocated to Eastern
Jewry the role of intermediaries between European and Oriental thought
in the event of a unified Europe under a German aegis.[31]

On one occasion the *Neue Merkur* took cognizance of anti-Semitism in
Germany which, as events such as the counting of Jews in the German
Army proved, continued unabated during the war years. Wilhelm Hausenstein undertook to trace its origin and continued existence within the
German fraternities.[32] But Hausenstein's sober reminder of continuing
anti-Semitism was drowned out, after the outbreak of war, by the intoxicating narrative of the fighting prowess of German Jews, as in an article
by the well-known sociologist, Franz Oppenheimer:

> In our country all parties have disappeared for the moment and
> the exaltation of the Social Democrats is in no way inferior to that
> of the other parties. . . . While Russia's down-trodden Jews go into
> battle only with great reluctance, despite all the flattery that the
> "little father" suddenly expends on them, the German Jews fight
> in the forefront for the common fatherland. A Jewish soldier,
> Fischel, was the first to take an enemy flag and the heroic death of

the irreplaceable Ludwig Frank, which can never be sufficiently lamented, will for all times testify [to the spirit] of the Social Democrats as well as the Jews.[33]

Franz Oppenheimer's article was symptomatic of the changes in the magazine that accompanied the outbreak of World War I. These changes were to be expected. The call to arms, at least on the surface, drowned out the voices of pacifism, and nationalism muted internationalism. The *Eichendorff Almanach* of 1916, page 97, for example, remarked on a new note in the *Neue Merkur*, "genuinely German and glorifying the Fatherland." But the reviewer should have been able to discern that this note of nationalism, superficially dominant, was usually contrapuntally accompanied by the quieter but very persistent note of the magazine's traditional cosmopolitanism and anti-war ideology.

Curiously, both attitudes were genuine. The espousal of nationalism was neither a forced marriage to escape censorship nor one designed to gain public favor. Rather, the editor of the *Neue Merkur* and his contributors sincerely felt that Germany's cause was just; that the enemy was temporarily misguided but would ultimately repent of his folly, and that the war must first be won by Germany before humanistic ideals could be realized. Shorn of their philosophical argumentation, many of the articles in the *Neue Merkur* argued (with a conviction as strong as Allied intellectual journals) that Germany was engaged in a war to end all wars, and that the world must be made safe for a Pax Germanica.[34]

Thus, while individual articles often contradicted each other, their total effect established a synthesis between two points of view. For example, a fairly strident attack on French expediency was balanced by praise of France's cultural contributions; an exposure of Allied cupidity was coupled with an admission of Germany's own transgressions, and one article breathing war-time chauvinism was leavened by the vision of a post-war United Europe. Often there appeared a nostalgic wish for a continued friendship with intellectuals on both sides of the front lines. In only one instance this moderation wore thin and the balance became precarious—in the articles on England. France, Italy, even Russia could be understood if not forgiven; "perfidious Albion," in Max Scheler's opinion, was the devil's disciple.

It was Frisch who apparently strove to make the magazine a forum for both a moderately nationalistic as well as a moderately anti-nationalistic point of view, often presented dialectically in the confines of a single article.[35] Naturally, not all topics received this triple illumination of thesis, antithesis, synthesis, but enough did for the reader to infer that with more space at his disposal Frisch would have liked this multiple exposure for all subjects.

Several examples will illustrate the method. Ludwig Brinkmann, the *Merkur*'s chief contributor from Spain, demanded that literature join the war effort.[36] "For at this moment only one single type of really timely literature is justified: the depiction of martial events, the analysis of strategic planning, its causes and effects and a critique of its implementation, in short pure military history." The humanistic rebuttal was presented by Ulrich Rauscher, in later years an advisor to President Ebert and German ambassador to Poland: "Literature . . . has become an exploited institution of the world's destiny and has lost, on the road to becoming [an object of] business speculation, its true dignity, its lack of purpose . . . . Wise men and fools alike forbid purposeless literature and support, whether intentionally or not, literature with an [ulterior] purpose, one with direct and expressed ties to the war."[37] Wilhelm Hausenstein attempted a compromise between the two extremes.[38] Conceding the difficulty of determining the boundaries between politics and art, he pointed to the examples of two contemporaries, Heinrich Mann and Wedekind who had successfully bridged the gap. By drawing on the spirit of Lessing and Kleist, they were perpetuating a tradition which "quivers downward from the most abstract playfulness of the arabesque to the desire for effect upon immediate things at hand, a desire that is anchored in the profoundest depth of life itself."

Frisch similarly balanced war and anti-war sentiments. On the one hand Carl Hagemann's report from the Carpathian theatre of war, Hugo Schulz's from the Northern sector of the Austro-Russian battle front and Walther Heymann's posthumous "Letters from the Front," all understandably partisan and occasionally militaristic, rejoice in every triumph of the Central Powers.[39] But a short story by Arnold Zweig, significantly called "Der Mann des Friedens," makes the case for pacifism. It pictures the tragedy of war in quarters where it might be least expected; a judge in a small German town, "who considered a peaceful existence as the only natural state of affairs,"[40] becomes mentally deranged under the impact of World War I. Similarly, Paul Adler's prefatory note to an essay by Charles Péguy is strongly pacifistic. It lauded the Frenchman's opposition to the "war-mongers" and, by implication, condemned all war: "Charles Péguy . . . died in September 1914 somewhere near the Marne or Oise in a battle against us, the victim of a somewhat errant bullet, at that sharp boundary between a German and a French offensive. Almost simultaneously with Péguy there died on the German side one of Péguy's translators and friends, Ernst Stadler, professor in Brussels till the beginning of the war and a poet well-known to the younger generation."[41] It should be added that the acerbity of these remarks is even greater in the German original; the carefully phrased words *eine einigermassen abgeirrte Kugel* mean both an errant bullet and a wayward one. The censor must have lacked or wanted to lack the ear for *double entendre*.

A dialogue between a front soldier and a man unfit for military service advances, dialectically, both militarism and anti-militarism.[42] Also Paul Zech's "Sommernacht" (Summernight), a series of army impressions, may be read as a combination of these two opposing views. Before the battle the troops are beset by strong anti-militaristic misgivings: "Stronger than ever one feels the torture of loneliness, the isolation from everything that is peaceable, enveloped by love, and divine . . . We rebel: to know that we are fragments of this giant enterprise, a screw in the great death-machine, a screw which must not come loose and which noiselessly, invisibly helps to turn the entire apparatus."[43] But these and similar misgivings are swept aside by the triple-fold glow of the orders to advance, by the "cheers of ten thousand victorious voices. . . . by the hurrahs for those souls who were privileged to enter eternity on such pinions." Yet a few days after the battle "the agonizing days of the marshalling area" have returned; the dreams of peace, the regrets about the *Triumph der Zerfleischung* (the triumph of internecine war).

A selective sampling of other articles will complete the physiognomical sketch of the war-time *Neue Merkur*. Many of them display a surprising readiness for national self-criticism. Franz Oppenheimer, for example, argues that Germany, from a sociological view, has just grounds for waging war, but shows that all the other nations will find much justification on their side. While he deplores the guerilla warfare of the Belgians and French, he reminds his readers that Germans and Austrians have conducted the same type of warfare in the past. In another article he exhorts his readers to judge Russia *sine ira et studio*.[44]

Several other articles address themselves to the applicability of international law in wartime and most of them concede that the Allies had no monopoly on transgressions.[45] Paul Adler's preface to an article by Unamuno, critical of Germany's astigmatism to present-day Spain, concurs with Unamuno: "We should very much welcome it, if a certain class of Germans were to benefit from the reading of it."[46] Efraim Frisch continues this note of *mea culpa* in a preface to an article by George Bernard Shaw, "Killing as a Sport." "This [i.e., Shaw's reproof] does not only apply to the English."[47] Frisch's remark is, however, the only conciliatory note towards the British. Max Scheler, promulgating a German prejudice which goes back to the Romantics and beyond, charges that the British have elevated "cant," a variant of hypocrisy, to a devilish code of national behavior. Ernst Wolff, "Oliver Cromwell und die Anfänge des Imperialismus," also invokes the infernal regions in a diatribe against modern British imperialism, while Wilhelm Hausenstein, in a somewhat tortuous analogy, describes the Germans as successors to Napoleon, who are continuing Napoleon's crusade against the British and their power politics.[48]

Another group of articles, particularly striking through the diversity and prominence (or subsequent prominence) of their authors, examines various inner conflicts posed by the war. How can an international social ist assuage his conscience as he fights against his proletarian brethren, asked Eduard Bernstein, one of the authoritative historians of the labor movement. How does a member of a union dissolve this conflict, queried Adolf Braun, himself a prominent leader in the union movement. How does an intellectual steel himself to fight a kindred spirit, demanded Max Hildebert Boehm, later a professor at the Universities of Jena and Göt-tingen. It is interesting that all three writers gave the same answer—the Socialist Bernstein, the union-leader Adolf Braun, and the ultra-conserva-tive Boehm who was then, as he told me in an interview of 26 July 1962, a member of the Young Conservatives, led by Clemens von Klemperer and Möller van den Bruck. (He was, incidentally, quite surprised and pleased that he had a chance to be heard in the liberal *Merkur*.) They all came to basically the same conclusion: we socialists (unionists, intellec-tuals) have a stake in the survival of our nation and must defend it. But let us prepare in soul and mind for a peace in which we can implement our ideals.[49]

This pragmatic *modus vivendi*, surely understandable, becomes tragi-comic when advocated by a pacifist. Kurt Hiller, when submitting his article "An die Partei des deutschen Geistes" (To the Party of the Ger-man Intellectuals)[50] obviously felt that he was putting himself into a highly equivocal position. In a letter to Frisch of 8 January 1915 he ex-plained some last-minute changes on the galley proofs: Of late he was being considered a "militarist" in the literary circles of Berlin and must therefore painstakingly avoid all ambiguity in these matters. "I ask of you *urgently, to retain these inserts inviolate*; every word has been thought through, and I can only take responsibility for the whole, if not one word of it is missing. In that case, to be sure, I shall gladly bear the responsibility." Hiller's temporary recantation of pacifism went so far as to make him suggest that his article be reprinted as a pamphlet for mass sales. Out of honest conviction he had written: "Let us condemn war: one *must* condemn it, but let not a single German condemn *this war*." As he admitted to me, rather ruefully, in an interview of 28 June 1962, he had been less than consistent in this article of 1915.

One contribution reflected the war-time intellectual adjustment of the *Neue Merkur* more than all others, Wolfgang Heine's "Maturing for Peace" (Reife für den Frieden). A Social Democratic member of the German Reichstag and, during the first year of the Weimar Republic, Prussian Minister of the Interior), he wrote not only with great intelligence but with unusual candor; and he links, in the confines of a single article, most of the subjects which other writers had discussed in separate ones. In a future Germany, he argues, common interests must prevail over special privileges; peace must remove all discrimination against the workers and farmers who have carried their full share of the burdens of war. "This war has discredited both blatant militarism and antimilitarism." Those who advocated internationalism have been proven wrong; but equally wrong is a racist nationalism in dealing with other peoples, or party chauvinism at home, practiced by the conservative parties in the past.[51]

Most articles on the spirit of Germany and on German patriotism are predictable in content—including Frisch's editorials. They range from Norbert Jacques' claim that Germany is more tolerant than the Allies to August Mayer's denunciation of a United Europe as a chimera, from Albrecht Mendelssohn-Bartholdy's scorn for the excesses of the language purifiers to Ludo Hartmann's plan for spreading German and German culture by teaching both to Russian prisoners-of-war, from a prediction of Italy's continued support of the Central Powers to a post-facto analysis of the reasons for her defection.[52]

Two contributions, however, stand out through the prominence of their authors and the weightiness of their content. Martin Buber's "Bewegung; Aus einem Brief an einen Holländer" (Movement; from a Letter to a Dutch Citizen) crystallized the response of the liberal intellectual to the transition from peace to war. We are not under the spell of a form of mass suggestion, Buber states, but have dedicated ourselves to a sober spirit of resolve and willingness to sacrifice, "to an unreserved faith in an absolute value—for which to die would mean the fulfillment of life."[53] This value is not to be equated with patriotism, national feeling or the like, but is an autonomous emotion. Forces, of which this war is but a symbol, have awakened a kinetic movement; it is the task of the intellectual-spiritual forces to give this movement momentum and direction. Buber's article ends with an unanswered question; at mid-stream the shore is dimly seen but left uncharted: "I see at the heart of this war the kindling of a great regeneration, of which I cannot speak as yet."

The other article has become so well known that a summary becomes unnecessary. Thomas Mann in his "Friedrich und die grosse Koalition" (Frederick and the Great Coalition)[54] pointed a parallel, whose applicability has been much and ardently debated, between Frederick the Great and his enemies in the Seven Years War (1756–1763), and Germany and its opponents in World War I. With some dubious historical facts, an unexcelled prose style, and a single subtle sentence (plus a less subtle subtitle) which brought home the parallel, Thomas Mann laid most of the onus for the war at the doorsteps of the Allies and, somewhat cynically, reminded his compatriots of Frederick's dictum that success sanctifies the means for its achievement. Whether this article is, as Soergel argues, "a German's quest for clarity about German and European questions of the moment," or "a small historic artifice in its strange mixture of sound critical reflection and untempered patriotic allusions," as its own author adjudged it nearly forty years later,[55] for the *Neue Merkur* and Efraim Frisch the procurement of this article meant a pinnacle of achievement.

Taking the war-year issues of the *Neue Merkur* in their entirety, it would be wrong to say that the magazine was representative of *the* state of mind in Germany; at best, it was the voice of the liberal wing of an intellectual elite. But the very fact of its continued appearance with little change and negligible harassment was characteristic of Germany in World War I, just as the absence of a similar magazine was symptomatic of the Second World War. Whereas the *Neue Merkur* continued to publish foreign authors, kind judgments of the enemy peoples (with the noted exception of the English) and abounded in enjoinders against lasting hatred, the German publications of thirty years later extended the concept of total war to the realm of the spirit.

2 *From War to Inflation*

1919-1923

In 1919 the *Neue Merkur* recommenced publication in a Munich which, to the chagrin of its staff, had ascended politically to the capital of the short-lived Räterepublik and descended culturally to the status of a town in the provinces. Events had twisted Thomas Mann's phrase "München leuchtete" into a parody of itself. The lights of its festivals and its glow as a city of artists were extinguished; in their place coruscated minor volcanoes which alternately erupted and lay dormant until one of them, which proved to be not minor at all, burst out from Munich, spread all over Germany, and consumed both. The *Neue Merkur* accompanied its city on the first stage of this journey into night, though it had long ceased to exist when the incendiary bombs gave the locution "München leuchtete" its ultimate grisly meaning.

In those years the *Neue Merkur* recorded the travail of both Munich and Germany; it represented, in the words of Ferdinand Lion, its most frequent contributor, "the quintessence of the Weimar Republic, and that is the finest tribute one can pay it." Less happily, it also represented or reflected Weimar's ineffectualness; in Weimar and in the intellectual circles of Munich and other German centers good efforts were being vitiated by a lack of faith in their effect. To what purpose, one may ask, were the exhortations in the *Merkur* urging support for the new republic and a renascence of German culture and learning when beneath these brave rallying cries were the mute or even audibly whispered admissions of a foredoomed defeat? "Our deals and our dealings," Joachim Friedenthal wrote, "everything we undertake in despair, cynicism, greed for life, in constantly renewed hopefulness is already the disguised, wildly defensive agony of a dance of death."[1] Frisch, in the very first editorial after the revival, carried this Böcklinesque mood, via a different metaphor, into his magazine: "Our reascendancy has been removed into a distance inaccessible to our eyes today."[2] Such prophecies may, by being uttered, hasten their own fulfillment; at any rate, it is certain that this mood of despondency pervading the magazine subtracted from its effectiveness and at times impeded its program.

Yet Frisch himself, despite this pessimism, was a courageous man. The very act of launching or relaunching a magazine in the Munich of 1919— and Frisch was but one of over twenty publishers to do so—demanded much fortitude. Munich was perhaps the most chaotic city in a turbulent Germany. Thanks to the close intertwining of its history with the rise of National Socialism, the steps of its dissolution have become general knowledge: the reverberations of the November revolution; the attempt to establish a separatist state in Bavaria; the murder of its first *Minister-präsident* (Prime Minister), Kurt Eisner, on 21 February 1919; the proclamation of a Räterepublik (Soviet Republic) and a Communist Räterepublik on 7 and 15 April respectively; its overthrow on 1 May; and the random and arbitrary arrests which accompanied each violent transition.

For a history of the *Merkur* the parallel history of publishing is even more pertinent. In theory a proclamation of 2 November 1918 by the German Commander-in-Chief and one on 11 November by the People's Delegates (Rat der Volksbeauftragten) ended all censorship and brought Germany, as its press joyfully reported, greater personal freedom than any of its enemies and substituted for supervision from above a responsibility only to the German people and each person's own conscience. In practice, bayonets often made individual consciences a dangerous luxury.[3]

The triumph of actual restraint of theoretical freedom began on 25 November. On that date the Berlin editorial offices of the *Vorwärts* were occupied by rioting Spartakist sailors; on 5 January the publishing houses of Mosse and Ullstein, the editorial offices of Wolff's Telegraphenbüro and the *Vorwärts* were taken forcibly by the Communists. On 16 January, a day after the assassination of Karl Liebknecht and Rosa Luxemburg, the military occupied and destroyed the editorial rooms of the *Rote Fahne* and riddled the presses with machine gun bullets. On 21 February, immediately following the murder of Kurt Eisner, forces of his government occupied all Munich newspaper offices and put out the next issues themselves or forced the staffs, occasionally at bayonet point, to follow their publishing directives. The same day, the Socialist Bavarian Government reintroduced pre-publication censorship. On 3 March a general strike broke out which stopped all printing presses, but by then, anticipating the strike by just a few days, Frisch had managed to publish the first post-war issue.

This minor miracle in the history of magazine publishing was the result of unflagging effort and of two years' planning. Incredible and quixotic though it may appear, Frisch, in the midst of war, had applied for a discharge from the Austrian Army on the grounds that he wished to resume publishing his magazine! He initiated his request late in 1917, still clung to his hope in May 1918, when he utilized a furlough for exhaustive discussions with his publisher, and optimistically reported to his friend Richard Beer-Hoffmann on 9 May that "the prospects for the continuation of the *Neue Merkur* have brightened; the laying of the foundations may possibly occur in the very near future."[4]

Unsurprisingly these plans came to nought. But when Frisch returned to Munich during the revolutionary days of November 1918, as he reported on 9 May to Ludwig Brinkman, the *Merkur*'s Spanish "correspondent," he immediately opened negotiations with the Georg Müller Verlag. When he found the new owners, a clan of opportunistic ironmongers, the exact opposites to the late Georg Müller, he exercised his contractual option to take over the magazine. Only a missionary zeal could have dispatched him on such an uncertain enterprise. This zeal, coupled with a belief in the success and efficacy of the magazine, suffuses a letter to Ferdinand Lion of 26 March 1920: The *Neue Merkur* was not an ephemeral publication as were so many newly founded publications; it had a financial basis and would probably outlast many of them. In Germany the present moment might not be particularly favorable, but this would only serve as a spur, "because we know that we are needed. Nor do I doubt that we shall slowly but surely make our way."

It now seems incredible that Frisch, who had returned to Munich in November 1918, initially set the publication of the first post-war issue for 31 January. As it turned out, the appearance of the magazine even by 1 March required an incredibly speedy settlement with the Georg Müller Verlag and unceasing editorial work. In a letter of 5 January 1919 to Beer-Hoffmann, written on the quickly produced stationery of his own publishing house, he admitted as much. The magazine had once and for all passed out of the hands of the Müller Verlag. An independent publishing house with sufficient means had been founded, which besides the regular issues, would print brochures with political and cultural contents in line with the aims of the magazine.[5] He had enlisted Dr. Hausenstein as co-publisher in order to gain a larger circle of contributors and readers. Among the limitations imposed by circumstances, Frisch lamented, were the cutting down of page numbers to be able to sell at a price within reach, and the shortage of living quarters, which forced the editorial staff to establish its office in Frisch's small apartment with the publishing house in Pasing, a small suburb of Munich. Improvisation was the order of the day!

Two important acquisitions stand out in Frisch's letter: that of a patron and also of a co-publisher-editor. The former was Heinrich Fromm, a wealthy Munich businessman who dealt in hops and was the first in a long line of the magazine's financial supporters. It is hard to picture Frisch in the role of fund raiser, yet he succeeded time and time again in finding backers for an enterprise which obviously could not return the initial investment. The question suggests itself why Frisch succeeded. From all the evidence there were traits in his complex character which drew people magnetically, even if it involved, as with backers and contributors, a considerable measure of personal sacrifice. With his curious mixture of aloofness and charm, he usually captivated those with whom he abandoned his native reticence—while others found him detached, icy, and as Johannes von Günther put it, "a literary snob."[6] He impressed, even overwhelmed, friends and acquaintances by a combination of almost antithetical qualities. He coupled dignity with Austrian unconstraint and joviality; Mrs. Hausenstein said of him in an interview of 13 October 1961 in Munich: "He was a figure from the Old Testament who could be wonderfully roguish [*espiègle*]." By his charm, crusading spirit, and persuasiveness—again and again his associates stressed his gifts as a conversationalist—he successfully solicited, in this *bouquet*, a dealer in hops, an owner of an art gallery, and a manufacturer of wooden bathroom accessories.

Frisch's acquisition of a co-editor, on the other hand, was unplanned and entirely fortuitous, though it subsequently appeared to competitors, reviewers, and uninitiated contributors as a strategic alliance of two complementary talents, of "a well-known essayist and a leading art commentator," as the *Westfälische Zeitung* of 14 April 1921 analyzed their joint editorship. Actually, by Ferdinand Lion's testimony, given in an interview of 25 September 1961 in Zurich, their agreement could not have come about more casually. At a social gathering at the home of the philosopher Rudolf Kassner, Frisch developed his plans for reviving the *Merkur* at length and to changing audiences; he suddenly received not only sympathetic support, but also some thoughtful criticism and some excellent, spontaneous suggestions from Wilhelm Hausenstein, a regular contributor in the past and then art critic for the *Münchner Neueste Nachrichten*. They continued their conversation in a corner of the room; late in the evening Frisch asked the company to toast Wilhelm Hausenstein as his co-editor.[7]

This toast remained the only formal token of their partnership; they never drew up a contract nor formally divided responsibilities. By inclination and training Hausenstein always edited articles on the fine arts, and Frisch those about the theater and Slavic literature; copy on other subjects was divided evenly. They ultimately consulted on all mss., but invariably and specifically edited political articles jointly. Hausenstein, until 1920 a registered member of the leftist Unabhängige Sozialdemokratische Partei, at first argued for a firmer political commitment of the magazine. Frisch occasionally acceded to these requests; it is likely that the *Merkur*'s support of Eisner's concepts after his assassination stems from Hausenstein's influence. On the last page of each issue both signed as responsible editors, though in the absence of one, the other co-editor would assume responsibility for both. The division of labor, although seemingly haphazard and unsystematic, was effective.

The collaboration was beneficial for both men. For Hausenstein the *Merkur* was an important stepping-stone in a brilliant career; he later became co-editor of the *Ganymed* (together with Julius Meier-Graefe), literary editor of the *Frankfurter Zeitung*, author of fifty-six separate monographs on art and literature (despite his enforced silence from 1936–1945), ambassador of the Federal Republic of Germany to France, and President of the Bavarian Academy of Fine Arts. He accumulated honors including the Hebel Prize, the Grand Order of Merit with Star from the Federal Republic of Germany, and the Insignia of Grand-Officer of the French Legion of Honor.

For Frisch and the *Merkur*, Hausenstein's editorship meant, as Frisch had hoped, the addition of many valuable contributors, among them the historian Willy Andreas, a friend of Hausenstein's from college days, the poetess Annette Kolb, and the music critic and translator Hans Deinhardt. Also as art critic on the *Münchner Neueste Nachrichten*, a job he held concurrently with his editorship until 9 June 1920, Hausenstein was able to solicit contributions from the artists and art historians Hermann Erhard, Hermann Esswein, Hermann Uhde-Bernays, and Julius Meier-Graefe. The latter, in fact, turned over to Hausenstein for pre-book publication his study of van Gogh, the first and still respected biography of the painter.

Finally, through a series of events which for the most part antedate Hausenstein's editorship, he gained the philosopher Max Picard as contributor. In Picard's own words, at an interview of 25 September 1961 in Neggio near Lugano, their acquaintance began like this:

> I had been invited to give a lecture, the first talk of my life, on *Bauernmalerei* [peasant art], in the gallery of the art dealer Freiherr von Bernus in Munich. I was then only twenty-five and

beset by stage fright, a failing that has never deserted me. In my stage fright I refused to mount the podium. Finally, out of the sea of dark people who were urging me on, emerged a face radiating light. This man did not expostulate with me, but shoved me gently onto the podium. And I started my speech. Later a young reporter congratulated me upon my lecture and told me that my gentle persuader had been Rilke. The next day I read, deeply moved, the review of the reporter: "Yesterday a young man with completely white hair spoke . . . with a heavy Badensian accent, but with words like those on the banderoles of old pictures." Thus my friendship to Rilke and Hausenstein dated from the same day. When years later Hausenstein asked me to contribute to the *Neue Merkur* I was glad to comply; between Frisch and me there never had been a warm relationship: an estranging element always stood between us.

It is fair to add that Hausenstein was unable to swell subscriptions considerably; he also caused, as with Rudolf Pannwitz, the occasional defection of a contributor. But on balance the addition of Hausenstein was a gain for the *Merkur*. His "discoveries" usually stayed loyal to the magazine even after his departure; he himself remained a steady contributor and diligent "recruiter" after his retirement as co-editor. At a time when they were needed most—later it became a matter of prestige to appear in the *Merkur*—he brought qualified writers to its pages.

Until the final months the relationship between Frisch and Hausenstein was unusually cordial; even their ultimate disagreement and separation was rooted in pay and principles rather than in personalities. The memoranda between the two are, in fact, characterized by a bantering bonhomie and a caustic gallows humor which is exemplified by the following "history of a rejection." An inquiry into the possibility of having an essay published was received by the editorial staff of the magazine. The essay, of general biological-philosophical content, was entitled "Teleology in Nature Studies."

Hausenstein, aghast, turned the letter over to Frisch with a five-word pencilled notation: "Um Gottes Willen nicht! [Heavens no!] Hausenstein." Frisch, probably more to amuse his co-editor than to assuage a would-be contributor, gave a fine gloss to his rejection note: he could not, unfortunately, consider the article's publication, since the essay, as a kind of delicate propaedeutic of scientific methods, should address itself, for best effect, to a "closed circle." He was having the manuscript returned with compliments and thanks.

When the break between the co-editors finally approached, the negotiations were carried out as befitted gentlemen. The magazine's straitened circumstances became a contributory reason, if a minor one, for Hausenstein's resignation. In a letter of 8 August 1921, he demanded the entirely reasonable remuneration of RM 550 per month. Frisch could not comply; the available funds simply were not sufficient to pay two editor-publishers. Given the altruism of both Frisch and Hausenstein, an equitable compromise on finances might have been found, but they clashed and separated on principles.

Curiously the falling out came after—and as a result of—the passing of the magazine's most severe crises; it led to a contention between the two for editorial *Lebensraum*. By the end of the second post-war year of publication, in March 1921, Frisch and Hausenstein had reconquered for the magazine, under their own colors, the heights of prestige it had enjoyed among intellectuals as an adjunct to the Georg Müller Verlag. By upholding the most rigorous standards, sometimes at the expense of a deadline or even an entire issue, they had elicited laudatory reviews from many influential papers and journals in Europe, among them the *Crifalco* of Italy, the *Nouvelle Revue Française* and the *Journal du Peuple* of France, the *Telegraaf* of Holland, and such German papers as *Leipziger Tageblatt* and the *Süddeutsche Presse*.[8] For many established writers, publishing in the *Merkur* had become a matter of pride rather than pay: other magazines often would have paid considerably more. A young writer accepted by Frisch and Hausenstein usually felt that he had arrived. Ivan Goll, for example, wrote Frisch on 20 July 1923: "I shall become one of your collaborators with great pleasure and interest, since I consider your magazine one of the very few in Germany that adheres to its standards." And W. E. Süskind, in an article published in *Welt und Wort* almost forty years after his first contribution to the *Merkur*, vividly recalls "the ineffable shock . . . when my paternal friend and benefactor, Efraim Frisch, printed *Tordis*, my first story deserving serious consideration, in his greatly distinguished magazine, the *Neue Merkur*."[9] In addition, the magazine's political profile attracted numerous essayists of the democratic left.

A few excerpts from pertinent letters tell the story of the *Merkur*'s transformation from petitioner to grantor—and, with it, of the declining necessity for two editor-publishers. The first stage is reflected in letters of 4 and 10 October 1919 respectively; Hausenstein urgently solicits contributions from Hermann Erhard, Frisch from Stefan Grossman. "Nothing more or less is at stake here than the continued existence of the style of the *Neue Merkur*, in short its spiritual life," writes Hausenstein, while Frisch pleads his difficulty "of finding suitable contributors for a magazine as individualistic as ours." But on 5 July and 22 December 1921 respectively, roughly two years later, Frisch informed Ernst Krieck, a literary historian, that his article, though accepted, would have to wait its turn for publication because of the abundance of manuscripts; he told Hausenstein that an extra thirty to forty pages of material was in type at the printer's. From then on Frisch and Hausenstein only approached authors if they sought a specific type of contribution. With the desperate search for contributors at an end, however, discussions between the two editors about editorial matters grew more contentious; with less work at hand the responsibility undertaken by the one diminished that of the other.

Hausenstein attempted to save the partnership by formalizing it. Having reconsidered, in all calmness, matters between them, he approached Frisch with very specific proposals which could regularize their working relationship. He asked to either be assigned the editorial responsibilities for every second, or at least every third issue or for a certain number of pages in each issue, especially treatment of all matters concerning art, which were of European concern or at least transcended the local German scene. Asking for complete independence in his editorial work, Hausenstein assured Frisch that he would not act against the latter's intentions. Not being able to accept an honorarium of less than 550 Marks he would, however, accept additional duties at the behest of his co-editor.

In case these proposals were unsatisfactory, Hausenstein saw no possibility of preventing future disagreements, to which he did not want to subject himself or Frisch. He closed the letter in the hope of a clear-cut solution at their next meeting. No accord was reached at the next meeting beyond the agreement to continue the co-editorship until the expiration of the publication year. The dissolution of the partnership was announced in the first issue of Vol. V: "With the conclusion of the last publishing year Dr. Wilhelm Hausenstein left the staff of the *Neue Merkur* on amicable terms, in order to assume the editorship of *Ganymed*, the yearbook of the Marées-Society. He will remain, as he was in the past, a regular contributor of the *Neue Merkur*."[10]

As a public announcement it was a fair enough account of the separation. In its prediction it proved to be accurate: until the end Wilhelm Hausenstein, with more than a dozen-odd articles, continued to be one of the magazine's most frequent contributors. Also, by commending it to the Deutsche Verlags-Anstalt, he became, as will be seen, its temporary savior. He and his wife remained intimate friends of Fega and Efraim Frisch; shortly before the magazine's demise on 6 June 1925, Frisch thanked Hausenstein for being "loyal to me for so long"; Hausenstein, the next day, answered: "Dear Frisch, you cannot imagine what a comfort to me are the special words of friendship at the beginning of your letter."

Frisch's acknowledgment of Hausenstein's long loyalty also paid tribute to his steadfastness during the many crises they had jointly endured. These crises deserve to be briefly recapitulated; in these years the history of the *Merkur* reflected to a large degree that of the country. The many strikes, for example, that debilitated the enfeebled German republic also effectively crippled the *Merkur*. In 1919, as the following notice indicates, the issue immediately following the initial issue was delayed for two weeks by a general strike in Munich:

To the Readers of the Neue Merkur

As a result of the general strike which shut down Munich print shops for quite some time, this issue, unfortunately, appears late by 14 days. The next issues will be published regularly and on time, if the situation permits.

Editor and Publishing House of the *Neue Merkur*

As late as 25 April 1924 Frisch reported to a contributor, Ernst Robert Curtius, that one issue of the *Merkur* had lost its timeliness and much of its effect through a local printers' strike.

More seriously however than strikes of printers, railroad workers, and distributors was the harassment of the magazine's contributors. Klabund, on the way to Munich for editorial conferences with Frisch, Hausenstein, and other publishers, was "erroneously" placed in protective custody as many others were at the time of the Räterepublik and its fall.[11] He was kept in a Passau jail for several months before being allowed to return to Switzerland. He had been overtaken, as Frisch's informant put it, "by the German destiny."

Richard Wiener, known to Frisch as an author of the Georg Müller Verlag, was unable to submit a novella in person because the Kahr government, as he wrote in a letter to Frisch on 26 September 1920, "arrested and jailed me and finally extradited me from Munich . . . all because of my friendship to Dr. [Walter] von Hollander."

Finally, in its first post-war issue, the *Neue Merkur* fulfilled a sad obligation by publishing an obituary, a twelve-page commemorative article by Wilhelm Hausenstein on Eisner, a valuable contributor.[12] Eisner, of course, had been assassinated. A like fate was to befall another frequent contributor, Gareis, who was assassinated in 1921.[13]

Some minor crises of the *Merkur* were less dramatic, but even more typical of its difficulties and the state of affairs in Germany. The alternating relaxation and tightening of censorship in Bavaria can almost be charted from the successive volumes, even issues of the *Merkur*. Frisch and Hausenstein by no means lacked courage; in accepting a controversial article by Otto Flake, they told him that they were fully prepared to take the risk of being banned. Because it sailed so close to the wind, however, the *Merkur* often had to trim its sails until the political tempests subsided. For example, in a letter to Arthur Holitscher of 22 July 1919, written about three months after the violent overthrow of the Räterepublik, Frisch confessed that Hausenstein and he had exercised "particular restraint" in the political and polemic articles of the July issue.

The threat of censorship, reprisals, or simply the instability of political institutions in Bavaria also inhibited some of the contributors. To the editors' chagrin, Hermann Esswein at the very last minute withdrew an article, "Political Remarks of a Non-political Person" out of considerations of personal and party loyalties. In a letter to Frisch of 28 November 1921 he wrote: "Again all sorts of fateful blows (if somewhat on the grotesque side) have crashed down upon my poor party friends, so that at this time I would prefer not publishing anything which might be interpreted as irony directed at the Social Democratic Party."

A similar communication from Friedrich Sternthal, the *Merkur*'s Berlin political correspondent, clarifies not only this particular difficulty of the *Merkur*, but also, perhaps, a debated point in German history. On 30 December 1923, he wrote to Frisch as follows: In the middle of September, when he received the impression from a confidential speech by Stresemann that a revolution [Umsturz] was imminent in Bavaria, Sternthal stayed, at the last moment, the mailing of an article he had promised Frisch, not wishing to subject him to the dangerous consequences of such a publication. As far as is known, the contents of this Stresemann speech have never been made public. Does not Sternthal's brief summation indicate that Berlin had strong indications of the imminence of Hitler's *putsch*?

The most persistent disease of the *Merkur*, and one that proved fatal, was its lack of sufficient funds: this symptom recurred so often that one can cull examples at random from the editorial files. "I very much regret that the financial basis of your enterprise permits only limited rates which will make frequent collaboration on my part inordinately difficult" (Alfons Paquet). "I resign, because I cannot live on 180 Marks a month" (Betty Paintner, editorial secretary). "I know from experience that bad magazines have abundant means. . . . It [therefore] does not matter, if the *NM* is getting these paragraphs for nothing" (Franz Blei). "We have to save on postage" (Frisch to Ernst Bloch). Finally, a pencilled note of Frisch's on a letter by a certain Walter F. may stand as a sign of hard times; the original letter reads, "I request some back numbers of the *Neue Merkur* together with your rates for subscriptions and advertisements." Frisch added: "Schnorrer! Nichts senden!" (Sponger! Send nothing!)[14]

The reasons for the *Merkur*'s inability to sustain itself were its low circulation (never higher than 1500), and rising costs. "Because of rising costs," Frisch wrote Hausenstein on 22 December 1921, "I cannot even add four pages, as I did at times in the past." The rising costs were, of course, beyond the control of the editors, but why did their subscription drives meet with so little success? The times were scarcely opportune for a publishing venture of this kind. Even the *Neue Rundschau*, with a printing of over 4000, the giant among German literary magazines, was at that time not completely self-supporting. In addition, the price of the magazine was prohibitively high for many potential readers.

Also Bavaria, due to its location physically, and at times spiritually, isolated from the rest of Germany, was a remote Helicon. Two friends of Hausenstein's, Gustav Pauli and Friedrich Ahlens-Hestermann, both non-residents of Bavaria, had not heard of the resumption of publication of the *Merkur*, although they had eagerly waited for it. Ahlens-Hestermann, a painter residing in Blankenese, added on 30 June 1919: "Up here in the Far North, regrettably, the products of South German intellectual and artistic life are shown and represented much more sporadically than, say, before the war." Frisch was aware of Munich's unpropitious location: "the small distribution of the *Merkur* in Berlin," Frisch wrote on 1 April 1922 to Dr. Vollert of the Gyldendalscher Verlag, "is a plight attributable to the peripheral location of our publishing house and our distributors." Yet Frisch's occasional attempts at relocation were desultory and never progressed beyond vague plans.

Revenues from advertising were usually satisfactory. Sometimes as many as twenty pages of advertisements, mostly from publishers, followed the editorial pages; obviously a reader of the *Neue Merkur* was a likely purchaser of their books. Another, if smaller, source of income was the sale of reprint rights. The *Frankfurter Zeitung*, for example, which for a year and a half had not even taken notice of its rebirth, suddenly discovered the *Merkur*, asked for reprint rights for its *feuilleton* pages, and from 1921 onward received galley proofs of each issue as a matter of routine. Other papers, among them the *Prager Presse*, followed suit. Yet even with these additional sources of revenue, the financial structure of the *Merkur* remained precarious; a memorandum, such as Alfred Vagt's of 13 November 1921, announcing a sudden drop in advertisements, could unhinge it for a few uneasy days. The concerns of the publishers were, therefore, at least equally divided between editorial cares and fund raising.

Yet the atmosphere in the editorial office—in 1920 Hausenstein and Frisch could move it out of the latter's small apartment to the fourth story of an apartment building in the Theresienstrasse—was far from gloomy. One of the staff members, Rudolf Nutt, a journalist and editor for over fifty years, wrote this author in 1961 that it was the nicest editorial office that ever existed. Between eleven and one, the editorial offices were the center of literary life in Munich.

Hausenstein's departure meant no real caesura in the magazine's history, but with the next year of publication Frisch himself modified his editorial policy. Instead of carefully balancing each issue between various genres, fiction, nonfiction, and poetry, and between various fields of interest, he devoted four of the twenty-one issues of the fifth and the (incomplete) sixth *Jahrgang* to special topics. Each special issue was intended as a crusade; each represented one of Frisch's most fervent concerns.

The first one was the so-called *Auslandsnummer* (foreign issue), a series of articles about conditions in England, France, Holland, Italy, Russia, and the United States, discussions of English and French literature, and a short story by Martin Buber with a Polish setting.[15] Frisch, in effect, devoted this issue in its entirety to his most noble pursuit, the rapprochement between Germany and its erstwhile enemies. The response to this issue was immediate and extensive. The reviews in newspapers and magazines all over Europe stimulated replies, rebuttals, and ripostes; it was precisely the dialogue Frisch had hoped for. In the months to come not only intellectuals, but practical men of affairs as well, particularly in Germany and France, followed the lead of the *Merkur* to espouse similar aims. With its first special issue and sequential articles, the *Merkur* sutured, incompletely of course, some of the wounds left from the war.

The second special issue, that of August 1921, broached the "Jewish problem."[16] It was by no means an apologia for Judaism, but for once the *Merkur* modified its stance of detachment in regard to this topic. As Frisch's wife and his niece, Dr. Bella Schlesinger, tell it, the insidious growth of anti-Semitism in Germany and, specifically, in Bavaria, had goaded Frisch into shedding his reservations and into taking up arms. In a way the issue on Judaism was a direct response to the deliberate attempt of the Bavarian government under Gustav von Kahr to poison the political and intellectual atmosphere.

The next special issue, the combined November-December number of 1921, was devoted exclusively to literature.[17] Frisch always chafed under the limitations of space which often precluded acceptance of lengthy novellas and of poetry.[18] He finally decided to skip one issue to double up on the next and assume his favorite role, that of an "Intendant der Literatur," as Karl Otten called him in an interview of 9 September 1961. Frisch managed this issue superbly; he reverted to earlier years and actively solicited for it. The results were gratifying: Heinrich Mann, Regina Ullman, Josef Ponten, and Robert Musil contributed short stories; Bert Brecht, Hermann Kasack, Friedrich Leopold, Arnold Ulitz, Friedrich Sieburg, Klabund, Rudolf R. Binding, and Johannes R. Becher poetry; Alfred Döblin, Hans Carossa, and Oskar Loerke self-contained excerpts from novels in progress; Paul Adler an act from his latest drama; and Bernhard Diebold gave the entire issue an inner cohesiveness with an essay of literary criticism.

The final special issue, the so-called Rhineland number,[19] was the tribute the patriot Efraim Frisch paid to his country, which in his opinion was being maltreated by the French occupation and in danger of losing the Rhineland permanently. Its subtle appeal to the better nature of the French, its avoidance of all catch phrases or inflammatory speeches, its completely factual articles on Rhenish geography, economy, and history, all skillfully interwoven with Paul Ortwin Rawe's "Bekenntnis Zum Rhein" (Rhenish Credo)[20] and Wilhelm Schmidtbonn's "Reise nach Orplid,"[21] an emotional drama of German immigrants forced to leave their homeland after an (unspecified) war, made this issue an ideal propaganda instrument; the naked emotional appeal was concealed beneath the covering cloak of unexceptionable reasonability. The German Foreign Office, much to Frisch's satisfaction, bought numerous reprints of this number.

Apparently Frisch took particular delight in the success of his special issues. The reason is patent: These four issues sharpened the profile of the magazine and defined the convictions of its editor. Here, as on many other occasions, the magazine (as Ferdinand Lion has put it) represented the Weimar Republic.

The special issues had yet another effect on the tenor of the magazine. By bringing together, between the covers of a single issue, proponents of divergent points of view, the editors intensified the controversies within the magazine. Both Frisch and Hausenstein knew, of course, that controversy is the lifeblood of a newspaper or magazine. Frisch, an expert on the theater, saw to it, for example, that debates about its nature and function often became an exchange of brilliant parries and thrusts which lent the *Neue Merkur* the excitement of a fencing ring. Likewise, Robert Müller's riposte to Thomas Mann's attack on Activism was submitted as a result of Frisch's explicit solicitation.[22] As he told Leo Matthias and

Müller in letters of 27 and 14 February 1922 respectively, Frisch felt compelled "to bring about a judicious correction of certain distortions in Thomas Mann's article" and "to confute certain crass inaccuracies."

Most controversies were conducted with a certain largesse and left little or no acrimony. Thomas Mann, for example, far from being offended by Müller's attack, responded to Müller's closely reasoned refutation with a compliment.[23] Count Richard Coudenhove-Kalergi, the founder and for many years president of the Pan-Europe movement, in a similar spirit of amicability took no exception when his declaration of faith in technology called forth a lengthy critique by Leo Matthias, who took him to task for "identifying technological progress with progress in general."[24] The criticized author remarked, in an interview of October 1961: "Matthias took an entirely reasonable point of view; it is more than possible that technology will some day destroy our culture. And the certainty of finding alert and enlightened criticisms of previous articles in the *Merkur* was one of the attractions for contributors and readers alike."

The same spirit pervaded the debate between Rudolf Pannwitz, who advocated a united Europe, and Robert Müller, who championed "one world."[25] Although not convinced of Müller's argument ("I see here a factual misunderstanding; geography is for me only a *conditio sine qua non*"), Pannwitz welcomed controversy as a means of keeping issues before the public (in a letter to Frisch of 22 December 1919). Otto Flake wrote in a similar vein a sober and objective reply to Döblin's annihilating critique of his novel *Stadt des Hirns* (Cerebral City) – though his letters to the *Merkur* became noticeably cooler for a while.[26]

Ferdinand Lion took a different view of the *Merkur's* family feuds. "All the contributors," he said in an interview of 25 September 1961, "were always anxious to knife another." Some of the controversies support Lion's view. When Alfred Döblin found his own work attacked—Friedrich Burschell had taken exception to the historical inaccuracies in his novel *Wallenstein*—he replied with considerable heat: "The worst [element] among the public are the critics. Just as a voluptuary profanes the secrets of love, they profane a work through their glance and their touch."[27] As we know from the editorial correspondence, the first version of the riposte was even more heated. Acting upon Frisch's suggestion, he requested a return of the article about Burschell for revisions: "I shall enlarge it," he wrote, "and remove everything that refers directly to B."[28]

The most violent controversy never saw print. Leo Matthias treated a favorable review of Hiller's *Aufbruch zum Paradies* (Departure for Paradise), by Hans Poeschel,[29] as a personal insult. Finding that it controverted his own article about the philosopher Leonard Nelson, he wrote Frisch, in a letter of 4 August 1922: "Words fail me to label such

disloyalty. It is almost German." Frisch, in his reply to Matthias of 12
September 1922, for once did not ask a critic to submit a rebuttal: "What
harm does it do if someone [i.e., Hans Poeschel] enjoys Hiller's book;
even his opponents might find likeable and honorable traits in his character. How very German among German authors is this arranged family
hatred! And how powerless does it render them vis-à-vis the closed ranks
of pedantry and brutality." Frisch probably felt that Leo Matthias, one
of his most contentious contributors, would have made this discussion
too lively. But upon other occasions he encouraged controversy, perhaps
even a little of the "knifing" about which Ferdinand Lion complained.
For the readers of the *Merkur*, however, it was (and is) an exhilarating
experience to watch the combatants, spurred by contradiction, continuously reach greater and greater mental heights. When the *Merkur*, in
1923, went into its state of suspended animation, the penchant for family
feuds died. Under the aegis of the Deutsche Verlags-Anstalt the *Merkur*
would acquire still greater respectability, but lose some of its zest and,
one is tempted to say, amateurish fun and abandon.

The road towards dependency upon an older and stronger brother began in 1922. In September of that year, Frisch had to subjoin his own
publishing house, for financial security, to a larger one, the O. C. Recht
Verlag of Munich. The inflation in Germany was well under way. In 1921
a single issue of the *Merkur* sold for RM 5.50; in January 1922 it cost
RM 10; in April, RM 19; in May, RM 24; in September, though now subsidized by a larger publisher, RM 30; in October, RM 60; in November,
RM 130; and by January 1923, it had risen to the astronomical height
of a half-million RM. With his financial reserves devalued, Frisch had to
seek funds elsewhere; through Joachim Friedenthal, the chief editor of
the house, he opened negotiations with the O. C. Recht Verlag and at the
same time, in August 1922, asked for financial aid from his cousin,
Israel Ber Neumann, a Berlin art dealer. On 27 July Frisch sent a letter
to the Department of Internal Revenue in Munich which spelled the end
of his career as publisher but the temporary survival of the *Merkur*:
"We wish to inform you that the firms of Israel Ber Neumann and the
publishing house of O. C. Recht have deposited in cash 70,000 M. each
for the unrestricted use of the business managers."

What follows is tragicomic. Both the O. C. Recht Verlag and its newly
acquired journal relentlessly slithered down the *glissade* of the German
inflation; by the time the magazine reached the newsstands its paper
was worth more than its price. Conversely, the payments to its contributors, no matter how carefully adjusted to the emergency scales of
the Schutzverband deutscher Schriftsteller (Authors' Protective League),
had grown miniscule upon receipt.[30] Their ire brought forth some of the

choicest barbs in the polemics-studded editorial correspondence. "In order to put an end to the ridiculous mailing and returning of a simple ten-million Mark bill," Hanns Braun began a tirade in a letter to Frisch on 23 September 1923. "Your behavior disgusts me," thundered Friedrich Sternthal. And Leo Matthias, on 6 February 1922, was even less subtle: "I have sent the money [i.e., 5000 M. for twelve pages of copy] back to the publishers and suggested a use for it which is generally accorded worthless paper."

At the end of the January 1923 issue, the O. C. Recht Verlag divorced itself from the magazine; the brief marriage, as happens so often, had foundered because of finances. A short postscript to the last issue, however, announced that the magazine was not dead, but had merely gone into enforced hibernation beneath a cover of worthless million-Mark bills:

To Our Readers and Friends

Because of the most recent enormous rise in production and operating costs we have been forced, unfortunately, to interrupt the publication of our journal. For almost six years, through a war and all the convulsions of this peace, the *Neue Merkur* has carried on its quiet and tenacious work and attained a position of pre-eminence. But confronted by a development in whose wake every enterprise is smothered which is not directly concerned with making a profit, its means no longer suffice. Those who, out of an idealistic interest, have not shunned sacrifices to maintain a representative German magazine, are no longer able to sustain a deficit which . . . with the growing devaluation of the Mark, would but steadily increase.

Given the reputation and wide distribution of the *Neue Merkur* we may speedily resume our task, if—and only if—our present subscribers not only renew, but also help us acquire an increase in new subscribers. We are convinced that for many who are in sympathy with our intentions a mere hint will suffice. . . .

We conclude with this issue the fourth quarter as well as the year of publication 1922/23.[31]

3   *The Message of Mercury*

Part I

Despite Efraim Frisch's exuberant commitment to the revival of the *Neue Merkur*, the mood of the magazine itself, reflecting that of defeated Germany, was somber. A note of resignation and pessimism had crept in and it accompanied the magazine until its demise.

Frisch's first post-war editorial set this mood. After welcoming the end of the war and the revolutionary upheaval as well as the birth of a new Germany, he lashed out sharply at his countrymen for past and present transgressions and at the Allies for creating, by similar sins, the grounds for a new world conflict. The dreamers of Germany's world domination, he argued, had turned into the day's pragmatic politicians (*Realpolitiker*) and materialists; in their effort to do business as usual, the conservatives still appealed to shopworn national emotions; the old and new German politicians showed no spirit of sacrifice or magnanimity, but continued, rather, the opportunism and the exploded and discredited dreams of German power. He felt, further, that the Allies seemed bent on repeating Germany's errors of yesteryear. The undoing of Germany was, in part, politics without intellectual and spiritual background; but the Allies were retaining *their* war-time militaristic leaders in government.

The Germans had suffered from hybris in their imperialistic war aims; they should have fought for a stable Europe, made no territorial demands or, at the least, seized the Allied offer for negotiations after the defeat of the Russians, instead of driving out the devil with Beelzebub by supporting Lenin and the soviets against Kerensky. The Entente's European policy appeared at that time equally dubious: the continuing blockade and the resultant starvation in Central Europe, the unconciliatory attitude towards the new German government, the denial of self-determination to German nationals, and a forcibly imposed peace indicated that the Allies, too, might fail at their hour of destiny. Perhaps, Frisch warned, it may be necessary to support the defeated enemy as a future ally in a fight for the preservation of the old economic and social order:

> Above all, the implementation of justice is promised us ("But the law cannot be carried out," says St. Paul). There is still no common bond. There is still a need for sacrifice, long, conscious renunciation. A long slow descent. Day by day the little that has gladdened and elevated us will disappear. Spectacles of the most oppressive kind. Have no illusions. Grow internally, toward other values, towards a new entity. Our reascendancy has been removed into a distance inaccessible to our eyes today.[1]

Given this resignation, why, one may ask, did Frisch and Hausenstein trouble to edit a magazine that continued to pledge itself to a "renewal of the German spirit"? Did, perhaps, the editors share the conviction of their young contributor, Coudenhove-Kalergi, that one must think black, but act white?[2] Whether held consciously or not, only such a principle, coupled with their initial compulsive dedication, can explain the dichotomy between the above despairing editorial and a prefatory note to the *Vorläufer* which, beyond restating the principles of the magazine (above all its impartiality in artistic and literary movements), lightened the somberness of the editorial at least into a chiaroscuro:

> We who have long regarded the flight of intellectual and spiritual values from politics as the prime cause of the disintegration which led to decay and collapse, need now no other attitude than the reaffirmation of our original convictions which were dedicated to the concentration and renewal of the spirit. In Socialism we see not only no divisive force but, on the contrary, the bond missing for so long which is destined to effect a new structure of society.[3]

This mood of faint hope breaking through despair was that of all Germany; never before or after was the *Merkur* so delicately attuned to the times and environment, nor, conversely, so much subject to their discordancies.

In short, during these years of crisis the articles and literary works in the *Merkur* tried to interpret the amorphousness of its times, surroundings, and own history. Their instability induced topicality; their painfulness induced self-analysis; and both occasionally provoked flight from reality. At this time the *Merkur* asked a series of questions—consistently and in startling variations: How did war come? Who is to blame? What was its true face? Why did we lose it? How do we bind up its wounds and avoid its recurrence? Which inner values will compensate for the loss in German prestige and territory? Which directions—in politics, literature, art, education, and philosophy—will lead to their attainment? And though some articles directed themselves only peripherally to these topics or even seemed to lead away from them, the magazine as an entity returned to this basic inquiry with a determination inspired by a searing past, a dissatisfying present, and an ill-boding future. Frisch, often without immediate reason, told his staff repeatedly that they were fighting a lost cause. He also felt that redemption, if it should arrive against all hope, could come about only through solving these seven questions.

The analysis of the causes of war, though accurate, for the most part limited itself to generalities; Frisch wisely rejected speculations upon specifics. The perspective was lacking and the documentary evidence still unavailable to the public. This policy, however, reduced these analyses—and not only by today's standards—to truisms and commonplaces. Rudolf Kayser, for example, predicted in a letter to Frisch of 8 July 1920 that his essay would be highly successful, since it "expressed for the first time what thousands now feel." But "what thousands now feel" rarely startles through originality and, in fact, Kayser's observation that nationalism, especially among the intellectuals, led and will lead to war, seems trite, if not banal. The same applies, if slightly less so, to remarks by Karl Bröger and Bernhard Diebold[4] that German leadership suffered from stupidity and hybris rather than ill will and hence stumbled into a war not of its seeking. Frisch, merely in passing, pilloried Prussian leaders and rejected their protestations of innocence in the rush to war.[5] Friedrich Sternthal's conviction, though often repeated, is still pertinent, because of the timeliness of its warning. He argued, from a historical perspective, that the rise of militarism in Germany since 1871 had brought about his country's destruction: "Germany must remember that it has confused, for more than fifty years, power and strength; it thought militaristically and destructively rather than statesman-like and creatively." And he warned: "Germany cannot prosper under militarism."[6] Despite their superficiality these early articles on the causes of war had their momentary usefulness: They counterbalanced the shrieks on the far right, audible in even those first post-war months, that war came as the result of a giant Allied conspiracy and that culpability rested with Germany's enemies alone.

In its own exploration of guilt the *Merkur* frequently reverted to its war-time policy of stating a middle course after a clash of antitheses.

Alfred Döblin, in an article which he himself described, in a letter of
23 December 1918, as "red-hot outpourings" (and which the *Neue Rundschau* had rejected as "too impulsive") accused the Allies of bearing the
major part of the guilt: "Undoubtedly the goal of the war was the expansion of power; it was a modern war of conquest. The fault is with the
other side; they should never have let it come to this [i.e., they should
have made some concessions to Germany]." In the very same issue Arthur
Holitscher argued the other side with equal heat: "Knaves misused us—
us, the people, for their knavish tricks."[7] He accused himself for not having fought against war more actively and admitted, remorsefully, that the
hatred his country expended on the enemy should have been directed
against "the truly guilty" at home.

Most articles represented shades of opinion between these two extremes.
Frisch and Hausenstein, while denying Germany's sole or major guilt,
repeatedly scored their country for turning imperialistic with the peace
of Brest-Litovsk. Their moderation was typical. Benno Reifenberg, for
example, warned against the prevailing mood of *mea culpa*, but conceded
that Germany *had* sinned.[8] Friedrich Sternthal, after denouncing Allied
aggression even after the peace treaty, reminded his readers of Germany's
breach of a treaty, the non-aggression pact with Belgium.[9] Thomas Mann,
who combined idyll with politics in his epic, "Gesang vom Kindchen, Ein
Idyll," spoke of the "guiltless-guilty fatherland" which "beats its breast
in contrite self-accusation." And he added: "Even if . . . [our opponents]
were no better, still Germany was evil / For times were base, and but too
faithfully served them thy people."[10]

A. Mendelssohn-Bartholdy, who had been a member of a special committee charged to write a memorandum on the question of war guilt, rendered, after the official acceptance of Germany's sole responsibility for
aggression, an almost classic verdict:

> A convalescence in the traffic between nations . . . can only come
> about, if precisely those states that are powerful militarily become
> convinced, through public opinion, that the methods of 1905,
> 1908, 1912, 1914 were ruinous; those of Paris, London, and Rome
> no less than those of Vienna, St. Petersburg, and Berlin. In this
> sense the question of guilt is, indeed, the most important European
> concern of our times.[11]

Germany's self-analysis, as recorded in the *Merkur*, was remarkably
astute; its validity remains unchallenged by more recent diagnoses. Most
of the findings elaborate upon one basic symptom; the paranoiac fluctu-
ation between two extremes. "They [the Germans] oscillate between two

dangers: to have no order at all or *just one* order which deadens the flesh and the spirit," said Erich von Kahler.[12] Unlike the Dutch and English they lack moderation, argued Wedderkop and Sternthal respectively.[13] Historically, maintained Karl Gareis, they have smothered their revolutions by a violent *volte-face*—and, as in the case of Luther, both action and reaction were often spearheaded by the same person.[14] They waver between ideal and reality (Felix Braun),[15] between optimism and pessimism (Helmuth Plessner),[16] between love and hatred for England: they alternately say of the English, "Look how repulsive they are . . . and oh, if we could only be like them" (Frisch).[17] And Rudolf Pannwitz argued that this oscillation is but the outward manifestation of an intrinsic inconsistency:

> In addition [there is] the German, especially Prussian, peculiarity of feeling compelled and obligated to dedicate oneself to a cause while wishing, at the same time, to keep oneself tightly under control. This results in a devotion by halves, a feeling that its rendering is a sacrifice. And one feels resentful and mutinous against and humiliated by the person to whom one has offered this sacrifice. Through this process devotion becomes dishonest and turns into subservience. But subservience, a basic drive, fulfills itself by breaking a man's pride which, itself a basic drive, avenges itself [by turning on] devotion.[18]

German subservience was castigated by several additional articles. "They gladly, all too gladly, accept leadership," mourned Friedrich Burschell.[19] And other authors detailed this charge; Flake found his countrymen too deferential to its generals and experts,[20] Kahler to each government in power,[21] and Stefan Grossmann to its press.[22] Grossmann had charged that the German press wanted domination over its readers; he strikingly proved his point when he announced (in a letter to Frisch, n.d.) that the article had led to his dismissal from the editorial staff of the *Vossische Zeitung*. Finally, Rudolf Pannwitz, deploring German stridency in the past, admonished his country: "*Lieb Vaterland, halt's Maul!*" (Dear Fatherland, keep thy trap shut!).[23]

These harsh judgments upon themselves, only occasionally relieved by pride in the German past and the national talent for art, music, and literature, followed the trial of a harsh war and an equally harsh peace. The *Merkur* castigated both. In all the post-war years, when "the experience of the trenches" was openly or subtly glorified by countless German authors, many of them among Germany's best, the *Merkur*, with but one exception, painted only its grimness. It stressed, as one might expect from

a magazine of its type, the devastation of the spirit more than that of land
and people. While the excerpts of Hans Carossa's "Diary from the Rumanian Front," for example, show, sometimes with medical exactitude,
the physical sufferings of civilians and soldiers,[24] many others, such as
Otto Flake's short story "Die Qual" (The Torture), are concerned with
the agony of the mind. In Flake's tale a young man feels his mind being
poisoned by a chauvinistic high school teacher who perverts history and
literature into instruments of envenomed propaganda.[25]

Karl Bröger, a poet whom the Nazis were later to distort for their own
propaganda, surveyed the total devastation of the spirit: "The effect of
the war has been identical on the physical and the spiritual terrain.
Everything is riddled by bullets, the mind a field of artillery craters
stretching over the face of the earth. What has become of the Reconstruction Commission for this desolation?"[26] A few issues later, Werner Richter transmuted a feverish soldier on horseback into an apocalyptic vision:

> Finally your ears are filled with noiseless but incessant shrieks—
> by which the fever announces itself. And while they swell, dissolv-
> ing consciousness, you see, ever more clearly, a nameless evil in
> the relentless sun, perhaps a giant hen brooding as if possessed or
> a monstrous, love-crazed female ape that burns to cinders every-
> thing that comes within the reach of her insidious embrace.[27]

How much has Werner Richter presented here out of the perspective of a
genuine poet! Lou Andreas-Salomé exclaimed in a letter to Frisch of
7 August 1920.

Unfortunately, too many German poets, no less "genuine" and heeded
far more often, labored to reveal the supposed glamour and glory of war
beneath its grime. The *Neue Merkur* all but once barred their products;
in a poem by Rudolf Binding, however, the note of *dulce et decorum est*
. . . remained undetected among more dirgeful poems. The title, "Stolz
und Trauer" (Pride and Sorrow) should have been preparation, however, for lines such as these:

> Wie leicht wird nun alles. Es ist, als hübe das Sterben
> die Leiber sanft aus den Armen der Erde empor:
> wie man einer Mutter ein Kind abnimmt.—
> Die Stimmen der Sehnsucht verstummten.
> Gestillt auf immer war das Verlangen nach Fernem.
> Besinnung wurde langsam hinausgetragen
> wie ein Licht. Nur das Auge
> wandte noch einmal

> ewig sich auf zum erblindenden Himmel.—
> Dann kam der Tod, der alles einfach macht.[28]

Death in battle rarely has such grace.

The reasons for Germany's loss and losses were the subject of much speculation. Surprisingly, the *Neue Merkur* did not bother to controvert the legend of the stab in the back; instead it cast the blame where it felt it belonged. Four of the most respected historians and political scientists among its contributors as well as Frisch himself explored Germany's weaknesses during the war. Although Frisch had suggested, in the very first post-war issue, that Germany had committed suicide by continuing the war after the Russian defeat instead of entering into negotiations with the Western Allies,[29] Willy Andreas blamed Hertling, Reichskanzler and Prime Minister of Prussia, for this failure.[30]

In a subsequent article, Andreas expanded on this topic. To Germany's detriment, the military had moved into a vacuum of power; the Emperor, his constitutional advisers, and especially the German civil service had defaulted in their responsibilities. He conceded the competence and conscientiousness of German officials, but found them wanting in initiative and independence: "Finally this civil service had to become a nail in Germany's coffin when it was thrown on its own resources as a result of incompetence in higher quarters, when they were called upon to win a world war, when it was faced with the task of *governing* instead of *administrating*, of *leading* instead of *serving*. . . . Finally it feebly succumbed in its fight against the jurisdictional infringements of the military."[31] Civil authorities also erred, as Otto Flake argued, in their fiscal policies; they protected big capital and hence encouraged the war profiteers.[32]

The *Merkur* was ready to admit Germany's transgressions in war; however, it found Allied conduct in peace equally reprehensible. Often the *Merkur* cleverly used contributions or reprints of prominent foreign authors, for example Shaw, Keynes, and Waldo Frank, to bolster its own editorial position; to the same end it solicited contributions from German authors, such as Mendelssohn-Bartholdy, Willy Andreas, and Lujo Brentano, who were well-known abroad. Through their pens it attacked virtually every provision of the treaties of Versailles and St. Germain, the "farcial" ineffectualness of the League of Nations and its exclusion of Germany, the dismantling of German industries and the acquisition of territory, the denial of self-determination to its citizens, the oppressive occupation of the Rhineland and the Ruhr Valley, and, finally, the demand of reparations from a country whose citizens were starving.

These and similar protests, original then but hackneyed now, need no elaborate summary. But even then their tone and source were more important than their content. And the critical tone in which the Allies were berated was unmistakable; they were called "poison brewers," "dictators of Versailles," "hypocrites," "roguishly virtuous"—this by Thomas Mann[33]—"arrogant, unconscionable victors," "[authors of] a web of infamy, breach of faith, deceit, coercion, and nonsense." All of these invectives reflected a bitter disappointment with the Western Allies. Albrecht Mendelssohn-Bartholdy, who had gone to Versailles with some hope for a new Germany and, in an undated letter to Frisch, had even written most optimistically about a new form of its government, had in despair joined the chorus of accusers and pessimists one year later. He had come to feel that Versailles foredoomed the Weimar Republic.

The intemperance of these attacks was deliberate. As evidenced in reviews, both foreign and domestic, the *Merkur's* democratic and moderate stand was, by then, clearly understood. Since its sharp protests could not be misunderstood as the voice of rightist revengists or of anti-Western Communists, its editors, in order to assure themselves of a wider echo, preferred thunder to gentle rebuke. It has undoubtedly become necessary to enlighten, *in a suitable manner*, the *Merkur's* circle of readers about the ominous meaning and presumable development of the hitherto established facts, Frisch wrote Mendelssohn-Bartholdy on 12 May 1919. He well knew that "this circle of readers" included such foreign statesmen as Masaryk, Gallarati-Scotti, and Aristide Briand, who would distinguish the democratic and usually moderate voice of the *Merkur* from the choir of the Nationalists. By its sudden and rare immoderation he wished to shock them and other Allied leaders into an awareness of their folly and its probable results. Frisch knew all too well that by ignoring this appeal from their closest friends in Germany, the Allies were giving a weapon to their worst enemies. Frisch had found evidence for such apprehensions right in his editorial correspondence.

On 30 December 1919 Luis Brinkmann, the *Merkur's* Spanish correspondent, had written Frisch a remarkable letter in which he first advised him to publish, in his *Auslandspost*, preponderantly adverse foreign reports about Germany, so that the Germans would know where they stood, and then offered some suggestions on how to arouse the Germans to a war of liberation. It is small wonder that Frisch, convinced that Allied intransigence would but strengthen the Nationalists, had grave concerns about the policies of Germany's former enemies.

In fact the stance of the Allies smothered the *Merkur's* budding affection, its reversal of war-time bellicosity. Its attitude towards former friends and foes provides, in effect, a fascinating perspective on the "foreign policy" of Germany's liberal intellectuals. Their warmest approval, and the *Merkur*'s, was reserved for those small nations who were new creations, such as Czechoslovakia, or who had been inactive during the war, such as Holland. Thomas G. Masaryk, for example, was the only foreign head of state ever to be reprinted in the *Merkur*.[34]

Similarly the *Merkur* continued its cordiality towards Austria: it advocated in its pages, as did many intellectuals on both sides of the border, a speedy fusion of the two neighbors.[35] Nothing demonstrates Frisch's conviction on this topic more dramatically than his unsuccessful attempt to solicit the help of Hugo von Hofmannsthal for this cause. In a letter of 22 May 1919 he reported to Hofmannsthal, whose acquaintance he had made during the war at the house of Beer-Hofmann, the results of a conversation with Ludo M. Hartmann, the Austrian ambassador to Germany. According to Frisch, Hartmann had complained that German-Austrian unification was not championed warmly and emphatically enough by its advocates and hence had no resonance. Frisch now suggested that an appeal by Hofmannsthal, to be published in the *Merkur*, would on the other hand leave "the strongest impression."

In a letter of 10 June 1919 Hofmannsthal sent one of the most illuminating letters of refusal in the history of the magazine. After commenting on a book he received from Frisch and in return calling his attention to the recently published *Untergang des Abendlandes* by Oswald Spengler, he proceeded to explain the reasons for his refusal to comply with the editor's wish. In the first place, essayism, its form of expression and way of thinking as a mere formal truth of thought and at most a momentary truth of temperament, had long become questionable to him. Moreover, he found it very difficult to take up any position on the problem of Austrian annexation itself. To Hofmannsthal, the arguments in favor seemed empty, the promoters of the *Anschluss* typical politicians, only able to think two-dimensionally, unaware of the physical and fatal problems of, for example, a state of sixty to eighty millions! From such "politics" he wanted to divorce himself, even if it meant unpopularity as a writer and person. Frisch could have done worse than reprint this letter, though going counter to his own opinion, as a contribution to the discussion of "German-Austrian Union Now."

Against Italy, the "deserter" from the ranks of the Central Powers, the *Merkur* maintained an undisguised and understandable *Schadenfreude*, that peculiarly German joy in the misfortune of others. Harry Kahn, in an article entitled "Italienischer Katzenjammer" (Italian Hangover), delighted in the slighting of Italy at the Peace Conference; Giuseppe Prezzolini, a well-known Italian essayist, concurred—and was gently rebuked in the Italian press for his lack of national feelings.[36]

On the momentum of its war-time hostility, the *Merkur* at first continued its sharp criticism of the English. Only towards the end of 1922, perhaps as a result of Lloyd George's reversal of his anti-German attitude, did more complimentary descriptions replace such invectives as "the British and their cant," the "hypocritical" or "Machiavellian" British.[37] Rob Rab, an author for the *New Age*, the close English equivalent to the *Neue Merkur*, opened the way for the *Merkur*'s "conciliation" with the British Empire. Though Rob Rab wrote more in censure than in praise of the English, he did strike at some German prejudices against Lloyd George and other British statesmen.[38] Mendelssohn-Bartholdy, at first antagonistic towards the British, in later articles praised two British political leaders, Lionel Curtis and Edward Fry.[39] Most telling, however, was Frisch's plan, revealed in a letter to Alfons Paquet of 21 April 1920, of publishing a special English-language issue. He intended it as a "depiction of Germany's domestic situation and foreign relations for the benefit of English readers." By June 1922, the projected date of publication, the financial crisis of the magazine had, however, barred this final stage on the road from complete Anglophobia to qualified Anglophilia.

The *Merkur*'s attitude towards Russia seems to defy logic; it vacillated from issue to issue. Panegyrics to the new Russia alternated with denunciations of its tyrannical government; the shades of opinion ranged from White Russian to parlor pink. On one end of the spectrum blazed the articles of Alfons Paquet who, disgusted with the Western Allies, had suddenly "discovered" Russia, the East, Pan-Slavism, and a cultural consanguinity between Germans and Russians. "The West," he announced categorically, "has little to give us at this state of our search except the invitation to help ourselves. Looking West, our disappointment is large and definite. Many European thinkers seem to agree, gradually, that the East will mean more for the future of Europe than the West." He also presaged a new flowering of the arts amidst the liberated Russian people and a cross-fertilization between them and the Germans. The Germans, he felt, would lend their eastern neighbor their industry, skill, and drive; the Russians, in turn, "will make us conscious and develop our slumbering spiritual forces . . . [through] the great thoughts of their character, which is striving upward with the vigor of youth."[40]

Otto Flake and Kurt Hiller, taking the opposite position, scoffed at such rose or pink-colored views of Soviet Russia and at German intellectuals who, like Arthur Holitscher, "try to cover up the despotic experiments [of the Soviets], because they wish for Communism." And Maxim Gorky's article "Russische Grausamkeit" (Russian [i.e., Soviet] Cruelty), anticipates the reports about Nazi concentration camps.[41]

Frisch's own views were only obliquely expressed and may even have escaped some of his readers. In an article on Dostoevski he mildly ad-

monished the Soviets for misusing that author's works as justification for
their domestic policies and for their abandonment of international Marxism in favor of Russian nationalism. But his letters are more sharply
critical of Russia's new masters. Yet, despite these convictions, he accepted outspokenly pro-Russian articles and rejected others which wanted
to refute the former.[42] What, one may ask, were his motives for doing so?

The many purely reportorial articles about Soviet Russia and its literature and culture were, of course, meant to satisfy a voguish curiosity of
Germany's intellectuals; the reasons for the controversial articles were
more devious. The *Neue Merkur*, a faithful satellite of the Weimar Republic, was clearly emulating its *Schaukelpolitik* (wavering policy) between East and West; the pro-Russian articles of Paquet and others were
the Rapallo Pact of the *Neue Merkur*, an implied threat to the West that
its harshness might drive Germany into the arms of the Soviets. Ernst
Robert Curtius, the *Merkur*'s "discovery" and its spokesman on "foreign
policy," perhaps inadvertently divulged this hidden intention when he
wrote in the *Auslandsheft*: "Young Germany is turning to the East and
its back on the West. . . . The sympathies for Bolshevism which a part of
our youth displays is but an outer symptom of this change." He implied
that only a reversal of Western policy could reverse the Germans' ideological drift to the East.[43] The *Neue Merkur*, by its ceaseless controversies
about Soviet Russia, meant to make the same point. As magazine editors,
Frisch and Hausenstein wished to demonstrate that a consistent argument
can be forged out of planned inconsistency.

Of all Germany's former enemies, the United States fared best and
worst in the pages of the *Neue Merkur*. Not a single word reminded readers of America's hostile participation in the late war; the U. S. Expedi-
tionary Force that had tipped the scales escaped the *Merkur*'s occasional
censure of the various Allied armies. The fire withheld from its soldiers,
however, was discharged all the more violently at the civilians of the
United States, from the President on down. Wilson's alleged failure at
Versailles and the short-sightedness of his isolationist opponents in the
Senate elicited several broadsides;[44] scattered shots were fired at all the
supposed blemishes in the American national character.

The Americans, Felix Braun maintained, "have drawn the lot, unique
in the history of all people, of receiving a period of civilization immediately after an initial period of barbarism; they completely lack, using the
concept in the sense of Spengler and Thomas Mann, an era of culture."
They were completely materialistic; their cities, in the words of Paquet,
were totally corrupted: "Noch so jung, und schon so krank / Ist die Stadt
am Michigan. / Grosses Herz Amerikas / Zornig mittendurchgerissen,"
he wrote. (Still so young, and yet so ill / Is that town on Lake Michigan. /

Large heart of America / Torn asunder wrathfully.) Robert Müller found
the United States a melting pot and, as early as 1920, New York's subways
hopelessly crowded. Waldo Frank, in describing his compatriots as materialists in search of idealistic facades, proved Winston Churchill's advice that criticism of the United States should be left to Americans,
"because they do it so much better."[45]

Luckily for the maligned Americans, an occasional article such as Otto
Flake's concentrated on their virtues, their realism, ingenuousness (in
the sense of Goethe's "Amerika" poem), their irony and noninvolvement
"which will some day supplant the sentimental and *petite-bourgeois* German character."[46] Perhaps even more luckily, the most vituperative article, which analyzed the Americans "as I see them," as overbearing, as
attached only to physical comfort, and as "gigantically inadequate,"
probably was self-defeating, since towards the end its author, Adrien
Turel, conceded that he had never been in the United States.[47]

None of the articles about Germany's former enemies were as suasive,
even missionary in tone, as those about France. The *Neue Merkur*, in the
words of Max Rychner (in a letter to Frisch of 11 May 1922), took the
leading role in Germany in regard to the problem of German-French relations; at its behest intellectual leaders on both sides of the border explored the rift between the two peoples and methods for bridging it. Once
begun, the discussion spread to groups and individuals, newspapers and
magazines, in all parts of Europe. For once the *Merkur* spoke for many
on a subject vital to all.

In its pursuit of better French-German relations, the *Merkur* turned
successively historical, censorious, and conciliatory. The magazine explained the historic basis for past and present feuds between the two
countries, castigated those who perpetuated the traditional enmity and
lauded those attempting to bury it. The historical presentation, a brilliant, impelling, far-ranging yet disciplined series of articles by Ferdinand Lion, an Alsatian sympathetic to both cultures, cleared away some
past misunderstandings. Why, many German democrats had asked, do
none of the major parties of revolutionary France support a revolutionary Germany? It is simply political convenience and fear, Lion argued.
"An empire [as a form of government] would isolate Germany, make it
impossible as an ally, and sharpen its party conflicts." He added: "The
empire is a pointed dagger which, however, once it bounces off [its tar-
get] has been overcome, while a [German] democracy of the masses will
always appear invincible."[48]

Lion echoed the frequently voiced charge that the victors were lacking
in magnanimity. But he coupled this accusation (as did Frisch in a prefatory note to Lion's "Verstandespolitik") with the reminder that Germany

had likewise been less than generous in 1871. While both denied that this historical "parallel [was meant] *ad usum delphini*"—they undoubtedly realized that their German readers were in no mood to be lectured to—these deft and subtly inserted reminders gave the lie to the denials.[49]

Where the *Merkur* could not condone, it condemned. Poincaré, Clemenceau, Foch, and all other advocates of a rigid policy against Germany, transgressors in the French army of occupation, chauvinistic iconoclasts in Alsace-Lorraine, tactless French diplomats who had failed to send a note of condolence after Rathenau's assassination, Germanophobes amongst the French intelligentsia: they were the targets of diatribes, protests, and even invectives.[50] "Debased France!" thundered Ernst Bloch. "The victors have gone too far," protested Friedrich Burschell, and Otto Flake warned:

> More tragic than the Bavarian puerilities is something else: the French attitude to the [German] Republic. No help, no well-intentioned gesture, nothing. More than others the French ought to comprehend that a form of government which has supplanted a flesh-and-blood tradition, cannot become a [national] experience unless it has some success in its foreign policy.
>
> The nationalists ask: of what use is the Republic to us. And they answer: none at all. It is unbearable, how blind the French are to the fact that an easing of the German burden is in their own interest.[51]

Exasperated with the official French policy, the *Neue Merkur* began, in its *Auslandsheft* of June 1921, a series of direct appeals to French intellectuals. As his first spokesman Frisch chose Ernst Curtius, whose opinions on the subject he shared entirely. What you write about the mode of *rapprochement* with France, Frisch wrote in a highly complimentary letter of 5 July 1921, exactly corresponds with our intentions. Frisch's choice of spokesman turned out to have been an inspiration. The Marburg professor, then virtually unknown to the general public and hence not identified with any party or splinter group, enjoyed, on the other hand, the most profound respect of writers and literary historians on both sides of the border. Curtius entitled his article "Deutsch-französische Kulturprobleme" (German-French Cultural Problems).[52]

He began his appeal with the evocation of a happier past, the years immediately before World War I. At that time "the educated youth of Germany and France had found a path to one another, spontaneously and without a party program, on the basis—truly the only natural and feasible one—of shared new experiences, which they discovered with surprise and

gratification. . . . Never before were the prospects for mutual understanding as auspicious as at the moment when the world war broke out." But,
unfortunately, the rapprochement "was destroyed before blossoms could
ripen into fruit."

Curtius found the young Germans of 1921 indifferent to France. Some
had turned for inspiration to the East, to China, India, or to Russia and
Bolshevism; others to the pedantic alternative of cultural nationalism. To
recapture their attention, France would have to give evidence that, by
drawing on its old traditions and an inexhaustible vitality, it could continue to make new, conspicuous contributions.

But the young Frenchmen were equally loath to embrace their German
opposite numbers. The animosity of war had erased shared intellectual
experiences. "Often hatred has spread even to the sphere of literature
which we once considered a common meeting ground." And not only the
ultra-nationalists in France, but nearly all French publications and authors, yes, even such intellectual leaders as Paul Claudel, were perpetuating the stereotype of the bloodthirsty German, solely and completely
responsible for the war. The few dissenters in France, for example Romain Rolland, who were trying to mediate between the two peoples, were
treated as pariahs.

According to Curtius, the one group in France opposed to French nationalism, Henri Barbusse's Clarté group, unfortunately offered no work-
able solution. Based on "an extreme, now completely anaemic schemati-
zation of eighteenth and nineteenth-century rationalism," this polemic or
pacifistic activism proposed an internationalism which was utopian to
begin with, and demanded, moreover, a *sacrifizio dell' intelletto*.

Withal, Curtius wrote, there was a possibility, if no more, for a renewed understanding. The Germans must accept, without reproaches, the
reality of French hatred and hence refrain from all unilateral attempts at
rapprochement. To do otherwise would not only be undignified, but also
injudicious, a misreading of the French national character. Unilateral
attempts on the part of the Germans would discredit them among the
most desirable Frenchmen and result in their embarrassed and indignant
withdrawal. Initiative must be left with the victorious nation; the intellectual leaders of France must combat the monstrous image of Germany
and the Germans which circulated at the time in the minds of their compatriots. If the French, impelled by a new attitude towards Germany, then
extended a friendly hand, hopefully the Germans would clasp it.

An escape from the present impasse, Curtius concluded, was possible
only "through an unprejudiced intellectual analysis of the whole range
of problems . . . [and] a dispassionate, objective penetration of the facts
of national psychology and cultural biology." In such a joint exploration

of their mutual problem, participated in by the best minds of both Germany and France, Curtius saw a chance for a new beginning.

Skillfully, through a footnote ("The *Nouvelle Revue Française* is continuously increasing its efforts to accord German matters a dignified and unprejudiced valuation"), Curtius put an address upon his appeal. In its next issue, through a summary, the *Nouvelle Revue*, then France's leading intellectual journal, "acknowledged receipt"; four months later it replied in full. The respondent was André Gide, who borrowed the title for his riposte from Curtius' article, quoted him at length, and informed him in advance of his intent. The letter, partially preserved through a note from Curtius to Frisch of 19 October 1921, announced an essay in which Gide would make very long and important citations from Curtius' article in the *Neue Merkur*. He still hesitated to make it appear as an integral translation, but believed, presented in this manner, it would be read and *carry* much further. As Gide implied, his article was meant to serve, in part, as a vehicle for spreading that of Curtius.

Gide began his discussion on a more optimistic note than had Curtius: "Numerous minds, and the very best—I mean the most truly French—are beginning to look with different eyes upon intellectual relations with Germany." The French were beginning to realize, he continued, that their isolationism towards Germany was working to the detriment of France— if for no other reason than that ignorance of one's enemy is dangerous. More important, in stupidly isolating themselves from the Germans, the French might become isolated; by failing to take advantage of German advances and discoveries, they would certainly retrogress. Gide felt that the French had steadily lost ground, intellectually and morally, since the end of the war.

The self-imposed isolation also extended to the arts and letters, Gide stated further; examples for France's fatuous imbecility in these fields could be cited *ad infinitum*. But the French spirit, if it turned upon itself, would lose all measure of comparison, its taste—and then the regard of other countries. Even then, as Curtius had said, the Germans were turning to the East.

How could this trend be arrested? Gide felt that Curtius was right in warning against both obsequious Germans and naively rationalistic Frenchmen of the Clarté group. At last a voice from the other side of the Rhine reassured the French that the Clarté members represented the German public as little as their opposites represented France. Curtius hoped, just as did the French, for a resumption of intellectual rapport between the two countries; a French author, Albert Thibaudet, had likewise demanded a restoration of cultural passageways. "May the *Nouvelle Revue*

Française be able to help in this; perhaps no task exists today which is more important."[53]

As Gide was able to inform Curtius (this letter is also preserved as an appendix to a 15 December 1921 letter from Curtius to Frisch), his essay evoked a tremendous, if critical, response: In all camps they were talking of the article about the *Relations*, etc., and of Curtius' in consequence. He had not bothered to send the articles, since they were, for the most part, singularly stupid, completely insignificant, or deliberately and most maddeningly incomprehending.

The vehemence of the debate led to its prolongation. The *Nouvelle Revue* returned to the subject several times; in newspapers and journals, Massis, Fortunat Strowski, and René Johannet arraigned themselves against, Paul Souday, Pierre Mille, and Jean Guehenno for Curtius and Gide. And the French public wrote numerous and copious letters to the editor. In Germany, Frisch and Curtius, delighted with the first results of their campaign for rapprochement, decided to continue it. As early as 15 November Frisch informed Gide of his intention of "returning once again to your most convincing article"; four days later Curtius approached Frisch with a concrete suggestion. He advised Frisch, emphatically, to return to Gide's article in the January issue, especially since the French nationalists and the German Clarté partisans with whom Gide was unpopular would probably stab him in the back. Curtius thought that an answer in the form of a brief commentary by Thomas Mann would be appropriate. He was sure that Mann, who had had some very bad experiences with the German literary chauvinists, would take a line consonant with that of the *Merkur*, and that it would be pleasant if in this manner Gide and Mann could be brought together. The commentator, whoever he might be, should, of course, write in assent, else the whole thing would misfire and matters would be worse than before. The newly spanned bridge was still feeble and had to be built well and circumspectly.

Frisch concurred. On 23 November 1921 he invited Thomas Mann "as the most fitting person known to me" to respond to André Gide. Thomas Mann accepted the invitation; as he intimated, it came most opportunely: He would utilize this opportunity to return an attack by Mille in *Le Temps* with a poke in the nose and, moreover, to say, from his own point of view and always in full accord with Curtius and Gide, what needed saying since the *Betrachtungen*.[54]

The brief commentary that Frisch and Curtius had envisioned became, much to their delight, an eighteen-page, 6000-word essay, "Das Problem der deutsch-französischen Beziehungen" (The Problem of German-French Relations).[55] As so often with Thomas Mann, the finished work outgrew his initial plan. In its skillful blend of waspish attack on his critics, dignified espousal of rapprochement, and simultaneous defense and modification of his political stand in the *Betrachtungen*, the article advanced both the cause of the *Merkur* and Mann's own. Despite this important dual function it has, surprisingly, never been reprinted.

In his opening paragraphs Thomas Mann expressed his enthusiastic approval of Gide's "Preface to Armand," published in the *Merkur*, and "Les Rapport Intellectuels" and of Curtius' "German-French Cultural Relations." He particularly sympathized with Gide who, having taken a stand somewhere between the nationalists and the "Clarté-Pacifists," was being misunderstood by all. Gide found himself in "a situation, which, like few others, enjoys our sympathy."

Who, in Germany, Mann asked, took a similar stand? Who condemned the "domestication of the intellect, the Roman Catholicism of the spirit . . . a European accord paid for by the sacrifice of the depth and the height of the human soul and by the acceptance of a pacifism bespewing the nation . . . the alternative of nationalism and internationalism?" Who advocated the position of a "national cosmopolitanism?" "In the name of the Lord it was my voice."

But Thomas Mann felt his words had been distorted by his French critics, notably by Pierre Mille. He had not, as Mille charged him, "glorified war" in the *Betrachtungen*, aligned himself against democracy, or deserted the cause of European internationalism for German chauvinism. Rather had he described war as abhorrent and condemned the abuse of such terms as democracy, truth, and justice—but by no means the concepts themselves. When the best minds of France, such as Gide and Thibaudet, then demanded the removal of politics from the realm of the intellect and a return to a traditional French spirit of *sens critique* they meant nothing else than the "sense of freedom that surges through the *Betrachtungen*," his own revolt against the enslavement of the mind through politics. Also the *Betrachtungen* were not an attack on France, Thomas Mann maintained. If Mille had read the book itself rather than a summary of it (Mann at this point impaled his adversary on the barbs of his sarcasm), he would have found that its Francophobia extended to the French pseudo-intellectual bourgeois, of which Mille and *Le Temps* were good examples; to the France of Poincaré, not to the true France; the "douce France" of their dreams, the France which a common artistic-metaphysical heritage united with Germany. But hatred had strewn disunity among the heirs; the young Germans of that day had grown indifferent to France. To what avail was military power which Germany, thank God, had lost, if a country such as France had grown sterile culturally?

The Allies had defeated Germany physically by starving it into submission through the blockade and spiritually through the propaganda about the virtues of democracy. As the result of the one, 90% of the children had curved spines, and as a result of the other, the German people, who believed Allied propaganda, suffered from an indescribable disappointment. They were convinced that the League of Nations was a gigantic swindle. But something more basic needed to be said about Germany's relation to the West and its traditional rationalism.

Mann continued that it had often been conjectured that the German brand of Greco-Roman humanism was but a superficial stylization of Goethe's paganism, and that recently André Suares had extended this argument. He maintained that Nietzsche, despite appearances, was even less French or Greek than Goethe and far more German than he "because [Nietzsche's] spiritual home is the Orient." Perhaps Germany's post-war receptivity to Eastern influences was indeed the victory of Germany's latent Orientalism. On the other hand, the explanation may be simpler: Germany and the rest of Europe, conscious of their moral bankruptcy and the crisis of traditional humanism, were seeking elsewhere for new values.

For the crisis was acute, far worse than that in the eighteenth century, when rationalistic, utilitarian scholasticism and optimistic progressivism (symbolized by Goethe's Wagner figure) were threatened by an Augustinian longing for a *redire in se ipsum*. The present threat originated from the East and was continued by Nietzsche.

Tolstoi's extreme anti-humanistic, anti-literary, anti-rhetorical conception of academic subjects took on German, Faustian forms in Nietzsche. And Nietzsche, Thomas Mann found, continued to be the guide for Germany's young intellectuals:

> Everything coming from Nietzsche—and everything comes from him—the entire point of view, striving, and experimentation of our best young men, their struggle to bring about a new morality, religiosity, community, an incarnate humanitarianism as well as this mystical willy-nilly motion [*Umhergetriebenwerden*] of, for example, certain roaming groups in the German heartland, reminiscent of psychic phenomena of the Middle Ages: what has all that still in common with humanism, with smooth rationalistic rules for politics and morals, with "exploration of natural laws for the good of society," with the Mediterranean model, with Latin and rhetoric, with French Hellenism, with humanitarian democracy.

Thomas Mann considered it a paradox that the war did not elevate this world view to preeminence, but the moribund nationalism of the pseudo-intellectual bourgeois, or its alter ego, international pacifism. But neither the one nor the other had as much as an obituary left to say; neither could lead to a new understanding between France and Germany, because they were political in nature. "The relations between the spiritual spheres of the two people cannot recover from their miasma without the removal of politics from the more elevated French mentality or without the liberation of the *sens critique* which is nothing but freedom, freedom and humanity."

Mann also addressed himself, briefly, to the question of guilt ("All of us, all of Europe are mired in guilt up to our ears.") and to a refutation of the arguments of the Activists, a group of militant, left-wing pacifists, who spread "hopeless confusion." As might be expected, the debate therefore continued as a colloquy between Thomas Mann and the Activists, who deluged the *Merkur* with protests. Kurt Hiller, in a letter of 16 February 1922, denounced Frisch for printing such a "superficial misanthropic discussion" and "precious trash" and for rejecting a refutation by Berta Lask which "might have inwardly touched Thomas Mann, reached him, perhaps shaken him." Robert Müller accused Mann of dealing blows to the Activists intended for his brother Heinrich "who has never called or shown himself to be an Activist." He, too, offered a refutation of Mann's article "in which he, regarding Activism, makes mistakes which are downright frivolous." Frisch accepted this article.[56]

Müller began with a homage to Thomas Mann. Many of his ideas, he felt, were self-evident; "yet they needed saying by Thomas Mann in his splendid grandiose formulation. . . . It is perhaps inestimable what Thomas Mann did here for his German contemporaries." But the ideals he expressed were identical to those of the Activists: "one could believe that Thomas Mann were one." Müller then redefined the goals of the Activists as pacifism, youth movements, reform of education, greater sexual freedom, social, agricultural, and penal reforms, and, finally, international understanding with full retention—not abjuration—of national differences. Between the ideals of Activists and Thomas Mann's he spotted only one major divergence: Mann abjured, while the Activists demanded, the unity of moral and political action.

Mann, who had seen proofs of Müller's article, declined, in two successive letters to Frisch of 17 and 27 February, to send a riposte: Robert Müller's essay was decent and intelligent, he wrote. Mann would have liked to have added a few statements of principle, but it was indeed too late. To reply at that time to Robert Müller's article would not make much sense and little would come of it. Let it, by all means, make its impression unhindered. Frisch himself had told Mann (in a letter of 14 February) that a continuation of the discussion didn't seem very essential.[57] Except for Curtius' subsequent reports on the French-sponsored international meetings at Pontigny,[58] Frisch thus terminated, as far as the *Merkur* was directly involved, the crusade for better understanding across the Rhine.

The discussion, however, continued for a long time. André Gide and Thomas Mann began an exchange of friendly letters on the subject; French and German authors visited each other for the express purpose of implementing the rapprochement (René Laurent called on Thomas Mann; Curtius, on Gide), and numerous magazines, approving of the *Merkur*'s campaign, kept it alive. By the summer of 1922, summaries, replies, and ripostes had appeared in Amsterdam, Berlin, Brussels, Halle, Milan, Paris, Prague, and Strasbourg, to give a random sampling. With characteristic understatement Frisch informed Mann, in a letter of 10 May 1922: "As far as I can tell the discussion has spread far and wide." Tragically, it left precisely those circles unmoved—on *both* sides of the border—that could have carried out its intent. The effort to improve relations between Germany and France was the *Merkur*'s boldest and noblest gesture; for the history of the two countries it signified merely one of a multitude of missed opportunities.

Indeed, within a few months after their campaign, Frisch and his staff divined its futility. In other articles on France, the constructive suggestions diminished and the futile warnings increased. "Germany's existence," wrote Friedrich Sternthal, "is [also] a question of France's destiny. . . . It is now one minute to twelve."[59] Frisch, finding the official French attitude towards the fledgling German republic unsoftened, warned that "the dangers of German nationalism cannot be painted in black enough colors."[60] And writing to Baron Benoist-Mechin on 3 March 1923 —exactly sixteen and one-half years to the day before France's declaration of war on Nazi Germany—Frisch declared he was glad to find in the writer's essay trains of thought which harmonize with those so often "advocated by us." But of what use is all this, if the policy-making government officials and the ruling parties of France still wanted to have nothing to do with this point of view? Virtually repudiating the *Merkur*'s past efforts, Otto Flake inserted the following dismal observation into his article "Politische Ferienbetrachtung" (Vacational Thoughts on Politics):[61] "What does it [really] mean, to have a rapprochement with France? The few little articles which were exchanged back and forth! We need rapprochement on a material basis; the intellectual one then will take care of itself." The quest of the *Merkur* for German-French friendship ended in despair.

The *Merkur* covered four other major developments abroad: the birth of Bolshevism, Fascism, intense nationalism in the colonies, and the la-

bors of the League of Nations. In reporting on them, the *Merkur* realized
its ambition of linking "the topical with lastingly valid observations."[62]
These reports also serve as a further measure of its editors' despair.

Despite its occasional and sporadic flirtation with Russia, always for
the benefit of the unrepentant West, the *Merkur* in truth feared rather
than loved Bolshevism. Frisch, with obvious satisfaction, accepted Maxim
Gorky's exposés of Bolshevic cruelty. They are very important in judging
certain traits in the Russians as the negative side of their so frequently
stressed community spirit, he wrote André Germain on 20 June 1922.
Still more to the point, on 20 October 1919 he informed Arthur Kauffmann, an intimate friend, that he took a public stand against imitating
the Russian method at the very time when the high tide in Germany, especially in Munich, swept along even superior minds.

In three separate articles by Rudolf Kayser, Richard von Moellendorff, and Otto Flake,[63] the *Merkur* analyzed Bolshevism as a desertion
of Marxist principles and a continuation of Russian imperialism. Otto
Flake, as early as 1920, accurately described the Soviet Union as follows:

> Question: Does today's Bolshevism correspond to yesterday's prin-
> ciples? The repeal of the right to strike, the introduction of the
> death penalty, the creation of a huge military apparatus: these
> were not part of the principles—all these phenomena were part of
> the old order and have persevered. And Bolshevism has grown into
> something quite different: a factor in the history of the world
> whose function seems to be to cut European nationalistic imperi-
> alism to the quick through an alliance with the national passions
> of the suppressed peoples of Asia. Socialism is, among other things,
> part of this approach, but in how modified a form!

Flake also implied that Soviet Russia was a threat, not a promise. And
while the *Merkur* often conducted a Rapallo policy of its own through the
pen of Friedrich Sternthal, it was by no means overjoyed with the Rapallo
Pact itself: "Perhaps it is already too late for the treaty to profit either
party very greatly. . . . From a Russian point of view concluding a treaty
with Germany at Easter was a master-stroke . . . but one must question
whether Germany chose a favorable time for concluding a treaty."[64] That,
on the other hand, the *Merkur* would and did denounce the Machiavellian
plan of some German generals to restore German greatness by an all-out
attack on Russia, scarcely needs to be said.[65]

The rise of Italian Fascism likewise evoked disapproval and apprehen-
sion. In particular the *Merkur* condemned Bolshevism *and* Fascism for
distorting both art and literature. "One must not," Otto Flake protested,

"commandeer as witnesses long-deceased authors such as Hölderlin who would, for certain, never have become followers of Lenin."[66] Tommaso Gallarati Scotti, the distinguished Italian statesman, protested in a similar vein against the Fascist exploitation of Dante.[67] Hausenstein registered physical revulsion upon witnessing, about a year before Mussolini's assumption of power, a Fascist parade in the streets of Florence. "The spectacle of the Fascists appeared to be the diletante convulsions of epigoni, something exclusively reactionary and unoriginal down to its foundations. No, that surely is not the future of Italy. I felt nauseous."[68] Leo Matthias expressed disgust at the deceitfulness of the Fascists, "their mask of loftiness";[69] Sternthal at their violence: "Explosions, fires, murders, destruction of every kind: these are the traces of Fascism." The same writer also discerned in 1922 the rise of Fascism in Hungary, and, immediately after Mussolini's accession to power, ventured to predict the possible spread of Fascism all over Europe. He foresaw its attraction to the young and all others "inclined to a heroic, romantic frame of mind," its successive flirtation with the House of Savoy, the Papacy, and capitalism, and, finally, its fall. "But until this fate has come to pass, the Romanticism of such a movement can have caused many disasters."[70] In its assessment of Fascism abroad, the *Merkur* was deadly accurate.

The *Merkur* also feared a catastrophic collapse of the colonial empires. Josef Ponten, in a lengthy book review, castigated European misrule in the colonies; Count Coudenhove-Kalergi predicted its results: "In the long run this expedient [i.e., pillage, exploitation, and slavery] must fail: for its inevitable consequence is a gigantic revolt of the slaves which will sweep the Europeans from the colored colonies and hence topple Europe's cultural base in the tropics."[71] Sternthal, finally, drew conjectures for the time after the collapse of the present empires. He bleakly foresaw civil wars, chaos, penetration by Japan and Soviet Russia.[72]

The League of Nations, the *Merkur* felt, constituted no reason to mitigate its pessimism. No less a person than Mendelssohn-Bartholdy, one of Germany's delegates to the League, denounced it as a useless, ineffectual debating society; Pannwitz believed it doomed from the start.[73] On this topic, however, the *Merkur* offered a positive, perhaps even utopian alternative—the creation of a United Europe. "But any reform has to begin with the insight that the present basis makes any prospect of a speedy revision and appropriate improvement almost impossible," Frisch commented. The implication is clear that the League of Nations must give way to a more cohesive unit.[74]

Count Coudenhove-Kalergi, the founder of the Pan-Europe movement, also used the *Merkur* for the propagation of his ideas; Pannwitz, his close friend, proclaimed that "Germany or England or France is our father-

land; Europe our motherland."[75] And Flake visualized a time when "it
will be all the same to what country one belongs, because political and
customs boundaries will have disappeared."[76] It would, however, be
wrong to overestimate this note of optimism in the *Merkur*'s dirgeful re-
cital of foreign affairs. In one of them, Sternthal aphorized: "In these
post-war years optimism is the rarest form of insanity." When he, upon
one occasion, forgot his own witticism and became optimistic, Frisch
sharply edited his report and, in a letter of 8 June 1922, begged him to
discontinue "his optimistic positivism."[77] Frisch was absolutely convinced
that the *Merkur*'s presentiments would come to pass. "Efraim Frisch was
invariably sad," Rudolf Nutt, one of his staff members, related in an interview of 11 December 1961. "It was a sadness feeding on the after-
effects of the pre-war and war years and on the premonition of a sinister
future. Frisch knew that he was fighting a lost cause. Without anything
having happened, he often left the editorial offices completely defeated."
Like Cassandra, Frisch was mourning the future.

Most developments inside Germany also entered the *Merkur*'s debit
column, which invariably registered the continuation of past mistakes
and the commitment of new ones. Among traditional German liabilities
it listed militarism, Prussianism, nationalism, and an endemic conserva-
tism that smothered Germany's revolutions. And of these it feared the first
the most. "The spectre" of war and militarism, to use Max Picard's metaphor,[78] still haunted those post-war years; the *Merkur* again and again
demanded its permanent exorcism.

Friedrich Sternthal described the ghost in an article entitled "What Is
Militarism?" as "less a state than an attitude and a credo. Militarism is
not the existence of a huge army, but the subordination of all other points
of view beneath the military, the penetration of civilian life by military
concepts and value judgments."[79] Other writers, often using Sternthal's
definition and Picard's image, sought the ghost in a multitude of places.
Hanns Braun spotted it in the new German Reichswehr; Otto Flake in
Germany's demand, at the Spa conference, for universal military training; Kurt Hiller and Oskar Loerke saw it wherever the call to arms was
raised. To Loerke, universal military training was "the worst and most
evil [institution] ever designed by man."[80]

Perhaps some writers went too far in their pursuit of the ghost. Stefan
Grossmann saw evidence of militarism in the imitation of war-time head-
lines, Burschell in the singing of "military and bardic songs," Alfred
Polgar in the children's game of "nation."[81] But no one today can argue
with Sternthal's warning in the article cited above: "There is no salvation
for Germany through militarism. Surely we have tried it long enough and
in vain, and every new militaristic experiment could bring us, at most,

the euphoria of a temporary success, which is followed by death—the death of Germany as a nation." Today, with Germany truncated and its national unity shattered as the result of its militarism, we can appreciate Sternthal's clairvoyance.

Many blamed Prussia for the persistence of militarism and its disastrous consequences in the past. The three principal attacks on Prussia came from the *Merkur*'s inner circle: Frisch, Hausenstein, and Sternthal. Frisch pilloried the Prussians for shrewdly and demagogically blaming the lost war on the revolution, the Jews, or anyone else handy, while in truth Prussia "made, conducted, and lost the war." Not dividing Prussia, Sternthal held, was one of the cardinal errors of the November Revolution, and Hausenstein, who had elsewhere denounced German and Prussian hybris, the result of 1871, as the worst conceit in history, now warned that Prussia had lost its viability and that "German history, if it [still] includes a better future, can no longer be the history of Greater Prussia." It may be significant that these three major attacks on Prussia appeared pseudonymously.[82]

Also, given the *Merkur*'s militant liberalism, its attacks on its political enemies appear mild. Resentments smolder in the correspondence; upon one occasion only do they burst into flame upon the pages of the magazine. When Rathenau was assassinated, Heinrich Simon, in his obituary, lashed out at those parties "who suffer from the conceit that they have the sole right to the appellation 'German.' "[83] Sternthal decided to exploit the occasion for "the proper treatment of this entire decaying class of society which, in the first place, made this political assassination possible," as he put it in a covering letter to Frisch of 30 June 1922. His article did this and more. He pilloried "the glorification of the past, in the press, the schools, the universities, the meeting halls." And he placed Rathenau's murder at the doorstep of the reactionaries, the demagogues of the Deutschnationale Volkspartei, the bourgeois infested with feudalism, and, in a final burst of invective, the murderers "from a little boys' masturbation society."[84]

Despite the usual mildness of the attacks on reactionaries, it was clear that the *Merkur*'s war against its political enemies was continuous. Frisch and Hausenstein at times suppressed criticisms of the Weimar Republic, even where justified, if the reproof could conceivably furnish ammunition to the rightists. Hans Roschenbusch's article "Politics and Freedom" which completely set forth Frisch's own doubts "in freedom as a political postulate" was nonetheless rejected in a letter of 23 January 1920 because of its accidental agreement with the rightist "party line." The editors of the *Merkur* published, in 1919, a forceful attack on Weimar political parties by Alfred Döblin.[85] A year later similar caustic comments by Max

Picard, a valued contributor, stayed buried in the files.[86] For identical reasons an article by the painter Albert Lamm, a friend of Hausenstein's, was rejected in a letter of 27 March 1920, and a column by Sternthal severely edited. Your criticism of Rathenau, Frisch wrote on 1 May 1922, would bring the *Merkur* into the company of people whose allegiance it emphatically did not need. Unlike many politicians of the Weimar Republic, Frisch and Hausenstein did not deem it undemocratic to deny help to its grave diggers.

Yet their love for Weimar was not blind. They perceived a multitude of ailments and diagnosed many of them as defects inherited from the revolution that mothered it. In an inimitable and untranslatable pun, Burschell said of the revolution: "Es war kein Staat mit ihr zu machen, es war mit nichts ein Staat zu machen." Robert Müller found that Weimar had failed in the realm of the spirit; Felix Braun and Karl Gareis deplored that it had fallen short as a political and social revolution. Gareis found that German revolutions usually—during the Reformation, in 1848, in 1918—came historically too late and accomplished too little. The original revolutionaries, he argued, turned into tomorrow's reactionaries and into "the executioners of their own offspring." In 1918 the revolution presented Germany, overnight, with a democracy, but the fruit was overripe and had lost its flavor. He predicted that Germany would pay a bitter price for allowing its revolution to run dry before it had run its full political and social course. The truth of his prophecy was testified to when rightist fanatics assassinated Gareis about six months later.[87]

The *Merkur* and its editors obviously had greater respect for the revolutionaries of the Räterepublik than for those of the November Revolution, although they probably agreed with Ernst Bloch in his assessment that the establishment of a Soviet-style government in Bavaria, "the most un-proletarian state in Germany," was arrant nonsense.[88] Also the *Merkur*'s sympathy for Kurt Eisner and his political aspirations emerged immediately after Eisner's assassination. Ernst Hierl, a Munich educator, prefaced his disquisition entitled "Forbidden Student Essays" with a memorial to Kurt Eisner "who took the life of the young generation seriously as [our hopes] for the future."[89] And Hausenstein himself wrote an eight-page obituary in which he praised Eisner for precisely the qualities that he, in other discussions, found lacking in the politicians of Weimar and Berlin: "political inventiveness in the grand manner, a precise sense of timing, the imagination of a statesman, a talent for improvisation, a universality which connects him with the Encyclopedists, facility . . . in administrative matters, a decided gift for political technique and . . . a special insight into the machinations of German imperialism."[90] Immediately after publication of this article, Picard congratulated Hausenstein:

His words about Eisner sounded as if no one at all had written about Eisner before; it was like a discussion between Eisner and Hausenstein. Others who wrote about Eisner were transformed into an audience, distant and mediocre.[91] After more than forty years of controversy about Kurt Eisner, Picard, in an interview of 25 September 1961, saw no reason to retract a word of his spontaneous praise of Hausenstein's obituary.

Initially the *Merkur* extended its cynicism vis-à-vis the revolution to the Weimar Republic, its offspring. Only when the editors and contributors came to realize that the two alternatives to the Republic were dictatorship or anarchy did they rally to its support and exchange cynical pejoration for constructive criticism. But in 1919 Hausenstein still spoke of the "drearily desolate world of the Weimar constitutional government"; Döblin of its opportunism; Hermann Esswein of its negligible superiority over the monarchy. Hermann Wendel, a Social Democratic delegate to the Reichstag in 1912, drew a seemingly roseate picture of Germany's new foreign policy, then destroyed it with the acid of his cynical last sentence: "But don't I hear someone laughing out there?"[92]

Germany's new government, some of the early writers found, "ailed from its prime foundation," to borrow a phrase from A. E. Housman.[93] A pseudonymous article (by Erich von Kahler) thought its constitution externally derived and hence foredoomed. To be viable, the author argued, a constitution should take on "the unique, naturally grown form [befitting] a specific group."[94] Arthur Salz, writing about a year after the revolution, put the same thought more concretely: "Is [our agonizing condition] then based on the fact that we have parliamentarianism . . . without the parliamentarians to carry it out, just as we have a magnificent structure of a republic but only novices as its tenants?"[95] In the view of the *Merkur*, however, the most serious flaws of the German constitution were its lack of protection against its internal enemies and a too centralized form of government. Bruno Altmann was shocked by the abuse of freedom of speech by the very officials sworn to uphold the republic:

> To allow public officials, here in Germany, freedom of opinion towards the [existing] form of government, to concede to them the right to form coalitions for the sake of combating the republic—means digging the grave of the republic. The next step of these officials will be to launch an attack on the republic *by means of their official powers*, as, indeed, has happened, everywhere in numerous court judgments. Thus there exists the embarrassing anatomy of a monarchistic civil service inside the republic, [maintained by] . . . the letter of constitutional law. Thus it could happen that the Bavarian *Regierungspräsident* [Governor] Kahr could

wish for the fall of the republic as the day of his greatest happiness
and that the Minister of the Interior, when challenged about this
statement, could cover [Kahr] by invoking Article 118.[96]

Mendelssohn-Bartholdy and Hausenstein, who feared the revival of
Prussianism, saw grave dangers in the unitarian form of the new government. "We shall have a federation! The best of us [Germans] demand
it," predicted the former. "We, however, want a federalistic Germany,"
Hausenstein added. "For Germany will be federalistic from Cologne to
Vienna, and from Bozen to Königsberg—or it will become its own self-
negation." A year later Hausenstein reported the results of his warnings:
"From the point of view of the Berlin unitarianism my [program of fed-
eralism] has become something like national treason."[97] Hausenstein
never wavered in this conviction even during the Nazi Regime.[98] By then
the charge of treason had become less academic: in 1936 the Nazis banned
his books, in 1943 all of his publications of any kind.

Hausenstein's tone in the first article had been carping and sarcastic;
in the second, exhorting and imploring. The change signified the *Merkur*'s new editorial policy toward Weimar. Usually such a reversal occurs
gradually, over several issues; in this instance it happened not only within
one issue, that of October 1920, but within the confines of two articles by
a single author: Otto Flake's "Republic Germany" and "Perspective." In
the first article, Flake predicted, accurately if somewhat cavalierly: "In
a certain sense we are living today in 1820 anno Domini. And if the democracy proves to be incapable of giving form to its ideas then the reactionary nationalists will take over the assignment." But between the writing of this and the second article, Flake and the staff of the *Merkur*
received a salutary shock through the Independent Socialist Congress of
1920 in Halle. Flake, while at the Congress, discovered that the Bolshevist
wing was interested in neither ideas nor intellectuals. Stunned, he called
on members of the intelligentsia to support the new democracy: "The
events of this congress force the German intellectuals, who do not altogether bypass politics as the means to put ideas into effect, to a revision of
their judgment about the [German] democracy. All our instincts warn us
against surrendering the rest of our liberalism in order to give a free rein,
for the time being, to a dictatorship." Since the Communist camp is now
out of the question, it "can only be the democratic one." And he closed with
the admonition, taken from Rathenau's address, "Democratic Development," to become more patient in one's demands on the new government
"and more modest."[99]

With the exception of an occasional relapse ("this farce of a republic following upon the farce of a monarchy," Hausenstein once wrote in exasperation) [100] the *Merkur* reserved its acid for the enemies of the Republic, its approval and well-meant criticism for its friends. It approved the thrust of Ebert's policies and the export program of Robert Schmidt, Minister of Economics. But far more interesting is its cautious criticism of the Weimar Republic. To many of its readers, as the editorial correspondence reveals, these criticisms appeared eccentric and capricious; in retrospect they can be read as a nearly complete catalogue of Weimar's weaknesses.

Some of the *Merkur*'s assessments were obvious even then; they surprise less because they were accurate than because they were so detailed and well-documented. The *Merkur* repeatedly attacked the multiple-party system, the cowardice and incompetence of Germany's new politicians, the unpreparedness of the Social Democrats for political rule, the social inequity of financial legislation—especially the laws pertaining to taxes, cartels, and stocks—the helplessness of the government in the face of hunger and inflation, the dual standard of justice—light sentences for the rightist assassin and counter-revolutionaries, severe ones for liberals and leftists—the Bavarian censorship laws—administered by customs officials the hypernationalism and radicalism of some political parties and the particularism of others, and, finally, the sparsity of effective social legislation. The *Merkur* also continued to criticize the government's rearmament program, the Civil Service, and the centralized form of government.

These evils were rather obvious. The *Merkur*, however, was equally attuned to the subterranean tremors of the Republic. It clearly registered major disturbances beneath the surface which other journals missed entirely or described only fuzzily. Among these were the growing disaffection of powerful groups, disaffection not from one party or the other, but from the political structure of the Republic itself. Harry Pross, in a book chronicling the fall after the event, has called this process "the destruction of politics": "To deny the necessity of parties altogether and to stick obdurately to a position outside any party whatever was, simply, an impossible position, the preparation for mob rule." And he traces this development to the Empire, where the citizens' political ambitions were thwarted: "The divorce from reality and especially the divorce from the necessity for testing the grandiloquent ideas one pursued through actual work-a-day politics: these conditions favored two modes of procedure. First, apathetic behavior, a complete indifference towards everything connected with politics; secondly, radical actions that aimed at the uprooting of politics." [101] Thirty-five years earlier the *Merkur* had come to the same conclusion and had begun to counteract both modes of procedure.

Oskar Ewald struck hard at the traditional political apathy of Germany's intellectuals, "who suffer from the delusion that the printed word relieves them of [the necessity for] action":

> For it is the lack of responsibility, the missing commitment which caused the degeneration of modern intellectuality into a sterile technology of concepts. Its attitude during the war has proven this. Modern intellect remained inwardly unmoved by the most horrible of all realities and clothed it all the more adroitly and unrestrainedly with an apparatus of ideological and phraseological constructions which deceived an unsuspecting world until its destruction was completed. The basic error which subjugated this irresponsible intellect is the delusion that thinking carries with it no obligation. . . . Therefore the intellectuals can help us little at this turning point of eras at which we stand. Only those true minds can do so who draw on the prime source of real existence and constantly renew themselves from it.[102]

Putting it more simply, Flake described the history of Germany as the recurrence of short periods of awareness in a long, sound sleep.[103]

Ewald had lauded the Activists as an example of responsible intellectuals. Most articles about them conceded their responsibility and the praiseworthiness of their pacifism, but questioned, at the same time, a program "which runs counter to that of all the present . . . parties," as Kurt Hiller, the founder of Activism, had himself written in the *Merkur*.[104] He had even admitted, in a letter to Frisch of 27 August 1920, that he was "inflexibly anti-democratic and extremely pacifistic."

Sternthal thought such a program dangerously romantic and, using language almost anticipatory of Harry Pross, condemned the Activists as romantics of reason and their reactionary opponents as emotional romantics. Both, he said, start from the same false premise: "Sie verkennen was ist" (They misunderstand what exists).[105] And Flake pleaded with the Activists to work through an organized democratic party; isolation, he felt, would bring destruction to them and the Republic.[106] No similar appeals were addressed to the many other groups in Germany that debilitated the Republic through their politics outside the political system: the anti-Republican Youth groups, the "*All-deutsche*," (a group working towards the hegemony of all German-speaking people), the veteran organizations, etc. They, the most dangerous destroyers of politics, were not among the readers of the *Neue Merkur*.

Instead, the *Merkur* labelled other groups as additional threats to the Republic. Among the intellectuals, as Ferdinand Lion and Robert

Müller pointed out, were not only apolitical and suprapolitical elements, but also determined enemies of democracy. Lion named the political Expressionists; Müller, prophetically astute, singled out the poet Gottfried Benn. Hermann Esswein, himself a devout Catholic, feared political Catholicism as a danger to both the Church and to German politics; Alfons Paquet warned of Rome's continuing tyranny over Germany. Nothing, however, alarmed the contributors to the *Merkur* as much as a weakening resistance to the disease of dictatorship.[107]

Otto Flake, in his polemic of 1920, "Die grossen Worte" (Grandiose Words), was the first to detect it; he diagnosed the condition more fully in his "Reise in die Zeit" (Journey into the Present):

> We were sitting on the veranda; a woman said: "Is there no-one strong enough that he can lead [us] out of the chaos; can't you imagine a new Bismarck, a social, spiritual, religious savior, an exponent of the will to regulate?" No one dared make an answer, for this circle included none of those naive and harmless *Deutschnationalen* who do not see the problem of the demonic but believe instead that it suffices if everyone puts aside a part of his wishes and subordinates himself to the whole.[108]

And it was again Flake who spotted Germany's susceptibility to a dictatorship of the proletariat. After Ludwig Rubiner had advocated it as a defense against the powerful reactionaries, Flake countered: "The demand of a pledge of allegiance to the Moscow International, the exclusion of all those who side with socialism without making a pact with the Sowjet-system: that is a self-appointed papacy."[109] And Frisch, in the first post-war issue, enjoined his countrymen, both laborers and members of the middle class, to avert the predicted class struggle by returning to a spiritual community of interest beyond the "purely economic pursuits."[110]

In tracing the history of the *Neue Merkur*, we come now to its most puzzling aspect and the magazine's greatest shortcoming: while it correctly discerned the theoretical danger of a rightist dictatorship, it ignored, beyond a few casual and mostly ineffectual phrases, the National Socialist Party, its concrete embodiment. This sin of omission is all the more amazing since the party's tempestuous introduction to the public at large occurred in Munich: Hitler's speeches in the Hofbräuhaus, his march on the Feldherrnhalle, his trial and (mild) sentencing. His infamous march passed, in fact, within blocks of the editorial offices of the *Neue Merkur*.

Before examining the reasons for this failure, one must, in fairness, delimit its extent. The following *aperçus* although they do not deal with the Nazis proper, show concern for the activities of the Rightists. In May 1920 Rasso Bergmann defended Moritz Schwind against the charge of the "Swastika-ites" (*Hakenkreuzern*) of being an Eastern Jew; in November of that year, O. M. Mittler sarcastically advised the Munich censors to switch their attention from books "that smell, even in the slightest, of extra-marital love" to the works of Houston Stewart Chamberlain. A few months before Oskar Ewald had also condemned Chamberlain as "an inimical influence."[111] In August 1922, Sternthal expressed the fear that Italy's Fascism might spread to other parts of Europe; in February 1924 (while Hitler was on trial), Hausenstein had unpleasant visions of swastikas on the walls of public toilets.[112] Two months later, Wilhelm Michel wrote: "Whatever assaults the Republic today in the name of the Hohenzollern or Wittelsbacher, whatever dishonors, befouls, or denies the German soul beneath the emblem of the swastika or the Red Star: that is the barbaric, teeth-grinding resistance against the German reality."[113] Sternthal, in June 1924, after the first electoral upswing of the Nazis in the spring of 1924, derided the Nazis as void of a single new idea, as the bodyguards of heavy industry, large estates and high finance, and as unsuited to fulfill the German search for a spirit of national community: "A spirit of community is only possible under the symbol of an authority. But this is lacking. Neither the swastika nor the fasces of the Fascists are the symbol of authority; but only the symbol of violence." Hans Poeschel called Munich "the metropolis of the swastika," and quoted Frisch's theory about the origin of the Nazi symbol. In August 1924, Hans Prinzhorn, curiously enough, mocked Hitler's actions as farcical in comparison to Mussolini's statesmanship. In October of the same year, Willy Haas deplored that the political discussion of the young, "those hordes and hordes with their swastika and death-head flags, their Sowjet stars and military caps," were politics by billy-club. Elsewhere in the article he gave a one-page summary of the Nazis' program against the Jews. And not until its final issue, in September 1925, and then only obliquely, did the *Merkur* mention the Beer Hall Putsch: "The Duce, as early as 1923, at the time of the Munich November Putsch, made his own actions contingent on the effect of the events in Germany upon the French."[114]

That, in its entirety, constitutes the *Merkur*'s treatment of the National Socialists. Not one complete article is devoted to them; at a rough estimate ten times as much space is given to the Activists, a politically insignificant group, than to the ultimate destroyers of the Republic. Also, one's puzzlement is heightened by the fact that Frisch considered even these few scattered paragraphs and sentences excessive. When Ewald, a valued contributor, offered a more comprehensive treatment,

Frisch rejected it sight unseen. Ewald had written "This second part [of my essay, "The Spirit of Politics"] also contains a critique of Fascism, foreign and domestic" (letter of 13 September 1924). Five days later Frisch answered him: "Just of late I have published so much basic political material of this type—an essay by Benedetto Croce about the same subject is imminent—that I, at present, must regretfully desist from it." Croce's article, it should be added, confined itself to Italian Fascism.[115]

The question obtrudes itself whether Frisch, his staff, and contributors underestimated the enemy and hence made light of him. It certainly appears so at first glance. Writing on the anniversary of the Beer Hall Putsch Frisch, in a letter to von Wedderkop of 15 November 1924, looked back on it with humorous detachment: "Munich is only boring now and is likely to remain so until they hatch something witty." And in the 9,000 mss. in the editorial correspondence, the name of the party or of its leader occurs precisely two times. Once Emil Preetorius wrote, rather breezily, in a letter to Frisch of 24 July 1923: "Addio! . . . Give my regards, for the time being, to Hitleria [i.e., Bavaria], so invigorating despite its knee-pants and swastika." Preetorius added to the humor of his greeting by spelling "Hakenkreuz" (swastika, literally cross with hooks) as "Hackenkreuz" (cross for chopping). The second mention of the party was made by Willy Andreas. In a covering letter to Frisch of 14 January 1924 regarding an article, he promised that everyone would notice that he did not think much "of Hittler [sic] or Bavaria." Preetorius' light-hearted pun and Andreas' misspelling speak for themselves.

Despite all appearances the *Merkur*'s failure, however, stems less from its editor's lack of political acumen than from a peculiarity of his temperament. Frisch, in short, was intensely aware of the threat, and whenever his vigilance relaxed Munich and his mail were there to remind him of it—even though the letters did not mention its name. Some of the letters are, in fact, classical documentation of the rise of Hitler. As early as 30 December 1919, three months after Hitler had become a member of the German Labor Party, Luis Brinkmann, the *Merkur*'s Spanish correspondent, answered a request for a contribution by stating that his contemplated article would reflect his sole political credo, a Machiavellian foreign policy, a thoroughgoing socialism and the arousal of the people's spirit towards a war of liberation. The ideals of the League of Nations, conciliation between peoples, and so forth had become repulsive to him. He found the Germans' whining that they had to regain the trust of other countries particularly distasteful. Brinkmann was sure that survival in this dreadfully bitter struggle for existence was predicated on the greatest possible mistrust of other countries. Only then would they treat Germany with some caution, some consideration. What he hoped for, what he saw Germany in need of, was a savior, not a prince, someone who, born in a manger, possessed the blind trust of the masses. Frisch, needless to say, asked for no further contributions.

A month earlier Frisch had had another brush with Fascism. In a lapse of vigilance he accepted an advertisement for Adolf Bartels' jaundiced *History of World Literature* and promptly received, in an open postcard dated 5 November 1919, an unbridled admonition from Kurt Hiller. The advertisement, Hiller protested, had struck him like a blow over the head. How could Frisch accept it? Didn't he know that Bartels was a completely stupid, Teutonic, rowdy anti-Semite? A supra black-white-red pogromist of literature? A man beyond discussion between educated people? Hiller's protest continued for three more choice sentences. This time Frisch sent an abject apology.

Upon another occasion Frisch "regretfully" returned a ballad that had been submitted on 6 March 1922 by Otto Sauber, an erstwhile functionary in the Räterepublik. The poet had indicated his change of political convictions by signing his letter "Mit deutschem Gruss." Finally we can judge, from Frisch's letter to Director Kilpper of the Deutsche Verlags-Anstalt, how seriously he regarded Hitler's Putsch. The letter was written on 13 November 1923, four days after the uprising. His work had become very much more difficult by the situation in Munich which, in his opinion, had still not settled once and for all. He was forced to ask himself, again and again, whether a change of the place of publication, if only temporary, would not be advisable. Frisch did not carry out his plan.

Frisch, in short, ignored the National Socialists—despite his insight and trepidation—because by temperament he could do nothing else. "Frisch had the grandeur of an old Jew," Ferdinand Lion told me in an interview of 25 Sepember 1961. And continuing, he quoted Frisch's exact statement about the Nazis, since reported to me by three other sources: "If they come to power, Germany is doomed. But they are too subaltern for notice." Of their unholy alliance with certain industrialists he said: "One hand befouls the other." Frisch's fastidiousness explains, if it does not excuse, his aversion to fighting in their mire. For Frisch and his magazine, the Nazis were beneath notice or even contempt.

The *Merkur* found a practical as well as altruistic answer to the destructive criticism of Right and Left. It bluntly announced that the impending execution of the Republic by either the rightists or leftists could only be stayed through social and economic reforms. "If the [German] democracy proves incapable of realizing its ideas," Otto Flake said, "then the reactionary nationalists will take over." Or, Rudolf Kayser warned, if the German people did not want a Russian brand of proletarian socialism, completely unsuitable for Germany, "then the obligation of the middle-class groups is all the greater to support a socialistic philosophy which will dominate the future."[116] Impelled by the urgency of its message, the *Merkur* spelled it out not only in essays but also in book reviews (e.g., in Poeschel's "Eine Arbeiterbiographie"), novellas of social protest (such as Hans Siemsen's "Die Geschichte meines Bruders" and Flake's "Byk"), and even, as witness a commemorative article on Theodor Fontane, through the words of an author dead for more than twenty years.[117]

With but two exceptions the various contributors were in remarkable agreement about the causes and cures of social and economic inequities. To start with the exceptions, Count Coudenhove-Kalergi argued that technological progress, not greater socialization, would eradicate economic needs; Felix Braun, that "we need neither revolutionary nor socializing tendencies, if we but become reacquainted once again with our souls."[118] All the other contributors felt that the perpetuation of unrestrained capitalism and the system of large, landed estates would doom the Republic, but that a modified capitalism, with strong social reforms, would assure its survival. Flake, pessimistic about Damaschke's land reform, insisted that some land reform and expropriation of the supercapitalists had to come to avert a revolution; Pannwitz called for ideas "that do not presume to shatter capitalism, but endorse it even and wish to retain it in part, that prepare the way for pruning its excrescences and for its subordination to fixed assets [*Realwerten*]. We need [ideas] in short, that comprehend it and thus strip it of its magic [*entzaubern*], ideas which, through their theories end its absolutism in practice and set an earthborn master over the metaphysical usurper."[119]

Flake and Pannwitz blamed the capitalists and the middle class for the social and economic abuses; Hausenstein redressed the balance by attributing them to the failure of the Social Democrats: "We experienced a social democracy that struck from its program its unique part, the socialistic one, and espoused, in parliament, the inherited and questionable part which would acquire its sense and essence only through socialism."[120] But to both camps the *Merkur* incessantly addressed demands for various social and economic reforms, from more just tax laws to overtime pay scales. Also its most important request, a free secondary and university education for all, was periodically repeated.[121] Harald Landry, condemning all social and economic criteria for admission, coined the slogan: "Die Hochschule dem ganzen Volk" (College for all the people).[122] And Flake, whose pen, as will become apparent, the *Mer-*

kur frequently used as the sword for its crusades, demanded the *Abitur* for the "future Sanscrit scholar" as well as "the future street cleaner," in fine "the most ruthless equality of education." But, as an afterthought, he denied that free passes to an expressionistic exhibit (donated by the Frankfurt city government) constituted education "for the masses . . . for those slaves of want."[123] Anticipating Brecht, Flake argued that a full stomach must come before art, especially if the art works are expressionistic.

In combating anti-Semitism, the *Neue Merkur* engaged the Nazis and other extremists of the right on yet another issue. One entire number, several specific essays, and numerous isolated paragraphs lifted the modern veil from the ancient face of anti-Semitism and revealed its ugliness. Yet the unmasking was too genteel. In turn serious and un-smilingly humorous, defensive and aggressive, subjective and suicidally objective, advanced by Jews and gentiles, all the apologias in the *Merkur* (except the fictional ones) lacked the one element that the opposition consistently exploited: emotional appeal.[124] Frequently despite their brilliance they even lacked ardor. The explanation for this zestlessness is simple: Frisch was of two minds about airing the subject, and his ambivalent attitude communicated itself to his contributors.

They could scarcely overlook his doubts. Plans for the special issue lay dormant for more than a year. One month before the deadline Frisch, in a letter to one of its authors, considered cancelling it. In soliciting material for it, his approach, for the only time in his career, was coy or casual. To his close associate, Ferdinand Lion, he addressed in a letter of 19 June 1921 a "timid request"; to Otto Flake he wrote on 22 June 1921, while in the midst of planning his issue: "I think that at some time I will take a position on the Jewish question, after all." And when the special issue finally appeared, Frisch prefaced it with the caveat, surely rare in the history of publishing, that it would probably be "of little use."[125] If this was Frisch's conviction, why did he bother?

As Lion told me in the September 1961 interview, the number on Judaism was a defensive reaction; it was, specifically, Frisch's direct answer to Kahr's anti-Semitic polemics and policies. Even so, two mental reservations inhibited Frisch: as a loyal patriot of the Republic he de-tested an additional divisive issue; as a German or Austrian *and* Jew he would have preferred stressing the links between the two traditions rather than the ruptures.[126] Hence this remarkable prefatory note, which shows nothing more clearly than Frisch's inner struggle:

> Our readers will find in this issue, from the circle of our steady contributors, a series of articles about the "Jewish question." At

such a critical moment in German history, to be sure, we consider raising this question and the method of doing it as a less than constructive multiplying of German difficulties at home and abroad and of little use in other respects as well. But faced by the growing brutalization which has refashioned also this "question" into a dubious political tool, we thought it fitting to contribute something to its clarification. We did not aim for an agreement among the articles, which could easily have been achieved, nor did we intend an *enquête*. Through the statements collected here and through additional essays by Thomas Mann and others in one of the next issues we hope to achieve a standard of discussion which befits the dignity of thoughtful and intelligent human beings.[127]

Frisch, in his own lead article, achieved this standard. The Jew, Frisch maintained, constituted the last surviving European myth, a myth from the Middle Ages, kept alive by a pettifogging, venomous pseudo-science. The myth, he continued, had most visibly affected certain Jews in Germany; it had reshaped them in its own image and left them either cynical, self-abasing, self-hating, resentful, or with exaggerated nationalistic feelings towards Germany or Palestine. Those who perpetuated the myth used religious arguments, he continued, against the Jews, but usually only as a means for inciting hatred. And while the earlier inquiry of the churches: "Shall the Jews become Christians?" was not without some logic, Frisch thought it should be changed into a more appropriate one: "Are the gentiles going to remain Christians?" There was all the more reason to ask, because modern anti-Semitism was often but a pretext for anti-Christianism, as witness the neo-pagan Wotan-worshippers—who are anti-Christian despite their arrogated appellation of Christian Socialists.

Frisch stated that their new racial philosophy, shared by other groups, documented nothing but the method by which majorities stamp minorities as aliens and aliens as enemies. In French and English literature, the Germans may profitably have looked for a similarly distorted image of themselves. But the plight of the Jews was far worse; virtually *all* literature about them was war literature. It registered fights "which were never a struggle of equals nor one involving mere theories," but a defense against such practical threats as boycotts, expulsion, the stake, and pogroms.

Nothing much had changed in the sterile, uninformed arguments of the anti-Semites nor in the general treatment of the Jews, the article contended. The two alternatives of enforced segregation or enforced integration had returned as the choice between assimilation or Zionist nationalism. Frisch suggested the existence of a third alternative: Judaism, far from being a petrifaction of a pre-Christian stage, has a continuing cultural and religious mission. Everywhere. It lives on as the embodied hope in man's happiness on earth, a hope unrequited by Pauline Christianity which has proven itself ineffectual in interhuman relations. Indifferent to human suffering, such as the pogroms in Russia, often perpetrators of the *consensus omnium* about the Jews, many Christians, as one suspects, enunciate the most lofty, transcendental demands because they are incapable of fulfilling the most mundane ones of everyday existence. But Judaism, with its God-imposed obligation towards the community, envisions man's future perfection—a *voluntary* compliance with God's laws—in concrete social terms within the context of its temporal religious philosophy. In the words of Jeremiah, "He judged the cause of the poor and the needy. Is not this to know me, says the Lord."

Through an excerpt from the *Brenner*, a Catholic journal, Frisch had a non-Jew confirm his belief in a continuing Jewish mission. In passing, he also used the author, Karl Dallago, to dispose of Houston Stewart Chamberlain's racial theories as erroneous interpretations of "race," "Arianism," and the Jewish religion. As a corrective to Chamberlain's distortions, Frisch urged his readers to study Eastern Jewry where beneath an unprepossessing surface of poverty, intellectualism without content, and the slovenliness of overcrowded quarters, courses a rich, even enchanting cultural life. Obviously recalling his own experiences, Frisch described the ritual of the ghettos, their folklore and narratives, their customs, games, theatricals, and festivities, their veneration for the lay scholar, and their timeless, non-causal, unhistoric, and hence everpresent faith in divine providence.

First the Eastern Jews, Frisch observed, then Jews everywhere, came to realize that the fall of the ghetto walls liberated them but also cut their roots. Some Jews responded by denying their heritage; others, through accepting it, acquired a greater sense of responsibility towards their new cultural environment and a better perspective of it. But among all European Jews, as their number increased, there also increased the intensity of the question: Where do I belong? It is a question born less out of occasional setbacks on the road to emancipation than from the immanent Jewish query about the significance, essence, and direction of Jewry.

The Jew who stepped out of the ghetto, contended Frisch, was at that time a bridge between Orient and Occident. As such he was often misunderstood. Western Judaism was often equated with political and religious liberalism—just because it emerged from the ghetto during the Enlightenment—and Eastern Jewry, less emancipated than its Western counterpart and hence more alien-looking, often was painted as a caricature. "One should cease, at long last, to speculate about the abstract

concepts of Jew and Jewry and to fight a phantom of one's own creation."
Frisch also advocated that Germans should try to recapture their ability
to assimilate others, lost perhaps during their colonization of the East;
they should open up toward the Jews whose emancipation was attributable, after all, to German ideas and German culture.

Post-war anti-Semitism, Frisch continued, had no foundation in fact; it
was incited, most likely, by interested parties to divert the people from the
country's real problems. And in this lay its dangers. But to those adherents of anti-Semitism who would say that a stand against the Jews was
essential to strengthen thereby the national sentiment, one must answer
that national unity cannot be found through something negative; by combating such figments as "Jewish Capitalism," "Jewish Socialism," and
even "Jewish Imperialism," the German spirit invoked against them would
be debased into an empty ideology.

Frisch at this point missed, if narrowly, the opportunity to raise his
article from an academic discussion—of unquestionable brilliance but
dubious effectiveness—to a telling counterattack against the anti-Semites.
"One is tempted," he wrote, "to shift from such a really undemanding,
negative refutation of what the Jews did *not* commit to a designation of
the guilty who have a vital interest in promoting this new canker." Instead of giving in to this "temptation," Frisch concluded his essay, otherwise so distinguished, with a condemnation, redundant for the *Merkur*,
of European nationalism, including its Jewish manifestations, and with
the advocacy of a Pan-European structure to which the Jews would contribute their universality, social experience, and temporal religious
philosophy.

Frisch's essay may be read as a thematic index not only for the "Jewish
issue," but also for all disquisitions on the subject throughout the *Merkur*.
Broadly the themes encountered in the magazine are the Jewish character, anti-Semitism, Zionism, and the position and prospects of German
Jewry. The most extensive studies of the first topic, which by no means
produced an altogether flattering portrait of the Jews, were contributed
by Rudolf Pannwitz and Count Coudenhove-Kalergi. Pannwitz, while
deriding the anti-Semites, nonetheless repeated, occasionally with approval, some of their charges. "The worst about the Jews," Pannwitz
wrote, "is their dynamic tension and expansion which lacks sufficient
substance, their ecstatic fervor without an abandoning love for the soil.
They are aloof from things concrete, which they cannot really grasp. . . .
Thus they become an impure and dangerous mixture of semi-oriental
sensuality and semi-oriental spirituality, the victims of claustrophobic
insecurity who end by losing their balance and degenerate into materialism and cynicism. Their worst feature is their extreme intellect-directed

sensuality."[128] It is of interest that Frisch, in a letter dated 17 December 1919, had specifically solicited Pannwitz' contribution.

Count Coudenhove-Kalergi, whose father had already been a life-long champion of mutual understanding between Christians and Jews, assessed the Jews more favorably. In a sub-section of his essay "Krise des Adels" (The Crisis of the Aristocracy), he described the Jews as the new leaders in commerce, journalism, and literature and as a new aristocracy, actual or potential, which was destined to supersede the old and decaying feudal nobility.[129] He claimed that the Jews, some honest, some corrupt, had achieved this status, an aristocracy of the intellect, by a process of natural selection: the timid and opportunistic had defected; the weak had been extirpated. As socialistic political leaders (Lassalle and Trotsky), philosophers (Bergson), composers (Mahler), scientists (Einstein), the new aristocrats of the mind were bestowing precious gifts upon Western Europe.

Where there is much light, Coudenhove-Kalergi continued, there is much shadow. As a result of centuries of inbreeding and persecution, the Jews had produced strong characters of high intelligence and spineless sciolists; selfless idealists and crass materialists; the dynamic, intellectually alive and the morally courageous; but also the psychologically brittle and the physically weak and cowardly. But their flaws, he predicted, would disappear with the cessation of persecution, with sports, and rural resettlement in Palestine.

As in Coudenhove-Kalergi's essay, the *Merkur*'s praise of the Jews outweighed the derogations through greater persuasiveness. If, as one article argued, Christ was a victim of Jewish nationalism, his philosophy, as another essay pointed out, could only have grown on the soil of Judaism. If, on the one hand, German-Jewish businessmen indulged in sharp practices, the most idealistic German politicians and statesmen, on the other hand, also came from the ranks of the Jews. If one contributor found all or some Jews hypersensitive, cowardly, flippant, clannish, or with lots of nerve (an approximate translation of the Yiddish word *Chuzpah*), others pointed to their sensitivity to their fellow men, their bravery in World War One, to the serious purpose of Jewish writers, e.g., Brod, Holitscher, and Werfel, to their adaptability, and to their urbanity. If, as Hanns Braun argued, Jewish writers had infected recent German literature with an overemphasis on cerebration, they also held a potential remedy: their spirituality (*Gottes-Erfassung*).[130] From these and other pairs of opposites—in which a debater's religion by no means determined his point of view—the reader at that time could draw but one conclusion: that the Jews, collectively, had both the virtues and failings of the average man. One wonders whether this was not precisely the impression Frisch wished to create.

Most refutations of anti-Semitism appealed, as Frisch's "Jüdische Aufzeichnungen," to logic and reason.[131] It was illogical, Herman Esswein protested, to judge a drama by the religion of its author; it was unreasonable and infantile, as Bruno Rauecker demonstrated, to blame the Jews for the lost war and the revolution; was not, Otto Flake speculated, hatred of the Jews a psychological reaction to a bad conscience, or, as Coudenhove-Kalergi surmised, merely the traditional distrust of the rustic for the urbanite?[132]

Occasionally the *Merkur* tried sarcasm. Don't blame everything on the Jews, Esswein advised the anti-Semites, you will give them megalomania! In answer to an attack on the "anti-Royalistic" Jews, Mendelssohn-Bartholdy asked in mock seriousness: "Was Schiller perhaps under Jewish influence," Rasso Bergmann and Ernst Hierl ridiculed discrimination and segregation; Alfred Döblin, as a practicing physician, prescribed a measured dose of Jews for a country's well-being: "Otherwise it will burst from indigestion." And he gently implied that all anti-Semites were feeble-minded.[133] If he was right, the *Merkur*'s reasoned arguments and clever barbs could scarcely be expected to penetrate the minds of the opposition.

Curiously and incomprehensibly, the *Merkur* expended not only space but, occasionally, even commendations on avowed anti-Semites. Hans Blüher's answer to an unfavorable review in the *Merkur* was printed in full, despite the disputant's unvarnished admission that the reviewer, Leo Matthias, "correctly senses in me an anti-Semite."[134] Nor did Blüher's antagonism towards the Jews prevent Frisch from placing his book on a list of recommended readings.[135] Frisch also passed a report of his English correspondent, Rob Rab, who described the *New Witness* as "clericalistic, anti-Semitic and humorous" and recommended it to the readers of the *Merkur*.[136] But the *Merkur* reached the final turn of a convoluted objectivity when it also recommended Theodor Haecker's *Satire and Polemic* which denounced the *Merkur*, by name, as a "Jew magazine." This time it was no oversight as it had been with the unfortunate acceptance of an advertisement of Bartels' book;[137] among Frisch's private papers is a printed review of Haecker's work which lauded its anti-Semitism. Surely one may question at what point, precisely, objectivity becomes self-destruction.

As a cure for the many difficulties of the Jews, some contributors advocated Zionism; others rejected it. Arguments pro and con were about evenly divided and sometimes, as with Frisch's essays, appeared within the same article. These arguments have since become so familiar that they do not require a detailed summation. Basically the Zionists espoused a state in Palestine as the only practical and feasible homeland for the Jews, theirs by reason of history and religion, as a haven against oppression, a center for spiritual renewal, and a balm for Jewish pride. The anti-Zionists considered a homeland unnecessary or impractical or, at the least, Palestine highly unsuitable for it. They also regarded Zionism as a deplorable form of nationalism and the Jewish spiritual mission as essentially diasporic. What remains of interest today are the various predictions made about Palestine; at this writing most have proved wrong. "Palestine will be a socialistic state or none at all," said Hermann Kranold. "When the Mohammedans and Christians will undertake their bloody expulsion of the Haluzzim," Sternthal predicted, "the English will watch with folded arms." Elsewhere he stated: "Zionism will always be nothing but a feeble subterfuge for the Jews of Western Europe." Flake warned that Hebrew would be inadaptable for modern usage. Döblin prophesied that Palestine, smaller than the Mark Brandenburg, "can be no more than a symbol." Paquet predicted its success; Judah L. Magnes foresaw continuing conflicts with the Arab nations.[138] Today these last two statements seem to remain as mutually exclusive alternatives.

The longest and most weighty article on German-Jewish mutuality was written by Ferdinand Lion for the special issue of Judaism. His essay "Deutsches und jüdisches Schicksal" (German and Jewish Destiny) sounds today like the brilliant retelling of a hopeful dream which, once shared by millions of all faiths, has been twisted by the Jewish catastrophe into a nightmarish parody of itself.[139] Here are its opening sentences:

> No matter what happens, whether Jews and Germans draw closer to each other or part as enemies, their bonds will, in reality, remain the same; they are constants. For they share the same fate . . . they are both peoples of suffering. . . . [But] neither was created for suffering; on the contrary they love, they need the earth, a full existence, joy, creativity, brightness and unhampered development, but destiny drives them from their course into sorrow, destitution, exile, contempt, restriction.

Lion wrote that the Germans and the Jews shared so many fateful characteristics, a spatial and temporal adaptability so developed, that they often lost their own profile—as witness their architecture and politics. The true profiles of these two peoples, both toys of destiny, could only be glimpsed when the Jew worshipped in the circle of his family and when the German lost himself in his work. These two peoples also shared the ability of re-emerging from obscurity, the Jews after the Middle Ages and the Germans after the Thirty Years War.

Lion concluded with a declaration of hope. "These two blessedly unblessed people hold each other convulsed in love or hate or love-hatred." What will be their mutual destiny? "The best of each, always expecting the miracle, sigh–while wrestling–into the ear of the other people, as though [the other one] were the celestial angel: 'I leave you not except thou bless me.'" By tacit agreement, this article was not discussed by author or interviewer at our meeting in September 1961.

Several regular contributors to the *Merkur*, surprisingly, never debated the "Jewish problem," though they could logically have been expected to do so. In fact, three of them were invited to contribute to the "Jewish" issue. "I have no desire," answered Max Picard on 21 January 1920, "to cite moral or metaphysical arguments against that dreadful anti-Semitism. I only wish to tell you how stupid this anti-Semitism is. It emanates from no one but a stupid kind of person." Friedrich Burschell gave a different reason in a letter to Frisch of 14 February 1920: He had had the intention of writing about the Jewish question, but had given it up, for he would scarcely have found anyone among the readers of the *Merkur* to convince. And to adjust, even in the slightest, to the tone of the others, was completely impossible. "Spengler is an opponent; the others, good Heavens!"

The case of Thomas Mann's conspicuous absence is more complex. In this instance neither secondary works nor the voluminous editorial correspondence could supply the needed facts. I learned later that all negotiations about an article between Thomas Mann and the editor-in-chief, Efraim Frisch, had been conducted over the telephone.

Briefly, the history of the essay, entitled "Zur Judenfrage" (About the Jewish Problem) is as follows. The August 1921 number of the *Neue Merkur*, a special issue devoted to Judaism, had promised a future article by Thomas Mann on the same topic, but none ever appeared. Many years later, in 1951, a book by a Mannheim dealer in bibliophilia mentioned that the article had been submitted and then withdrawn by Thomas Mann: "He suddenly [after reading proof] decided to withdraw the article. Via telephone he gave instructions that he would come by the printer's, in order to pick up the ms. and to be present at the destruction of the set type. In this half-an-hour 35 copies were run off."[140] This curiosity, apparently once in the possession of the scholar Martin Sommerfeld, ultimately found its way into the Thomas Mann Archive in Zürich, where I read and inspected it. Its type face was obviously that of the *Neue Merkur*. Its content, a more negative evaluation of German

Jewry than that of the articles in the special Jewish issue, gave no hint as to its publishing history. At this point I decided to arrange three interviews: one with Fega Frisch, the widow of the editor; one with the writer and librettist Ferdinand Lion, a friend of both Frisch and Mann; and one with Alfred Vagts, former editorial assistant under Frisch.

Mrs. Frisch, interviewed on 10 September 1961 in Ascona, recalled only that her husband had been "äusserst aufgeregt" in 1921 about an article by Thomas Mann. Knowing now Frisch's opinion of the article, I felt justified in surmising that the *editor* rather than the author had withdrawn it in the course of the press run. The next interview, conducted on 28 September 1961 in Zürich, apparently confirmed this assumption. Ferdinand Lion told me at that time: "The special Jewish number caused some discord with Mann. Frisch was too much of an idealist to accept an article not consonant with his standards." When I told Dr. Lion that the article *had* apparently been accepted, in fact even been set in type, he clarified his statement by saying that he was positive that the final prohibition of the article came upon specific orders from Frisch. As a friend of both men, he added, he had heard this version from each side.

My third interview, over a year later in Sherman, Connecticut, revealed that Dr. Lion's disclosure was true—but not complete. On 25 January 1963, I talked with Alfred Vagts, once a prominent German Expressionist poet who even rated inclusion in Gottfried Benn's anthology, but who is now (unbeknownst to most German scholars) an American military historian emeritus at the Institute for Advanced Studies in Princeton, New Jersey. Professor Vagts told me an astonishing story: "As to the special Jewish number this could be said, and I believe that my recollection is somewhat more accurate than that of Ferdinand Lion. . . . The essay by Thomas Mann was, let us say, the most critical [pronouncement] which Mann said about this problem and went even beyond the [Reflections of a] Non-Political Man. . . . Nonetheless his contribution was accepted, after all it was Tommie's responsibility, as Frisch put it. However, it came back from the author's proof-reading with so many deletions that the editors saw in this reduction sufficient reason, to reach an agreement with the author to omit it. I heard—this is hearsay—that Mrs. Mann had been behind the deletions." Although I am not at liberty to divulge Professor Vagts' source I can say, unequivocally, that his informant was in a most favorable position to supply such intimate knowledge.

Professor Vagts also recalled that a member of the editorial staff (I surmise that it was he himself) asked the printer to run off thirty-five copies of the already set article. This explanation appears to be the final piece in the puzzle; Professor Vagts' recollection, both complete and consistent, now clears up an elusive detail in the history of the *Neue Merkur*. Also the first publication of my findings in the *German Quarterly* evoked so much scholarly interest in Mann's "self-censored" article as to lead, forty-five years later, to its publication. This, in turn, led to further debate, still in progress, as to the circumstances surrounding its submission and withdrawal. An early contribution to the controversy, a study by Dr. Kurt Loewenstein, takes issue with some of Professor Vagts' (and my) presentation. But in an addendum to his article, written in collaboration with Alfred Vagts, Vagts illustrates the basics for his argumentation and Kurt Loewenstein revises his first opinion and basically substantiates my interpretation.[141]

The Nazi years wrote the final commentary on these three "noncontributors," who each in his own way wanted to ignore the existence of "the others," as Friedrich Burschell put it. They burned the books of the Catholic, Max Picard, of the two Protestants, Friedrich Burschell and Thomas Mann, and they expelled the Jew, Efraim Frisch—who *had* contributed but had been of two minds in doing so.

As a remedy for anti-Semitism, intolerance, and many of the other ills of the Weimar Republic, the *Merkur* suggested a thorough reform of the German educational system. "Educate each German youth in such a way," urged Sternthal "that . . . he, while fighting an opponent, respects him as much as himself and his own partisans."[142] To bridge the differences between the classes and to strengthen the foundations of democracy, the *Merkur* urged a free high school and university education for all; it supported the educational theories of Gustav Wyneken and Friedrich Wilhelm Foerster as a successful fusion of humanism, religion, and democracy. In a devastating article, the magazine rushed to Wyneken's defense when he stood accused of a morals charge.[143] To blunt the differences between the religions, the *Merkur* recommended a change of religious instruction in the high schools. Ernst Hierl, a teacher at a Munich Realgymnasium, argued, in essence: Religious instruction, yes; instruction in *a* religion, no![144]

Two main obstacles, several contributors contended, remained as barriers to an effective democratic education: the entrenched conservative educators and the *Studentenverbindungen* (fraternities). The former, Hierl remonstrated, inhibited a more democratic relationship between teachers and students and a free expression of opinion by either; the latter had been and continued to be, as Romain Rolland charged, the mainstays of any reactionary, counter-revolutionary, anti-democratic organization.[145] Otto Flake, in a memorable hyperbole, called the student body at Munich "8000 students, each with two bullets and one gun."[146] As a salutary corrective to the bellicose *Studentenverbindungen*, Oskar Ewald advanced a new student movement in Austria, the *Christo-kraten*, who tried to live by the principles of the Sermon on the Mount.[147] But Harald Landry felt that the best student organization was none at all; let each student, on his own, progress "from highest consciousness via virtuosity to a second state of naturalness, from sharpest intellect to a liberation of the instincts."[148] Frisch, however, demurred at this. Was not such an exhortation, he asked, a return to the Bismarckian ideals of achievement and competence? Frisch asked for new values.[149]

Frisch's postscriptum re-echoed the principal spiritual and philosophical quest of his times and his magazine; immediately following the war years the phrase "geistige Erneuerung" recurred in the *Merkur* like a refrain. When used, it often remained vague and ambiguous; "geistig" meant, in turn, spiritual, philosophical, intellectual, religious—or an amalgam of some or all of these. And "Erneuerung" of course signified any ideological direction championed by the writer. But while the ambiguity of terms precluded a head-on clash, the various writers divined each others' opinions sufficiently to indulge in some of the liveliest and most tempestuous controversies in the history of the *Merkur*.

Up to a point all philosophical articles followed a pattern—before the evocation of a specific "renewal" inevitably led them into different directions. The war, so the articles ran generally, had crippled not only the bodies of men but also their spirits; the materialism of the post-war years had swept away the last remnants of idealism (many writers called this loss "Entgeistigung").[150] It was useless to try to restore the ideals of the past; they all had failed. Each writer then detailed this charge by attacking one or more of the lights that had failed. Concretely in an editorial preface to an essay by Masaryk, Frisch and Hausenstein chided his "narrow rationalism."[151] If Hausenstein's opinion, expressed in a letter to Frisch of February, 1920, had prevailed, the article would never have been published. Frisch also turned against the *Erkenntnistheorie*, which Erich von Kahler also condemned.[152] Alfred Döblin derided orthodox religion as a superstition of heaven and hell and, like many other writers of the time, as a handmaiden of the ruling castes and large industrialists.[153] Felix Weltsch, examining freedom of the will and divine grace, judged a philosophy or theology based exclusively on the latter as potentially dangerous.[154] And the ethical system of Leonard Nelson, according to Leo Matthias, foundered on the dilemma of trying "to build on reason without a God and without a proof for the existence of an inner moral law."[155]

One philosophy, that of Oswald Spengler, created a united opposition among the contributors of the *Merkur*. At least twelve articles took issue with him, fortified by arguments from religion, history, philosophy, science, and personal experience. By 1924 the subject had been covered so thoroughly that Frisch showed no enthusiasm for further contributions and little regret that a refutation of Spengler by Thomas Mann went to the *"Tagebuch"* and *The Dial* instead of the *Merkur* (as he informed Director Kilpper on 27 March 1924).

Ferdinand Lion opened the *Merkur*'s attack on Spengler's *Decline of the West* by disputing his historical facts and his "arbitrary" periodization of history.[156] Was it not equally correct, Lion asked, to call the rise of Christianity the renewal rather than the end of the Roman period? Lion even disputed the accuracy of the title of Spengler's book: the decline of the West was in reality only the decline of the Wilhelmine empire and Spengler's book was its swan-song. In this assumption Lion erred; it turned out to be one of the processionals towards Weimar's *Götterdämmerung*.

It was Robert Musil who, no less critical than Lion, nonetheless conceded Spengler's troublesome pertinence and pertinacity.[157] "It is a work of significance, with a life of its own," he said. "If one attacks Spengler, one is attacking the times that gave birth to him and which he now gratifies [by his book], for his faults are theirs." And he closed his essay with an appreciation which is not completely invalidated by its irony: "I profess publicly to Oswald Spengler, as a token of my affection, that other authors make less mistakes only because they lack the range . . . to accommodate so many." Between these tokens of tempered admiration, Musil enumerated the mistakes of the book. Spengler, who had frequently relied on "mathematical evidence," was to Musil no more a mathematician than "a zoologist who classifies dogs, tables, chairs, and equations to the fourth power as quadrupeds." His mistakes in mathematics, a subject Spengler taught, he felt were not only errors in particular details but also characteristic faults in his way of thinking. He arrived at the same conclusion when he examined Spengler's interpretation of reality, spatial theory, and the contrast between culture and civilization.

Spengler's entire philosophy was severely criticized by Rudolf Kayser, who deplored the destructive effect of Spengler's nihilism and scepticism upon German literature, as well as by Helmuth Plessner.[158] "It is a philosophical impossibility," Plessner argued in refutation, "to compare the present in which we live with what has come into existence. . . . The principle of relativity also applies to historical measurements; the planet on which we live changes its position and the system in which it moves again changes its place towards an unfathomable direction."

Despite its resistance to Spengler, the *Merkur* was unable to escape his influence or at least his terminology. The concepts of "end of a cultural epoch," "the decline of Europe," "the decline of the West," were not only quoted but often also treated as realities. Frisch, despite his own and his magazine's militant stand against Spengler, invited him (in an incompletely dated letter of 1920) to fulfill his verbal promise for a contribution. Spengler never complied; perhaps he found the *Merkur*, upon closer examination, too hostile to his ideas. If that was, indeed, the reason for his refusal, a still closer reading would have revealed to him a partial agreement beneath the apparent hostility: the *Merkur*, while rejecting his covert German nationalism, shared his cultural pessimism.

The partial endorsement of Spengler was involuntary and subconscious. What the *Merkur* proclaimed as its philosophy or philosophies—as part of its quest for a spiritual renewal—was quite different. Pannwitz, for example, predicted the dawn of a new age if the philosophy of Nietzsche ("who has created a new world") were put into practice.[159] He posed the question: "What to do?" And he answered it himself as a true disciple of Nietzsche:

> Have no ideals, but live and create ideally. . . . Above all one must act and create personally, positively, and directly. No longer [endure] narrowness, philistinism . . . libertinage and exploitation. Turn everything in such a way and to such fruitfulness that it can and must be affirmed. Whatever one recognizes as hostile one should turn to the advantage of one's higher purpose. . . . If such a spirit gradually also takes hold of politics—of political theorists who will someday supervise or carry out practical politics themselves—we can hope for an immeasurable improvement.

Pannwitz remained alone in his evocation of Nietzsche. As if in refutation, Albert Steffen, in an article following almost immediately upon Pannwitz', identified anthroposophical philosophy with a renewal of the spirit.[160] Other contributors, such as Rudolf Kassner, Felix Braun, and Thomas Masaryk, equated it with a revitalized form of Christianity.[161] Surprisingly, Alfons Paquet, himself a Quaker, expected this revitalization from the Russian Orthodox Church; Ernst Hierl from groups outside organized religion. Leopold Ziegler found elements in Buddhism that offered new answers to Western man; Hugo Horwitz in a return to a community of male citizens similar to that envisioned by Socrates.[162]

Walter Strich demanded a "spiritual renewal" in politics. To many contributors this meant an evolution from a democracy to a pantisocracy. Kurt Hiller, somewhat dogmatically, demanded "a purified aristocratic idea; not the will of the majority [shall be] the law-giver, but the will of the intellectuals [*Geistwille*]." (Otto Flake subsequently rejected Hiller's plan for a "dictatorship of the Aristoi" as unrealistic.) But Count Coudenhove-Kalergi came to Hiller's defense by devoting an entire article to the coming ascendancy of rule by an aristocracy of the mind over a rule by the people.[163] The author stated in an interview of 10 October 1961 that he viewed the present rise of a privileged intellectual elite in Russia and of a "brain trust" in American politics as practical proofs of the accuracy of his prophecy of more than forty years ago.

Truly the locution "spiritual renewal," heard so often in the *Merkur* (and in Germany), was no more than a slogan. By careful elaboration Julius Meier-Graefe, Hanns Braun, and Hans Deinhardt made clear what they meant by "spiritual renewal" in and through the fine arts, the theatre, and music—although the term itself became tautological.[164] But what did Herman Uhde-Bernays mean, for example, when he wrote of "artistic renewal" (in an article significantly entitled "Auferstehung" (Resurrection): "We know that in the depth of the peoples' existence there slumber mysterious forces, whose awakening life is carried upward to the surface of the day like the rising air bubbles above the clear mirror of a well."[165] Here the term had lost all meaning; eventually Hausenstein and Frisch discouraged its use. Hausenstein spoke of the word *geistig* as "discredited by silly misuse";[166] Frisch complained that "the word *Erneuerung*, much misused, is being fashioned into party slogans, almost into waste paper."[167]

The two co-editors rejected, but did not try to explain, the Germans' sudden predilection for the term and the concept. Hanns Braun did: "Thrown back upon ourselves, poor and disdained, we expect, from the spirit within ourselves, which we have disavowed for so long, our future and our happiness."[168] Writing forty years after Braun, Max Tau made a similar observation: "Many in Germany tried to compensate for the defeat in war through the rediscovery of spiritual values."[169] Many more among Germany's intellectuals, however, used "spiritual values" as an escape from the lost war rather than as a compensation for it.

In this sense much in the *Merkur* was "escape literature," a comfort to the individual, but—as all the plethora of escape literature printed in Germany—a danger to the Weimar Republic. Its best minds, lulled by the palliatives of distant and romanticized times and places, became unresponsive to the demands of the perilous here-and-now. With surprising inconsistency the *Merkur* frequently dispensed such comforting palliatives while at the same time warning against their use. "We Germans," cautioned Albert Steffen, "turn in aberration to the West and to the East. We are on the look-out for American success and become worldly-minded speculators or we lose ourselves in oriental mysticism and become transcendental visionaries."[170] Bernhard Diebold's warning was even more pointed:

> Many think, mistakenly, that the Old World has been reduced to ruins and that the decline of the West is inevitable. We pant beneath the dust-cloud of the military collapse and believe that we shall recover only in foreign climes. But instead of immigrating to India or Africa we try to transplant lotus flowers and palm trees into European farmland. . . . There are far too many who open their ears and their trust to the ancient Chinese instead of listening to the subterranean springs of our own soil.[171]

Otto Flake's "Reise in die Zeit"[172] was, finally, a declaration of war against Germany's escapists. He admitted that his own journey started out as a flight, an escape from printer's ink, a sick democracy, Bavarian politics, and Munich's cultural decline into nature and, via Tieck's *Der blonde Eckbert*, into the world of the German Romantics. But in the industrial city of Pforzheim he realized that "turning back is impossible —as impossible as regaining our lost religiosity." He scolded the Germans for their flight to metaphysics: "They believe that *Innerlichkeit* is enough." "On the contrary," he expostulated, "it is our task to show [our efforts] on the outside, to make them visible, to become active." He also condemned "the German tendency to use hard toil as an escape," "the flight from the revolution into the neutrality of work." And he summarized:

> On this evening someone found the right word for our resignation: one must withdraw into the world of the spirit. How clear it became that every new philosophy is but a reaction and a flight. . . . But at precisely this point I decided to resist, not just on my own behalf but for all who think.

A page later he stated his objections:

> One must not pit the world of the spirit against reality or separate the one from the other. I demanded, on the contrary, that we project our inner energies outwardly, that we shape life and its realities, specifically politics, society, human activity of every type, and restrict metaphysics. . . . I joined a few determined thinkers who agreed with me that the flight into the realm of the spirit must be replaced by an advance out of it in order to emerge,

finally, from the literary, the spiritual, the timeless and the non-committal.

These and similar warnings remained unheeded, even in the *Merkur*. Again and again various writers sought to escape the dreariness of post-war Germany. They belatedly popularized, in the pages of the *Merkur*, the earlier retreat into abstruseness of Germany's experts in philosophy, theology, sociology, and the arts. They "fled" to America, "the last refuge of the white race,"[173] to the art and literature of China, India, Japan, the old Germany and the new Russia, to the philosophy of Gautama Buddha or Jean Jacques Rousseau, to the culture of the Aztecs, the North Germanic tribes, or the Middle Ages, and once even to the exotic charms of Samoan women.[174] While the subjects in themselves were unobjectionable—except, possibly, the panegyrics to the North Teutonic culture and religion[175]—their invocation as a haven from an unbearable reality was socially destructive. Immersed in them, the intellectuals became a group apart. "The majority of the intellectuals," Oskar Ewald complained, "deludedly think that the written word releases them from [the necessity] to act. . . . They lack a sense of responsibility."[176]

Did the *Merkur*, despite its enjoinders to the contrary, encourage this irresponsible flight from reality? In some instances it did so quite openly. The Hölderlin revival, Conrad Wandrey argued, gave the Germans a chance to "turn their reflections back to their innermost life"; Hans Poeschel even used the word "flüchten" (to flee) in a parallel appreciation of another nineteenth-century German writer: "The more painfully one experiences the crises and chaos of the present state of the world, the more strongly the need makes itself felt to flee this unrest, if only for a few hours. In this frame of mind we gratefully welcome [Stifter's *Nachsommer*]." Erich Jenisch similarly praised Chinese art as "the salvation and *refuge* [italics mine] from the aberration of European 'culture.'" Julius Meier-Graefe saw in all art "the means . . . for compensating us for our material losses and of elevating the might of our souls."[177]

In other articles the "escapist" quality took subtler forms; it was often suggested by a single word or phrase or by a pointed comparison. Vis-à-vis the harmonious world of Java, European culture appears atomized; compared to the religious arts of the Middle Ages, modern art reveals a "small soul"; the numerous books about the accomplishments of the primitive Germanic tribes had, according to Josef Ponten, a definite "ethical purpose: to wrest our culture from the ennervating embrace of the South."[178] One also suspects that the sudden increase of exotic settings in the *Merkur*'s fiction (which was symptomatic of a trend all over Germany—and in other European countries) and the many travel descriptions offered still another route of escape.

The dangers of such a flight from reality were illustrated nowhere more clearly than in a passage by Robert Walser: "I have given up the habit of reading newspapers, for the simple reason that I wanted to break myself of curiosity. . . . For me it is unprofitable to be informed of something every day on which I can exert no influence. That means a useless exertion of my brains which I forbid myself."[179]

In short, the magazine in those years resembled Janus more closely than Mercury. One of its faces, that of its political and social articles, was turned to the local and present scene; it carried the mien of a sentinel sounding the alarm. Its other face, shaped by many of its literary, aesthetic, and philosophical contributions, bore a far-away or retrospective look which lulled its contemporaries into complacency.

This latter shortcoming was also a strength; the *Merkur* often introduced and, even more important, often popularized, subjects—translations from recent Russian literature, for example—which would otherwise have remained *terra incognita* to most of its readers. In the fields of fine arts, theater, and music it combined this search for novelty and experiment with a rediscovery of traditional works. To both the old and the new art it applied the same philosophy of criticism: an eclectic and ingenuous approach, an "interpretation from the inside out," and a decided preference for the committed artist—*l'artist engagé*, to use a modern term.

The eclectic approach had become the *Merkur*'s policy with Frisch's very first editorial. He pledged his magazine to a position above the directions and movements of the arts and reiterated this declaration of neutrality after the war.[180] In practice, however, it was a militant neutrality; frequently the *Merkur* challenged reviews in which it detected bias towards a specific artistic movement. Willy Wolfradt, for example, defending Richard Seewaldt's change from his earlier Expressionistic style to an "unfashionable" Naturalism, declared: "It is mere prejudice to evaluate the . . . content of a work proportionate to its measure of abstraction from nature."[181] In the light of this review it was probably no accident that the term *Neue Sachlichkeit*, the direction which Seewaldt's canvasses approached, was invented and championed by G. F. Hartlaub, one of the *Merkur*'s principal contributors for art criticism.[182]

In a similar vein Wilhelm Hausenstein, disturbed by the fulsome praise heaped upon the works of Ferdinand Hodler, charged that the trend towards "monumentalism" and Swiss national pride, rather than sober judgment, had established their fame. When his rebuttal unleashed a war of words between the *Merkur* and the Swiss press, Frisch and Hausenstein learned to their chagrin that neutrality is no shield against attack.[183] Hausenstein, by urging that critics judge each art work in isolation—divorced from its time and movement—carried this principle of neutrality one step further. Since he himself did not always adhere to this method of criticism, especially in later years after his conversion, it seems likely that in protesting the encroachment of the "evolutionary method" into art, he deliberately overstated his case.[184] Nonetheless his request had some results. Though the *Merkur*'s articles on art did not abandon established labels, they constantly re-examined them and their applicability to a given work. Hausenstein himself, writing about Impressionism, concluded that "labels are bureaucracy"; Heinrich von Wedderkop, discussing Dutch art, argued that Rembrandt's greatness "protects it [Dutch art] against all systematization." And Otto Höver, comparing the Italian and the German Baroque, reclassified the latter as a "spatial rococo, a continuation of the late Gothic with different means."[185] This last judgment, written in a spirit of *se non è vero, è ben trovato*, was often symptomatic of the articles on fine art. Somewhat journalistic, occasionally "literary," they often defied conventional art criticism and thus forced the experts to re-examine their premises.

Hausenstein's request was also consistent with the *Merkur*'s second aesthetic principle, which was advanced in separate articles by Erich Jenisch and Robert Musil.[186] Jenisch called it "a new criticism." (The definite article, capitalization, and deification were to come later.) In writing the history of art, Jenisch contended, the mere knowledge of styles, names, and dates was inadequate; a logical or a psychological interpretation of art from the life and environment of the artist was likewise insufficient. The critic must learn to empathize with the mood of the work; by employing comparisons, by assessing "the artistic facts" objectively and avoiding a merely subjective appreciation [*Nacherleben*], he will allow the art works to speak for themselves.

Robert Musil's exposition (which, despite its importance, has never been republished), was more extensive and profound. Although in appearance it seemed a book review, it was in reality (as the author wrote Frisch on 17 September 1921) "an essay in size and through the importance of the subject." Musil like Jenisch rejected the traditional methods of art criticism; they were either witty or scholarly, rarely both, and intruded "concepts and related feelings furnished by the imagination of the beholder which do not belong to the picture." Instead he urged the adoption of a method used or, as Musil should have said more correctly, popularized by G. J. von Allesch in his *Wege zur Kunstbetrachtung* (Dresden, 1921): "Under the guidance of one's first impressions the total intention of the picture is divided into partial impressions [e.g., color, plane, spatial, figure, and object-relationships] and these are tested against the picture whether or not they are fulfilled in it. This method constitutes an experimental interpretation of the picture from the inside out . . . [accomplished] by attributing to it a tentative interpretation which is only accepted, if it does not fail at any point and does not lead to contradictions." He continued: "The determinants thus determine each other." Musil conceded that this method, too, had its limitations; a critic who was using it could, instead of verifying an assumption, merely pile error on error. He also doubted that anyone, including the artist, could ever explicate or even know an art work [das Kunstwerk an sich] completely. Nonetheless, he concluded, we will never again be able to forego Allesch's "pliable and resistant method."

The Merkur, at any rate, employed it extensively. The aforementioned article by Höver and Hausenstein's compact and cogent analysis of Grünewald's Isenheimer Altar most closely exemplified the method, but its application is also apparent in Hausenstein's essay about Renoir, Hans Kauder's review of books on medieval art, and in other articles and reviews.[187]

Virtually all critics concurred that the degree of the artist's commitment was one measure of his greatness. According to Frisch only the compulsive artist, driven "by the grace or wrath of fate," unafraid of "the martyrdom of proclaiming lasting values in a shattered world," could revitalize German art, stagnating as "an art for other artists." Hanns Braun, expanding upon Frisch's thought, explored the boundaries between artistic commitment and propaganda.[188] He also, in common with several other art critics of the Merkur, sought to define "lasting values" more closely. But here agreement among the various contributors ended. While Braun identified lasting values with religion and Hausenstein with Nature and God, Alfons Paquet, on the other side of the scale, expected them to blossom from the ideology of the New Russia. But Paquet, when he made this prediction in May 1922, did not realize that the brief period of free artistic experimentation in Russia had already ended.[189]

With artistic commitment its yardstick, the Merkur revaluated previous criticisms. Medieval art, even primitive wooden statues, was ranked above well-known but presumably less sincere art works.[190] In its enthusiasm for medieval art, the Neue Merkur, for different reasons, reiterated an artistic conviction of the Expressionists—long after it had eschewed their other views. For the critics of the Merkur, Vermeer exemplified the artist diminished by his lack of commitment and van Gogh his salutary counterpart. In this spirit von Wedderkop wrote: "Art is, ordinarily, purgatory. With Vermeer it is not." This sufficed, by Wedderkop's standards, to consign him to the special limbo, if not the purgatory, for artists. By the same reasoning Vincent van Gogh became the greatest artist of modern times.[191] In reaching this conclusion the critic, Julius Meier-Graefe, also set forth his and the *Merkur*'s criteria:

> In the meaning of the term with which we are conversant, Vincent never was an artist. Surely, one thinks, a heightened feeling of self-confidence is in [character]. Yet nothing was less pronounced in his case. And ease, lyricism, inventiveness, talent: all these he had to a lesser extent than the average. Only if we conceive of "artist" quite differently, as the highest [form of] selflessness, as the ability for complete self-sacrifice and for complete dissolution with world and mankind, as a moral person impelled only by a conscience which is purified by an ever deepening insight—then, to be sure, he was an artist, the greatest of our era.[192]

This new conception of the artist was also one of the major reasons for the *Merkur*'s disenchantment with Expressionism, with which it was so closely identified before the war. Many painters, which it formerly esteemed as committed artists, now appeared to the *Merkur*'s art critics as empty poseurs. "Expressionism," wrote Rudolf Kayser in an essay programmatically entitled "Das Ende des Expressionismus" (The End of Expressionism) "is everything but a voyage of discovery or a conquest, but merely an aimless immigration from the dying continent, a new form of *Europamüdigkeit*."[193] Frisch and Hausenstein, as Karl Otten told me in an interiew of 20 September 1961, turned from Expressionism "because they found its ethical tendencies inadequate." While they continued to publish appreciations of the formalistic innovations of Expressionism or of individual Expressionists such as Kubin and Beckmann, they henceforth dismissed Expressionism as a movement. The Expressionists themselves had demanded a committed artist; they were now weighed on their own scale and found wanting.

Otto Zoff's essay "Tizian's Dornenkrönung" (Titian's Crowning of Thorns) best illustrates the practical application of the *Merkur*'s aesthetic principles.[194] Conventional classifications such as Renaissance and Baroque are avoided; the repetition of the judgment by Tintoretto, Titian's contemporary ("a model of modern painting"), exposed the transitory nature of *all* classifications in the arts. Zoff's critical method followed that advocated by Robert Musil; an initial impression of the painting ("triumph of color . . . which eschews drawing and line") is tested against every part of the painting. After finding his initial judgment confirmed by the "foci of the picture," the color contrasts, the arrangement of the figures of Christ and his tormentors, and their facial expressions, he expands his impressions. He sees in the picture a "developing color symphony," the constant repetition of the same chords.

The degree of commitment which Titian brought to his subject is next examined. Christ, Zoff finds, dominates the painting, but not as the Son of God. The painting depicts "the passion of the triumphantly suffering spirit"; "a thinking and spiritual human being is crowned with thorns by the plebeian mass." Titian is the new man "who has partaken of the most dangerous poison: the experience of the nexus of causality." A sceptic, he was driven by a want of inner harmony; he did not believe in God. He lacked commitment; he could and did paint religious, profane, or classical subjects, with the same colors and in the same style. "A subject is a subject. Painting is painting. Business is business." And sadly Zoff concluded: "Since [Titian], life is more beautiful, lighter, mightier than ever. But it is without a goal. And thus it is, in spite of all advances, also the poorer." It is easy to understand why Frisch, as Otto Zoff told me, energetically solicited this article for the *Merkur*. It epitomized its editorial policy in the fine arts. And it was, therefore, particularly unfortunate that precisely this contributor—despite some merit, plainly an amateur art critic—provoked a merciless refutation by one of the best-known experts of the day, Heinrich Wölfflin.[195]

In the years 1919–23, only five articles on music appeared in the *Merkur*; none of them emulated the interpretative method advocated by its art critics. But they clearly evoked the other two aesthetic principles of the *Merkur*: the eclectic approach, by its impartial enthusiasm for Bach, Beethoven, Busoni, Mendelssohn-Bartholdy, and Arnold Schönberg, and by the criterion of artistic engagement in evaluating these and other composers. To Hans Deinhardt, Beethoven's music appeared as the "epiphany of the soul," as "purity and self-sacrifice, inspiration and work, wisdom and love." Mendelssohn-Bartholdy characterized his grandfather as "called to the service of the purest and most spiritual art. . . . His service was dedicated to a splendor beyond human rule. To it he willingly sacrificed his young life: *in serviendo consumor*." And Annette Kolb, as knowledgeable about music as about literature, saw in Busoni a composer similarly "possessed" by his artistic mission of preparing the music of the future. In each one of these evaluations (which are, of course, debatable as music criticism) the artist's dedication is heavily underscored.[196]

Two general articles on music, both by Hans Deinhardt, summarized the *Merkur*'s musical criteria: "Great music is, to some degree, always tendentious; it always bears traits of a world reform. It wants to contribute to the tension between subjectivity and objectivity; it is a philosophy of identity." Modern music, he felt, was lacking precisely in these qualities. Unlike the music of the Age of Romanticism ("the Romantic never *is*; he always becomes"), today's music was repetitive bargain-basement music. He prophesied that the music of the future, in the Age of Socialism, would be "without tonality, without tension between concord and dissonance, without modulation, without change of arsis and thesis."[197] Deinhardt did not make clear why the type of music he described would come as a concomitant of socialism.

In its theater criticism, the *Merkur*'s vaunted impartiality wavered before the repeated and determined demands of artistic engagement. Perhaps it is easier to remain impartial when an art work betrays its intent through sound and color rather than words. No matter what the explanation, the drama critics of the *Merkur* had definite preferences and even condemned eclecticism in others. Hanns Braun, for example, looking back upon the 1920 theater season in Munich, deprecated it as "eclectic triflings." He would have banned light comedies, no matter how excellent, as the cheap escape of a public "overfed with reality," and Wedekind as a panderer to the public's love of sensationalism.[198] Sternthal also had no patience with a selectively assembled repertoire. He lauded the Berlin *Volksbühne* for the discernible homogeneity of its playbill and derided the motley program of other Berlin theaters. He felt that a unified world view (not ideology) should control the selection of the repertoire.[199]

Robert Musil, reporting on the theater in Vienna, turned not only against Wildgans as a playwright, but against all "petit-bourgeois" (*Spiesser*) dramas as well.[200] And while the *Merkur* had conceded the excellence of some of the Expressionists in the arts and in music, Frisch published Sternthal's praise of Fritz von Unruh and Georg Kaiser very reluctantly and only after Sternthal had added the qualification that "we will smile at Kaiser's Expressionism in ten years as we do today at Sudermann's 'Naturalism.' "[201] And von Wedderkop, in an article on dramatic Expressionism that drew praise from Musil, categorically dismissed all Expressionistic playwrights: "Expressionism appears like an admiral on a sailboat with an auxiliary motor which he orders to go full steam ahead."[202]

The *Merkur* allocated to the theater a mission reminiscent of the one advocated by Schiller in his "Die Bühne als moralische Anstalt betrachtet." "It is the task of the stage," wrote Hanns Braun, "to hold up to . . . its age a mirror of its manners and a model of greater perfection." And he added: "In this [present] chaos the theater could prove to be one of the most important constructive elements in the [German] society of the future."[203]

Using this concept of the theater as its yardstick, the *Merkur* received few plays with favor. Musil, intrigued with the form and originality of

Werfel's *Spiegelmensch* (Mirror-Man), nonetheless found it wanting, "because emotions must be taken seriously."[204] Sternthal rejected the bourgeois heroism (again, over Frisch's protest) of Schiller, Grabbe, Grillparzer, and Otto Ludwig and (with Frisch's approval) of Kornfeld, Hasenclever, Toller, and Wildgans. The outdated heroism of the older writers, he felt, was as bad as the pathos of the moderns.[205]

Given this point of view it is easy to surmise which dramas met with approval. Naturally the *Merkur* heartily endorsed the dramas of George Bernard Shaw. *Man and Superman, Captain Brassbound's Conversion,* and *Heartbreak House* were lauded for their social responsibility. The latter work was praised by Alfred Döblin as "the work of a man who can, with a feeling of responsibility . . . say: 'I have experienced the war; it is still alive within me; I will not forget it or allow you to forget it.' "[206] Heinrich Mann's Napoleon drama, *Der Weg zur Macht* (The Road to Power) appeared to the reviewer as not only an exposé of the unbridled quest for power and "a lance broken for Democracy," but also as the presentation of "the tragic fate . . . which in the course of strong-fisted power-politics turned the avenger of the revolution into the murderer of his own ideals."[207] More examples for the direction of the *Merkur*'s drama criticism could be cited, but none more striking than its early appreciation of Brecht. Despite reservations about the drama's second half, Joachim Friedenthal welcomed *Trommeln in der Nacht* (Drums in the Night) as "the new dawn of German literature," and its author as a modern Lenz or Büchner. What of course so deeply impressed the reviewer about the play was the social consciousness, the outcry of a generation "whose soul has been interred."[208] And Sternthal wrote Frisch, after the premiere (in a letter of 6 January 1923): "Last night I saw something unutterably beautiful." Whatever the qualities of Brecht's play, it could be labeled "beautiful" only by a beholder completely empathetic to its social message.

Another group of articles may be read as a spontaneous symposium on the nature of the theater, in which the participants frequently commented and replied to each other's expositions. Franz Ferdinand Baumgarten and Robert Musil argued that the dramatist is paramount in the theater. "The stage must be the humble servant of the poet's word," declared Baumgarten. And Musil criticized Vienna for being a city of actors, not of theater and drama. Wilhelm von Scholz concurred. In a Philippic against the conquest of the stage by the creative arts (i.e., staging and stage decorations), he exclaimed that "the word was in the beginning—and the end." He termed the conception of theater as "total art" a misconception and was supported in this view by von Wedderkop, who ridiculed Wagner's *Gesamtkunstwerk* as "erschlagende Gesamtwirkung" (demolishing total effect).[209]

Joachim Friedenthal defended "total theater." "I am for literature as the intensified expression of everything human. In the theater, however, I am for theater, hence just as much for the actor, the iridescence of the stage, the harmony of the art of directing, and even for the increased manifestation of a special type of community spirit and sociability which, like a perfume, makes the atmosphere of the theater attractive or repulsive. The theater is not necessarily dependent upon pure literature. But the stage play always needs the stage, even when it is good, even when it is literature."[210] Following almost immediately upon Musil's coronation of the dramatist, Friedenthal's diminution of him to the rank of peer among peers kept the controversy alive. But it reached a fever pitch when Franz Blei reduced the status of the writers even more. Discoursing on the training of actors, he blithely and heretically conceded them the right of adding and subtracting lines in the interest of good theater. The author of the *Bestiarium*, the hilarious "sociological study" of German writers, took an obvious delight in twisting the tails of his beasts.[211]

But the people of the theater did not escape unscathed. The *Merkur*, in fact, reserved its most pungent criticism for a director, Max Reinhardt. Frisch, who had chafed under Reinhardt's tempestuous rule when he was a dramaturgist at the Deutsches Theater, and disliked Reinhardt's penchant for spectacular theater, published not just one but two chapters of Franz Ferdinand Baumgarten's book *Circus Reinhardt*. This director was, in the author's opinion, at first a great pioneer of the theater, but had ultimately turned into a megalomaniac. His theater-in-the-round, staged in a circus tent, Baumgarten felt, atomized the drama and turned the art of the classic theater into a modern artifice. "In Reinhardt's circus the downward glide of art to the plane of life took on visible forms and affected the public. . . . The drama loses its magic and becomes ineffectual. The most profoundly human tragedies, their effect tested by centuries, plunged to their death when they descended into the menagerie of the circus. In the Circus Reinhardt there remained even less of Hamlet than of the *Oresteia*. And Caesar found himself completely in the company of the mass and the market place."[212]

The *Merkur*, in essence, favored a socially engaged theater. Though it had little patience with the directorship of Reinhardt's rival, Otto Brahm, whom it found too preachy,[213] the magazine consistently rallied to the defense of those theaters who were attacked, often through cat-calls and stink bombs, for their advocacy of social reforms. Rarely was the *Neue Merkur* as unrestrained in its use of invectives as when it denounced the reactionary rabble as "loutish juveniles" and "scoundrels." "We are absorbed by the symptomatic nature of these ugly events," wrote Hermann Esswein.[214] He and Frisch may have sensed that history was holding a rehearsal in the theater.

4 *Mercury in the House of the DVA*

The *Neue Merkur* entered the haven of the Deutsche Verlags-Anstalt (DVA), one of Germany's leading publishers, via a back door. Wilhelm Hausenstein, dedicated to the magazine beyond his tenure as co-editor, mentioned its financial plight to various influential publishers, editors, and journalists. At a social gathering at the house of Benno Reifenberg, editor of the *Frankfurter Zeitung* and an old friend, he tactfully explained that the *N.M.* was to change hands and that Frisch, in order to be as strong as possible during the negotiations, needed additional capital.[1] One of his listeners was his host's brother, Ernst Reifenberg, senior partner of E. Reifenberg-van Delden & Co., Inc., a "factory of sanitary wooden articles, specifically toilet-seats."

Much to Frisch's surprise a very business-like letter dated 23 April 1923 with this imprimatur reached his desk when he was contemplating various schemes to refloat the *Merkur*. Ernst Reifenberg had reported Hausenstein's remarks to his cousin, Paul Lenneberg, a Berlin book dealer. The two cousins had agreed to make Frisch a proposition: Paul Lenneberg, anxious to switch from distributing to editing publications, offered to invest in the *Merkur* in exchange for an editorial post on the magazine "commensurate with his abilities." It was a take-it-or-leave-it proposition. Under no circumstances did the young man want to be considered as a mere investor, since he was primarily concerned with finding a lively profession which appealed to him.

Frisch accepted with joy, undoubtedly influenced by an offhand remark in the letter: Perhaps it was not unimportant to add that Lenneberg would marry the daughter of one of the Berlin directors of the DVA. In fact, the young man's nuptial plans, as it later turned out, proved to be anything but unimportant. In his correspondence with Lenneberg, Frisch found his prospective editorial helper "kind and extremely cultivated" (letter of 13 October 1923 to Adolf Löwenstein, director of the DVA) ; his ideas, such as inexpensive editions of good books, revealed, in Frisch's opinion, a great deal of resourcefulness.[2] But in the course of the correspondence the name of his future father-in-law, Adolf Löwenstein, more and more overshadowed that of the prospective co-editor. The original plan had changed. Paul Lenneberg would still join the editorial staff, but the *Merkur* would become a publication of the DVA. Negotiations switched to the main offices of the DVA in Stuttgart; as early as 26 July 1923, Director Kilpper sent out a simple contract to Frisch: the *Neue Merkur*, with slightly expanded format but with its editorial offices remaining in Munich, was to appear as a publication financed by the DVA. Although early in October 1923 Paul Lenneberg suddenly died, just before the appearance of the first new issue, this contract remained in effect. Frisch had never met Lenneberg, but because of him the *Merkur* survived for another two years.

Had Lenneberg lived, Frisch's relationship to his publisher, leavened by a personal contact, might have been smoother. As it was, after an initial era of good feeling[3] three major areas of sharp disagreement developed. They were finances, the exact relationship of the publication to its publisher, and the choice of contributors. The debates about all three were closely interlinked, but the *Merkur*'s inability to sustain itself financially was most often in contention and ultimately led to its demise.

Frisch, it must be conceded, entered the new relationship under a delusion. As he visualized it, he would be editorially as completely independent as he had been in his joint venture with O. C. Recht and as heavily subsidized as the *Neue Rundschau* was by the S. Fischer Verlag. In a letter to Karl Bröger of 17 December 1923, for example, he described the *Merkur* as being so situated that it could resume its task in an expanded format and in the same spirit. Through its transference to the Deutsche Verlags-Anstalt it had now, fortunately, been afforded the secure material basis upon which it could favorably develop. This expectation proved unrealistic.

The first indication of major differences came in a letter from Director Kilpper of 19 January 1924 when he tactfully but irrevocably rejected Frisch's request of a higher rate per page for Otto Flake ("We surely need not be ashamed of 6 Marks per page.") Frisch's intercessions to satisfy his authors became increasingly more frequent; successively he demanded, for example, 15 Marks per page for Ferdinand Lion and Hermann von Boetticher, 20 Marks for Robert Musil and Wilhelm Hausenstein, and 55 Marks for Heinrich Mann.[4] Director Kilpper disallowed each one of these requests. In a letter of 29 July 1925 Frisch complained to Hausenstein that he had difficulties with Kilpper each time the editorial staff demanded for the contributors an honorarium above ten Marks per page.

This complaint followed a spirited exchange between Frisch and Kilpper, first in letters,[5] then in a personal conference in Stuttgart which Frisch, writing to Hausenstein on 27 July 1925, summarized. The problem of the *Merkur*'s honoraria was a part of the real difficulties which remained unresolved despite frequent negotiations with Kilpper. The latter was of the opinion that not the publisher but the *Merkur* must meet the payments and gear them to its financial situation. And its limited circulation, still inadequate, also ought to impose restrictions on the demands of its contributors, who should be as interested in the preservation of the magazine as the editors. Kilpper's attitude considerably exacerbated the difficulties of his editorial work, Frisch complained. With a heavy heart ("I cannot take the responsibility for damaging you [financially]") he returned Hausenstein's submitted article with the advice to accept the higher fee offered by another publication.

In general, Frisch felt handicapped whenever he competed with the *Neue Rundschau* for the services of an author; his main competitor, as he complained to Director Kilpper in a letter of 18 June 1924, was paying —on information from its editor-in-chief— an average of thirty Marks per page. But Director Kilpper, sceptical of the figure, answered three days later: Despite esteem for the contributors, they must watch out that the honoraria did not rise from issue to issue or else the question would arise whether or not they could continue at all in this fashion. He explained his attitude more fully to me in a letter of 2 April 1962. The Deutsche Verlags-Anstalt had acquired the *Neue Merkur* in consideration of its literary prestige. But its high standard had soon proven to be a barrier against extending the number of subscribers. On the contrary, in each quarter the number of cancellations outnumbered the new subscriptions. Since a turn for the better had not seemed to be in the offing, it was agreed to cease publication. Despite certain economy moves—he operated his editorial office on sixty Marks per month—Frisch could not halt the decline.[6] His soft-hearted idealism foundered on the hard-headed business sense of the DVA.

Another point of contention between Frisch and Director Kilpper was the selection of contributors. The latter, in a letter of 17 June 1924, envisioned contributions "with a wide-reaching propaganda effect" such as Schnitzler's *Fräulein Else*, Shaw's *Saint Joan*, and essays by Thomas Mann. For such contributions, he added, he would authorize considerably higher expenditures. Frisch, whose greatest joy in publishing had always been the discovery of new talent, tried to skirt the issue by answering (on

18 June 1924) that his contributors, Musil for example, were first-rate authors, even if they did not have a "name" in the popular sense. Also the average reader was far less interested in a popular name than one generally supposed. But Director Kilpper was not to be diverted by commonplaces. Admitting the unsurpassed quality of Musil's article, even of the entire June issue, he nonetheless instructed Frisch three days later to attract new readers by name authors who produced an extensive effect. Most of its readers would gladly confirm that the contributions in the *Merkur* were excellent almost without exception. But the hard core of readers simply did not suffice to carry the magazine: the total income did not even come close to paying the honoraria of its collaborators. If, therefore, the magazine wished to attract new circles, especially the German bookselling trade, it was not enough that it offered excellence. It had to call attention to itself by more forceful means. Kilpper, in short, "placed the highest value" upon enlisting such names as Thomas Mann.

When it became apparent to him that Frisch pursued most of these suggestions only desultorily, Kilpper admonished him that "writers want to be wooed."[7] Even this suggestion failed to impress Frisch; Kilpper's preferences simply were not those of Frisch. At that time Frisch preferred D. H. Lawrence and Bertolt Brecht, just on the way to fame, to Schnitzler and Shaw, Alfred Neumann to Jakob Wassermann, Robert Musil to Galsworthy, and he esteemed Heinrich Mann as highly as his more famous brother.

In fairness to Frisch, it should be noted that he *had* made a serious if vain effort to obtain a contribution from Thomas Mann. Asked for his lecture on occultism, Mann replied, in a letter of 8 December 1923 that he could not offer anything from his lecture, since a bibliophile publishing house had a claim which precluded pre-book publication. Much to Frisch's surprise and Kilpper's chagrin, the lecture subsequently appeared in the *Neue Rundschau*. Reproached by Kilpper, Thomas Mann replied that Frisch had not asked for pre-book publication.[8] Having Thomas Mann's refusal before him later, Kilpper, in a letter of 14 February 1924, could only conclude that "writers are funny people."

All humor on the part of the publisher, however, was absent in the third major disagreement between editor and publisher, who strongly resented the fact that the authors of the DVA were neither sufficiently represented nor reviewed in its "house-organ." Here a basic misunderstanding between the two major parties concerned had obviously developed. Frisch, even while he was a paid employee of the Georg Müller Verlag, never permitted interference with his editorship of the *Merkur*; perhaps he should have explained his stand to the DVA at the beginning. As it was, he clarified his position only after Kilpper wrote him charging neglect of the DVA authors in the *Merkur*'s book review section. It might almost appear as design, he answered Kilpper on 9 January 1924, that so far almost no publications of the publishing house had been reviewed. But this was merely coincidence. He had no intention of *presenting the magazine as a magazine of the publishers*. Neither would he approve of disregarding, out of false discretion, a number of excellent and important new publications.[9]

This exchange was but the first of many. "Reminded" repeatedly of the availability of Ponten's prolific effusions,[10] Frisch sent, on 7 February 1924, a statement of principles to Director Kilpper. He would pay close attention to Kilpper's hint concerning Ponten. His reserve, however, arose from the consideration that he could not focus on one author alone without having the magazine acquire an odor of one-sidedness. Such a treatment would also not be very advantageous for Ponten's highly developed sense of self-confidence. But here, as always, he would let himself be guided solely by considerations of quality.

Frisch's sober replies to the DVA's importunities were, upon one memorable occasion, relieved by a *picaresca*, which Frisch carried off with the connivance of Wilhelm Hausenstein. Kilpper, in requesting a review of Georg Habich's *Medaillen der italienischen Renaissance* (Medals of the Italian Renaissance), had been particularly insistent. He had good reasons to be: the oversized folio volume on numismatics, containing 140 pages of text, 45 illustrations, and 100 pages of life-size, copper-plate facsimili, represented a huge investment on the part of the publisher, and sold at the respectable price of between 70 to 85 Marks. Even today it is the most authoritative and best book on the subject. But Frisch and Hausenstein obviously considered it a recondite bore and the latter poked fun at it in a review that sounded, on the surface, like the most extravagant praise. A few samples from the review will exemplify the deft deviousness of Frisch and Hausenstein. By leaving, under the guise of a typographical error, a space within the word *wunderbar*, they turned the commendatory adjective "wonderful" into the pejorative "devoid of wonder." Habich's text was damned by faint praise through characterizing it as written "in the quiet tone of objective instruction." "An apparatus of annotations," Hausenstein wrote, "supplements the explanations in the text [and satisfies] the scientific need for excursions." He even managed to hide, in a parenthesis within a lengthy sentence, Frisch's and his doubts about the appropriateness of such a review in the *Merkur* (". . . since it is not the business of the *Neue Merkur* to wreak specific technical criticism upon the detailed technical aspects of a publication.") In addition, Hausenstein's style aped the pomposity of his subject; at times it becomes sublime double-talk. And, in a final burst of playful exuberance—and as a last hint to the reader—he signed his review with the English word "Hobgoblin" as a pseudonym.[11]

The worst disagreement with the DVA, however, occurred after Frisch had submitted copy for the special literature issue of 1924. After Kilpper had noted that only two regular authors of the DVA were represented in it, he informed Frisch, through a letter of his chief reader, Martin Mörike, that he was "greatly disappointed." In vain did Frisch reply, on 20 November 1924,[12] that several of the other contributors had also published with the DVA upon occasion, that he was hopeful of attracting new talents for the DVA via the *Merkur*, that he felt constrained to vary his contributors to the last special belletristic issue, and that he would have tried to oblige Director Kilpper had he but been informed of his wishes before. All to no avail: the special issue caused a rift between editor and publisher that was never to heal. The correspondence between Stuttgart and München of the year 1925 was always business-like and often icy.

The growing estrangement often threatened to magnify minor annoyances into potential crises. Frisch apologized profusely in writing on 15 March 1924 when the haphazard proofreading of one of his authors, Ernst Bloch, necessitated considerable resetting. He spent an entire week at the offices of Meyer and Jessen, a Munich publishing firm, in order to avert a threatened lawsuit against the DVA which might have led to a further deterioration of his relationship with Kilpper. Hans Feist, one of Frisch's contributors and an out-of-favor author of Meyer and Jessen, had published a translation of an article by Benedetto Croce without proper authorization. Only after considerable pleading did Frisch persuade the aggrieved firm to accept a settlement from the *Merkur* instead of "exposing" Feist via a suit against the *Merkur* and the DVA.[13] Finally, as Ferdinand Lion told me in our September 1961 interview, Kilpper never forgave Frisch for the one and only piece of advice concerning book publishing that, contrary to the many astute suggestions he furnished, turned out to be financially disadvantageous: Frisch had dissuaded Kilpper from publishing the German translation of the works, "antiquated" in his opinion, of John Galsworthy.

These altercations developed, of course, only gradually and over the span of two years. At the time of the nuptials between the *Merkur* and the DVA, only one (insignificant) false note marred the festivities: a repetition of a contretemps of two years earlier. At that time Hugo Stinnes, the chief robber baron of German industry, had sent one of his underlings to Frisch with orders to "buy up" control of the *Auslandspost*. When Frisch had convinced himself that a subsidy from Stinnes would mean the sacrifice of editorial independence, he immediately broke off all negotiations.

Meanwhile, however, the rumor had begun circulating that Stinnes had acquired both the *Auslandspost* and the *Neue Merkur*; Frisch saw himself compelled to send out denials in three languages. Now, with the *Merkur* passing over to the DVA, a Viennese newspaper revived and embellished the rumor; not only the *Merkur* but also the entire DVA had become the property of the Stinnes cartell. A chorus of "how-could-you" letters flooded the offices of Frisch and Kilpper. With much annoyance, Director Kilpper issued an official disclaimer.[14]

In all other respects the publishing house was, initially, highly pleased by the acquisition of the *Merkur*. In an almanac celebrating its 175th anniversary, the DVA announced the acquisition with obvious pride: "Beginning in the fall the monthly, *Der Neue Merkur*, enjoying a firmly founded prestige, will appear under the [aegis of] the Deutsche Verlags-Anstalt. Thus a new circle of authors, especially of the younger generation, will ally itself with the Deutsche Verlags-Anstalt."[15] Enthusiasm received new impetus with the first press notices and "letters to the editor," which Frisch forwarded to his publisher.

The encomiums generally stressed two points: with its new lease on life the *Merkur* could continue to represent Germany favorably abroad and provide a suitable platform for its most distinguished writers. Ernst Robert Curtius, in a letter of 31 October 1923, commented on the representational qualities of the magazine. He hoped that the *Neue Merkur* survived the dangers of the coming winter. It was more important than ever, he wrote, that the German spirit should be decently represented abroad. And T. S. Eliot's *Criterion*, welcoming the revival of its German vis-à-vis, featured a two-page review of the first two (October and November 1923) issues by A. W. G. Randall:

> The reappearance, with the October number, of the *Neue Merkur* (Stuttgart: Deutsche Verlags-Anstalt), which had been suspended since the spring of last year, is an interesting example of the way in which, despite the financial, economic, and social chaos into which their country had been plunged, German intellectuals managed to keep their head[s] above water. If this particular review possessed any element of propaganda, either for internal or foreign consumption, one might well imagine efforts by interested parties to keep it alive, but such features happily seem absent. Nor does it show any of the extreme 'radical' tendencies of so many reviews started during or since the war. Finally it is not—even partially—an art-review, depending for its support on subscribers here or in the United States. The *Neue Merkur* is a monthly lit-

erary periodical which appears to cater purely to the instructed German middle class, and for this reason it seems to be worth rather more than ordinary attention.[16]

Randall then proceeded to an article-by-article review of the first two issues.

Dozens of notes, from the most diversified camps, welcomed the return of the *Merkur* as a boon to German writers. Hugo von Hofmannsthal's praise has been quoted in Chapter I; Thomas Mann's of 24 August 1923 is scarcely less impressive: "I have heard of the *Merkur*'s revival with satisfaction. . . . Not many outlets are under consideration [for the pre-book publication of *The Magic Mountain*], but the *Neue Merkur* is, of course, among them." "An oasis in the Munich desert," wrote Hans Poeschel early in 1924. "Congratulations," exclaimed Franz Blei (in an undated letter), "that you are publishing the *Neue Merkur* again, the best magazine we have." From Frisch's fellow editor, Max Rychner, came a similar note: "I congratulate you most cordially upon the revival of the *Neue Merkur*. Mens agitat molem, and your tenacity doubly impresses someone who knows of the difficulties of such an undertaking." Almost forty years later, Rychner reaffirmed these sentiments.[17] Gustav Kiepenheuer, the owner of a leading publishing house, volunteered on 22 November 1923: "I should not like to miss this opportunity to tell you how highly I esteem the *Neue Merkur* and that I consider it the only significant magazine in Germany."

The DVA reaped several additional advantages, beyond prestige, from its new publishing venture. Martin Lang, one of its principal editors, had just launched the publication of small, inexpensive volumes of twentieth-century novellas, in emulation of the clothback-bound books of the Insel-Verlag. The series, entitled "Der Falke," proved immediately successful; with the acquisition of the *Merkur*, the DVA could draw on still another hitherto largely overlooked wellspring of never republished short stories.[18] In fact, as the poet Otto Heuschele told me in an interview of 14 April 1962, the "Falke" sustained itself for two years on reprintings from earlier issues of the *Merkur* and on Frisch's personal and generously shared discoveries in obscure foreign and domestic journals.[19] Hence a kind of symbiosis came into being: novellas that had appealed to the readers of the *Merkur*, for example fiction by Josef Ponten, W. E. Süskind, and Arnold Ulitz, were immediately reprinted in the "Falke" as excellent publishing risks. Conversely, advance publication of distinguished DVA titles, such as the correspondence of Ferdinand Lassalle, poems by Heinrich Lersch, and excerpts from Alfred Weber's *Die Krise des modernen Staatsgedanken* (The Crisis of the Theory of the Modern State) often enriched the *Merkur*.[20]

There was one final mutually beneficial link between the editorial offices and the publishing house: Frisch, unofficially, became a consulting editor of the DVA. Much of the correspondence between Stuttgart and München dealt not with the *Merkur*, but with books of the DVA. Frisch, by common consent of the disputants, arbitrated, in a letter to Kilpper of 13 December 1924, a disagreement between an author, Arthur Salz, and the DVA. He frequently inhibited or urged the publication of literary works; it was on his endorsement that the DVA published Joyce's *Ulysses* in German translation. He also passed on each volume of the Falke, sometimes recommended younger contributors, e.g., W. E. Süskind and Karl Pagel, as editorial assistants, and channeled translations needed by his publisher to the staff of his *Auslandspost*.[21] As Rudolf Nutt put it in an interview of 11 December 1961: "We were, so to speak, the Munich branch of the DVA."

In its two years under the aegis of the DVA, the *Neue Merkur* changed its outward appearance slightly, its content and policy significantly. The alterations in its appearance were all salutary: a better grade of paper, the enlargement from 65 to 85 pages per average issue, and the gradual elimination of the small type face in full-length articles, a font that many readers had condemned as a strain on the eyes.[22] The changes in content and style were fivefold: a noticeable turnover in contributors; the cessation, with one exception, of all special issues; a decrease in poetry and book reviews; and a corresponding increase of theoretical and technical articles. A more intangible change but perhaps most damaging to readers' interest, was the curtailment of controversy in favor of more judicial exposition.

A change in contributors did take place, in part, at the insistence of the DVA. Frisch could not always resist the pressure, no matter how delicately worded, of including the favorites of the publishing house. "It would make Dr. Kilpper very happy," ran a typical memorandum dated 7 March 1924, "if Reinacher's most recent works [a part of a planned volume of idylls] would please you so much that you might like to publish them in the *Merkur*." As a result of such notes the works of Reinacher, Ponten, and a few other authors of the DVA, although often quite meritorious, nonetheless destroyed the balance of the magazine by the frequency of their appearance.

To make matters worse, the half-year interruption had decreased Frisch's regular contributors and editorial staff, or caused a diminution of their contributions. Thomas Mann, despite his promises, no longer submitted his works; André Gide, as Rudolf Kayser informed Frisch in a letter on 28 May 1923, had—because of the interruption—transferred the translation rights of *L'Avenir de L'Europe* from the *Merkur* to the *Rundschau*. Friedrich Sternthal (Dr. Usch) had, as he informed Frisch on 18 and 31 July 1923, received the post of foreign affairs editor of the Berlin newspaper *Montag Morgen*; the fact that Stefan Grossmann wished his collaboration he owed to the *N.M.* articles as Dr. Usch, he wrote. As a result of his new position his "World Chronicle" became less frequent and, as Frisch implied on 3 March 1924, less estimable: He would like to make sure, in Sternthal's interest as well, that the character of the "Chronicle" —intelligent, informed, and comprehensive—should be preserved. Alfred Vagts of the *Merkur* and Paul Marc (Franz's brother) of the *Auslandspost* had received, through Frisch's intercession, editorial positions with Albrecht Mendelssohn-Bartholdy's *Hamburgische Monatschefte für auswärtige Politik*.[23] Last but very important, Frisch "lost" himself as a contributor. In the final two years he wrote a very brief introductory note, a couple of lengthy glosses, but not a single editorial.[24] His friend, Wilhelm Hausenstein, while admiring Frisch's essay on Bruno Cassirer in the *Frankfurter Zeitung*, wrote him spontaneously on 25 May 1925: "What a pity that you do not write *more*." Did Frisch sense, after the deterioration of the initially excellent relations, that the DVA would ultimately abandon the magazine and hence was loath to throw good effort after bad?

Frisch felt he had good reasons for cutting down on book reviews and poetry. After Ernst Weiß had complained about the *Merkur*'s failure to review his books, Frisch replied on 15 August 1924: If he were to look at the last seven issues of the *Merkur*, Weiß would see how few reviews they contained. As long as the critics were of the quality they both knew, Frisch would rather do without them. Weiß should, on the other hand, consider what the French did. There the very best did not consider themselves above writing essays about the books of their colleagues. In Germany this was left to anyone and the reviews turned out accordingly. Behind this answer lay Frisch's frustration of convincing such well-qualified experts as Alfons Paquet and Wilhelm Michel, regular contributors of essays, to write book reviews as well.[25]

Although he did not say so, Frisch apparently had the same qualms about the quality of poetry submitted to him. The lengthiest explanation of his retrenchment policy, in a letter of refusal to Paul Graf von Thun-Hohenstein of 29 March 1925, concealed a general deprecation of German poetry beneath illogicality and verbiage: As far as lyric is concerned it is somewhat of an orphan of the *Neue Merkur*. He had published a few, to be sure, but in view of the prevailing abundance of submittals the ratio of poems in the magazine was not always satisfactory. He would prefer to publish none at all. As it was, Frisch contented himself with publishing poetic translations of lyric works (e.g., poems by Heraclitus and Paul Valéry)[26] and with an occasional poem by Richard Billinger, Hermann von Boetticher, Hermann Hesse, Klabund, Armin T. Wegner, Heinrich Lersch, or Eduard Reinacher—the last two upon the request of the DVA. Looking, however, at the German poetry of those years in rival magazines, the quantity and quality of those in the *Merkur* were rarely superior.

Much of the lyric was concentrated in the special literature issue of Oct./Nov. 1924, the only special issue to appear during the last two years of publication. Frisch, as he had done in the literature issue of 1923, managed again to assemble some of the most distinguished authors writing in Germany at that time. Paul Fechter's essay, since become famous, "Das Bekenntnis und die Dichtung" (Creed and Literature), was followed by Heinrich Mann's novella "Die roten Schuhe" (The Red Shoes); the posthumous—and first—publication of some of Kafka's aphorisms; a legend, "Irisches Heiligenleben" (Life of an Irish Saint) by Georg Munk (i.e., Mrs. Martin Buber); poems from Heinrich Lersch's *Mensch im Eisen* (Man in Chains), *Legende aus dem Ghetto* (Legend from the Ghetto) by Leo Perutz; short stories by Axel Lübbe, Arnold Ulitz, Ernst Weiß; a poem by Hermann von Boetticher; and Hermann Hesse's wonderful poem "Media in Vita," which the poet had submitted after a personal meeting with Frisch in Switzerland. The story, however, that again gave Frisch the personal satisfaction of literary discovery and brought admiring comment from numerous older writers was W. E. Süskind's "Tordis," the first publication of the then twenty-year-old writer. If Frisch indeed did him the honor, Süskind wrote me in a letter of 18 October 1961, of considering himself Süskind's discoverer, he was absolutely right.[27]

Frisch resisted the pressures of using important anniversaries as pretexts for special issues. He had an insurmountable aversion to anniversary articles, he wrote Erna Grautoff on 26 March 1924. Whoever read the *Neue Merkur* attentively would have found that it always bypassed such occasions as Ricarda Huch's sixtieth birthday. Frisch also decided, after long reflection, to scuttle a special issue he himself had conceived. On 11 April 1924 he had sent letters with identical text to various youth leaders requesting "a presentation of the tendencies, directions, also of the active views of the most important youth groups and their leaders. . . . A preview of the Germany of the future could be included." But exactly two months later he abandoned the project because of "technical editorial reasons" (letter to Professor Hans Freyer of the University of Kiel, 10 January 1924). Since the DVA had not demurred at this special issue it can only be surmised that the "technical reasons" were the content of the articles: in statements which the youth leaders published elsewhere they preached a spiritual divorce from the disdained Weimar Republic; Frisch was never keen on doing work for the enemy.

Competitive pressures forced two further changes upon the magazine. Through its financial backing by the DVA, the *Neue Merkur* had become a potential threat to the dominant position of the *Neue Rundschau* and its publisher, the S. Fischer Verlag. In addition, as we know through the testimony of Robert Musil,[28] the owner of the publishing house, Samuel Fischer, took an almost personal and violent dislike to rivals of his magazine. For both financial and personal reasons he immediately took counter-measures. By emulating Frisch's experiments and luring away his principal contributors by higher honoraria, the *Rundschau* tried to obscure the chief difference between the two magazines; that the *Merkur* was, basically, an independent publication, while the *Rundschau* was an adjunctive publication of a publishing house. Frisch found his rival's tactics of copying the public image of his magazine annoyingly effective.[29] In a letter to Willy Haas of 10 April 1924, he confessed that he was not taking pleasure in continuously sharing his collaborators with the *Rundschau*. He himself was not wooing the authors of the *Rundschau*, but if an author had established himself in the *Merkur*, this obviously was giving Mr. Kayser no rest. He had to have him. Naturally Frisch welcomed Haas' collaboration very much, but he was aware that this meant inviting the reproach that he was importing the authors of the Fischer-Verlag, while the opposite was true. Obviously, so Frisch continued, Fischer would like to be able to say: "You see the same people are writing for me," even though his aims were quite different.

Frisch felt constrained to write similar letters to Ernst Robert Curtius, to Ferdinand Lion, and to other contributors;[30] he also delayed the publication of works by authors who appeared in the *Rundschau* (letter of 15 January 1925 to Dmitrij Umansky). But, as he wrote Kilpper on 18 June 1924, additional measures were required to preserve the identity of the magazine. In contradistinction to the *Rundschau* he was then engaged, in the *Merkur*, in attracting informational material, in the widest sense of the word. As Professor Jacobsthal's contribution in the current issue exemplified, this position contrasted with a purely literary one which had already been discredited. Frisch rejoiced, as he told Kilpper, that this change of policy had brought him the collaboration of new writers such as Hans Prinzhorn, successful author of *Bildnerei der Geisteskranken* (Paintings by the Insane—Berlin, 1922) who felt more at home in the *Merkur* because its emphasis had shifted.

Frisch no doubt succeeded in giving the *Merkur* a new face through this change in editorial policy and set it apart from the *Neue Rundschau*.

But the increase in purely informational articles brought, as an unavoidable corollary, a decrease of speculative and hence controversial ones: He was striving to an ever greater degree to unburden the *Merkur* of speculative articles and to acquire contributions containing facts and their reasoned commentary, he wrote Willy Haas on 23 May 1924. But reasoned commentary, no matter how eloquent, rarely provoked the heated controversies that had enlivened the magazine in earlier years. It may well be true that the new editorial policy raised the standard and the tone of the magazine; at the same time it also became more languorous and dull.

Perhaps the *Merkur* could have weathered all ill winds directed against it, the icy ones coming from the DVA and the searing ones from its rival. But it was no match for the general tempest that swept all of Germany in 1925. To halt inflation, the German government ordered a currency reform which precipitated a deflation as disastrous to marginal enterprises as the inflation had been. The DVA, which might have been willing to support the *Merkur* a while longer had deflation not reduced income, told Frisch in the spring of 1925, during a conference in Stuttgart, that it could not support the *Merkur* beyond the current publication year.[31]

The news did not catch Frisch unprepared. As early as February 1925, anticipating the withdrawal of the DVA, Frisch had looked elsewhere for support. Upon his return from a trip to Stuttgart, Heidelberg, Darmstadt, and Frankfurt am Main he wrote Ferdinand Lion on 3 February 1925: "During this trip the enlargement of the *Merkur* has taken on shape. You will hear further details." Mr. Lion told me, in our 1961 interview, that Frisch had met representatives of the S. Fischer Verlag during his journey who had sounded him out about a possible merger of the *Rundschau* and the *Merkur*. "Unfortunately," Mr. Lion added, "all of us, notably myself and [Frisch's] friend Max Ettinger [the composer] dissuaded him from accepting the offer, at least not until the Deutsche Verlags-Anstalt had definitely abandoned the *Merkur*. But by then Samuel Fischer had changed his mind."

Mrs. Margareta Morgenstern recalled, in an interview of 10 September 1961, that Frisch had also negotiated, during this trip, with Director Kippenberg of the Insel Verlag. Otto Heuschele, though less certain about the time of these negotiations, believes that they ultimately came to naught because the Insel Verlag was too slow in reaching a decision (interview of 14 April 1962). In short, the *Merkur* foundered because one of its would-be saviors offered rescue too early, the other too late.

The obituaries took many forms. The *Steglitzer Anzeiger* of 24 September 1925 grieved that Germany's most valuable publications were falling victim to the dismal economic conditions; two days later the *Neues*

Tageblatt of Stuttgart wrote: "We learn, with distress, that this journal, so distinguishedly edited and intellectually so outstanding, will not be continued. A palpable gap has been torn into the rank of high-level German monthlies which devote themselves to politics and cultural affairs and which are none too numerous." And the *Criterion* of January 1926 said: "This interesting monthly ceased publication with the September number, leaving a gap in German periodical literature which no other review, unless it be the *Neue Rundschau,* entirely fills."[32] Even in death the *Neue Merkur* had to compete for attention with its powerful rival.

Frisch was not in his office to read the newspaper notices nor the many letters from friends, contributors, and subscribers. During his last month as editor he had turned the affairs over to his last and youngest editorial assistant, Hans Rhotert, and left for a prolonged sojourn in Italy. Mr. Rhotert, now director of the Linden Museum in Stuttgart, told me on 17 April 1962: "Frisch carried the *Merkur* more in his heart than in his mind. I suspect he was unable to be present when its doors closed."

5 *The Message of Mercury*

Part II

In a novella by A. M. Frey, the young hero, a symbol of Germany's lost generation, is consumed by one thought: "The war and its senescent face are still with us."[1] Printed in the *Merkur* immediately after it resumed publication in 1919, the story and theme could have served the magazine as *leitmotif* during its final years. With Germany still racked by the war's aftermath, the *Neue Merkur* continued to examine its causes and the possibility of a recurrence, but wisely refrained from discussing its conduct. The search was as persistent as in the months immediately following the Armistice, but the goals of the examination changed. While a few writers still explored immediate causes—for example, the clash of Austro-Russian interests in Galicia and Rumania and the German-British rivalry in Mesopotamia and overseas—most contributors now looked for basic causes and historic patterns.[2]

The scholarship in these articles was meticulous and results were superb. The *Merkur* had the good fortune of possessing in Albrecht Mendelssohn-Bartholdy and his assistant, Hugo Preller, two steady collaborators with access to the secret papers of the Imperial Foreign Office, an important and hitherto unexplored primary source which the Weimar Republic was then making available to a few selected researchers. Since the publication of these papers was at that time still incomplete and proceeded slowly, volume by volume, the readers of the *Neue Merkur* could peruse articles, based on the entire unexpurgated archive, sometimes weeks in advance of the appearance of the documents.[3]

Even today, when the divulgatory, perhaps sensational, character of these articles has worn off, one can still profitably read them for their conclusions. After following some of the diplomatic convolutions on the road to war, Mendelssohn-Bartholdy concluded that more than anything else—more than "British Imperialism," "Pan-Germanism," "Italian treachery"—the entire unfortunate concept of international diplomacy itself had made war inevitable. "If anything can be learned from these papers," he deduced, "it is surely . . . that the policies of the major powers were inseparably intertwined, that their common fault was the distrust in their diplomatic secrecy, the insincerity of their treaties and, most of all, the delusion of 'compensations' whereby one country sought an increase of power to compensate for the natural growth of another." He let Hugo Preller draw the moral from this, the necessity of finding "new forms of intra-national relations."[4]

In the same articles both writers drew corollaries to their conclusions. If secret and inept diplomacy had been one of the primary causes of war, then all nations were about equally guilty and Germany's monopoly on guilt was an absurdity. In time, scores of other contributors seized upon this argument. Perhaps original when Mendelssohn-Bartholdy first propounded it, this stand grew wearisome by repetition and by the predictability with which it appeared in articles written by the nationals of the erstwhile Central Powers.

What differentiated the *Merkur*, however, from many of the other countless apologias printed in Germany in the 1920's was the ready admission of Germany's failings. The warning of its American contributor, A. V. Velton, against "depicting [pre-war] Germany as angelic"[5] was conscientiously heeded. The *Merkur* remained responsible even while partisan. Germany had erred, Alfons Paquet declared, by being "a bit brazen, insatiable, and proletarian."[6] Friedrich Sternthal traced Germany's left-footed diplomacy not to simple ineptitude or the failing of other nations, but to national character. Vacillating constantly between hubris and a feeling of inferiority, so self-centered that he lacked all understanding for the peoples beyond his own horizon, the German was temperamentally unsuited for the game of diplomacy.[7]

Unlike its causes, the war itself received scant attention. Where references did appear they were, with but one exception (a half-hearted defense of the maligned Austrian Army), coupled with a pacifistic moral. So it was with Axel Lübbe's short story, "Ein Richter" (A Judge), Rudolf Nutt's deprecation of German war dramas, Felix Braun's review of Hans Carossa's *Rumänisches Tagebuch* (Rumanian Diary), and Sternthal's renewed criticism of German diplomacy towards the Kerensky government.[8] The most telling example of the *Merkur*'s pacifistic policy, however, was the curious editing of a work about another war. Offered the pre-book publication of an account of Kemal Pasha's flamboyant campaigns in the Near East, Frisch managed to extract a twenty-page article **from it which contained not a single description of a battle.**[9]

In a letter to Willy Haas on 21 April 1925, Frisch declared that he intended, in a book review, "to clarify, in a suitable manner, our muddied
relationship to the war and its aftermath." The review was never written,
but the *Merkur*'s acerbic commentaries left no doubt what his "clarification" would have been, either on the war or on its aftermath, the Peace of
Versailles. With the help of carefully selected writers, Frisch renewed his
indictment against the drafters of the peace treaty.

The article which probably most conformed to his own views was Alfred
Weber's "Die Neue Situation."[10] Frisch had made a special trip to We-
ber's home in Heidelberg to obtain it, and had himself helped in selecting
excerpts from a book-length manuscript.[11] Weber argued that "the new
German state is weak. The peace treaty, allegedly intended to rebuild
Europe, deprived Germany . . . of half its sovereignty [in dealing with]
other countries." The post-war German government lacked tradition,
Weber felt, and the chance of building one or acquiring prestige within
Germany "was dashed by the treatment it received after the peace." Weak
internally, ineffectual in foreign affairs, Germany could survive at best
as an "oligarchy . . . on a democratic basis."

Other predictions, based on the peace treaty, were even gloomier.
Friedrich Burschell foresaw a starving and destitute Germany degen-
erating into a "brutal military state"; Wilhelm Michel predicted anti-
democratic uprisings "in the name of the Hohenzollerns, Wittelsbachs,
under the Swastika, and the Sowjet Star."[12] And Friedrich Sternthal,
tracing this rise of nationalistic and monarchistic movements to French
oppression, bluntly predicted: "Without any exaggeration we can say
that we are racing towards a new world war with seven-league boots."[13]
The year was 1925.

Fearing another war and hopeful that international understanding
could avert it, the *Neue Merkur* extended its foreign coverage and re-
examined old judgments. The revaluations were not without surprises.
Despite its distaste for the Fascist government in Italy, the *Merkur*, probably impressed by Italy's friendly gestures towards Germany, dropped
its rancor.[14] It unexpectedly abandoned its hope of an Austro-German
reunification; Frisch and his staff were probably alienated by Austria's
growing disaffection with the Fatherland.[15] Both instances demonstrate
that the *Merkur* (always an accurate barometer of the atmosphere in Weimar) had become extremely sensitive (and sometimes overreacted) to the
"German policy" of other countries. When Sternthal very hard-headedly
advised his countrymen not to confuse political alliance with friendship,
he was, inadvertently, also admonishing himself and his colleagues on
the *Merkur*.[16]

An ever more cordial attitude toward England became evident in the

Merkur, especially after the election of its first labor government in 1924. At first, however, it appeared otherwise. After its rebirth, the *Merkur* carried an article by Hausenstein which revived war-time acrimony and invective. England was called the "anti-Christ of the continent," "the driving force among our enemies," "the classic, immanent foe of the continent," "Germany's antipode, now and forever." Hausenstein warned against the "Anglo-manic" British-oriented policy of the German Foreign Office and predicted an Anglo-French war in which the British would win.[17] Why, one may ask, did Frisch publish an article so obviously at odds with his own editorial policy?

It was one of the rare instances in which personal considerations dictated policy: as the correspondence shows, Frisch did not wish to reject a contribution by Hausenstein, his former co-editor and, more recently, his intermediary with the Deutsche Verlags-Anstalt. After a lengthy conference in which Frisch requested Hausenstein's permission to publish an "editorial polemic" against Hausenstein's point of view, the latter agreed to modify his article by incorporating and taking issue with Frisch's objections. Interestingly, their principal point of disagreement has retained its topicality into the present time: could Britain, despite its ties to its empire, enter into a continental union? Frisch had answered in the affirmative; Hausenstein, "surprised" by Frisch's opinion, considered after due thought the possibility of a British return to a continental union an erroneous idea.[18]

The article aroused considerable controversy. Gerhart von Mutius, the German Ambassador to Denmark, found it "brilliantly written and completely mistaken";[19] *The Criterion* pointedly ignored its anti-British bias and called it stimulating.[20] Perhaps T. S. Eliot and his staff sensed that the article no longer represented the *Merkur*'s attitude towards Britain: at Hausenstein's suggestion, Frisch had balanced it with a pro-British article by Ferdinand Lion in which the Alsatian writer defended Britain's policy of a European balance of power.[21] Yesterday's heresy had become today's editorial dogma.

Tensions between Germany and England, the two erstwhile enemies, were fading; the *Merkur*, in an article by Rudolf Nutt,[22] welcomed the disappearance of Germanophobes from British journals and the reappearance there of distinguished German writers. The *Merkur*, in turn, reopened its pages to British political essayists—the flow of belletristic contributions had never stopped—and published articles by H. N. Brailsford, the editor of the *New Leader*, and by H. G. Wells.[23] The one predicted the future of Britain's first labor government; the other the future of the universe. The politician, in forecasting the emergence of "public works, public housing, the recognition of Russia," proved right in his predictions; the novelist saw "no revolutionary changes for a long time to come!"

Hate of the British not only disappeared but slowly gave way to genuine interest and grudging admiration. A gloss praised Sir Thomas Barclay, a Liberal member of Parliament, "as a just man"; the writer tactfully illustrated the member's sense of justice with examples not culled exclusively from his pro-German voting record.[24] Nutt, mixing benevolence with humorous references to Freudian psychology, produced a delightful report on the suffragettes.[25] But Paul Graf Thun-Hohenstein apparently had difficulties with the new editorial policy. In a travelogue, very labored in its objectivity, he merely and unfortunately substituted a bad canard for a worse; his article turned the British scoundrels of yesteryear into amiable dullards.[26]

It was Lion who finally ushered in the new "policy" towards Britain, in a manner befitting the *Neue Merkur*.[27] In two related articles he not only expressed his admiration for the British and their political system ("England [is] a conservative-revolutionary state; it has the advantage of continuance; at the same time, however, a sense for change"), but he also shattered, irreparably, the *Merkur's* most cherished prejudice. The British, he concluded, were *not* hypocrites: "Morality, even where it camouflages selfish interests, remains a genuine postulate of the . . . [British] people," he declared. Thus ended, despite the somewhat pejorative subordinate clause, the *Merkur's* paper war against the British national character: not with a wail nor a whimper, but with an aphorism.

With one war ended, the *Merkur* began a new one. The next opponent was Soviet Russia. The Rapallo Pact had been signed; the West, presumably, had been properly aroused to the dangers of its neglect of Germany; hence the *Merkur* could abandon its own flirtation with the East. Fairly and objectively, but with obvious relish nonetheless, it intensified its criticism of the new Russia. "Do not confuse," Sternthal warned repeatedly after Rapallo, "political friendship with cultural friendship." Germany, he added, "must not open its doors to the new Russian culture, that *lucus a non lucendo*."[28] Adolf Grabowsky scratched the Bolshevists and found not Tartars, but Pan-Slavists. Richard Wilhelm observed Soviet influence in the anti-colonialism of "China, Persia, India, Arabia, and Morocco." Mendelssohn-Bartholdy, finally, in the printed version of an address before the University of Riga, called the Baltic people "outposts," "which stand guard at the border." He did not think it necessary to specify against whom they were supposed to be standing guard.[29]

The *Merkur's* attitude toward the United States did not change, but it crystallized, perhaps through the precise formulation of an American. H. V. Velton, a U. S. Midwesterner but a long-time resident of Germany, discerned two European interpretations of the American way of life: "a crass barbarism which accepts the pursuit of the dollar as sole ideal," and "the land of the future and of peace."[30] On either side of the time-honored debate, the *Merkur* continued to provide ammunition to contestants—occasionally through one and the same contributor. In successive articles, Nutt found, first, the growth of culture and "Europeanization" typical of the United States and then the Leopold-Loeb trial.[31] Leo Matthias, who after World War II was to write some of the most vituperative books against America, as early as 1925 sharpened his pen in the pages of the *Neue Merkur*. He returned from a sojourn in Mexico with the usual stereotypes about its northern neighbor ("hollow colossus," "a parasite despite a certain independence,") and with the prediction that democracy would break down in the United States and that Mexico would utilize the revolution there to throw off its bondage to the United States.[32]

But the *Merkur*'s final word was favorable. Writing about the muckrakers (Sinclair Lewis, Upton Sinclair, and Ludwig Lewisohn), Franz Schoenberner reasoned that a people as self-critical as the Americans had every chance to survive their ills. "An organism which produces such powerful anti-toxins to its poisons is half-saved," he maintained.[33] By a particularly cruel bit of irony, the author, so sanguine about American ills, became one of its victims. Schoenberner, last editor of the *Auslandspost*, a close associate of Frisch, and from 1930 to 1933 editor of the *Simplizissimus*, was crippled for life in a senseless attack upon him in his apartment building in New York.

The final essays on France followed closely the changes in German-French relations. In 1923 and 1924, while the French occupation of the Rhineland and the Ruhr further depressed German pride and prosperity, the articles reflected despair; by 1925, when Clemenceau and Poincaré were no longer in office and the more moderate Briand and Herriot were in power, cautious optimism occasionally lightened the gloom. At no time, however, could staff or contributors rekindle their enthusiasm or strong hope for a German-French rapprochement; French intransigence or indifference had proven, in their opinion, the ineffectuality of their pens vis-à-vis power politics. The fact that they needed this proof and reacted to it so strongly revealed both touching naiveté and profound sincerity.

The reactions of writers for the *Merkur* were also a gauge of German indignation in general and of Allied folly. If occupation policies drew criticism, not to say abuse, from proven friends and admirers of France such as Hausenstein and Curtius, resentment must have been nearly universal in Germany. If Hausenstein thought "hatred, scorn, and contempt" were "the most legitimate reactions to the official representatives of official France" and Curtius accused the average French intellectual of a dangerous indifference—what acrimony must the typical German have harbored who was far less sympathetic towards France to begin with![34] While Hausenstein, whose lot it ultimately became, after World War II, to pick up many of the pieces, still sounded his warnings ("a solution for the present situation must immediately be found"), his two worlds, Germany and France, were rushing towards mutual destruction.

The *Merkur* occasionally tried to recapture the mood of reconciliation apparent in its earlier issues, but its evocations lacked conviction and freshness. It may also have been that for a time, with new statesmen at the helm, the issue appeared less pressing. It reported yet another friendship meeting at Pontigny; cited still another author (here Anatole France) as an example of a different, better France; once more interpreted a French change of presidents, the resignation of "the vengeful [Alexandre] Millerand," as an easing of tensions; and speculated, for the last time, in a brilliantly sarcastic essay by Heinrich Mann, that the different political gravitation in Germany and France—the one towards the right, the other towards the left—might lead to a happy complement, "a promise of a fine future harvest."[35]

Iwan Goll repeated the same hope.[36] The differences between Paris and Berlin, he admitted, were greater than those between Paris and Honolulu. German sentimentality clashed with the realistic bent of the French "(a German sees all the beauty of Paris, a Frenchman all the ugliness of Berlin"); German pathos clashed with French irony and German introspectiveness with "the healthy normalcy of the French." But, he added, despite the fear on both sides to admit to these differences, they might melt away. "From below [i.e., the common people] might come the warmth to fuse the two people." Frisch himself, surveying the French press, saw "symptoms of a conversion." And returning with the summery glow of Pontigny still upon him, the *Merkur*'s reporter, Count Thun-Hohenstein, welcomed the passing of the Poincaré-Clemenceau era and the beginning of a new and more objective one in France: "Truth and Peace are on the march."[37] More than anything else, however, this brave formulation betrayed uncertainty; when one strongly believes in something, one does not feel compelled to insert slogans into a factual article.

The same uncertainty is noticeable in the *Merkur*'s reiterated advocacy of a United Europe. Once more Rudolf Pannwitz, Robert Müller, Thun-Hohenstein, and Lion wrote passionate appeals for "Union Now."[38] In gloomy colors they painted the alternative: dangers threatened Europe today; tomorrow they may destroy it. Or Pannwitz warned: "May Coudenhove's Pan-Europe reach its full effect and preserve peace on this continent, so that the last hell . . . may be spared us." In their chthonic picture of the other terrifying alternative, their vision of hope appeared dark and forlorn indeed. The efforts to keep this hope for peace and unity alive appear, therefore, all the more heroic. In the same article, Pannwitz hailed, in panegyric terms, the latest book of Coudenhove-Kalergi, *Pan-Europa*, as being "rationalistic without being materialistic"; "it is a high-minded, open-hearted . . . spiritualized Enlightenment." Only if Coudenhove's plan were implemented could mankind be saved from a descent to an ultimate hell. But it was left to Ferdinand Lion and to the *Merkur*'s very last issue to give this essentially political idea its most philosophical coloration. "All [the old countries] joined together would once more be young; this metamorphosis will lend an alibi to time."[39] It was—and is—not a bad exit line for a liberal magazine.

In looking at the Germany of the golden (or rather, gilded) twenties, *Merkur*'s prognoses became still gloomier. Lion, Burschell, and Paquet found the situation so catastrophic that they even thought hope lay in the very enormity of the catastrophe. They demonstrated, by alleged parallels from history, that a resurrection inevitably follows a low point.[40] "Despair has no place in Europe," wrote Lion, "and apparent misfortune should be blessed." Or, more simply, when things can get no worse, they must get better. The author could as easily have demonstrated that many times in history, when Man had thought himself at the bedrock of misfortune, the worst was still to come.

What troubled the writers in the *Merkur* was a multiplicity of seemingly unsolvable problems. The old ones had refused to fade; new ones further bedeviled the unsteady Republic. Once more, in a polemic which the author, Burschell, in an interview of 18 October 1961, termed one of his best political essays, the *Neue Merkur* pilloried "the triumph of raw militarism over a powerless citizenry"; once again it demanded, through Hausenstein, a reduction of the influence of what he called a Prussian spirit within the German Republic; it reiterated its charge against the German Communists as serving as the tools of Moscow, this time by trying to provoke a war between Germany and the Western allies.[41] It also restated its case against the die-hard reactionaries and against a people which, as Heinrich Mann mocked, "manages to have a history consisting of nothing but reactionary periods."[42] Mann singled out, in the *Merkur*'s war on reaction, the unreconstructed monarchists: Sternthal "the politically blind" industrialists; Alfred Weber the "pernicious reactionary brochures of Oswald Spengler which have harmed our fatherland"; and Poeschel certain educators who, like Martin Luserke, "were widening the gulf" between Germany and the other European countries by a dangerous concentration and glorification of the Nordic-Germanic past.[43] Criticizing the "Myth of the Twentieth Century" before it had been formulated, Poeschel attacked "the prevailing multiform concept of a purely German school of culture." A few years later, after the emergence of Goebbels and Rosenberg, he could have written "purely Aryan."

By some stretch of the imagination, Poeschel's article can also be read as one of the few indictments of National Socialism to appear in the *Neue Merkur*. Frisch, because he found the Nazis beneath contempt, usually chose to ignore their machinations. When he, therefore, bothered to attack the Communists, he expressed, perhaps subconsciously, a measure of respect.

As in the past, the *Merkur* not only raised its voice against the overt enemies of the Republic but also against the many who weakened it by their indifference. This time it made a direct appeal to the disaffected youth groups. An essay by Carl Brinkmann appealed, in its subtitle, directly to "the educated among its despisers." He asked the German youth groups of his time to recall the love and lovers of country among the German youth organizations of the past; he enjoined them to adopt, instead of "their scorn of East and West, even of the great mass of their own people," the patriotism and cosmopolitanism of youth groups abroad.[44]

Brinkmann concluded his essay with a plea "for reconciliation and brotherhood among the people of the land and its disaffected and despisers." It was a timely appeal. In views expressed in the *Merkur*, the Republic, already divided against itself, was split even further by new cleavages. In Weber's opinion, influential economic, class, and interest groups who had usurped powers rightfully belonging to the State were deepening the divisions between social and economic classes.[45] Hausenstein and Willy Hellpach observed an accentuation of religious differences; the former described "the calamity that has divided our people into a Catholic and Protestant mentality." Hellpach, State President of Baden, concurred, but hoped that this division might engender "enrichment and hope rather than dismemberment and calamity." His optimism, however, was cautious. Only if the Center Party, the party of "political Catholicism," would also become a party of tolerance, of religious understanding, and of Catholic acceptance of modern cultural values—only then could this hope be realized. Against custom but in deference to Hellpach's wishes (made known to Frisch in a letter of 29 December 1924) his full title was given in the credit line.[46] This request for full identification and the motive behind it, i.e., "to assume full responsibility," was as courageous as the article itself. His courage went unrewarded. The following year, four months after the letter was written, he placed fifth in a seven-way race for the Presidency of the Republic.

Like many another liberal journal, the *Neue Merkur* considered the election of Paul von Hindenburg an unmitigated disaster, a still further debilitation of the Weimar Republic. Unlike many of its rivals, however, the *Merkur* recognized Hindenburg's election for what it was, a continuation of national hybris. Wrote Sternthal:[47]

> In April this column stated: "With steadfast foolishness Germany has repeated to date almost every mistake of the past. This year, 1925, will decide whether we Germans find the heroic, sober road to self-control and self-imposed limitation." Since then Germany has ventured upon two romantic experiments. The first is the election of Hindenburg as Reichspräsident.

This observation appeared in the last issue of the *Merkur*. In analyzing, *ante factum*, one of the subtler causes of World War II, the magazine stayed in the van to the very end.

If militarism, Prussianism, reaction, and even the election of Hindenburg could be blamed on the enemies of the Republic, the *Neue Merkur* had to admit that many of the difficulties of the Weimar government were of its own making. For the *Merkur*, its loyal supporter, this was an increasingly bitter admission and always posed the same dilemma: Should a certain article or passage be published as constructive criticism of the Republic or be rejected as tending to strengthen the hand of its enemies? By a close perusal of the editorial correspondence it becomes clear that Frisch, with increasing frequency, believed that criticism would do more harm than good. At least in writing of the government, the *Merkur* of 1922 was beginning to "pull its punches."

Even so, the *Merkur*'s catalog of governmental folly was long and, by today's perspective, accurate if not complete. With hunger and destitution spreading in Germany (grimly painted by Burschell and Flake[48]), why had the government strengthened the very forces that had willfully caused the economic disaster, Heinrich Mann asked. Hiding bitterness beneath banter, he wrote:

> [The inflation], as one knew but has probably forgotten, came about because certain large entrepreneurs, mostly large industrialists, entered into international business deals which fortunately profited them but unfortunately did so at the expense of the German currency. When they finally repaid the borrowed money it was devalued to a fraction [of its former value]. This devalued money belonged to all of us; the values they had purchased with it belonged to them. During the occupation of the Ruhr they even had the government advance them the wages of their workers. . . . Hence these industrialists remained debtors of the country. And

the country—sure enough—indemnified them with the greatest part of a laboriously negotiated loan as soon as it arrived from America.[49]

Wilhelm Michel, in "Die geistige Krise in der Sozialdemokratie,"[50] also marvelled at the paradox of a government slighting its friends and favoring its enemies. Was it perhaps, he wondered, a case of leaning over backwards? "Only because [the Social Democrats] thought of themselves as representatives of merely one class interest could they indulge in the laxity of tolerating the re-emergence of the very forces that had proven to be the grave-diggers of Germany." In his list of particulars against the Social Democrats (their lack of a more conciliatory policy towards the churches, their dearth of new ideas, their lack of enthusiasm for leadership), Michel particularly stressed their neglect of school reforms despite a desperate need for more democratic education. In so doing he advanced an argument close to Frisch's heart; twice in the years of his virtual retirement from writing editorials, Frisch broke his silence to endorse democratic reforms in education.[51] Apparently this failure of the government—to help educate its potentially most active supporters—weighed heavily on Frisch.

Regarding education, the *Neue Merkur* offered a practical solution to a specific ailment of the Weimar Republic. The same may be said of Lion's repeated pleas for a more federalized form of government in Germany.[52] In general, however, the *Merkur* offered more theoretical advice than nostrums, from Burschell's call for a rededication to a life of hard work to Flake's admonition to copy the youthful vitality of the Americans, and to Lion's advice to pursue a global policy commensurate with Germany's geopolitical realities.[53] But one article, Michel's "Republik und Kaisergedanke," was neither practical remedy nor theoretical advice; at best it was belabored inspiration. Michel recommended an "imperialism of love and service," an investiture of the German people with the glamorous garbs of an emperor, and a republic with the unity of an empire and without particularism. The Weimar Republic, he argued, should utilize the myths of the imperial past.[54]

Despite its profession of noble sentiments this article was essentially inimical to the aims of the *Neue Merkur*. Its danger came not from its thoughts but from its language. The journal could, occasionally, afford to agree with the reactionaries without doing their labors. Thus when Alfons Paquet spoke "of the prison of our present, unbearably confined geography," he registered a legitimate, if debatable, protest without stooping to the rightists' slogan of a "people without land."[55] But when Michel used such mythical and essentially untranslatable dithyrambs as

"Schwertleite," "Bekenntnis zur deutschen Seele," "der Kaisergedanke drängt zu seiner Erfüllung," and evoked memories of Kaiser Rotbart (Frederick I [1123?–1190], as a symbolic figure of the resurrection of German power of hegemony) and the red imperial robe with the golden eagle—all in the name of strengthening the Republic—he, probably more than anything else, fed the discontent of the German people by calling attention to the mundaneness of the Republic. *The Criterion* of London judged this article to be "ephemeral."[56] To an Englishman analyzing its thoughts, it would undoubtedly appear so. But to a German, more likely to imbibe the toxin of its language than the elixir of its philosophy, it was, at that time, truly dangerous. It seems almost anti-climactic to relate that the author himself succumbed to his own intoxicating language. Michel ultimately decided that not the Weimar Republic but the Third Reich was the true heir of the Empire.

Fortunately, not all articles on Germany's democratic and peaceful pursuits were compromised by their monarchistic and martial language; Paquet forcefully resisted Michel's attempt to drape the Republic in the garb of the Empire: "Our world-wide tasks are, therefore, different from those of the Wilhelmine epoch. They are more noble, more humane, and yet, for all that, no less German."[57] Also, though the *Merkur* all too rarely took issue with the conquistatorial mission preached by the Nazis, it did berate the unreconstructed chauvinism of some of Germany's industrialists. Unbeknownst to these critics they were, by attacking "the blind knights of industry,"[58] also hitting out at the clandestine supporters of the National Socialists.

In these last years the *Neue Merkur* also virtually suspended its criticism of Germany's Communists; only once, in an article by Willy Haas, were they condemned—together with the extremists of the right—as operating outside the rules of a democratic society: "The politics of these young people—I saw hordes upon hordes of them with their swastika banners, death-head flags, Sowjet-stars and military caps on a hike through Thuringia this summer—their politics begin with a 'commitment' at sixteen or eighteen. . . . Discussions? Yes, indeed, but with the billy-club!" Haas also had a doctrinaire Communist say that there can be "no truly far-reaching, spontaneous people's movement, no national, ideological *levée en masse* without Communism at its base."[59]

Alfred Weber mentioned the Communist (and Fascist) danger in passing; his fear was that radicalism would grow in a State where much of the central power of the government had been usurped by special interest groups. His remedy for Communistic egalitarianism, an extension of earlier proposals by Coudenhove-Kalergi and other writers, was an oligarchic democracy. In modern terms, he advocated political leadership by an elected power-elite aided by a brain trust, and economic leadership by qualified managers. Clearly his plan anticipated developments in the major democracies, but he was equally astute in predicting that in the short run the German workers would be more susceptible to "sudden apostasies" and "catch-phrases" than to his plan.[60]

Weber implied that Germany's social structure would resemble an "oligarchic democracy." Outside of this prediction the *Neue Merkur* ignored the shifting sociological structure in postwar Germany. It did, however, occasionally survey the inconstant fortunes of German Jewry. In comparison to other Western countries, it found the status of the German Jew depressing. In Holland, as Hausenstein pointed out, there was virtually no anti-Semitism; in Austria, Robert Müller reported, it was becoming the monopoly of the extremist parties on the right (an argument he invalidated when, over Frisch's reservations, he praised Austria's past political leader, Karl Lueger (1844–1910), an avowed anti-Semite. In the United States, Franz Schoenberner found anti-Semitism on the wane.[61] But Germany, he declared, "infected by the same disease, shows none of the violent reactions which augur and aid a recovery." Thirty-five years later, attesting to the accuracy of his diagnosis, his nephew published a book significantly entitled "The Yellow Star."[62]

The most extensive treatment of the subject came from Willy Haas in the aforementioned article.[63] Couched in the form of a debate, it illuminated "the problem 'German and Jew' " from four different aspects. The first speaker, an Orthodox Jew, shocks readers to attention: "I am a National Socialist. Everyone wishing to call himself a 'Jew' must be one. And I hate Communism." In a brilliant satiric tour-de-force the imaginary representative of Orthodox Jewry then shows the coincidence of Jewish and National Socialist views; both seek segregation of the Jews, strictures against intermarriage, dispossession of the Jews (advocated in the Bible after seven years) and a resettlement of the Jews in Palestine.

An ideological anti-Semite (*not* a National Socialist) continues the debate. "The true meaning of anti-Semitism," he explains, "can only be . . . the annihilation of Judaism through a complete sterilization of the Jewish spirit." Reiterating the theses of Paul de Lagarde, he credits "the German soul" with the chemical properties of neutralizing the Jewish poison. German schools and German mates could even change Jews *physiologically*, he argued. "Strange and unique power of the German soul," he exclaims rhapsodically.

In this four-way debate, the assimilated Jew finds points of agreement with this view. He also welcomes a fusion of Germans and Jews, two peoples with "historic psychological" similarities: for instance Jehovah and Wotan, Samson and Siegfried, Ezekiel and Nietzsche, Isaiah and

Hölderlin, the longing for the promised land and the *Drang nach Süden* (Urge to the South). To these historic parallels he feels compelled to add one metaphysical difference. The Germans, though rooted in the reality of their soil and commonplace living, seek reality beyond the attainable: "in Italy and in the Thing itself." The Jews, on the other hand, living in a world of unreality, refuse, for the most part, to return to a possible reality, that of Palestine. Jerusalem has become a symbol of the ultimate spiritual world order; the diaspora, the inescapable historical destiny of Jewry. The Germans thus were the people for whom reality is not real enough, the Jews a people for whom unreality does not exist. If these two peoples should fuse, then—for the first time in the history of man-kind—the *logos* would become reality, the world would become the embodiment of the spirit.

A Catholic and a Communist conclude the debate. The former, forced into the role of critic and polemicist by the nature of the argument, lumps Jews and Wotan-worshipping National Socialists as arrested on the same level of disbelief. Both have had the chance for salvation and both have rejected it. Atheistic Communism, on the other hand, has erected a hierarchy which, absurdly, lacks a head, just as it did in the positivistic state of Comte. "After a thousand phantastic experiments Comte had to adopt the Catholic hierarchy as the final political means of salvation—because no other one exists." The Communist declares that the Communists did not want to socialize Jewish capital, but *all* capital, that they rejected the deportation of Jews as being equally absurd as the deportation of the Bavarians from their land in favor of the Irish, "the chief representatives of the extinct Celtic aborigines." He agrees with the Catholic that "the Germans were arrested on a level of disbelief." He does not, of course, equate salvation with Christian grace, but with Lenin's Communism.

Haas, in concluding his fictional debate, explained the absence of a debater from the National Socialist ranks. "One who debates," he commented, "no longer is one. As one of their leaders put it, 'one doesn't debate with animals, one kills them.' From his point of view, with full justification." In a letter to me of 16 July 1962, Haas considered this article prophetic: Quite a few correct assessments about the Nazis must have been in this article and a few prophecies that later became horrible facts. His claim is just. But it is equally true that his satiric barbs escaped even the sophisticated readers of the *Neue Merkur*. A reader, an executive officer of the Deutsch-Demokratische Hochschülervereinigung, who referred to himself as "an intellectual," asked on 22 November 1924: "Do you think this article was intended as irony?"

Tolerance for all faiths and militant opposition against all religious intolerance marked articles about religion. They stand in the best tradition of German rationalism. Nonetheless many are marred by a propensity for preachiness, a fault to which the *Neue Merkur* rarely fell prone. But it seems significant that the article which made the case for tolerance most convincingly, in the opinion of contemporary readers, was one on an entirely different topic, an account of Kemal Pasha's exploits. It chronicled, if tangentially, a Christmas Eve celebrated jointly in the desert of the Holy Land, by believers of all three religions. It deplored the strife between adherents of the three major religions and extolled the unorthodox joint celebration as a symbol of "their identical roots."[64]

Dogmatism, several writers felt, doomed all attempts to achieve religious harmony. Since such declarations were usually directed at Catholic dogma, they were, in a way, precursors of Ecumenism. Frisch, writing pseudonymously (F.), deplored religious intolerance in Spain: "The press of the Jesuits and bishops is performing an Indian war dance around the corpse of liberty."[65] Willy Hellpach, as State President of Baden a most authoritative contributor, couched his concern in more diplomatic but equally forthright language: "It would be unnatural, if the Center Party, which flourished because of persecution [of Catholics] during the *Kulturkampf* . . . would change from one day to the next into a party of tolerance, of understanding among the religions, and of Catholic adoption of modern cultural values." Having thus acknowledged the continuing prevalence of dogmatism and militancy, Hellpach ended on a more optimistic note: "The ripples of a new spirit are, however, discernible among the party's leadership."[66] At several points the article went beyond a conventional rationalistic advocacy of religious tolerance. He maintained that the diversity of religions could and should enrich rather than threaten European culture.

Hellpach's view was shared by three other contributors who also maintained that religion could help shape the future, if—and only if—it could rid itself of institutional calcification. Both the rationalistic Ferdinand Lion and the pious Catholic Felix Braun—to cite two totally different exponents—urged a return to Christian-Judaic ethics as a salvation for Western nations.[67] "Is it truly necessary," Braun asked, "to seek for profundities greater than those pronounced in the Sermon on the Mount?" Paquet saw the return of such basic ethics in the theology and absolute pacifism of the Mennonites and Quakers.[68] Curiously enough, at the very moment when these clarion calls for a religious renewal were being sounded, yet another contributor tried to interpret the reasons for their evocation. Kurt von Boeckmann, in an article which reached the *Neue Merkur* through the mediation of Thomas Mann,[69] viewed the new spirituality as merely the obverse of the new and crass materialism in

Germany. He saw it as still another consequence of Germany's post-war travail.[70]

In one short story, finally, which has since entered world literature, Isaak Babel's "Pan Apolek,"[71] the *Merkur* departed as far from established dogma as was then possible in Germany without alienating the majority of its readers. A tale of a picaresque painter, who immortalizes his patrons as saints, culminates in his unabashed retelling of the apocryphal story of Christ's copulation with Deborah.

The articles on philosophy focused more closely still on contemporary issues. Even when they were retrospective and dealt with philosophers of the eighteenth and nineteenth centuries, their authors were, nonetheless, preoccupied with controversies of the moment, most frequently with the virtues and failings of nihilism. Hence an article by Leo Matthias on Friedrich Heinrich Jacobi, a writer and philosopher of the Age of Goethe, culminates in the assertion that Jacobi was the first to use the term "nihilist."[72] Here the intent of making a half-forgotten author again relevant became so apparent that Lion, in writing to Frisch on 8 December 1923, demurred: Matthias destroyed the association of ideas (*sprengt den Zusammenhang*) ; he did not care for him.

Similarly, Nietzsche was praised as "a foil against self-destruction of this modern civilization," as a new Rousseau who "takes up arms against our present-day culture" and who "wants to facilitate a break-through of the truly creative forces." Gerhart von Mutius, the author of the article, attempted, in a later issue, an equally unconventional and modernized interpretation of Immanuel Kant.[73] Upon the occasion of Kant's two-hundredth birthday observance, he found in the sober philosopher the advocacy "not of domination, but of joint effort, not of power or subjugation, but of Eros." And Eros, he asserted, is "the source and aim, the center [of Kant's philosophy]." Kant, in this brief article, is conjured up from the underworld to protest the literal interpretation (*Buchstabendienst*) of his works and to affirm his love for the living spirit. In a letter of 10 June 1924 accompanying the article, von Mutius conceded that these were more his own thoughts than those of the historical Kant. A few days later he became apprehensive about publishing the article: Please return the small Kant marginalia, he wrote Frisch. In retrospect it seemed too "insignificant" and too "impertinent." He could have said, more accurately, that the article was too conjectural. It answered an unasked question: how would Kant have reacted, on his two-hundredth birthday, to the materialism and nihilism of the times?

Eugen Rosenstock authored a short article about Hegel which was similarly didactic. He used Hegelian philosophy to berate the devaluation of old philosophies—of Classicism, Rationalism, Liberalism, and Chris-

Wilhelm Hausenstein 1882–1957

*Reproduced by permission of Mrs. Margot Hausenstein
and Mrs. Renée Marie Hausenstein-Parry*

tian philosophy—now denounced, he noted mournfully, as a "Jewifica-tion" of Germanic myths.[74] But an article about Kierkegaard furnishes a still more telling example of confronting a nihilistic present with a more positive philosophy from the past. Armin Kesser, an unknown nineteen-year-old writer and, obviously, a Frisch "discovery," began his study[75] with a veritable diatribe: "In our times which classify anyone an idealist who has long, well-manicured fingernails and knows how to cross his legs elegantly, in these the most ridiculous of all times, he [Kierkegaard] may be a plain example of seriousness and commitment." "He teaches Man to bear his great isolation." When publishing this ar-ticle, Frisch must have already foreseen that Kierkegaard, though any-thing but obscure in the 1920's, was destined to become one of the most important philosophical guides to the next generations, for in a letter of 29 October 1924 to von Mutius he declared the extreme youth of Kesser was a decisive factor in accepting his work, and added that despite reservations he had published him because he believed that young peo-ple had the right to acquire and come to terms with valid philosophers—in their own way and from the atmosphere of their own thoughts. In his letter accepting the article, on 14 March 1924, Frisch expressed this feeling to the author.

The marshalling of philosophers of the eighteenth and nineteenth cen-turies was an indirect attack upon nihilism. But this attack also took direct forms. Rudolf Utzinger, in a gloss called "Zeitgesicht," contrasted the salutary and creative scepticism of Georg Lichtenberg with "the plump nihilism" of his own times, while Friedrich Burschell not only opposed the nihilists but even challenged them on their own terms. He expressed astonishment at "the dearth of nihilistic thinking": "I find little [thinking], at any rate no logical thought. Pessimists they are, but they are too enamored, for my taste, of their black prophesies."[76] The dan-gers of twentieth-century nihilism were apparent even then.

One further article tried to find a philosophical basis for an age-old and persistent reality, the differences and disagreements between the French and the Germans. Willy Haas, in a highly technical treatise, found this basis in the French predilection for "assimilation" and com-promise and in the German insistence upon attaining an ultimate solu-tion, even at the expense of a "Twilight of the World." French philoso-phies are evolutionary, German ones revolutionary.[77] Even then, A. W. G. Randall, reviewer of *The Criterion*, had misgivings about the form of the article: "the appeal is hardly to the ordinary reader,"he wrote.[78] And Haas himself, in an interview on 30 July 1962, admitted: "I would not write this *today*. At that time it was true, but one can no longer say this. France is [also] revolutionary. And Sternthal said [concerning this article]: 'We will live to see the German revolution; you will see how repulsive that will be.' "

One of the last articles with a philosophical theme, "Das Symbol der Odysseia," was also written by Haas.[79] Published in April 1925, eight years before Hitler's accession to power, it made an ominous prediction in the guise of a parable. A poet and a philosopher, after an endless and sometimes acrimonious debate about the respective merits of their respective professions, are asked to display their "wares" at a fairground—with tragicomic results. The article, despite its wit, is suffused by pessimism. Haas, probably with the rest of the imaginary circle gathered around the *Neue Merkur*, had ceased to believe that the admonitions of the philosophers—or poets for that matter—could divert disaster. In fighting nihilism the *Merkur* had, to be sure, not succumbed to it, but it had despaired of victory. Perhaps Ludwig Marcuse put it best in declaring that philosophy had run out of answers: "The basic occurrence, which the representatives of our century repeat in infinitely rich variations [and] often in the same words, is the loss of a universal absolute experience of meaning. Hence no self-evident meaning can be spelled out in literature or philosophy. . . . The entire century is searching for a meaning without finding it, and therefore is possessed by unrest."[80]

This mood of disquiet and unrest corroded the writing on spiritual renewal published during the *Merkur*'s last two years. In that period of "a horrible set-back [in which] shoddy money and . . . a calloused militaristic state are triumphant," as Burschell put it,[81] the cry for spiritual renewal became less frequent and was sounded but dimly. Frisch, in a preface to an article by Rosenstock, noted a twofold direction in the "mobilization of the spirit," one being a gradual discard of previous concepts and the other a new organization of knowledge and education (*Bildung*), which intends "to bridge the long alienation of people and spirit and to affect life directly."[82] These words, an assertion rather than an exhortation, ran parallel to an article by Poeschel which advocated a spiritual renewal through reliance upon Voltaire's philosophy.[83] Lion called this article "weak" in a letter of 2 January 1924. Its weakness, however, was not in the writing or thinking, but in its lack of animation. Where earlier calls for spiritual renewal at least *sounded* like clarion calls, this one began with a subjunctive ("Could not Voltaire . . .") and ended with a question mark.

At least these articles retained some hope in spiritual renewal. Otto Flake's warning, however, that a renewal could not be had for the asking sounded grim, and an essay by Kuno Mittenzwey amounted to a repudiation of the entire search for spiritual renewal.[84] According to the latter, the entire quest had proven quixotic: "The often invoked regeneration of the German spirit is, naturally, not going to be accomplished by reducing well-meant appeals to morality to the level of slogans or by a hardworking instructor serving up a revamped Hegel or Fichte in accordance with the demands of the moment. If the *esprit* of generations has been used up, we must likewise adjust our hopes to the work of generations. Renewal can never be an act of will, as little as real life can be."

This bleak realization caused preoccupation with spiritual renewal to become but another means of escaping the here and now. Flake clearly sensed this: "The forces [in our society] which are [at present] forbidden to turn to action flee into the realm of the spirit."[85] He could have taken his evidence right from the pages of the *Neue Merkur*. Confronted by "outer disintegration and chaos," Conrad Wandrey discovered in the writings of Stefan George "a pledge for the metaphysical wholeness of [our] people."[86] But dreams of spiritual renewal and preoccupation with literature are, at best, substitutes for life. Marcuse protested that preoccupation "with theory and morality *can* be [a form of] flight. But it is wrong to insist that they must be that under all circumstances, that the character of these two phenomena is exhausted in this (merely possible) function."[87] Perhaps so. But he obviously felt the necessity for such a protest, thereby proving the widespread existence of *Weltflucht* among his countrymen. Marcuse was never given to fighting straw men.

In addition to the articles on philosophy, the *Neue Merkur* carried numerous critical essays of a para-philosophical nature. Pacifism and its militant sister-movement, Activism, were repeatedly scored for their shallowness. Hausenstein, for example, writing under the pseudonym of Kannitverstan, ridiculed a jovial Dutch citizen, an enthusiastic admirer of Bertha von Suttner's manifesto, *Die Waffen nieder* (Lay Down Your Arms). The Dutchman reminded him of a "pacifistic union secretary of the good old times."[88] Iwan Goll similarly derided pacifists, activists, and even expressionists—to whom he himself belonged—as ideologists with whom "one has become surfeited."[89]

In an analogous vein the *Merkur*, in this case through Ernst Bloch, berated the pseudo-philosophies of Communism ("The Russians act philosophically, but think like uneducated dogs"),[90] Spengler's later and chauvinistic writings—this through no less a critic than Alfred Weber—[91] and the muddled thinking amidst the Youth Movement. "What mischief a young, talented chap can cause in his dark drive, when he is left without intellectual and spiritual help (I purposely avoid the word *Führung* [leadership]). One glance at thirty years of [it] and [their] role in economic and political life demonstrates this [observation]," wrote Franz Angermann.[92]

The French Feminist movement also drew its share of derision. Rudolf

Nutt wryly remarked that the average Frenchwoman harbored as little enthusiasm "for the vote as for motherhood. . . . They prefer to exploit their political and feminine capabilities in a different fashion."[93] Some further pointed barbs were aimed at commercialism as a way of life. Musil deplored the inroads it had made upon the theater; Rosenstock, upon all aspects of Western (and particularly American) society. He even anticipated the critical voices of today who constantly discover "hidden persuaders" behind Man's synthetic wants: "We no longer eat what is wholesome for us, do not put on clothes conducive to our health, do not read what we want, do not listen to what is important. Rather we hear the music that rattles down on us, read what is foisted upon and recommended to us, eat and drink what the organized market tosses before us."[94]

To lapse, for a moment, into less serious matters, the *Neue Merkur* reflected not only the spirit of the times but also its high jinks and fads which occasionally it took seriously beyond their deserts and, once, not seriously enough. Regarding the former, it twice featured lengthy physiognomical studies by Rudolf Kassner, such as his analysis of the face of Gustav Mahler; the only saving grace of his speculations was a liberal dose of self-irony or, at the least, of humor. Thus he has a banker say, in an earlier article: "Here you have the eternal connection between love or, rather, sensuality and money. And you will understand why money-people so frequently have phallic faces."[95]

The *Neue Merkur* may, perhaps, be forgiven for placing confidence in this extravagant revival of an eighteenth-century avocation to which even Goethe, though briefly, succumbed. When I discussed this article almost forty years later, on 25 September 1961, with Professor Max Picard, who had written in the *Merkur* on the same subject, he demonstrated that his faith in the science of physiognomy had remained unshaken. He wished it clearly understood that a book review by Frisch in the *Europäische Revue*, which called his and Kassner's systems of physiognomy related, was clearly in error.[96]

Another article, by Werner Achelis, not only defended physiognomy but made an equally impassioned argument for graphology as well. They were sciences, not arts, "to which one must be born," he maintained. And he warned of the charlatanism that accompanied their popularity—and from which their true practitioners were free, of course: "All those who feel they can rummage, at bargain rates, in Nature's secrets, are deceived citizens."[97] In a covering letter of 1 December 1924, Achelis described his article as a "clarification of the true meaning of medieval profundity."

The same author, less than a year later, got a further hearing in the

Merkur in order to defend astrology. After denigrating Einstein's theory of relativity, he espoused astrology. He postulated that "the so-called inorganic world has an inside" and he deduced from this an axiom for astrology, i.e., that there is an "identity or, respectively, an inseparable cross-relationship between astral and earthly substance which in Man coalesces as consciousness." Achelis concluded by saying that all these sciences—physiognomy, phrenology, graphology, and astrology—"are beginning, slowly but surely, to establish themselves."[98]

The only fad that deserved the serious analysis the *Merkur* accorded it was jazz. W. E. Süskind wrote a highly perceptive article on the "dancing generation." He called dancing to jazz bands a democratic pleasure, symptomatic of young people who had grown up in difficult times but were, nonetheless, growing into respectable citizens with a minimum of convulsions.[99] The article was dedicated to Erika Mann; Süskind, then but twenty-four, in fact owed his connection with Frisch to her, as he told me on 1 November 1961. Klaus Mann, her brother, wrote of Süskind's article in his autobiography: "In order to prove to Erika that her fictional murder [i.e., in Süskind's novella "Das Morgenlicht," *NM*, VIII, 870] was not ill-intentioned, he dedicated to her his first published essay, a study of the 'dancing generation,' which, proudly hailed by us all, appeared in Munich's eminent and erudite journal, the *Neue Merkur*. In this very civilly written article [he] tried to formulate the pathos and the philosophies of all the small circles, including ours, that were devoted to the fox-trot."[100] In the 1961 interview, Süskind, by then a political editor of the *Süddeutsche Zeitung* in Munich, intimated that the current generation of young Germans was not unlike that described in his article.

The *Merkur* viewed other fads with alarm. The popularization of psychoanalysis, to which the experts had contributed—or so, at any rate, Hermann Hesse felt—made it easy for "the normal people" to malign every genius as "a psychopath."[101] Adrien Turel added that psychoanalysis, in countries where it had become fashionable, was turning shallow.[102] Carl Brinkman expressed similar concern about sociology, implicit in the title of his article, "Soziologische Konjunktur" (Sociological Boom): "German sociological research which, in sharp contrast to English and French sociology, survived but in esoteric journals for experts, has now become a catch-word and a fashion."[103] And, according to Hermann Hesse, even preoccupation with a poet, such as Hölderlin, could have its legitimate and faddish aspects: "There was, indeed, even a Hölderlin fashion and the poet, by no means easy to comprehend, now often lies on the table of many ladies, next to the speeches of Buddha and the feuilletons of Tagore."[104]

One fad, which ultimately became an obsession in Germany, was unfortunately dealt only a passing blow. "We object," wrote Poeschel, "to the idea, now current in many forms, of schools [bent] solely towards German culture."[105] Here was the *Merkur*'s chance, only partially realized, of following the dictum of *principiis obsta*.

Poeschel's article was one of several devoted to education in the years 1923–25. They were exemplary. No doubt realizing that an already threatened future could only be salvaged if the German educational system molded a better informed and adaptable citizenry, Frisch published articles on education, from elementary school to university, that were as vigorous, uncompromising, and unambiguous as those in the most crusading years of the journal. He marshalled some of his most able writers for this campaign: Hausenstein, Hellpach, Thun-Hohenstein, Rosenstock, and Musil.

Among these excellent articles, one stands out—Musil's "Ein wichtiges Buch" (An Important Book). Under the guise of a book review,[106] Musil, who had written one of the most scathing indictments of German and Austrian high schools in literature, his novel *Die Verwirrungen des Zöglings Törless*, returned to the attack. His review, never republished since its appearance in the *Merkur*, dripped vitriol in the first paragraph. "With striking frequency one is looked upon as a tailor enlightened by the Lord if one expects an interest in mass education [*Volksbildungswesen*] outside of the groups immediately concerned with it. The average German intellectual is intellectually too refined for such problems." "Yet the future is entirely dependent upon them," Musil continued. The German educational system had grown no better since the time of the Empire. The spirit of the *Gymnasien* (high schools)—because their graduates rose to leadership in politics, civil service, commerce, technology, and landed property—remained "like a giant intellectual filter over our people." What this filter let through, Musil noted grimly, was "shot through with compromise, was backward-looking, complacent, torn and mended in many places . . . inferior." Nothing, he felt, had changed since the time of the Empire, "although our tasks, especially [since we live in] . . . a democracy have grown more difficult, though the dissolution of the Age of the Middle Class, which may already have set in, lies ahead of us."

Musil further stated that for these reasons mass education had become a sobering task for all, for with few exceptions nothing constructive had been done. Many qualified experts were indifferent; others were either ineffectual because they rode their own idealistic hobby-horses, or dangerous because they were partisans of Marxism, Nationalism, or Clericalism.[107] He concluded that von Wiese's book was, therefore, crucial: it provided some of the solutions.

The *Neue Merkur* did not confine itself to theory or "idealistic hobby-horses." Musil, apparently profoundly concerned with the subject, returned to it, briefly, in the unlikely setting of a discussion of the theater. He noted that the German institutionalized school system was resisting all progress and that the prevailing mode of mass education was little more than an expedient.[108] Franz Angermann's article, equally excellent and enlightened, set forth a more salutary method of popular education through a description of a high school for adults of which he was the assistant principal.[109]

On his campus, Angermann explained, thirty students between twenty and thirty years of age, none of them previously educated at a high school but fully employed, studied and worked together. The faculty consisted of a director, an assistant director, and two teachers. The students each had to pay according to income, about the earnings of forty working days. The deficit was made up through donations and by the State. Selection of students was made on a competitive basis and without regard to party affiliation. Angermann added wrily that this last principle was obviously being followed because the school was being attacked by both the radical right and left parties.

The curriculum of this school was not exclusively concerned with the imparting of information but with a humanistic outlook on life as well, and, to use a slogan, with education for democracy. Hence discussion classes were preferred to lectures, and topical to traditional subjects. Students enjoyed absolute freedom of speech, governed themselves, and learned to respect each other's point of view. Angermann ended his article with the hope that these students would spread the teachings of the school among their fellow-workers and associates after returning to their jobs. It urged the establishment of more schools on the model of the experimental school, *Dreissigacker*.

Frisch could not have been more in agreement. For the first and only time in the history of his magazine he endorsed, after a fire at the school, an extramural fund-raising campaign; at all other times he ignored such appeals.[110] Indicating that the school administration could not count on State subsidies for reconstruction work, he subtly underscored Angermann's complaint that the radical parties were establishing adult high schools for their own propagandistic purposes, while the democratic government and the moderate parties remained apathetic. In the context of his entire editorial policy, Frisch was stressing once again that Weimar failed to punish its enemies and to reward its friends.

The *Neue Merkur* addressed itself to the long overdue problem of a university reform through an article by Kuno Mittenzwey. He, too, welcomed the establishment of high schools for adults, but, in the main, focused his article on three unattained but desirable goals of a modern German university: a restoration of the vital link between academic pursuits and life; a conjunction between the study of historical facts and of a phenomenological investigation of the present; and a systematization—beyond mere positivistic research—of the isolated parts of a discipline and, ultimately, between various disciplines. Mittenzwey advocated reforming all universities in the spirit of these principles; all other matters then under dispute, such as involvement in professional training and methods of examination, appeared secondary.[111]

Hausenstein and Thun-Hohenstein added two further suggestions after trips abroad. The former returned once again to a previously voiced concern, the inimical influence of German fraternities. This time he held up Dutch students, unencumbered by fraternity badges, as salutary counterparts to their German vis-à-vis.[112] Thun-Hohenstein encouraged German universities to emulate the English system: "The English are constantly conscious of the fact that a young man of eighteen to twenty-four still needs being educated; hence the colleges at Oxford are educative institutions rather than mere institutions of higher learning."[113] It was scarcely surprising that this essay received praise in England;[114] it was disturbing that Germans ignored it.

The *Merkur*'s convictions on education appeared, occasionally, in writings on specific research areas. Eduard Allendorf, for example, consonant with Rosenstock's aforementioned recommendations, advocated a different approach to history.[115] He criticized the constant preoccupation with "historical systems," also to a lesser extent the exclusive concern with a history of ideas. He felt that the latter led to a "one-sided, cerebral presentation." He prescribed, instead, a concern with the living forces which affect history, "a turn from the history of subjects and events to that of the individual" in whom "the historical forces unfold, and direct."

Articles on the theory or philosophy of a social or natural science, however, were rare. More often than not they seemed to have been selected primarily because they were topical or fashionable. A disproportionately large number of discussions, for example, were devoted to sociological topics; the field was then enjoying one of its most productive, innovative, and popular periods. Alfred Weber's "Kultursoziologie" was the most basic presentation;[116] behind the multiplicity of human endeavors, he found certain "protophenomena." He thought he could apply to history Goethe's approach to nature, the way from complexity

to simplicity. Lion wrote on 2 January 1924 that Weber was worth all
the money the *Merkur* could possibly pay him: "He is formidable."

Obviously impressed, Lion, more and more inclined to abandon his
occasionally popular approach for a more scholarly one, applied "sociology of culture" in several articles of his own. One of them[117] grew so
brilliant that Frisch, in a letter of 3 November 1924, extravagantly
praised his contributor—and condemned the age which no longer was
able to appreciate such quality. He liked Lion's political articles very
much. He loved in them the apparent ease of tying together such decisive
points of view in politics which for the majority of people, even the
sophisticated ones, were a kind of practical, pragmatic affair, or conversely, became pale ideology. Living in times when quality is sensed
by all too few people, Frisch continued, he watched the appearance of
Lion's essays with the same recognition with which he saw everything
he valued go up in smoke in the *Neue Merkur*.

In "Europa und die Antike,"[118] Lion found that the old "protophenomena" of the Ancients which Weber had mentioned still had pertinence
—as an incentive and as a measure for achievements. In a similar vein,
Paul Jacobsthal began and ended "Zur Soziologie der heutigen
Griechen."[119] He denied the continuity of the ancient Greek tradition in
modern Greece. "Although the ruins of the temples stand on their soil,
[the past is] an alien [to the modern Greeks] as is the old Greek language
which they raised, in 1830, to their standard language. . . . The new
Greeks lack an inner relationship to antiquity." In addressing himself
to sociological conditions in Greece, Jacobsthal cited its agrarian, pre-
industrial, pre-capitalistic, and (more or less) classless society, the
heterogeneity of its people, and the close ties between rural and urban
population as the determining factors of Greek sociology. Although the
article appears dated today, it still retains many of the "excellent qualities" which Frisch attributed to it in writing to Curtius on 13 September
1924, when he thanked Curtius for "discovering" the author for him.

Another sociological essay, this time on Man in an industrial and
capitalistic society, was contributed by Eugen Rosenstock.[120] He found
Man not only possessing money, but also being possessed by it; work in
such a society was not only the sustenance of life, but its sense as well.
The soul of the enterprise absorbed the soul of the entrepreneur. America,
as might be guessed, was described as the most extreme example of this
tendency; there, even culture and religion had become the opiates of
a sensation-hungry society.

This essay, the one on modern Greece, and several others on foreign
cultures and social systems sometimes used the methods of an anthro-

pologist, although dealing with modern Western societies. Jacobson, who
had lived for many years in various parts of Greece, and Leo Matthias,
who administered an orphanage in Mexico, went at their task as if they
had to explore and analyze a primitive or extinct society. Matthias' article
has since become well-known as part of his book on Mexico.[121]

The beginning of another anthropological article, this one by Adolf
Fischer, a professional anthropologist, might indicate that involvement
with the *Merkur* was making a more closely knit group of its individual
contributors. Fischer used a sentence from Matthias' "Europäer, Amerikaner und Indianer" as his motto ("I believe that it is one of the principal tasks of an author to introduce [his readers] to the more important
but little or unknown peoples and cultures"). His article was devoted
to Ifé, the Yoruba kingdom, and especially the famous brass portraits of
its royalty in the fourteenth century. Today, with the wealth of subsequent studies about Ifé, Fischer's observations are less important than
the subtitle of his article, i.e., "a cultural problem," and his conclusion.[122] "European civilisation," he maintained, "is today at the point of
blanketing the entire globe. Irresistible because of its political power
and technical facilities, it draws alien peoples into its sway and presses
upon them the stamp of our superiority—by no means to the benefit and
comfort of those people." This Rousseauistic note appeared quite frequently in the *Merkur*. Fortunately its pessimism has to date proved
unjustified, at least so far as Ifé is concerned.

Sociological and geographical articles on Sumatra by Martin Borrmann, on the Orient by Adolf Fischer, and on China by Richard Wilhelm
were probably accepted as further experiments with "informational
articles";[123] Borrmann intimated as much to me in a conversation on
1 March 1962. None of them escaped the weakness of "informational
articles"; they proved to be ephemeral. The only observation on geography, or perhaps geopolitics, that stays fresh is Gerhart von Mutius'
interpretation of Leopold Ziegler's *Das heilige Reich der Deutschen*.[124]
Mutius rightly attributed two crucial theses to the book: that Germany's
central position "determined" not only the Germans, but also each German. He quoted Ziegler as saying: "Each German is a center; let each
German be one."

Mutius' article—and Ziegler's book—combined geography, philosophy,
and psychology. It was not alone in attempting such a sweeping approach.
Kurt von Boeckmann explained "lucidly," as Thomas Mann put it in
a letter of 22 February 1925, Dacqué's "refutation" of Darwin.[125] Dacqué
asserted that all living things originate from an antediluvian, amphibian
prototype and that Man retains memories of this experience in his sagas
of dragons, dinosaurs, the Deluge, and the like, and that Primitive Man

as revealed by human myths had knowledge of transcendental events and of magic. These rather preposterous hypotheses which, at that time, however, caused heated and most earnest controversies, again corresponded with Frisch's revised concept of his magazine. He wrote to Boeckmann on 27 February 1925 that Thomas Mann had been kind enough to give Frisch the manuscript which fitted in with his intention of giving more space to new and recent scholarly publications.

Other writing on psychology, whether or not involving myths, proved more terrestrial and less fanciful. Adrien Turel weighed the similarities and differences between Freud, Jung, and Adler; Ernst Bloch between the average person on the one hand and the genius and poet on the other.[126] In this article, as Bloch told me on 17 April 1962, he particularly had Thomas Mann in mind when he berated shallow authors: "The latter are incapable of experiencing [something], to stand up for themselves [a pun on the German expression "seinen Mann zu stehen"]. A surplus of life by no means oppresses their chest so that there is no conceivable reason to purge themselves of it by creativity." It is idle to ask whether Mann, a regular reader of the magazine, understood the subtle attack.

The natural sciences were all but ignored by the *Neue Merkur*; in truth they did not fit very well with the general tenor of the magazine. H. G. Wells's technological and unscientific prophecies were the closest the *Merkur* was to come to the natural sciences in its last two years.[127]

During this time the *Merkur*'s attitude on fine arts, music, and the theater did not change; its tone did. It became more tactful, less forceful. It did not try to please everyone, but it attempted, through less aggressive wording, to offend fewer people. Hausenstein's review of Georg Habich's *Medaillen der italienischen Renaissance* camouflaged all objections by an irony so subtle that it became evident only to the initiated.[128] In earlier years the *Merkur* would have been more direct. Occasionally the old verve broke forth when it criticized the new Soviet architecture ("monuments that can compete in ugliness with the Siegesallee"), but otherwise the editorial policy had become more politic.[129] Yet deference to the art-loving public and to publishers was not the sole reason for the sedate tone of the articles on aesthetics. The movements with which Frisch, Hausenstein, and their generation had been most concerned had become established and some of them were almost passé; the controversies had lost their immediacy and spontaneity. The most polemic articles about Expressionism in the fine arts, both pro and con, fell into the 1919–23 period. In 1924 and 1925, objective appraisals replaced, for the most part, partisan pronouncements.

Emil Preetorius, for example, mildly suggested that Expressionism might have a revival and become the art movement of the future.[130] Bloch expressed disappointment that Expressionism had lost its momentum and squandered its promise, but believed that it might regenerate itself: "More geniuses than we have Muses might have found work here: but even though the movement may have levelled off in Europe (and again not in Russia) . . . it still has not disappeared, just as little as all unattained greatness. It awaits a new army."[131] Only Iwan Goll, himself an apostate from literary Expressionism, cudgelled its counterpart in the fine arts. "An ism marks the period of struggle for an artistic form. When it has been accepted, the shouting stops and art begins. Or—it was not art! Of Expressionism, for example . . . one has become as weary as of Pacifism and Activism and it came and went with them." Elsewhere he added: "The Expressionist only painted *the* Kiss, *the* Woman, *the* Human Being: holy virgins with angular arms and rachitic chests—he painted Ideas and Pamphlets."[132] Apparently Goll's tone had at first been even more vehement; in a letter of 5 February 1924, he permitted Frisch to edit and revise the article: From Paris, he wrote, one possibly weighs too little what may be said and what may not.

The last period of the *Neue Merkur* also brought forth the first attempts to link Expressionism with movements of the past and present. Hausenstein, quite early, viewed Expressionism as a belated form of the Baroque: "We effect a substitute of Gothic and Baroque in the catastrophe of this war and peace: Expressionism."[133] Preetorius, on the other hand, viewed Expressionism as a (regrettable) precursor of Abstraction in art.[134] He came to this conclusion after examining the great exhibit of the Staatsgalerie in 1924. Starting with the thesis that "art needs nature as symbol for subjective drives," rather than reality chosen at random, he categorized Thomas and Böcklin as artists in whose work outer and inner world are a unit, Leibl's paintings as predominantly determined by nature, Marées' as the first break with nature, Liebermann, Slevogt and Corinth as throwbacks to an earlier, more harmonious age, and Marc, finally, as the end of nature depiction and the beginning of Abstraction. Abstract art to Preetorius was synonymous with a crisis in art: Marc "is the end of all representational art, for the common 'Something' is lacking, which is to be depicted and mastered: a 'Something' which an individual cannot invent, but which must confront the mass as a prototypal, familiar, lofty thing." Twenty years later, Preetorius reaffirmed this conviction (25 November 1961): "The crisis of art is the crisis of a subject." Another contributor of that time shared Preetorius' views. Hermann Esswein condemned the exclusive preoccupation with artistic form as "suicide and murder through algebra."[135]

With historical perspective came also discrimination of the qualities of individual artists; previously they had all too often been lumped together as Expressionists. Hausenstein, upon the death of Lovis Corinth, attempted with much justice to draw the dividing line between him and the rest of the Expressionists:

> Expressionism resembles the German revolution; it was not an action, but a reaction—a reaction to the War, a reaction of the War, not an original concept. Corinth represents a revolt out of the fullness of the positive—completely unpolemical, only positive; this Protestant of the North has no opponent at all. This is the most beautiful [achievement], that his paintings, his drawings oppose nothing and no one.[136]

Esswein tried a similar confrontation of artist and movement in the case of Max Beckmann: "The seemingly most modern Beckmann has kept faith with the art that mattered to us oldsters in 1895."[137] Esswein saw in many of his pictures the realization and fulfillment of an earlier Naturalism in its denudation of suffering humanity. Had he wished, he could also have grouped Beckmann with the artists of the *Neue Sachlichkeit*.

Finally several contributors attempted, since Expressionism had all but run its course, to correlate the manifestations of Expressionism in all the arts and, still more ambitiously, to relate it to the spirit of the times in general. Bloch, for example, concluded that Expressionism marked the most violent departure from traditional Western culture in all the arts: "So tremendous is the rupture between Leibl and Chagall, Wagner and Schönberg, Keller and Döblin as to be perhaps unprecedented within modern 'culture,' even within the entire cultural complex from Athens to Classicism, not excepting the most aesthetic Middle Ages."[138] Iwan Goll related Expressionism to its times: "In the war of phrases and billions [i.e., the inflation money] every German became an Expressionist, who expressed in *one* paper bill the fortune of the entire world. Ernst Toller, the Revolutionary, was an Expressionist. Ludendorff, the general, was an Expressionist."[139] These sweeping generalizations were, of course, all too often tours de force.

Outside of the cohesive and repeated treatment of Expressionism, the pages devoted to the fine arts appeared kaleidoscopic: they simply commented upon events in the art world. The acquisition of a Rembrandt painting by the Kassel galleries, for example, called forth a lengthy analysis by Hausenstein.[140] Similarly, the appearance of important books or the opening of major exhibits triggered writings on subjects as varied as Carpaccio, Phidias, the drawings of Michelangelo, or on Cubism and contemporary French art.[141] This last, again part of Goll's report from

Paris, made an astute prediction on the newest phase of Picasso's development: "Picasso is doing things which will keep the mouths of astonished
viewers agape for five years." If anything, this prophecy was on the
conservative side.

Reverting to a tendency of the pre-war years, the artists, art historians,
and art critics displayed much self-consciousness about their role as
critics, about art criticism and its theory. In quoting and adopting a
(debatable) dictum by Bela Balázs ("No art has yet achieved greatness
without a theory"), Musil set the tone.[142] As if in agreement with Balázs,
virtually every major essay on fine arts stated its theoretical premise.
Preetorius repeatedly asserted—finally in our 1961 meeting—that he was
writing as a creative artist rather than as art historian, and was therefore
less inhibited by a scholar's perspective. Yet some of his observations
(after Wölfflin's not entirely original)—for example, that the art of the
Romanic peoples is painting, that of the Germanic people drawing—posits
a definite (if mistaken) historic outlook.[143]

Hausenstein prefaced an encyclopedic article, "Zur deutschen Situation,"[144] with the remark that it can do no harm, but only good, if one
has, at the least, a theoretical insight to a situation. He then tried to fix,
in theory, the identity of the German. He blended art history with geography, history, and cultural history to find this identity and, in so doing,
arrived at some brilliant, always stimulating and startling, even daring,
observations: "If Germany is essentially medieval . . . then this fact expresses implicitly that the Gothic style and feudalism do not merely
belong to German history but to the unalterable substance of the Germans." Hausenstein further illustrated his "total" approach to the fine
arts through his essay, "Reise zu Carpaccio."[145] He interpreted the great
masters of the quattrocento through their historic, cultural, and geographical surroundings and concluded his essay with an aperçu which summarizes his method: "Where is now the difference between art and life?
Are both not one?"

Johannes Alt, on the other hand, argued for a more immanent interpretation of art works (which Hausenstein, incidentally, still applied when
he studied individual art works rather than movements or centuries). In
a not totally correct reading of Wölfflin and Gundolf, he used them as
authorities for such an approach.[146] Felix Braun, finally, in his "Wandel
der Kunstgeschichte" (Evolution of Art History), indicated that various
schools of art historians were seeking new ways of approaching art: "If
Dvořák arrived at a type of philosophy of art through art history, then
we observe in the second of the great German art historians of our generation, Wilhelm Worringer, as we did in his predecessor in Bonn, Karl
Justi, progress from an originally philosophical attitude towards one of

increasing plasticity."[147] The title of Braun's review was obviously most
apropos, although in equating Worringer's merit with that of Dvorak,
he may have done a disservice to both. The former was far more concerned with basic principles of art criticism; Worringer, in his *Abstrak-
tion und Einfühlung*, for example, related art to current popular taste.[148]

Music, always somewhat of a stepchild in the *Neue Merkur*, despite
its editor's love for it, was relegated to a single gloss, an observation on
Puccini as a bourgeois artist, during the *Merkur*'s last two years.[149] By
contrast, the discussions of the theater and its aesthetics increased in
number, thoroughness, and importance. Among these weighty discussions, Musil's unquestionably stood out. He had intended the essay as a
direct continuation of his two earlier discussions;[150] its contentual relationship to the earlier writings is obvious. Frisch, however, asked Musil
in a letter of 5 June 1924 to change the title to "Der Untergang des
Theaters" (Decline of the Theater).[151] The change strikingly indicates
Frisch's (and Musil's) reassessment of the cultural climate in Germany.

It was characteristic of Musil that he consistently tried to elevate his
essays beyond topical concerns to lasting observations. His third contribution on the theater was no exception. As a letter of 25 April 1924
indicates, he initially pursued a far more polemic intent with it. He was
going to send again a *Symptomentheater*, and did believe that various
things struck his attention during the past season which could stand
elaboration. Perhaps he also was going to use the opportunity to talk *pro
domo* against von Ihering and a few other symptomatic persons, only however, if this attracted him objectively, for subjectively it did not.

But four days later Musil announced a much more impersonal approach: "A completely independent article. . . . Its content: an analysis
of the crisis of the theater through a comparison with the crisis of culture
[*Bildungskrise*]." The article, with one exception, skirted all but one
direct reference to contemporary directors, dramatists, and critics.

Another letter, that of 8 June 1924, which offered some brief observations on the submitted article, also outlined the projected but unac-
complished continuation of the series. If the *Symptomatic Theater* was
to be continued, part IV would present practical examples which would
buttress part III: The uncomprehended new humor in the works of Jules
Romain; a production of an Eulenberg drama, in which the figures and
their actions did not matter, but rather the atmosphere; the very amusing
misunderstandings, which he, in person, experienced.

What Musil liked about the idea of such an essay was the uncon-
strained possibility of speaking *pro domo*, the chance to introduce some
variety into the discussion of matters of principles, and to lay at least
the groundwork for a future article. For what he liked to present, as

Symptomatic Theater part V, was an essay about prominent critical systems. Also, in continuations he would frequently turn to problems which existed independently of the theater, as well.

Musil's ability to transcend the initial intention of an article is also demonstrated in his last discussion of aesthetics. He fully realized the change of intent and direction. He had promised a review of Balázs's extraordinarily interesting film dramaturgy *Der sichtbare Mensch* [Visible Man], but while working on it, it had grown into an essay, remaining a review only by virtue of its point of departure. It was, in reality, a discussion of important aesthetic problems, which through their entire tenor, he felt, belonged in the *Neue Merkur*. In a letter of 22 December 1924 he added that he was naturally aware that on a relatively small basis great breadth had developed. But in the process many things were being said for the first time, and Musil was very well satisfied even with the current draft of his paper.

In short, Musil wished to develop his own system of aesthetics in these articles on the theater and film. In the one of 1924, he started with a grudging admission of the permanence of crisis in the theater, but he traced its then prevailing ills to the growing commercialism of the stage which forced upon it both sensationalism and banality. Technique achieved predominance over substance; "a good dramatist works like a factory engineer [today]"; the content had become a purpose in itself, for "material is heaped next to material, without a new spirit arising from their proximity." Having thus carefully laid his groundwork, Musil drew important social implications from the degeneration of the theater: it paralleled and was symptomatic of a general decline of *Bildung*. Specifically they both were burdened by an anti-intellectualism of thirty years' standing. "Impressionism already formed the prejudice that the writer must speak to [Man's] heart or some such organ, which is always thought of as lacking all connection to Man's large brain . . . a type of illiterate language." Also, he maintained, the most recent education was trying to shape not personalities but persons submerging themselves in the mass; in theater and literature this phenomenon was paralleled by a tendency towards "folk or emotion-language, hallowed and *festlich vereinen* [unifying through a festival mood]." This thesis, of course, was to be expected from the author of *Young Törless*. Finally, said Musil, the ennui with education expressed itself through the anti-literary method of staging, conducive to a type of "journalism of the stage." He saw no immediate remedy for the theater, perhaps because its malady was closely tied to a general cultural retrogression. He had only two concrete suggestions: improve theater and literary criticism, since currently "the essentials are neglected; we lack an ideological approach to complement

An die Leſer des Neuen Merkur

Infolge des Generalſtreiks, der die Münchner Buchdruckereibetriebe längere Zeit ſtillegte, erſcheint dieſes Heft leider um 14 Tage verſpätet. Die nächſten Hefte werden, wenn es die Lage zuläßt, regelmäßig rechtzeitig fertig vorliegen.

Redaktion und Verlag des Neuen Merkur

Georg Müller and Efraim Frisch at the Dedication of the gravestone for Otto Julius Bierbaum, Winter 1912, Waldfriedhof in Munich

Left to right: Kurt Martens (with white scarf), (behind, hidden, in fur cap) Gerhard Oukama Knoop, Georg Müller, (the man with the pointed beard is unidentified), Hans Brandenburg, (half-hidden by him) Hermann Croissant, (to the right of the gravestone) Gemma Bierbaum, Max Halbe, Maria Langer (painter), (woman in hat with feathers is unidentified), Dora Brandenburg-Polster (painter), Anna Croissant-Rust (writer), (hidden by her) Alfred Schuler, Mrs. Lisette Streml, Max Artur Streml (painter), (half-hidden) Efraim Frisch, Mrs. Oukama Knoop, Wunderer (mayor of Pasing).

(Courtesy of Handschriftenabteilung der Stadtbibliothek München, Richard Lemp, Director.)

a biographical one. Let us return to the cardinal responsibility of the theater, Man's preoccupation with Man."

Musil expanded upon his views of the theater in the essay on its budding sister art, the cinema.[152] Taking a book by Bela Balázs as his point of departure, he soon veered from his initial subject to make some basic observations on aesthetics: "The remarks which I am adding below apply mostly to the territory where [film and literature] converge and separate. The question whether or not the film is an independent art stimulated questions which [in turn] are common to all arts." His main thesis, discussed from a variety of aspects, was the view that "it is one of the basic capabilities of all arts to explode a normal total experience." His article was written at a time when fellow novelists, such as Dos Passos and Döblin, were beginning to explore the applicability of film techniques to the novel. But his main thesis applied to no one's fiction as accurately as to his own.

6   The Lyre
of Mercury: I

1914-1916

No period in German literature, except that of the Age of Goethe, is currently receiving closer critical scrutiny than the first decades of this century. Hence the addition of yet another "history of literature," based on a single magazine, to a bibliography already imposing would be superfluous and perhaps misleading. Many of the writers whose works appeared in the *Neue Merkur* frequently departed from their customary patterns; Frisch, its editor, delighted in publishing the unusual and unexpected. Measuring some contributions against the yardstick of Expressionism, for example, one might arrive at some curious conclusions about their authors. Judging solely on the basis of works published in the *Neue Merkur*, we would have to conclude that such a pioneer of Austrian Expressionism as Emil Alphons Rheinhardt was no Expressionist at all, that his equally influential countryman Oscar Maurus Fontana was one only sporadically, and that the Classicist Wilhelm Lehmann wrote stories with "Expressionistic excrescenses," as he himself, on 22 August 1962, described his novella "Der bedrängte Seraph,"[1] his only belletristic contribution.

The *Neue Merkur*'s literature, however, may serve as the source of a different type of literary history. As probably the only journal of its type whose entire editorial correspondence is extant, it projects, as if in arrested motion, the generic growth of various literary movements and experiments, the rise and (sometimes) decline of poets and writers, and, more often than not, the causes behind the solstice of movements and their representatives. While the journal's fiction and poetry were frequently symptomatic of the literary taste in Germany, the correspondence and subsequent interviews based on it often suggest the reason for the period's fickleness. A rejection note sometimes mirrors the tragedy of an author

or a movement that has suddenly become passé, a solicitation or acceptance of an author previously rejected attests to a development in him or
in his readers. Since the *Neue Merkur* had no program, it could change
with the times, adjust to new public demands, and occasionally, as in the
case of Brecht, could even channel them.[2] Because Frisch was intensely
attuned to his times and its tastes, yet stubborn enough in his convictions
not to try being fashionable at all costs, the reasons for his selections
become a legible chart of the currents and counter-currents in the stream
of German literature. In short, the belletristic part of the *Neue Merkur*,
together with the correspondence and statements concerning it, offer not
a history of literature but part of a history of literary tastes which, according to Henri Peyre, "must some day be undertaken."[3] The *Neue
Merkur* provides, in other words, a glimpse of the German literary
market place during the eight years of its existence.

Eight years is, of course, a minute span in literary history. Even so
the lifetime of the *Merkur* fortunately coincided with a particularly
fertile and imaginative period in German literature in which, following
a curious and readily discernible pattern, long, lean years were ex-
plosively relieved by a few years of superabundance. The *Merkur* existed
during these fat years and achieved through this favorable circumstance
quite a respectable record of longevity in comparison with many other
German literary magazines. Its relative longevity can be explained, in
part, by two factors: the excellence of its literature (on which it had no
monopoly) and the eclecticism of its taste. Precisely those magazines
that were wed to a particular movement died with it; the *Neue Merkur*
underwent several regenerative metamorphoses and proved slightly more
viable. These metamorphoses or processes of *stirb und werde* might have
come about accidentally, but they were, in fact, the result of choice
rather than chance.

The choice began with the selection of a title for the publication.
When Frisch proposed it to his publisher, the two founders knew from
the start that the name bound them to a tradition. One of the truly great
magazines in eighteenth-century German literature was the "old"
Merkur, Christoph Martin Wieland's distinguished journal *Der Teutsche
Merkur*, to which, at one time or another, nearly every one of Germany's
Classical authors had contributed. Few educated and sophisticated Germans, those most likely to read the newly launched magazine, would
miss the import of the title; if they did, helpful reviewers, such as an
anonymous one in the *Hamburger Nachrichten* of 4 April 1914 (page 4),
were ready to point it out. Also some of these knowledgeable readers
could be counted on to recall the policy of the old *Merkur*, enunciated
by Wieland in its first issue of May 1773 (I, v): "Withal we feel bound

to announce in advance that we shall not use any contributions that may be submitted without examination and selectivity, and that we shall, in making our selections, be guided solely by the public interest and not by considerations of persons and special circumstances."

Both Frisch and Georg Müller shared Wieland's conviction. When Müller launched, in 1903, eleven years of idealistic and inspired, if occasionally frenetic, publishing, he issued the following statement of intent: "In our times literary movements follow on each other's heels . . . and hence we shall be acting in the spirit of Goethe, if we pay homage to no direction at all."[4]

Frisch, as Müller's chief editor, subscribed to the same views; perhaps Frisch's appointment to the post and the unusual harmony between the tempestuous publisher and the withdrawn editor were both predicated upon a joint purpose. Hence the magazine, by definition, could not become what the *Grosse Brockhaus* of 1932 made it out to be, "a magazine in the service of early Expressionism." On the contrary, Frisch made a promise in the first issue which he fulfilled in every one: It is our task "to gather the seed of renewal from among all the values, old and new, from among all the camps, which no longer represent movements—and then to resow this seed."[5] Wieland, in the same preface of the *Teutsche Merkur*, had enunciated another publishing principle: his magazine would provide a forum for incipient writers, in order to bestir dormant or undecided talents. Although Frisch made no such commitment outright, he expressed similar sentiments in several letters. It soon became known that the *Neue Merkur* judged a work of literature on merit, and not primarily on the reputation of its author. By indulging his hobby of making literary discoveries, Frisch launched many distinguished or, at the least, respectable careers. By their own testimony Bertolt Brecht, Leo Perutz, Friedrich Sieburg, Gottfried Kölwel, and W. E. Süskind considered the *spiritus rector* of the *Neue Merkur* as their "discoverer" or "co-discoverer." It was not unusual for a young author, once he had been published in the *Neue Merkur*, to find previously closed doors suddenly ajar. As Süskind put it, in an interview on 1 November 1961, an author accepted by the *Merkur* had "arrived" in German letters.

This enlightened attitude paid Frisch a twofold dividend. It led to some of the most gratifying moments of his editorship; Felix Braun, the Austrian poet, told me on 18 December 1962 that Frisch experienced no greater professional fulfillment than when he had "discovered" a new talent. In addition, this policy gave his magazine a fresh image. From the very beginning, for example in the April 1914 review in the *Hamburger Nachrichten*, the phrase "new physiognomy" was used to describe the fledgling magazine. As, one after the other, new writers displayed their

talent in the *Neue Merkur,* its reviewers had occasion to repeat or vary
the phrase. It was a pleasant way of filling a column: to display acumen
by predicting success for a young author and to quote these predictions,
often much later, when they had come to pass.

In fact the frequency with which the *Neue Merkur* received critical
notice was to no small extent attributable to the sense of discovery with
which readers and reviewers could open its pages. "But we have Germans
again who can write," exalted the reviewer in the *Neue Badische Landes-
zeitung* of 28 October 1921. Then as now a critic likes to be present at
the birth of a poet or, even more so, at the birth of a nation of poets.

Also, by giving a writer a "start in life," Frisch frequently induced
some fierce loyalties among his protégés. Leo Perutz, Friedrich Sieburg,
Ernst Robert Curtius, and Ernst Bloch kept contributing when they could
command prices far higher than the *Neue Merkur* could afford. And they
rendered it a service which no amount of money could have commanded:
they acted as "talent scouts" for the journal. Curtius procured contributions from Gide and Valéry; Ferdinand Lion acted as middleman for
Thomas Mann; Mann, in turn, mediated between Frisch and Kurt von
Boeckmann.[6] This type of "chain-reaction" was, indeed, by no means
uncommon. Also young authors just accepted by the *Merkur* "spread the
word." Fontana recalled on 21 December 1962 that it is certain that the
youth of that time who were looking for a forum, selected the *Neue
Merkur* as their mouthpiece, especially since it was free of cliques. To be
sure there were Expressionistic journals, but that was a matter of fashion.
On the other hand, one saw that the *Neue Merkur* was not written for the
moment. A journal that wanted to advance 'young literature' did not, at
that time, exist. To publish the lasting within the transitory—how many
editors aim for that! Most are hunting for items salable on the literary
marketplace. Later in our conversation Fontana returned to Frisch's en-
couragement of the young: That was something new at the time that one
wanted to boost the young. At that time being young was no asset; one
tried to hide his age. Fontana, for example, concealed his from the
Literatur-Kürschner. Erich von Kahler, in an interview of 28 January
1963, put it still more succinctly: "It was the journal around which the
young people thronged."

In short the *Neue Merkur* pursued excellence, no matter where it might
be found. But since excellence is subjective and its hunters fallible, the
editors of the *Merkur* occasionally failed in their quest. Ferdinand Lion
told me on 25 September 1961 that the *Merkur* far too often published
Josef Ponten; this objection, from today's perspective, seems valid. Franz
Schoenberner relates in his memoirs that the selection of a work was
sometimes capricious and hurried along by the very human consideration

of a beckoning weekend excursion. Occasionally greatness may be thrust upon an author by an editor's sudden urge to commune with nature.[7]

Though the literary part of the *Neue Merkur* was not free of occasional mediocrity, of choices dictated by personal prejudice or caprice, of rare deferences to a publisher's wishes, it was innocent of yet another fault with which literary journals, past and present, are frequently reproached. The journal did not try to "manipulate" the taste of its readers; it erred from honest conviction rather than in an attempt to make "the worse cause appear the better." One would-be contributor, Karl Fischer, the co-editor of *Kunstwart*, began his covering (undated) letter to a novella with the less than ingratiating opening: If you should be inclined to make an exception and print a contribution of a non-member of your steady group of collaborators . . . . Such a group never existed.

The eclecticism of the magazine becomes apparent through a chronological reading of its literature. A perusal of the literary contributions to its war and pre-war issues leads immediately to the discovery of a major omission: with the exception of Strindberg's prologue to the comedy "Comrades," which Strindberg had originally withheld from publication, no work by or about a Naturalist appeared in the *Merkur*. Also, on the evidence of the editorial correspondence none was solicited and several critical articles were returned. The editors, despite their commitment to universality, had no choice. French, Scandinavian, and German Naturalism had, by 1914, passed its peak: its representatives, if they still wrote in that mode at all, were being identified with other magazines. The *Neue Merkur* could not risk being considered an imitation.

The seeming exception of Strindberg strengthens rather than invalidates this conclusion. When the *Merkur* included unpublished writings of the pre-Expressionistic Strindberg, it was hardly courting the criticism of being imitative. On the contrary, their publication was something of a "scoop." As chief editor of the Georg Müller Verlag, Frisch had shepherded the German translation of Strindberg's *Works* towards publication and tempered the eccentricities of Emil Schering, Strindberg's pedestrian translator and his irascible German copyright holder. Frisch made the most of his fortuitous role: first he conjured with Strindberg's name in announcing the founding of the magazine: "[We] have acquired . . . unedited material from Strindberg's literary legacy for original publication," he wrote in a "house-ad" preceding the first issue.[8] Then, inside this first issue, he redeemed his pledge by printing twenty-four letters, Strindberg's own highly revelatory commentary to five of his prose works, together with a two-page passage from his novel, *The Son of a Servant Girl*, censured by his publisher as "purple," but in reality an extensive and sensitive psychological exploration of human jealousy.[9] Finally Frisch and his war-time substitute announced, in a triumphant footnote, that Schering had unearthed another major item by Strindberg (at that time he was probably at the zenith of his posthumous fame) : "Written in the Fall of 1886 in Gersau on Lake Lucerne. Was to preface *Comrades*, but was deleted by the poet who wanted to preserve the unity of time of a comedy set in Paris. [The Prologue plays in Sweden.] Only now has [this prologue] been unearthed from his literary remains."[10] The *Merkur*'s brush with Naturalism may have been brief, but it was memorable.

In his quest to make the *Merkur* representative in all other respects—as well as original—Frisch turned it into a judicious admixture of traditional and experimental literature. Knowing that the fate of a magazine is usually decided within a year of its birth, he balanced the two with particular care in the first two volumes, which span the *Merkur*'s first period. Out of the same conviction he exacted tentative promises for contributions from Germany's leading authors; the aforementioned house-ad in the first issue listed their names. It reads like a highly selective "Who's Who" in pre-war German letters, although it is hardly surprising that many of the prospective contributors did not keep their promises—what an embarrassment of riches that would have produced! The astonishing thing is that so many did keep faith with a new and untried magazine.

To obtain some of his most distinguished contributors, Frisch heavily taxed personal loyalties and contacted friends and acquaintances. Christian Morgenstern, Frisch's best friend and literary mentor, did not live to see the first issue of the *Merkur*, but he left his friend a valuable heritage: the *Neue Merkur* was accorded the honor and prestige of publishing the first poems from Morgenstern's literary legacy.[11] Through the enduring friendship of Margareta Morgenstern, the poet's widow, Frisch secured the publication rights to ten of his unpublished metaphysical poems, which appeared throughout the first three volumes of the *Merkur*. Among them was the great and often since cited confessional poem, *Nachtlied*, with its beginning line, "Die Sterne brennen hernieder" (Nightsong; The Stars burn down). It was, as many reviewers noted, an impressive acquisition.

Reviewers were no less impressed by the contribution of another traditional and established German author. Frisch, who had become acquainted with Jakob Wassermann through their joint publisher, S. Fischer, and his chief reader, Moritz Heymann, was able to prevail upon Wassermann to grant the *Merkur* the serial rights to his new novel, the realistic, symbolistic narration of an artist's life, *Das Gänsemännchen*.[12] It held readers in suspense across the entire span of the first volume. The response of readers and reviewers was overwhelmingly favorable; only a few found fault. Among the critics was Max Mell, who related on 20 December 1961: In my opinion *The Little Gooseman* was too hefty a chunk, a bit too heavy to carry. Despite the general success of the novel, Frisch, in retrospect, must have come round to Mell's opinion. He did not again approach Wassermann for another contribution. Also Frisch must have sensed, even at the height of Wassermann's success, that the traditional, realistic German prose narrative had run its course. Wassermann, once among Germany's most prominent authors, is virtually forgotten today. As Frisch was to demonstrate time and again in future years, he could discern, even when momentary taste seemed to point in the opposite direction, which works would endure. Committed through his house-ad to publish only works of enduring quality or experiments of great promise, Frisch may have suppressed principle for expedience when he solicited *Das Gänsemännchen*. If it was a compromise for the sake of popular appeal, it was the last one.

Paradoxically, traditional authors far less gifted than Wassermann occasionally found favor in Frisch's eyes and were published after the decline of the plot-centered novel and novella had long become apparent to far less discriminating critics. A careful perusal of Frisch's essays and of these works explains this inconsistency. Greek antiquity and the Italian Renaissance held an obvious fascination for Frisch which sometimes distorted his critical judgment. Hence some superb, inventive re-creations of these periods, for example Max Krell's "Die Frangimani," appear alongside such feeble, long-forgotten works as Andreas Schreiber's Renaissance novellas, "Der Bischof von Valencia" and "Die arme Vaubonne," all too reminiscent of Conrad Ferdinand Meyer; Eduard Kehlmann's short story "Hellas," a contrived attempt to confront Hellenic ideals, championed by a German high-school boy, with the materialism of the twentieth century; and Hermann von Boetticher's less than inspired poem to a Spanish Renaissance figure, "Don Juan's letzte Liebe."[13] Frisch, in subconsciously deviating from his quest for literary excellence when lured by his hobby-horse, proved that even a great editor—which he undoubtedly was—succumbs occasionally to human foibles.

Otherwise when Frisch solicited or accepted works by established and traditional authors, he sought and attained both quality and variety. Max Dauthendey's "Nächtliche Schaufenster" is, for example, a glittering and intoxicating specimen of Impressionism at its best; Dauthendey confines the scene of his story, for the most part, to a single street corner in Berlin, but the palette of his temperament splashes upon this monotone the colorful "impressions" of the far corners of the earth: "Upon a placard I saw one night the huge head of a tiger. Underneath it was written 'India in Berlin.' The speckled head of the tiger gazed out from yellow bamboo shoots and was a taut cat's head, and above it rested a painted pale-blue heaven. For a while I felt then that I was traversing the jungles of India."[14] August Mayer, in free translations of poems from the *Greek Anthology*, deliberately superimposed the poetics of the Stefan George circle upon the Greek originals.[15] "It appeared advisable," he wrote in a prefatory note, "to forego an external imitation of the ancient form and to attempt a solution which is close to the true function of the ancient models through means at the disposal of our own language. [This true function is] vividness and revitalization."

The Austrian, Oscar A. H. Schmitz, used a Neo-Romantic frame (fairy-tale themes, a depopulated world, a ghostlike lover) to bring about a modern, deliberately absurd and spurious, dialectical confrontation between metaphysics and natural sciences. He resolved his novella, "Eine heimliche Geschichte" (An Eery Story)[16] in a manner familiar from the writings of the Neo-Romantics. At the end of the tale, the hero realizes that his fantastic adventures have been a dream. Though it might be argued that of the three representatives of tradition only Dauthendey is likely to endure, it is obvious that Mayer and Schmitz met one of Frisch's criteria for acceptance. By applying the stylistic devices of established literary movements to contents hitherto not attempted by other representatives, they extended their limits and "conducted experiments of great promise."

The last example of traditional literature in the *Merkur*'s early years met both criteria; it had enduring qualities and was experimental. Hermann Stehr's novella "Das entlaufene Herz"[17] is one of the enduring examples of that much abused term *Heimatkunst* (Regional Literature) which has so often served, in the more recent past, to lend dignity to shoddy sentimentalism or a mythical nationalism. Stehr's work is neither. It is regional art in the sense that the term might be applied to Thomas Hardy or Katherine Anne Porter. When this novella was recently republished,[18] several German reviewers pointed out its timelessness. "How far," wrote Karl Boegner, "does Hermann Stehr's grandiosely eery, thoroughly Silesian story rank above the pseudo-art of the 'Blood and Soil' trash [*Blut und Boden Kitsch*]. Spirits emerge from elemental depth."[19] Though the story has deep roots in its "homeland," the soil of Silesia, its basic theme, the demonic drive to motherhood of its unwed heroines, is timeless and universal.

The acquisition of this story demonstrates that skill *and* luck determine the quality of a literary journal. The author had first offered the novella to another journal; its editor, not impervious to the narrow morality of his times, rejected it. As Stehr reported in an unpublished letter to Marie Oehlke of 6 November 1913 (kindly furnished by Wilhelm Meridies), just then the *Leipziger Illustrierte* had turned down his *Entlaufenes Herz* in consideration of "the not unobjectionable subject" which had been "treated with exceptional artistry." The devil should fetch morality, so Stehr wrote, if it had as swinish a nose as the readers of the *Illustrierte*. He was itching to write a story that started: "I am about to tell a story which is really designed only for swine and jackasses, but could profitably be read and perused by human beings as well." As a less drastic means of self-rehabilitation, he offered the novella, completely innocuous by modern standards, to the *Neue Merkur*. Its editor was less puritanical and more courageous.

As the foregoing examples illustrate, Frisch redeemed his pledge "to preserve old values"; his service to the "newer writers," primarily to the Expressionists, exceeded his promise. Names which are now standard entries in the history of Expressionism and works which now typify the movement sparkled across the pages of the *Merkur*'s first two volumes of 1914–16. Among them were, chronologically, Alfred Döblin's "Die Nachtwandlerin" (The Woman Sleepwalker), Arnold Ulitz' "Die vergessene Wohnung" (The Forgotten Apartment), Kasimir Edschmid's "Das beschämende Zimmer" (The Embarrassing Room)—possibly the most ecstatic affirmation of life in Expressionistic literature—and Paris von Gütersloh's "Der sentimentale junge Mann."[20] And interspersed among these early manifestations of Expressionistic prose were a score of poems which, like those by Ulitz, had already achieved the expressiveness of the new movement or, like the poems by Klabund, were groping toward it or, as exemplified by Kölwel's and Ehrenstein's, were already modifying and modulating Expressionism.

In the pages of the *Merkur* the development of Expressionism, insofar as it did not antedate the magazine, unfolded with particular clarity. Frisch's eclecticism, his belief that literature was never static, but rather elastic, expansive, and experimental, made him accept contributions from all the allied or warring camps and sub-groups of Expressionism. He published Gottfried Benn and Kurt Hiller, Alfred Döblin and Otto Flake, and allowed opponents such as the last two to use the *Merkur* as their arena. Frequently, as exemplified by Döblin and Flake, he sent assuaging letters to both combatants.[21] His interested nonpartisanship made him a confidant of all the camps and his magazine and correspondence a limited but uncolored and dramatic record of the movement's dominance and decline.

Frisch's relationship to two writers as different from one another as Döblin and Ulitz offers us a new perspective on the development of the movement. The prima facie evidence consists in the acceptances and rejections of their literary works. From Döblin, Frisch accepted the novella "Die Nachtwandlerin" (April 1914), another novella "Die Schlacht, die Schlacht" (April 1915), a self-contained narrative from the novel *Wallenstein* entitled "Predigt und Judenverbrennung" (February 1920), a scene from the drama "Die Nonnen von Kemnade" (Nov./Dec. 1921), and an episode from *Berge, Meere und Giganten* entitled "Die Balladeuse." He rejected, in 1919, passages omitted from Döblin's *Die drei Sprünge des Wang-Lun*, in 1921 a film script, in 1924 a factual account of a court case, "Klein Nolte."[22] In short, Döblin's creative works (apart from the essays mentioned in earlier chapters) appeared from the very first number through 1923, when he was abruptly dropped from the list of contributors.

Frisch's letter of 24 February 1919, in response to a request for a recommendation from Anton Kippenberg, director of the Insel Verlag, explains his initial enthusiasm:

Among the very questionable contributors to the *Sturm* Döblin, who joined their ranks quite by accident, had aroused Frisch's attention through his tenor and attitude, above all through his excellent reply to Marinetti's futurist manifesto. Later, after the foundation of the *Neue Merkur*, he had had much success with Dr. Döblin's novella, entitled "Die Nachtwandlerin." The novel, *Die drei Sprünge des Wang-Lun*, he rather considered the best work of prose fiction published in the last ten years. Frisch considered Döblin, truly, an independent spirit and, something still rarer, an intuitive artist. What one called Expressionism was, in his case, intrinsic and natural. The editor once had made his acquaintance in Berlin and his personal impression only served to reinforce that of Döblin's works. The latter was a man in his thirties then and in his profession served as doctor to the poor. He was one of those rare artists who the older they get, gain steadily in true spontaneity and intrinsic ingenuousness. This assessment might appear too subjective; even so, Frisch would not be able to express it differently. Several chapters from the poet's new historical novel i.e., *Wallenstein*, which he had had the opportunity to read strengthened his conviction that Fischer was not the right place for the works. He himself would like to apply for Döblin's works if the condition of the publishing house, which was still in its beginnings, would permit him to do so. With Döblin, Kippenberg would make a significant acquisition for the Insel Verlag. Frisch wrote few such panegyrics.

The letter, in conjunction with other information, reveals much about Frisch's attitude towards Expressionism in general and Döblin in particular. He scorned the outcries of the poets who were symptomatic of Walden's *Sturm*; upon one occasion he called them "Krämpfe" (convoluted writings),[23] and in later years he allowed Paul Fechter to polemicize against them.[24] His reservations regarding "convoluted" Expressionists are echoed in his remarks that Döblin's Expressionistic style comes naturally; the obvious corollary is that it is mannered or unnatural with many other writers. His admiration of *Wang-lun* as a finished novel also clarifies his rejection of the parts submitted to him. Apparently Döblin, not always the best critic of his own writing, had for once identified the weakest parts of his novel and had deleted them from the complete work, but thought them adequate as independent pieces for a magazine. Frisch obviously did not concur.[25]

On the other hand, Frisch must have concurred with Döblin's conception of Expressionism. In one article entitled "Der Epiker, sein Stoff und die Kritik"[26] Döblin comes close to a definition, though he would probably have used a less ambitious and more personal term. Even though it answers a very specific rhetorical question regarding the germination of his novel *Wallenstein*, it has validity considerably beyond an argument *pro persona*:

> [Was] it an inclination to breathe air into non-living, dead matter? Not at all. No dead matter came before my eyes; the Thirty Years' War is for me as much of a sealed book as it was twenty years ago. Empathy? That is something I know nothing about, but still I sense that it was the exact contrary: 'expathy.' Empathy entails loving genuflexion, personal effort and the urge and volition to be just. . . . But since I took no notice of the Thirty Years' War, prevented from all participation in these undoubtedly interesting events by a blinding light from within and inner occupation, how should I have gained empathy? . . . I had sought for stimulants, stimulants to set me free. I sought, strove for a midwife to deliver [my work], for forceps. Those were the documents, the books. [But] they were not my content."

Reality as the midwife of an inner vision—there are worse ways to define Expressionism.

Frisch's agreement with Döblin's definition may be assumed all the more readily since he had a hand in its inception. He suggested, rather subtly, that Döblin rework the first draft of his article, originally a short defense *ad hominem* against Friedrich Burschell's attack on *Wallenstein*. Döblin took the hint. On 11 February 1921 he wrote asking for the return of the "Burschell" article; he wanted to enlarge it and remove everything that referred directly to B.

Agreement also seems likely in the case of yet another article, an essay about Döblin's works by Alfred Endler. In a letter of 5 August 1922 Döblin suggested its publication: Frisch complied immediately. Once published, the article lost much of its appeal for both of them. Endler can't write, wrote Döblin on 27 November 1922, he was still young and still very much at odds with himself. But they accepted its substance. Endler hypothesized: If the "collected works of a writer permit us at all to draw conclusions about his development, then that [of Döblin] seems to have proceeded in exactly the reverse order of the average Expressionist—from remoteness to proximity of reality."[27] Although Endler's apodictum appears today somewhat of a simplification, it does roughly describe Döblin's development. And precisely at the moment when Döblin reversed this trend, Frisch lost interest in him. Apparently Frisch demanded of Expressionism that it couple the quest for new forms with that for the new man, to borrow Walter Sokel's terms.[28] He approved of Döblin's "proximity to nature" and rejected him when he thought, mistakenly, that he was becoming a writer *desengagé*. In retrospect it is easy to see that Döblin, far from seeking the comfort of a flight into the future, was coming to grips with one of its most catastrophic dilemmas, the quandary between man's advances in technology and his moral inertia.

Frisch's disillusionment began with Döblin's submittal of "Die Balladeuse," a fragment from his novel *Berge, Meere und Giganten*. The editor seemed to harbor little enthusiasm for it. Pleading the story's dependence on the total novel and its length—actually no greater than that of many others—Frisch asked for a substitute. Döblin, on 25 August 1922, answered with a detailed and highly illuminating defense of his story:

> Dear Mr. Frisch: Indeed, if you do not like the episode of the Ballad, just let it go. I don't want to give away the other [episode] either; something in it does not satisfy me. An episode is never a novella, but I thought that all the important perquisites are provided, and, after all, people understood the piece when I presented it at a private reading in my house! Perfectly; for *in essence* it has a novella-like compactness, the depiction of a terrible individual fate, of a horrible, unique occurrence. That *must* be understandable, but I am already taking the same [apologetic] line of the failures. The ballad singer who does not reappear here, the tyrant, the friend who is disengaging himself from him: those two play the central roles; everything [else] about him, about [the novel's] content are non-essentials; the obscurity there is of no consequence. Ergo: please reexamine

the wild, heinous piece (it is worse than the 'Burning of the
Jews' in *Wallenstein*). You will probably see through this struggle
of the male and female animal—and surely not with pleasure; it
cost me nervous energy to look these things in the face. Therefore I will certainly be angry with you, if you put up resistance
(in Freud's meaning [of the word]); after all I just wanted to
give you—unsuccessfully?—some pleasure.

> With best regards,
> Yours, Alfred Döblin.

In view of this letter, Frisch could only refuse publication at the loss of
a contributor.

The printing of "Die Balladeuse,"[29] however, only postponed the
inevitable. When, in 1924, the finished novel appeared, Frisch was
appalled. In asking Harry Kahn to review the book on 17 June 1924,
he made no secret of his displeasure. It would be necessary, he argued,
to publish something about Döblin's new novel. Not knowing Kahn's
point of view, he himself had to confess his horror when faced with this
withdrawal into the future and a certain "Super-Spenglerism," so much
so that Döblin, whom he esteemed very highly, now almost had been
spoiled for him. His probably very subjective attitude, however, should
not prevent him from doing justice to the magnitude of the task and the
achievement. Frisch was waiting for Kahn's opinion.

Harry Kahn shared Frisch's view. He called the novel (in a letter of 2
July 1924) a gigantic and obscene piece of cowardice (*riesige Etappen-
schweinerei*. But he never submitted a review. When Max Krell's essay
about contemporary German prose presented the opportunity to rectify
this omission, Frisch let it pass unused. Krell, without a demurrer on
Frisch's part, dismissed Döblin with a single sentence—after a discussion of "responsible writers": "Döblin—aber Döblin stellt einen Fall
für sich dar." ("Döblin—but Döblin is a chapter in itself.")[30] The appearance of this essay, Frisch's rejection of "Klein Nolte," and the dis-
continuation of all correspondence between Frisch and Döblin all fell
within the same month, April 1924. It was no coincidence.

Frisch's relationship to Döblin illustrates one more editorial principle. Whether right or wrong, Frisch's decisions as to literary contributions were his, exclusively. With the exception of those issues he could
control but incompletely during his military service and three other
issues edited by Wilhelm Hausenstein alone, Frisch had final say on
all matters pertaining to literature. In the case of Döblin he received
contrary opinions when he included him and when he dropped him. On
10 November 1919 Kurt Hiller wrote Frisch that he would be more

than pleased to contribute to the *Neue Merkur*; if for no other reason
than to paralyze what he considered the dangerous effect of certain contributors (e.g. Döblin!). And on 12 March 1924 Ernst Bloch wrote
regarding the publication of *Berge, Meere und Giganten*: What did
Frisch think of Döblin's novel? He himself was completely overwhelmed.
When he saw Döblin the day before, he had hugged and kissed him. If
only Döblin were not the political writer Linke Poot as well! Frisch,
although he respected the judgment of both Hiller and Bloch, allowed
neither the detractor nor the admirer of Döblin to influence him.

At first glance, however, Frisch's relationship with yet another Expressionist seems to be inconsistent, if compared to his treatment of
Döblin. The development Frisch had condemned in Döblin he welcomed in Arnold Ulitz, a prominent Silesian writer. The obvious—and
obviously false—explanation for this contradictory attitude appears to
be personal friendship. Letters of Frisch to Ulitz, especially that of 7
December 1922, statements by Mrs. Frisch, and, conversely, a letter to
me from Ulitz on 15 April 1962, all testify to the mutual liking and
respect between the author and the Frisches: Every visit of the *Neue
Merkur* at that time, he wrote, was for him a human and intellectual
enrichment. Mrs. Frisch also gave him many linguistically valuable tips
for his translations from the Russian, especially of Alexander Block's
"The Twelve." But the frequent and enthusiastic acceptance of Ulitz'
writings can scarcely be explained on the basis of friendship alone;
Frisch, upon innumerable occasions, sent rejection notes even to his
best friends. Hence it becomes necessary to examine closely Ulitz' change
during his years as a contributor. Such an examination will open yet
another perspective on Frisch's (and the *Merkur's*) attitude toward
Expressionism.

Ulitz' development can readily be traced through his numerous contributions. The first, two poems of January 1915, show all the conventions, but little of the essence, of Expressionism. In one of the poems,
"Schlafende Frau," the syntax and vocabulary are pronouncedly Expressionistic; the third strophe, for example, begins: "Du wanderst viel-
leicht durch funkelnde Stadt." (Perhaps you wander through [a] sparkling city.) But the incident, the narrator's observation of his sleeping
wife and his speculation upon her dreams, is firmly rooted in reality.
One of the last two poems contributed by Ulitz (published in 1921)
begins, on the other hand, on a realistic note: "Ich bin so müde vom
Leiden der letzten / Durchschrieenen Nächte." (I am so tired of the
suffering / of the last raucous nights.) But it ends on a surrealistic one:
"Löscht doch in mir aus das Wer, / Bis ich ganz verschwinge / Und in
einer Säule Sonnenstaubes / Bewußtlos singe." (Expunge in me the

Who, / Until I utterly disappear / And in a column of sun dust / Unconsciously sing.) [31] The difference between the earlier and later poems reflect a development in Ulitz that had set in with his novel *Ararat* of 1920,[32] probably his most important work: a progressive departure from realism and a greater predilection for abstract imagery.

His fiction is even more revelatory. Ulitz' first story, "Die vergessene Wohnung," unfolds a psychological study of a woman's mental deterioration after the death in battle of her common-law husband, and bears many of the outer accoutrements of Expressionism. ("The city towered in the gradual onset of dusk with its unlit houses and many steeples which were grey as concentrated night, and she was frozen and completely extinct."[33]) Yet these appear only sporadically and are adornments of a realistic and essentially autobiographical novella. In an interview on 11 October 1962, Ulitz admitted as much. This woman lived once, and he had known her well. The forgotten apartment had been his student quarters; he had lived way up in the drying-loft which painter friends of his had decorated in the most inexpensive and fantastic manner, with a painting of Iphigenia by Feuerbach as "show-piece." His father, on a visit from Kattowitz, seeing the furnishings, the cigarette butts lying everywhere, and the storage rooms that made up the other stories of the house, thought his son had totally gone to seed and threatened to remove him from the university. The apartment, and its reflection in the eyes of two generations, Ulitz assumed, would probably be recognized easily by me, when I read the novella. One might add that few visionary flights in the novella distance us from this reality.

In his next novella, "Die Flucht nach Indien,"[34] Ulitz adheres, in the main, to the same style and subject matter: A middle-aged intellectual, brought to realize by the outbreak of World War I that he is a coward, commits suicide on a boat to India; he finds that he may be able to escape the war but not himself. Ulitz converts a sad fate into tragedy by making us see that his hero's self-understanding misses the mark: Cowardice, in a senseless war, is justified. In one stylistic device, the insertion of an emotion-charged Expressionistic poem ostensibly written by the hero, Ulitz does show a modicum of development towards greater abstractions.

More than eight years elapsed before the appearance of Ulitz's next story, "Der verwegene Beamte oder Was ist die Freiheit," (The Daring Civil Servant, or, What Is Freedom),[35] in which a Prussian official flees the constraints of his position for a brief nonconformist's life and a spectacular nonconformist's death. In this story, too, autobiography nurtured the plot. The model for the daring civil servant was still living, but the story also pictured the precariousness of his own civil service status as a high-school teacher, Ulitz told me on 11 October 1962. But throughout, biography and autobiography give way to inner visions: "The park quivered with life, growth could be perceived with one's nose; fertility rolled across the fresh soil like a colt, chestnut trees held up their buds like plump fists." Frequently Ulitz used subject-object reversal: "The next day intoxicating May fell upon him." Examples of prosopopoeia also permeate the story: "A painful ringing tore the silently flowing time." Moreover, as Ulitz told me, the hero's name, as in so many Expressionistic works, becomes a sobriquet; Flondersug, termed "a unique name in Germany" by the hero, is in reality a *Schüttelreim* (Spoonerism) for *Sonderflug* (Special Excursion). All these characteristics add up to a dramatic metamorphosis of style in Ulitz' writing.

"Das wunderbare Schiff,"[36] Ulitz' final contribution to the *Neue Merkur*, marks the completion of his evolution. His stylistic features are stretched to the limits of their potential: "Die Sterne [waren] krank" ("the stars were sick"); the visions, as that of the magical ship, become realities; the names such as Turrwull and Löma, hero and heroine, are no longer suggestive sobriquets but evocative exoticisms. When Ulitz briefly afterwards reverted to writing Silesian folk literature, it was probably because the style of his middle period had reached its consummation.

Why did Frisch endorse this development even to its logical extreme? That he did so is clear in his letter to Director Kilpper of 1924; Frisch, in fact, reserved his most lavish praise for "Das wunderbare Schiff," a story that ultimately became the opening chapter of *Der Eroberer*, Ulitz' most consistently and resolutely Expressionistic novel.

It appears likely that Frisch spotted a constant within Ulitz' development which, doubtless, assured Ulitz the continued favor of the *Merkur*'s editor. As Werner Mahrholz puts it: "A fullness of experience and experienced suffering which border on barbarity and wildness force him to write."[37] Or, as Ulitz put it, less tortuously, in our 1962 interview: "I simply wrote what I felt compelled to write." In short, his stories, no matter how unrealistic, never equivocated; through all stylistic convolutions the engaged poet clearly speaks. In "Das wunderbare Schiff," for example, all his sympathies are with the poor, despised, clownish outsider; in "Der verwegene Beamte" the newspaper editor becomes a victim of human inhumanity, a symbol at once pitiable, accusatory, and terrifying. The evocation of the editor, Schottländer, "murdered by Nationalists," is reminiscent of Ulitz' *Ararat*, in which a Christian-German officer is resuscitated from the depths of despair through the ministrations of a Russian Jewish rabbi. Ulitz sides with the stepchildren of this world. "Meine Sympathie für Juden geht durch alle meine Werke," he told me. His sympathies for the wretched, his choice of the Jew as their symbol, were bound to strike a responsive chord in Frisch.

There is direct evidence to support this inference. In October 1924 Frisch assigned an article, "Der metaphysische Roman (Ponten-Ulitz-Lübbe),"[38] to one of his regular reviewers, Hans Poeschel—hence to someone who represented, if in the widest sense, editorial policy. Poeschel wrote: "Demonically objective, like a Büchner or Grabbe, free of revolutionary resentment, free of hate, but with burning soul Ulitz has written here [in the novel *Das Testament*] the history of the ordeal of the German intellectual in particular, 'the poem of poetry's collapse.' " What Poeschel describes as passionate compassion indeed permeates Ulitz' work.

Frisch's reaction to the various stages of Döblin's and Ulitz' evolution is detectable from their contributions, the editorial correspondence, and in personal interviews. By comparing these reactions and Frisch's assessment of other Expressionists, we can arrive at a further significant conclusion about Frisch's attitude towards the movement, one which may even be symptomatic of his times.

Walter Sokel, in his excellent 1959 examination of Expressionism, assesses the movement as follows: "Utter failure or at best ephemeral success was the fate of former Expressionists who placed the ethical ideal, the gospel of moral regeneration, in the foreground. A very different kind of success came to those Expressionists who had never concerned themselves with hope for 'the new man,' but had developed new forms in which to express their despair."[39] This is a literary historian speaking, drawing a correct judgment long after the event. But Frisch, from his contemporary vantage point, came to a different conclusion. The editor, adjudged by many as "endowed with the nose of a bloodhound" for all shifts in literary trends, rejected the "formalists" and published the advocates of the "new man." Hence Frisch appreciated Döblin as a seeker after new human values and rejected him when the form (as Frisch mistakenly thought) became his paramount concern. He upheld Ulitz because he thought he spotted, beneath all experiments, an abiding concern for human regeneration. And so it went with others: the formalist Benn was dropped, the reformer Becher wooed;[40] the middle-class poet Pulver was not reinvited after 1921, but Heinrich Lersch, the spokesman of the laborer, carried to the last.[41]

Three other Expressionistic poets, contributors to the first two volumes, invite—if for other reasons—juxtaposition and comparison. By reading them for contrast, a procedure which the perusal of the bound volumes of any belletristic journal automatically suggests and one as multifaceted as the *Merkur* almost compels, we can draw further conclusions about the magazine, the literary market place, and Expressionism.

Of the temporary type of Expressionist, Sokel says that many "merely copied a few devices of modernism, but remained basically old-fashioned in their form."[42] Gottfried Kölwel's poetry, which appeared in the last war-time volume and again in the first post-war year, perfectly illustrates this observation—as the poet himself came to realize. In an autobiographical sketch he virtually admits as much: "What an impetuous, headstrong period of youth! With all the strengths and errors of the times! What was strong, natural and simple remained."[43] Kölwel's biographer, Ernst Alker, puts it even more concretely by referring to Kölwel's "expressionistically oriented early period [and] the linguistically conservative period that followed."[44] As we know from the unpublished correspondence between Kölwel and Martin Buber, his "literary mentor," the poet arrived at a conservative language, more germane to his nature, through the guidance of the Jewish theologian.[45]

The change in Kölwel occurred, demonstrably, in 1921 or 1922. In his "Nachtlied,"[46] we find the following Expressionistic strophe, strongly reminiscent of Werfel:

> Seligster von allen Söhnen
> Bruder auch vom fernsten Ding
> aufgelöst zu lauter Tönen
> Schwebte ich im blauen Ring.

(Most blessed one of all the sons / brother of remotest things / all dissolved in nought but tones / hovered I in azure rings.)

When Kölwel's poem "Gewitterhymne" (Hymn to a Thunderstorm) appeared,[47] his poetic vision, though not his metaphors, followed more traditional paths:

> Donnernd
> stürzen die Scherben des Himmels
> hinter erschrockenen Wäldern hinab.

(Thunderingly / the shards of heaven tumble / down behind startled woods.) Then, on 10 September 1920 he submitted a story, "Der Schlüssel" (The Key), a traditional village tale of a hard-hearted housewife and her abused servant girl, who exchanges her enslavement for a brothel. Kölwel, in a covering letter of that date, said of the story that, in its form, it was "free of all ballast": He was awaiting the publication of a prose volume, with which he was striking out into new directions. It was his intention to help guide a modern, disintegrating, chaotic prose if not back to, at least toward, an archetypal purity. At one time people like Kleist, Peter Hebel and others had drawn on the existence of this source. The story was rejected. Although the *Neue Merkur* was eclectic, and Frisch, as Alker correctly points out,[48] highly esteemed Kölwel—and Buber for that matter—he stopped short of publishing experiments moving in the direction of the nineteenth century.

The spontaneous Expressionist is exemplified by Joachim Benn (a cousin of Gottfried Benn), whose death in war at age thirty-two occurred at the very beginning of his literary career. Elsewhere I have detailed his biography; it had to be based, in part, on scattered records of the City of Munich, which indicates his present obscurity. Benn deserves better of us: as columnist of the *Frankfurter Zeitung*, he was one of the first critics to apply the term "Expressionism," originally confined to the Fine Arts, to the realm of literature. As "Franz Marc's prophet" (Rudolf Geck so called him in an obituary in the *Frankfurter Zeitung*[49]), he occasionally reached, in his few short stories, the luminous and extravagant coloration and expressiveness of Marc's paintings. The opening paragraph of his "legendary tale" entitled "Elfriede"[50] exemplifies his style:

> The Spring dragon had been lying above the house for seven days and seven nights. Its tail whipped the flanks of the high tenement cage so that they, rocking gently like the walls of the car of a balloon, rattled all their windows. In the meantime its mouth howled into the chimney and into every crevice of both exposed walls. It was as though ghosts were screaming who, circling incessantly, were fighting one another in overcrowded skies; or as if a child were breaking out into crying. In between, at regular intervals, a hollow drone, as if a fish, swimming in the void beyond, was venting unbearable pain through a sigh.

Expressionistic prose is rare: "In reality only a few authors represent Expressionism in the realm of prose writing."[51] Joachim Benn was one of these few. In his prose, Expressionistic style was natural and appropriate.

By comparison the poems and short story by Albert Ehrenstein, separated from Joachim Benn's contribution by the span of about one year, are shown up for what they are: excellent in themselves but their Expressionism imitative and spurious. There have been, in the past, several reasons for questioning the label of "Expressionist" which has been affixed to Ehrenstein's works by all histories of modern literature. For one, in an age when virtually every Expressionist expounded his theory

of the movement, Ehrenstein mentions the term but once in his entire
work—and there, in the grotesque *Kimargouel*,[52] he lampoons the term
and the movement. It seems equally significant that Mrs. Walden, when
publishing a history and anthology of her late husband's Expressionistic
magazine, *Der Sturm*, omitted Ehrenstein, one of its most frequent
contributors.[53]

The most compelling evidence, however, is internal. Against the background of Joachim Benn's prose, suffused in Expressionism, Ehrenstein's
contributions display but an Expressionistic façade—and that only sporadically. Ehrenstein's first poem in the *Merkur*, "Der ewige Schlaf,"[54]
for example, at least retains the extravagant vocabulary of Expressionism, though its vision goes little beyond that of, say, Hölty in his poem
"Rosen auf den Weg gestreut." Ehrenstein begins his poem:

> Ich war der silberschenklige Schenke
> und schenkte den weltentrückenden Wein.
> Bin ich entwirbelt schon dem Freudentanz der Zeiten,
> hat schon die Lust sich drohend umgeschwungen
> in Trauer?

(I was the silvery-limbed cup-bearer / and poured the wine that trans-
ports from the earth. / Have I already whirled away from the joyous
dance of time, / has already pleasure turned, with menace, / into grief?)

But by the time Ehrenstein reached the seventh and final strophe
almost all vestiges of Expressionism disappeared:

> So lass auch du die purpurne Gebärde,
> du bist der gute Tod,
> ich bin ein Häuflein Erde.
> O komme bald und menge mich
> Erde in die Erde.

(So stop you too that purple gesture, / you are gentle death / I am a little
dust heap. / O come you soon and blend me / dust into the dust.)

In Ehrenstein's short story, "Wodianer,"[55] the flirtation with Expressionism is equally sporadic: only at the end do we have a glimpse of
Expressionism or Surrealism. As the passive hero commits suicide, he
hears the voice, in a slightly Czech accent, of the eternal tram conductor.

It may well be that in Ehrenstein we have an example of poetic mim-
icry, a protective coat to assure publication. Ehrenstein, who was driven
all his life by a compulsive and deeply honest urge to be heard, may have
instinctively and successively adopted various guises to assure himself a

hearing—as here in the *Merkur*. Alfred Beigel, author of the only monograph to date on Ehrenstein, comes to a similar conclusion.[56] He argues
that Ehrenstein used this new literary movement as a guise, to assure
himself publication both for the sake of his message and for eking out a
bare existence as a freelance writer.

After the publication of "Wodianer," Frisch rejected all further manuscripts by Ehrenstein, although the two remained good friends, as
indicated in a letter of 21 December 1933 (now in the Wiener National-
bibliothek). Might it have been that Frisch sensed Ehrenstein's disguise
and preferred, in the long run, an unabashed traditionalist to one sailing
under the false colors of Expressionism?

Another author, not mentioned before as either a traditionalist or
modernist, and certainly not as an Expressionist, must be included here
as one of Frisch's most important discoveries of new talent. Robert
Walser, eternal vagabond and roustabout, classified in histories of literature all the way from a precursor to Kafka to a harbinger of Dylan
Thomas, came to Frisch's attention as early as 1906 when both resided
in Berlin. Frisch was then dramaturgist for Reinhardt's Deutsches Theater; Walser was staying at the residence of his brother Karl, decorator
[*Bühnenmaler*] for the same theater. As Fega Frisch related to me in
1961, Walser, the eternal outsider, felt at home in the company of Frisch
and his friends: "In our circle, to which the Stuckens, . . . also belonged,
Walser appeared to feel at home."

Frisch recognized Walser's unique talent immediately; he published
Walser's "jewels in prose" from the first volume of the *Neue Merkur* to
the last. Thus Frisch became, together with a very small but highly select
group of writers—Musil, Kafka, Morgenstern, Hesse, Blei, Brod, Hofmannsthal, Walter Benjamin, and Stefan Zweig, one of Walser's earliest
champions. Their combined acumen and Frisch's zest for experiments
led to Walser's publication then and, indirectly, to today's "Walser
renaissance."[57]

Walser's first contributions were six small, disconnected "Prosa-
stücke."[58] The late Carl Seelig, Walser's friend and the editor of his
collected works, called them "a unique interplay of irony and solemn
sentimentality for nature, of demonism and childish naiveté, of metro-
politan pertness and rural bourgeois solidity."[59] The irony in the sketch
"Hanswurst" (Clown) is unmistakable; the solemn description of nature
is pervasive in "Spaziergang" (The Stroll), where he evokes the picture,
"it was as though heavens were a cheek aglow with happiness and bliss");
the demonism, anticipating Kafka, prevails in "Eine Stadt" (A City), his
naiveté in "Ausgang" (Carefree Walk), his impishness in "Stellungs-
gesuch" (Job Application), hints of rural bourgeois solidity likewise

in "Ausgang," where even the dogs of a farmhouse wish a good morning to the narrator by nuzzling him.

Two other works by Walser appeared in the course of the first two *Jahrgänge*. In the novella "Sebastian," Walser tells in whimsical language, and ironic detachment, but with symbolic profundity how a detective traps a murderer into confession by suddenly confronting him in a mask, a replica of his victim's face. Several months later, in June 1915, Walser contributed an autobiographical "Reisebeschreibung," in which the poet, with his attitude of *dolce far niente* appears almost as a reincarnation of Eichendorff's "Taugenichts" (Ne'er-do-well).[60] It is fair to add that Walser's naiveté and naturalness were completely genuine. On 12 October 1962 in Zurich, Max Rychner recalled an illustrative incident for me: "When Hans Trog, editor of the feuilleton of the *Neue Zürcher Zeitung* in 1920, held a public reading of works by Walser, the latter came there, took a seat in the first row and applauded his own works with boundless enthusiasm." Today, in reading Walser's ingenuous prose amidst the often studied Expressionistic works in the first volumes of the *Neue Merkur*, one feels as if a wide-open countryside and a mysterious green forest were set down amidst stylized gardens and crowded cities. Yet his stories also abound in unobtrusive symbolism that anticipates Kafka. Perhaps out of this realization the present-day *Merkur*, in a way the successor to its namesake, recently republished "Sebastian," together with an intriguing commentary and a fictional continuation by Peter O. Chotjewitz.[61]

Like Walser's, several other literary works defy easy qualification. It is surprising, however, that they were written by authors whose niche in the history of literature seems to have been carved long ago. But it was one of the most striking characteristics of the *Neue Merkur*, especially in its early volumes, that representative authors broke forth with unrepresentative works: Max Mell with a psychological novella; Heinrich Mann with a drama; Frank Wedekind with a historical drama about Bismarck; and, after the war, Thomas Mann with an epic.[62] Max Mell told me on 23 December 1961 that he had intended this particular story for the *Neue Merkur* from the start, "da es [das Werk] abseits lag" ("since it was off the beaten track"). As Mell implied, it was outré, not only for the times, but also for him. Each of the other authors, the brothers Mann and Wedekind, might have said as much.

Mell, generally classified as a "Viennese Neo-Romantic," radically departs, in his short story "Die Brille" ("The Spectacles"), from his conventional works. Though told with Mell's usual classical restraint, transparent syntax, simple language, and dialectically colored dialogue, the story arrives at a climax of physical and psychological horror totally atypical for him: a blind girl, the tragic heroine of the story, gouges the remaining eye of her pretty, one-eyed playmate. Only in rereading the story do we realize how various seemingly trivial events mark the heroine's psychological deterioration and, cumulatively, motivate, in a manner reminiscent of Schnitzler, her final burst of rage and jealousy. Max Mell, son of the director of an asylum for the blind, had observed them in depth.

To find any story of Mell's in a prominent journal was strange in itself; Frisch reported to Kilpper (in a letter of 27 December 1923) that most of Mell's stories had appeared in ephemeral publications, while Soergel stated that the Austrian, as a short-story writer, was virtually unknown.[63] Yet even cognoscenti of Mell's previous stories must have been startled by this one. No doubt the effect was what Frisch intended. Chance played a major role in the acquisition of this short story. Mell and Frisch, though both Austrians, had met in 1906 at the Monopol, the famous gathering-place of Berlin's artists and writers. Then dramaturgist for the Reinhardt Theater, Frisch frequented the Monopol in the company of the Reinhardt troupe. When he founded the *Neue Merkur*, he remembered his Berlin acquaintance and requested an article from him: "Was erwartet die neue Generation von der Zukunft Österreichs?" ("What does the new generation expect of Austria's future?"). This article, announced in a "house-ad" of the first number, never materialized. As Mell told me on 20 December 1961 he had not been able to write the Austrian article because of the stresses of war. Frisch had been insisting, so he had sent him "Die Brille," which had been intended for the *Neue Merkur* even before it fully took shape. Since the subject was off the beaten track, the *Neue Merkur* was the logical magazine for it. The story had gone through a long process of genesis, but a reason for molding it was needed and Mell discovered that in the newly founded magazine. Here the term "literary market place" seems particularly apropos. Not only did the founding of a magazine provide the final impetus towards artistic creation, but the author then submitted it in place of a political prognosis.

The other two "excursions" by established authors must be numbered among Frisch's less happy choices. Heinrich Mann, who contributed a drama, "Die große Liebe," did not take his dramas as seriously as his prose; in his autobiography he says that his period as a playwright provided him with easier years than his very strenuous ones as a novelist.[64] And even among his dramas, "Die große Liebe," which was premiered in Berlin in 1913, is one of his less memorable. It repeats a theme which Mann in other works elaborated upon more skillfully, "the impossibility of reconciling human weakness with the true and ardent love which expresses itself in a work of art."[65] Its inclusion in the *Neue Merkur* probably sprang from Frisch's desire to be among the first to publish a drama by Heinrich Mann.

It is hard to fathom why four acts of Wedekind's five-act play, "Bismarck, Bilder aus der deutschen Geschichte,"[66] were published. The drama can scarcely be defended on literary grounds. Coming from an experienced playwright, its exposition seems amateurish: Otto von Bismarck and his wife, under the thinnest of pretexts, reflect upon their past and narrate events which may perhaps be new to the audience, but are, as is painfully obvious, well-known facts to the partners in the dialogue. Bismarck: "Do you, perhaps, recall the dream which I told one morning in Spring?" His wife: "Certainly I remember. . . . ." Bismarck: "I dreamt —I will never forget this. . . ." And he proceeds to tell the dream once again. Also the dialogue is stilted, the humor heavy-handed, and the continuity obscure, even for an intelligent reader of 1914 well-versed in history. After all, fifty years had by then elapsed since the Prussian wars against Denmark and Austria, the subject of the drama. Wedekind himself must have felt that the drama lacked discipline; in readying it for publication in book form he added the sentence: "For the purposes of presentation it will prove necessary to make some cuts or to skip one or the other tableau, since the author was more concerned with exhausting the dramatic impact of the negotiations than to adjust them to the limitations of one evening in the theater."[67]

What, then, induced Frisch to publish the drama? No doubt he was, to some extent, influenced by considerations of the literary market place and by personal predilections. Wedekind always aroused interest; the play, which he had dedicated to Bismarck's biographer, Maximilian Harden, marked such a radical change in the iconoclastic Wedekind that it had value as a literary curiosity. Also the rights to it were easy to acquire, because the Georg Müller Verlag was just then (1912–21) publishing Wedekind's collected works. Furthermore Frisch highly esteemed Wedekind and published two laudatory criticisms of him—at a time when few articles devoted to literary criticism appeared in the *Merkur*. One was a very detailed appreciation of a scene in Wedekind's *Marquis von Keith* by Thomas Mann, the other a defense of Wedekind's morality by Bruno Frank. And in 1920 Frisch published yet another article, Kurt Martens' memoirs of the recently deceased author.[68] In themselves, however, these explanations are scarcely adequate to explain the publication of so flawed a work as the Bismarck drama.

More likely, political rather than literary or personal reasons were the predominant factor in Frisch's decision. He himself consistently tempered his war-time patriotism with a spirit of conciliation. Precisely this largesse and reasonableness grace the Bismarck of Wedekind's drama.

Is it not likely that Frisch wanted to suggest, through publishing it, the same moderation to the inept government of his times?

In the works of famous German authors Frisch frequently sought the atypical; in those of foreigners, the exotic. With the exception of a historical scene from a drama by Martin du Gard,[69] Frisch chose works of great foreign authors that gave his readers and, probably, himself a respite from the calamity of war. In this the *Neue Merkur* was not alone: it was the time when Stucken, for example, "discovered" South America; Hauptmann and Hesse, India; Klabund, China. In the *Merkur* the foreign works, by origin, style, and intent worlds apart, had the exoticism of their setting in common, whether it was Paul Claudel's icy and Utopian Caucasus in "Tête d'or" [*Goldhaupt*]—a work revived in 1967, most successfully, by the Odéon Theatre in Paris; Otto Rung's intrigue-ridden Egypt in "Fadl Paschas Schicksal"; Micha bin-Gurion's (Berdyczewski) legendary Palestine of Biblical times; or Michail Prischwin's "Bilder von der Steppe," which combines descriptions of the Russian steppe with visions of the Arabian desert.[70]

Together with these four translations from, respectively, French, Danish, Yiddish, and Russian, the *Neue Merkur* offered several German works as further escape routes from the uninviting Europe of the times, such as Klabund's recreation of Chinese poetry, Leo Perutz' short story about Cortez' conquests, "Der Tod des Meisters der Materie," and Norbert Jacques' "Jangtse-Tagebuch."[71] Finally, Arnold Ulitz' aforementioned story of a German's flight from the war suggests that this galaxy of works with an exotic setting was, far from being fortuitous, a sign of the times.

In any discussion of the foreign literature published in the *Merkur*, the quality of the translations requires comment. Frisch, a translator himself, once expressed the opinion that a work in translation becomes, if it has intrinsic worth and the translator is not a charlatan, an integral part of German literature.[72] In his magazine he tried to prepare for such a happy transplantation. He entrusted belletristic contributions—though not always articles and essays—to some of the best translators in the field: i.e., translations from the Russian to Alexander Eliasberg, Arnold Ulitz, and to Fega Frisch, his own wife (one of the nominees for the 1962 translator's prize of the Deutsche Akademie für Sprache und Literatur).[73] For the translation of poems from *Leaves of Grass* he acquired Hans Reisiger, whose Whitman translations Thomas Mann considered the equal of Schlegel-Tieck's Shakespeare translation and whom Gay Wilson Allen, author of the *Whitman Handbook*, praised as one of the world's truly great Whitman scholars and translators.[74] This work is now regarded as a classic. For translating Paul Claudel's work, Frisch secured

Jakob Hegner who, according to Soergel-Hohoff, "translated, printed, and performed Claudel, when his manuscripts, in France, went still from person to person in handwritten copies!"[75] Finally, the masterly (post-war) translations of D. H. Lawrence were undertaken by Mrs. Else Jaffé-Richthofen,[76] Lawrence's sister-in-law—at Lawrence's own behest, as Mrs. Jaffé told me on 19 July 1962. "Translations are outrages," she added. If she is right—and she well may be—Frisch and the *Neue Merkur* at least tried to reduce the extent of the outrage.

The final point to be made about the pre-war and war-time *Neue Merkur* is, properly speaking, no longer part of the magazine's history, yet it has much relevance for the subsequent history of German literature. Many works by important authors, first published in the journal, underwent considerable change before they appeared as books. Hence the *Merkur* sometimes took on the character of a repository for original versions of literary works. One example is particularly striking. Arnold Zweig's novella "Der Mann des Friedens" appeared first in the May 1915 *Merkur*; the version in Zweig's *Ausgewählte Werke* now bears the title "Helbert Friedebringer" and the marks of considerable revision.[77] In a letter of 10 October 1962, Arnold Zweig so informed me and added about the first version: "I had written it in January of 1915 before I had ever experienced the war personally."

A close reading of the two versions reveals the principle behind Zweig's severe editing of the original. The omniscient author who in the first version considered all participants about equally guilty shifted, in the second, more blame for the outbreak of World War I to Austria. Germany's conduct of the war and the war-time attitudes of its population are now condemned more sharply. By means of an insertion, an account of the hero's trip through Germany, the contrast between the spirit of Weimar and Potsdam is delineated. The fanatic militancy of the women and youngsters at home was not only uncovered but also commented upon and, finally, condemned far more sharply than earlier by the hero's son, disillusioned during his military service. Through the addition of a few summary sentences, Zweig also reveals his hero's fate. In short, by changing his story Zweig underscored its moral implications and the symbolic significance of his hero, the prototype of the better German and European.

Doubtless these changes made for a novella more cohesive in form and more cogent in its philosophy, but they also entailed some sacrifices. The hero, by becoming more humane, became less human. His weaknesses— his egoism, his tyrannical streak—perhaps undesirable in the moral exemplar he became in the second version, had lent him greater credibility as a character in the first. His alienation from his son, motivated psychologically in the first version, results in the second from his ideological fight against all proponents of the Wilhelmine monarchy. This new motivation ennobles him, but at the same time also makes it more difficult for the reader, presumably a less lofty creature, to identify with him. The publication of the second version, therefore, did not render the first, now extant only in the pages of the *Neue Merkur*, in any sense obsolete.

7

The Lyre
of Mercury: II

1919-1923

At first glance the belletristic part of the post-war *Merkur* (1919–23) appears to be a replica of the earlier volumes. Again it produced a judicious admixture of experimental and traditional literature, the same impartiality vis-à-vis the opposing literary camps, the same cosmopolitanism in its publication of foreign literature. And it featured well-known authors in atypical works once again: the philosopher Ernst Bloch in remarkably well-told anecdotes ("Philosophische Anekdoten") and the fiction writer Thomas Mann in a quite unsuccessful classical epic, "Gesang vom Kindchen."[1] But if we examine the *Neue Merkur* more closely, especially as a barometer of the literary market place, we will discern that the Expressionists, during the intervening two years, 1916–18, had suddenly become the "Establishment" and that three new forces, the post-Expressionists or mutators of Expressionism, the resurgent traditionalists, and the exponents of *Neue Sachlichkeit* (New Objectivity), had moved into the van. Hence the balance was maintained, in part, by a reaction of tradition against the modernists, whereas before the modernists were the insurgents.

There is abundant evidence that the Expressionists had "arrived" during the last years of the war. Only a brief time before, as Karl Otten pointed out recently, "a new generation of publishers and discoverers . . . among them the Georg Müller Verlag" and "journals in which the opinion of the few can find refuge and solidify" had been necessary to bring the representatives of the new movement to public attention. "Works were printed which quite clearly went counter to public taste and to which the readers of the traditional publishing houses would have issued death certificates."[2]

But Otten's description, as we now can see, applied only to the early years of Expressionism. After the war and until about 1925, most Expressionists modified their style; they had become more traditional. Also, though they still did not appeal to a mass audience, they had conquered enough German readers to make the publication of their works "good business." The more moderate revolutionaries had become fashionable.

In the letters emanating from the editorial office of the revived *Merkur*, these authors were not only solicited but wooed as well. Hausenstein, for example, in a letter of 2 February 1920, invoked joint military service with Gottfried Benn, a brief period in Brussels, to gain a contribution from him. In turned out to be Benn's famous poem "Schutt."[3] Frisch, on his part, accepted in writing on 22 June 1922 a group of poems by Johannes R. Becher after the most cursory of readings;[4] they appeared in the *Sonderheft Dichtung* of November/December 1921. This special issue was, in fact, symptomatic for *all* the issues of 1919–23; at least half of the belletristic contributions were Expressionistic in nature. Old contributors, such as Döblin and Ulitz, mingled with new ones, including Paul Adler, Martin Buber, Oscar Fontana, A. M. Frey, Iwan Goll, Hermann Kasack, Heinrich Mann, Max Pulver, and Armin Wegner, the last being one of the few writers whose prose was as unmistakably Expressionistic as his poetry. In short, the Expressionists, on the evidence of a single but highly representative magazine, had carried the day.

The *Neue Merkur* also supplied one hint for its triumph. If it is true, as Paul Pörtner maintains,[5] that the successors by their extremism become the pacemakers for their predecessors—or, to put it bluntly, that later poets make yesterday's revolutionaries look conservative by comparison, then the *Merkur* provides evidence for just such a phenomenon. Dadaism, the logical extreme of some Expressionists' penchant for artistic suicide, burst upon the literary scene while Expressionism was on the verge of a breakthrough. Otto Flake's hostile commentary, "The few talents among the Dadaists will soon outgrow this first, rather infantile, stage for something important," and André Gide's "Dada" which, though not unmindful of the necessity for such a phenomenon, labeled Dadaism "Operation Demolition," both testify to the discomfiture it caused.[6] The annoyance with Dadaism probably mitigated the annoyance with Expressionism.

It is hard to find a common denominator among these diversified Expressionistic works; unmistakably, works predominate which attempt to transcend the boundaries of Expressionism. As Günter Blöcker describes this phase of Expressionism, "it becomes manifest, that of every literary movement only that remains which no longer entirely belongs to it, that it only matures in those instances where it secretly defies the dogma which it assumes it is serving."[7]

The departure from dogma took various directions. In Klabund's "Flieder" (Lilacs)[8] the poet, in exploring the thoughts and feeling of a man dying, like himself, of tuberculosis, combined with unique success the stylistic elements of Impressionism and Expressionism. The psychological exploration of a dying man's mind is reminiscent, in its sharp analysis, of Schnitzler's famous impressionistic story *Sterben* (Dying). Such details as the hero's desperate attempt to cling to life by draining from it the last physical impressions—the smell of a flower, the feel of a tree—parallel passages in Schnitzler. Frequently, though, these impressions are but the springboard for expressionistic metaphors or visions. The intensity of his love for nature and for a woman begets "the fragrance of lilacs that drifted up to his heart"; the eyes of his beloved are transformed into a heaven in which the protagonist blazes forth as a star: "The Algiers Observatory registered its coruscation as the appearance of a new star."

Heinrich Mann's novella "Der Jüngling," Hans Reisiger's "Blitzschlag im Frühling," Wegner's "Der Knabe Hüssein," Ernst Weiß' "Die Verdorrten" progress—each in its own way—so far beyond Expressionism and towards realistic genre pictures of the post-war period that the variations all but obscure the Expressionistic themes.[9] Mann's picaresque tale of a young man's retrogression from young idealist to opportunistic actor, unravelled through his adventures with three different women, evokes Expressionistic conceits only in some descriptive passages, when Mann exalts his lovers: "The cold, moonlight, and the countryside trembling away into the distance seized the motionless couple like the sounds of things that had never existed." But with the exception of a few such passages, the story realistically, sometimes even sardonically, depicts the world of the theater, post-war Munich, and a Zurich unaffected by war.

Reisiger's debt to Expressionism is traceable only through the ecstatic tone pulsating through his dirge for the revolutionaries of November 1918. He begins his story in the manner of a report: "The roof of the newspaper emporium was burning, and from down below approached the rumbling of the flame-throwers." However, in the closing of his "sketch," as Reisiger calls it, a blending of reality and its transfiguration in the mind of the heroine lend Expressionistic ecstasy to an otherwise senseless and brutal struggle to the death: "A blinding glare of fire devoured everything that flashed through her mind. . . . And suddenly a stream of ardent tenderness burst from her." This startlingly successful balance of realistic reporting and intense feeling was the result of artistic intent, as Reisiger wrote me on 21 September 1962: The form corresponded to his efforts (respectively, inclination) to bring to life the so-called "monological dialogues" of man with himself—an effort that later was to earn him the appellation "poet of internal monologue."

Wegner's narrative, set in Turkey around the time of the battle of the Gallipoli Peninsula, destroys with the stylistic devices of Expressionism one of its favorite conventions. Unlike the many Activistic works in which the hero, shocked and chastened by the experience of war, emerges as a militant pacifist, "Der Knabe Hüssein" chronicles the debauching of a sensitive, horrified eleven-year-old into a war-lover, honored and admired by his compatriots. He becomes a *topos* of his times: "Hussein stormed across the hills, down the plain, through a country mangled by horror, which lay cowering beneath the grey skies [and] with his foot stepped upon the eyes of corpses." This story marked not only a departure but also an inversion of the conventional Expressionistic story of development: the "New Man" is a man of war rather than of peace; Wegner, a dedicated pacifist, obviously intended it as a warning against a false optimism of the Activists. It was a dangerous device; to the unsubtle reader, the horror of a young killer-in-uniform is drowned out by the vivid retelling of his heroic adventures, a warning easily misread as approval. Did Frisch later realize the dilemma? When Wegner, who remained a valued contributor of lyric poetry, requested (on 1 July 1922) a review of his new volume of novellas, in which "Der Knabe Hüssein" was the title story, Frisch, curiously, neither answered nor complied. Did he wish to avoid the repudiation of a story, published in the *Merkur*, which, however excellent and experimental, seemingly approached the romantic battle scenes of Ernst Jünger, Germany's foremost apostle of war?

Ernst Weiß fused a new realism and a close observation of the post-war years—"his stock had risen, meanwhile, from 700 to 825"—with a physician's clinical dissection of his characters. But the inner life of his characters is frequently evoked in the dithyrambic conceits of the Expressionists. "All passion turned tremblingly into indescribable rapture; he loved her like a high-pitched tone before the deepest depth which bestirred her summer-moist flesh, and both were as an inaudible high, penetrating vibration at the conclusion of their love at the end of the attainable world . . . his silence later on as one with the silence of the forest, her trembling, so maidenly, as one with the trembling of the wind-brushed birch tree." Weiß's involvement with his characters, often camouflaged beneath the detachment of the physician, stands revealed in a letter to Frisch of 30 March 1922. He was sending Frisch a story, "The Withered Ones," on which he had worked, with long interruptions, for five years. It was therefore possible that the work did not possess, especially in the opening sections, the cohesiveness and simplicity for which Weiß was striving. The genesis of five years, uncommonly long for a story of thirty *Merkur* pages, resulted, one suspects, from the author's involvement with his characters. As he suffered with them he reverted, *malgré lui*, to the expressiveness of his earlier works—at the expense of simplicity. Weiß, one of the few reviewers of the *Merkur* who cajoled Frisch into printing a favorable review of a Dadaist (Melchior Vischer), apparently bade his farewell to Expressionism only after overcoming a persisting predilection for the style of his earlier period.[10]

In all of the foregoing stories, Expressionistic passages appear side-by-side with realistic invocations of the present or recent past. Oscar Fontana, frequently described as a pioneer of Austrian Expressionism,[11] used a different approach. In an attempt to lend permanence and universality to a depiction of the contemporary scene—a purpose that made him gravitate naturally to the like-minded editors of the *Neue Merkur*— he fused the strict structure of the traditional historical novella with the style and language of Expressionism. In these crypto-historical novellas he always wrote of the distant past but meant the present. As he put it in an interview of 21 December 1962, in these four novellas he had tried to be the voice of generations that experienced war and had arrived at a new mental attitude. They all had started with a precept of the world in which one had not expected war, a war which, however, came after all. These stories, Fontana said, were not anchored in any ideology, but in human concerns, a word and a concept which at that time had been very much wrinkled and debased, but with which they had grown up. These generations represented a search for salvation, for extrication from confusion. Therefore the story "Der Kreis" (The Circle) also belonged to this group. It showed how someone led a second life, a new life, which arrived, however, at the same destination as the first. They could not help being what they were.

Essentially this is the thesis of Fontana's first contribution, "Der Tribun auf der Flucht,"[12] an account of Gaius Gracchus' assumption of the tribuneship in Rome. Recalling the bloody assassination of his brother Tiberius and foreseeing his own failure, the tribune-elect and erstwhile "social reformer" flees to the countryside to escape the unwanted office and himself. A chance meeting with his ex-wife convinces him that "our destiny is inescapable." Gaius follows the messengers from Rome: "Yes, I follow my summons as Livia followed her summons." By casting his historical narration into the tight form of a traditional novella, but by telling it in the familiar style of Expressionism, Fontana manages to make it timeless: "He felt as though a colossal, collapsed rocky desert was receiving him who was transformed into the ancient and holy she-wolf and he was offering her teats to prostrate, hungering mankind." The reformer, even though he despairs of success, even though he recognizes that "the fight for the leavings in the masters' bowls is eternal," cannot abandon the sick, the hungry, the needy. In 1920, after social reformers such as Eisner had been assassinated and Leviné had been executed for advocating a new social order, Fontana's story of Tiberius and Gaius was not only timely but timeless as well.

In his last contribution to the *Neue Merkur*, "Die Nacht in Mantua,"[13] Fontana again uses a historical episode to make a humanistic appeal. His novella is a fictionalized version of the life and death of Salomon Molchos (1500–1530), a pretended Messiah whose amazing prophecies brought him the protection of the Pope and the crowned heads of Europe. Fontana imagines his meeting with Charles V, "the ruler of the earth." The Emperor cravenly betrays his own human and humanistic impulses and abandons the Jew to the stake of the Inquisition; unlike Gaius he foresakes his destiny: "Then he was like his ancestors, nothing more than an emperor, hard, old, shriveled, dull, a slave to his work, of which he knew in nightmarish dreams that it was no true work, that his true work and all true achievement had been born and had died for him that night in Mantua." Immediately after writing his story, Fontana, in a letter of 15 July 1924, explained its universal human and humane intent to Frisch in response to an inquiry. Döblin's famous "Burning of the Jews" he only knew from hearsay. He therefore believed that no reminders of it could be present. The non-Jewish elements in the Jewish context Frisch had found he did not deny, he simply was more interested in transporting the content into a general human area. It had been a purely Jewish reference which had drawn his attention to the subject, Meir Wiener's *Messiah* (Loewy, Vienna). This collision of two powers took hold of him, even though he found later, in Grätz's *History of the Jews* that Salomon Molcho probably had been a conscious and unconscious impostor. The myth had grown so strong in him that it could absorb no further historical truth, so that the power politician Molcho became his shoemaker Salomo. In spite of this fact he did not think that he wrote entirely in an unjewish fashion. The willingness and compulsion to serve was one of the great Jewish forces, he felt.

In this story, actually published during the third phase of the *Neue Merkur*'s existence, Fontana again intensifies the more emotional passages through Expressionistic images and vocabulary. As the Emperor meets the Jew, in his jail cell, Fontana describes his reaction: "Then heat and cold was in Salomon; he melted, he froze; he was a fiery river; he was a block of ice." Similar passages recur in two of Fontana's earlier contributions to the *Merkur*. These two novellas, though well-written, represented no departures from Expressionism. "Das Abenteuer" achieves its climactic passage in the neurotic compulsions and fevered visions of the hero; "Himmel und Hölle,"[14] the reunion and reconciliation between murderer and victim in the beyond, adheres completely, in setting, structure, and style, to the Expressionistic movement. A review of 30 August 1922 in the *Kieler Zeitung* (page 21) summarizes this latter novella, an excursion into transcendental realms: "Of the further contents of the issue we shall mention Oscar M. Fontana's novella, which, in bizarre progression, spins a tale of human redemption."

Of the numerous Expressionistic poems some, such as Gottfried Benn's "Schutt," Johannes R. Becher's "Aus Vernichtung," and Klabund's "Ballade vom Schlaf der Kindheit,"[15] have become too well known; others, such as the poems by Max Pulver, Alfons Paquet, Hugo Jacobi, and Friedrich Leopold, have proved too unviable to warrant separate discussion here. Nor do the poets' letters add materially to an understanding of their poems; it is, in fact, remarkable how rarely poems, in contrast to fiction and essays, were accompanied by elucidations. One poem, however, today neither a standard staple of all anthologies nor forgotten, but illustrates the development of literary taste in the *Merkur* and probably amongst the German literati generally. The poem, Iwan Goll's "Ballade in Innsbruck,"[16] is a litany for a dead peasant woman. Expressionistic and traditional means are blended in a new synthesis. Goll, who had until about 1920 represented Expressionism at its most typical and, occasionally, at its best, still utilized it for the close of his poem, a vision of the hero's dead mother performing her daily tasks in heaven. He also reached for Expressionistic effects in lines such as "Und all die müden Bäume der Straß / bekreuzigen sich" and "Der Bach gefriert vor Angst, / . . . die Sonne platzt." (All the tired trees of the road / made the sign of the cross; the brook freezes in fear, / . . . the sun explodes.) But in its first half, a sardonic protest against the exorbitant cost of death, Goll uses a new technological vocabulary, "im internationalen Speisewagen" (in the international dining car), "Totenwagenagentur" (death-car travel agency), "Kontrollkommission" (control commission), "Agrarbank" (Agrarian Bank), and clothes the speech of the bereaved son in realistic dialect: "Mutter, die rote Kuh hat gekalbt" or "Das Heu ist herinnen noch vor dem Sturm" or "Was bollerst du, bammelst du, kicherst du?" (The red cow has calved; the hay is in before the storm; why are you so noisy, why do you dangle, why do you giggle?)

Frisch, who frequently was rather dilatory in publishing poetry, printed this ballad immediately. On 16 September 1922 Goll wrote Frisch. He thanked him most heartily for publishing his poem so quickly. Goll asked specifically for a change of title to "Innsbruck Ballad," if that was all right with Frisch. On 20 July 1923 Goll added: He was working with Frisch with great pleasure and interest, since he considered the editor's magazine one of the few in Germany maintaining standards. The quick publication of the poem and the mutual esteem of author and editor probably indicate that their literary tastes, at least at this time, were not far apart.

Two works, written by Frisch and Hausenstein, further prove that the editors were deliberately moving the literary part of their journal in a direction beyond Expressionism. The first was a novella by Frisch, "Der Weg durch den Traum." I have tried elsewhere to interpret this complex, psychologically involved narrative;[17] here we are concerned with its *locus standi* within Expressionism. It is Expressionistic in its dithyrambic language which occasionally spills over into verse, in its egocentricity—the whole world is moved to help the hero gain cognition and self-knowledge—and in its protracted visions which are parables of his real life. But it is also in these visions, in "the way through the dream," to quote the title, that Frisch parts company with Expressionism. In previous Expressionistic exploitations of dreams the work, as in Strindberg's *Dream Play*, never left the convention of the dream or, as in Toller's *Man and the Masses*, let reality at the end dispel the visions. Frisch breaks the Expressionistic convention by the strength of his psychological insight: the dream is stronger than reality, or, rather, the dream is reality. As the hero, in his moment of self-realization, stumbles forward mentally, he physically falls and dies, crushed on the cobblestones.

While Frisch showed his aesthetic convictions by precept, Hausenstein explained it in critical articles. His notable essay of February/March 1920, "Die Kunst in diesem Augenblick" (Art at this Moment),[18] which heralded three others with approximately the same views (by Rudolf Kayser, Conrad Wandrey, and H. von Wedderkop), said, literally, that Expressionism was dead. A letter from Hausenstein to Ludwig Rosenberger of 24 August 1920, commenting on the results of the article, revealed still more about the editors' view of Expressionism at that time. His statements and those of Kayser had been, of course, exploited as testimonials in a reactionary press. Though predictable, this consequence was no reason for withholding these views. Nowhere had it been a question of "going back" but rather a "going beyond this moment," no matter what the reactionary press had implied. Particularly Hausenstein himself had not advocated a return to Impressionism, but an advance beyond Expressionism into the future, an advance that had long been realized in artistically progressed countries such as France. Beyond its value as a program for the *Neue Merkur*, this letter is, to the best of my knowledge, also the first hint of the dangerous alliance of Expressionism and radicalism. Most critics saw the explosiveness of the mixture only in retrospect.

Despite Hausenstein's protestations to the contrary, one of the *Merkur*'s departures beyond Expressionism was a retreat—if not to impressionism, then to the classical tradition. The *Neue Merkur*, in this respect, conformed to a general trend in German literature. In doing so it published some unforgettable novellas by Hans Carossa, excellent short stories by Rudolf Borchardt, and Felix Braun and, for the rest, emphemeral contributions by authors prominent in their day but practically unread today. By and large, therefore, this advance beyond Expressionism ended in a cul-de-sac.

Yet Carossa, Borchardt, and Braun, the three notable exceptions, added a new dimension to the *Neue Merkur*. Carossa himself was intensely aware of the fact that his two contributions, "Die Krippe" and "Die Forelle"[19] (later parts of the autobiographical novel *Eine Kindheit*), appeared as primitive folk art in a museum of modern art. When "Die Forelle" was published in the so-called "Sondernummer Judentum," Carossa wrote to Dora Brandenburg on 17 September 1921 that "The Trout," in such intellectual Israelitic surroundings, appeared a bit as if it had dropped out of the sky." His comments about the appearance of "Die Krippe" seem equally apt. His unpublished diary bears a 1921 entry on the appearance of "The Crib" in the *Neue Merkur*. It struck him as if one had placed a wax candle between electric arc-lamps. It was a graphic way to contrast naiveté and sophistication.

The publication of these two stories by Carossa, incidentally, exemplified yet another editorial criterion: excerpts or parts of larger works were published only if they had intrinsic unity. The editors frequently rejected even those by prominent contributors, if explicatory prefaces were needed. In the instance of Carossa, Frisch was so convinced of the cohesiveness of the stories apart from the larger work for which they were planned that he, who was meticulous in classifying literary genres, either himself subtitled them "novellas" in the table of contents to Volume V or accepted Carossa's own designation. (Carossa, who occasionally left his nearby physician's office for a brief visit to the editorial rooms of the *Neue Merkur*, might have been present when the index was compiled at the end of the publishing year.)

Recently the opportunity presented itself to verify Frisch's assessment of the stories as autonomous works against Carossa's original intention. Carossa's daughter, now the executor of his papers, was able, a few years ago, to decipher her father's original diary of World War I, the unedited source for his famous war-time memoirs, "Siebenbürgisch-rumänisches Tagebuch," parts of which were also pre-published in the *Neue Merkur*.[20]

Here, under the dateline of 6 September 1917, at Radautz, Bukowina, is a most illuminating entry which was not utilized in the published version of the "Diary." Carossa was reflecting on how quickly his work on *Eine Kindheit* (A Childhood) ought to progress in this room. Again some connections had become clear to him. It was only a matter of not making everything too tight, too condensed, of letting the contents stay lightly in a loose order, so that light and air could enter through the cracks and crannies of the structure for the sake of the recipients. The reader should not be mistreated through a depiction which was too pedantically thorough and which left him without the chance of taking an active part. His power of imagination was to be stimulated into certain directions and not bound or paralysed. Today, in reading Carossa's finished novel, it becomes clear that he carried out his intent of constructing it with numerous interstices.

Like Carossa's novellas, Rudolf Borchardt's "Geschichte des Erben" (Story of the Heir)[21] is reminiscent of an older prose style. Whatever innovations Borchardt may have achieved in poetry, his novellas recall Heinrich von Kleist's nineteenth-century tales. Borchardt's admiration for Kleist's life and works, his facility in re-creating the style of great writers of the past, and the Kleistian density of his sentence structure, which one of the earliest reviewers called "dramatically explosive in its compressed impetus,"[22] suggest that Borchardt consciously reverted to the model of Kleist. The plot of the story, however, appears to have a more modern ancestor. The hero's symbolic name, Adam, and his act of renouncing his inheritance for the sake of finding his own "new destiny," propel the story close to the Expressionists' quest for the new man.

Felix Braun's two novellas appear still more traditional. Braun's *Merkur* review of Carossa's poetry of about the same period was a theoretical advocacy for the return to Classical and Romantic German tradition;[23] in his two novellas he fulfilled his own aesthetic demands. They are curiously nostalgic and romantic; Ferdinand Lion, for that reason, disparaged one of them in a letter to Frisch of 5 March 1922: Braun's novella, which Achim seemed to have written in 1817, he thought bad. But Lion, possibly the most cerebral intellectual among the *Merkur*'s contributors, failed to recognize that of their kind they were small masterpieces. The first, "Die Magd vom Chiemsee,"[24] presents a harmony of Man and Nature which is reminiscent of Adalbert Stifter: the harvest season restores fertility to an unhappy servant girl on a Bavarian farm. The virtually plotless story perfectly balances nature description with insights into the mind and soul of a distraught girl. It earned Braun, as he reported to Frisch on 28 November 1920, enthusiastic encomiums from

Hugo von Hofmannstal and from a wider public: He had not found that much of an echo for a long time.

Braun's second story, "Wunderstunden,"[25] revives the convention of the utopian or revenant village in the language of the late Romantics. ("The Vienna Woods are beautiful; the beech trees with grey or black trunks and green-golden leaves make it so gentle, and the dear, tender larches remove all those anxious feelings, with which the deep forest, as we walk through it alone, pierces our quivering souls.") What distinguishes this story from similar ones of its kind is the essential nature of Braun's mysterious village. The narrator frankly admits at the end that it has no substance in reality, but reflects, rather, poetic imagination spilling over into life. Since it contains autobiographical touches, its genesis, the beginning of such a poetic conceit, is almost as important as the finished work.

An investigation of the genesis of "Wunderstunden" was suggested by Braun's letter of 12 May 1921, in which he told Frisch he was sending his last story, which probably fell into his lap from the skies. Forty years later, on 23 December 1961 in Vienna, Braun explained this rather mysterious remark and the genesis of his story. In the spring of 1921 he was waiting in front of the University of Vienna for his friend, the poet Franz Karl Ginzkey. Strolling down on the ramp students, male and female, couples, young and old, went by. He heard fragments of their conversations. Finally a young couple passed by, happy with springtime. He heard only one word of their conversation which sounded like *kunterbunt* (particolored) or *Wunderstunden* (miraculous hours). The reverie-like word implanted itself into his imagination like a seed. When his friend finally arrived, the story already stood before him in a firm outline. It was finished a few days later.

Frisch's acceptance of the story, so different from the more modern works that surrounded it, completed the genesis. Its appearance brought mixed comments. Outside of Lion's perjoration, there was some favorable reaction, as the author was able to report: In a few days the two stories which appeared in the *Neue Merkur* would be published, together with a third one, by Ruetten and Loenning in Frankfurt, Braun wrote Frisch on 4 January 1923. He owed this literary success, "the only one in years, solely to Frisch and the *Neue Merkur*." It was the strength of the magazine that any single issue was likely to contain something for every educated reader, no matter what his literary taste.

Yet in his wish to make the *Merkur* representative, it is likely that Frisch, in the instance "of the classical revolution or restoration," tried too hard. Except for Carossa and Braun, the contributions of the tra-

ditionalists were undistinguished and sometimes came dangerously close
to being sub-literary. While Frisch's errors in this respect were no
greater than those of his contemporaries—the traditionalists in the *Neue
Merkur* were all widely read—the sureness of judgment here deserted
him for once.

Rudolf Binding's poems, "Stolz und Trauer," criticized elsewhere for
their subtle glorification of war, will serve equally well as examples of
overrated works. The last verse of "Ruh-Spruch" (Maxim of Rest), for
example, though nontendencious, illustrates all the weaknesses of his
lyrics, his unerring instinct for the trite metaphor, a self-conscious striving
for traditional forms through the use of obsolescent syntax, a spurious
profundity, and a penchant for a typographical effect by diminishing
the length of successive lines until but one stressed syllable remains:

> Einem Ende treiben zu die Völker.
> Eine Sonne nur geht über allen
> Menschen hin. Es blüht und stirbt
> alles gleichen Sinnes. Und im Ewigen
> ist das Gute
> wie das Böse
> gut.[26]

The pompous turbidity in Binding's poetry carries over even into his
letters. In one, dated 3 June 1919, he offers his novella, "Die Keusch-
heitslegende" (Legend of Chastity),[27] in terms which are, in turn, con-
descending and incomprehensible: He would like to see his most recent
work, "The Legend of Chastity," published in a magazine before it appeared as a book of the Inselverlag. In this attempt he was hoping for
the *Neue Merkur*, since it was one of the few journals which fortunately
did not find the salvation of politics solely within politics.

The novella itself, a precious and gratuitously symbolistic, laboredly
ironic tale of a young girl's realization that innocent nudity attracts less
attention than provocative clothes, received much favorable comment at
the time. The *Leipziger Tageblatt*, in an unsigned feuilleton of 25 August
1920, called it "a tender beautiful fruit on the rarely blooming tree of
this writer. . . . Upon its first appearance in the *Neue Merkur* this small
piece of prose fiction delighted me." The adjectives in this laudation and
the verb *entzücken* (delight) appear rather suspect. Little needs to be
added, despite Johannes Klein's recent apologia for this work, to the
judgment by Claude David who speaks of Binding's "Reiterallüren"
(horseman's mannerisms), "elegantem Dünkel" (elegant conceitedness),

and says of his novellas that "they push forward to a type of mannerism which today is scarcely bearable anymore."[28]

Josef Ponten, who also appeared consistently in the *Neue Merkur*, falls into the same category. His many contributions straddle two periods of the magazine's publishing history, its time of independence and its years under the aegis of the Deutsche Verlags Anstalt. During the first period, of course, Frisch was solely responsible for Ponten's collaboration, although Ponten, at that time wooed by many journals, was not averse to applying considerable pressure. When Frisch accepted Ponten's novella "Derselbe oder die Geschichte einer Narbe" (The Same One, or, The Story of a Scar),[29] but demurred against putting it into a special literary issue, Ponten protested and prevailed.

The exchange is interesting because it shows how an editor who had less honoraria to offer than his competitors sometimes had to compromise —not in quality, but in publishing policy. On 9 November 1921, Frisch wrote Ponten that he liked "The Same One," but it appeared questionable to him, whether one could let it pass as a novella. It was not that he wanted to start a subtle investigation of the form, but the story might not be completely befitting for the "literature" issue. Ponten, beneath exquisite politeness, threatened to reclaim it and sell it to the *Neue Rundschau*. He regretted that his novella—whether novella or not, as long as it was art—had not been given space in the issue devoted to "contemporary German literature." To enter into competition with the others, this was precisely what had attracted him and for that reason had withheld the story from the *Rundschau* and offered it to the *Merkur*. He believed, after having read quite a few of the works in the magazine, to be able to enter into this competition without qualms.

Since he was already planning for next spring a second volume of novellas entitled *Salz* (Salt), he feared to be getting into a bit of a squeeze with his publications, as had been the case with the "Boy Vielnam," and he wanted to retain his freedom of disposition over "The Same One" for a while longer. He wanted to give it to the one who could publish it most quickly.

Frisch capitulated. On 23 November 1921 he wrote that, although space in the literature issue was very tight, he had decided to find room for Ponten's novella. He stressed that it was a sacrifice, since he was not to exceed the norm set for this issue. This concession was meant to prove to Ponten that he was making every effort to accede to the author's wish. Later, when Director Kilpper of the DVA, the publisher of Ponten's works, lent his forceful voice to Ponten's pleas *pro domo*, as documented on the following pages, the pressure became even more intense.

Before and after the transfer to the DVA, Frisch acted as a sort of Maxwell Perkins to Ponten in his unlikely role of a German Thomas Wolfe. Like his American contemporary, Ponten proved incurably prolix; Frisch generally pruned his contributions, possibly saving some of them from the grave of sub-literature. Ponten's "Rheinreise," at first sub-titled, according to his letter of 10 August 1920, as "Erziehung zum Manne," is a case in point. Apparently even Ponten, by all reports a rather vain man, had some misgivings himself. In the same letter he said: The length might induce some misgivings—a large-size novella, as he was accustomed to writing it, needed, as it happened, a fuller treatment. Frisch, through a telephone call or by means of a letter of which no copy was retained, must have used the metaphor of a swing to indicate to Ponten that his novella contained too many retardations. On 14 October 1920 [date inferred from the dateline "Donnerstag"] Ponten accepted Frisch's suggestions, in fact rather generously. Their opinions were congruent, as became apparent from Frisch's picture of the swing, otherwise he would not have been able to comply with the editor's wish. The latter must have meant the aberrations and retardations, the rocks thrown into the brook of the narrative, so that it might rush on all the more strongly. But perhaps there were too many, or rather, too voluminous ones. By 25 October 1920 Ponten had complied. He announced that he had cut the story by four pages and had deleted, specifically, large parts from the narration of the voyage proper, where too many "swings of the pendulum" had previously occurred. With those cuts, he concluded, he believed he had found the right solution.

Ponten undoubtedly had improved the story; this tale of a journey into maturity of an eighteen-year-old boy remains, despite a certain preciocity at the end, one of Ponten's readable efforts. The other one of this period, "Derselbe," which Frisch had only reluctantly included in his special literature issue, is not. It is a convoluted tale that breaks over the attempt to combine the Romantic *Doppelgänger-motif* with a proto-schizophrenic state of mind, and descriptions of the Alpine landscape with metaphysical speculations about the nature of evil. It merits Hellmuth Himmel's assessment of its author: "Ponten is unable to contribute anything to the . . . form of the novella."[30]

The publication of numerous other writers, as traditional as Binding and Ponten, was prompted less by considerations of style and form than of subject matter: several stories continued, in fictional form, the political debates of the *Neue Merkur*, and, in some cases, surpassed them in the graphic description of the contemporary scene in Germany. This was true of Friedrich Sieburg's story of German inflation, "Der verwunschene Dieb," and, even more pointedly, of Otto Flake's two novellas, "Die Qual" and "Byk."[31] Their inclusion proves that a magazine devoted to both politics and literature cannot always sharply separate the two.

In "Die Qual" Flake describes the poisoning of young minds, during the first years of the war, by a super-patriotic school teacher and the inevitable disillusionment. In "Byk" he unfolds all the miseries of a defeated Germany through the adventures of two returned veterans, jobless, hungry, and desperate, who are drawn into the clash of extremist groups of the right and left, the *Freikorps* and the Communists. Flake, in commentaries to "Byk," separated by more than forty years, has stressed its archetypal elements. He wrote to Frisch on 21 April 1921 describing the heroine as an archetype. But he believed that this encounter with Eternal Helpfulness or the Feminine did not determine the man. On 15 April 1962 he added that the motif of the returnee preoccupied his mind as a saga motif, as a motif close to the Romantic narrative, even to the fairy tale, even though he attacked it in a modern fashion and took the contents from events of the day. But it is likely that Flake's contemporaries (and also his many post-World War II readers) liked his works more for their topicality than their typicality. On 22 May 1920, shortly after Flake had abandoned his disastrous flirtation with Expressionism, Kurt Hiller wrote to Frisch that he thought extraordinarily much of Flake, especially since he had withdrawn from writing belles lettres. Flake's novellas in the *Neue Merkur* stand at the borderline of fact and fiction.

Ironically a story with even fewer literary pretensions and a style still closer to reporting became one of the most memorable pieces of fiction in the eight volumes of the *Neue Merkur*. In a letter of 17 November 1922 to Frisch, its author, Hans Siemsen, rejoiced about its acceptance for completely altruistic and nonliterary reasons: Because it is good, he wrote, if people are forced, again and again by every means, to come to terms with the concept of prison. In "Die Geschichte meines Bruders,"[32] Siemsen eschewed all rhetoric, even lent the story-teller in the narrative his own name, and included him in his closing pejoration: "But it is we who regulate this world. It is we, who build prisons." Because of its very simplicity and unpretentiousness, the story enchanted some of the most astute contemporary critics. That prestigious English journal, *The Criterion*, commented: "The most interesting contribution to this number is a story by Hans Siemsen, . . . which goes to show that German can be written with the simplicity of form and the subtlety of content that distinguish Anatole France's prose. To one who daily endures the tortures and unravels the twists of the attempts of the German professors to appear profound, this story comes like a release from oppression."[33] And T. S. Eliot, the magazine's editor, in a letter to Frisch of 12 January 1923, expressed his personal appreciation of the story by Hans Siemsen of which he thought very highly. These views of Siemsen's story seem to have prevailed. Karl Boegner, a regular reviewer for the prominent German book review journal *Bücher-Kommentare*, wrote upon its republication: "Hans Siemsen's touchingly unvarnished 'Story of My Brother' belongs to the most beautiful realistic narratives which this reviewer has ever read."[34]

The return to a tradition before the moderns was reflected not only in the literature of the *Neue Merkur* but also in its literary criticism. In the earlier pre-war volumes, German literature of the eighteenth and nineteenth centuries was all but ignored; in the years 1919–23 some of Germany's best-known scholars were solicited for occasional contributions on this period. Adolf von Hatzfeld wrote a commemorative article upon Gottfried Keller's hundredth birthday (June 1919); Walther Harich one on the hundredth anniversary of E. T. Hoffmann's death; Max Picard attempted a philosophical explanation of Matthias Claudius; Hans Poeschel wrote an appreciation of Stifter's "Nachsommer"; Conrad Wandrey, one of the literary historians close to Stefan George, devoted an essay to Hölderlin, who was then of considerable interest to the "Georgeaner."[35] He also assayed yet another definition of Classicism and Romanticism by applying Wölfflin's categories to literature in refutation of Fritz Strich's book, *Klassik und Romantik*, of which the gloss purported to be a review.[36]

Most of these articles have become obsolete or commonplace through subsequent scholarship. Their abiding interest consists in a unifying theme which runs through the tangential remarks of their authors. We need only cull a few of these marginalia to detect their drift. Picard commented upon a passage from Matthias Claudius: "Oh, where today is the beautiful earth and the beautiful sky and holy religion. They have been chased from this world." Conrad Wandrey said, in the opening paragraph of his essay on Hölderlin, "The bitter turning point which only seemed to threaten with hardships and losses, now brings to light buried depths." Poeschel began his gloss on Stifter: "The more painfully one feels the crisis and chaos of the present-day condition of the world, the more we feel the necessity to flee from these disturbances, if only for a few hours. In such a mood we gratefully welcome the reemergence of Stifter's 'Late Summer.' " It becomes clear that the sudden preoccupation with the German past, through its literature, was a flight from the present.

This impression is heightened through the sporadic quotes from authors of the past. The quotations from Jean Paul, for example, had apparently all been chosen as admonitions to later generations: "Therefore dawn in rose-color, ye morning of the new times, and as on the morning of yore let the rainbow of peace arise in the West behind the receding Deluge."

Analogously the "Fragment eines frommen Gedichtes" (a translation by Alfred Neumann of an Old French poem of the twelfth century) shows sorrow mitigated through an ultimate consolation.[37] It was the publication of this poem that apparently led a perceptive critic to the conclusion that the *Neue Merkur* and similar journals, formerly devoted to vanguard literature, were now constructing still another refuge from the uninviting present through the poetry of the past. When it appeared, the critic in *The Criterion*[38] remarked: "These [translations by Hermann Hesse in *Die Neue Rundschau*] and the translation of a 'pious poem' from the Old French, 'Quant il solleiz converset en leon' in the December [1922] number of the *Neue Merkur* are among the many signs that the Germans, in the midst of material disaster, are harking back to an earlier, simpler, and more spiritual time." The observation, though true, was, however, only part of the truth.

The *Merkur* looked, Janus-like, both backward and forward. This tendency can best be seen in Rudolf Pannwitz' brilliant review of Hugo von Hofmannsthal's narrative (not the libretto) of *Frau ohne Schatten* (Woman Without a Shadow).[39] On the one hand he correctly shows that the story is "something classical, exceedingly restrained, something that perfects the most noble tradition"; on the other hand he defines it as the harbinger of a new direction in German literature: "The times thought that Hofmannsthal had stood still; in reality he has advanced, but no one advanced with him." This estimate has, of course, not yet been accepted among scholars of literature.

Interestingly enough, Hofmannsthal himself suggested Pannwitz as a possible contributor to the *Neue Merkur*. As Pannwitz himself wrote me on 30 October 1962: For the connection with Frisch and his journal, he could thank Hofmannsthal. This information is confirmed by Frisch's letter of 14 November 1919, in which he acknowledges Hofmannsthal's recommendation of Pannwitz. Hofmannsthal's recommendation of the previous June, which would have been most revelatory, unfortunately was lost on his summer vacation trip, wrote Frisch.

By assuming its Janus-like outlook, the *Neue Merkur* discovered, or helped to discover, three post-Expressionistic writers who were still in the vanguard of German, if not European, letters long after the *Neue Merkur* had ceased publication. They were, in the order of their publication, Bertolt Brecht, Robert Musil, and Oskar Loerke.

The initial contact between Brecht and Frisch was established through Lionel Feuchwanger. In an undated letter from Munich, one of the few to be sold at auction in 1943, Brecht wrote that Feuchwanger had told him to send something to the *Neue Merkur*. Brecht had selected some very simple stories. After the acceptance of "Bargan läßt es sein" (Bargan Gives Up), Brecht called on Frisch in person. In an article in *Akzente* a few years ago, Ferdinand Lion recalled these visits (although he erred as to Brecht's age at the time): "Attracted by Frisch's personality travellers arrived. . . . Brecht, not yet twenty, brought poems, all with the same subject, swamps and quiet waters. People did not as yet divine anything of his later development."[40]

The publication of the novella "Bargan . . ." (and later of the poem "Vom Schwimmen in Seen und Flüssen")[41] aroused much attention and comment. Frisch apparently was quite enthusiastic and must have told Brecht, since another letter from Brecht (also cited in the catalog "Auktion 41") says: I am happy that you like the story 'B'. By Brecht's own testimony, the novella helped start his rapid ascent to success. In an undated letter to Frisch, written, according to internal evidence, between 1 September and 21 October 1921, he reported that publication of the novella in the *Neue Merkur* was evidently very useful for him. If the editorial correspondence is indicative, the resonance was indeed formidable. With the exception of a few who found Brecht's matter-of-fact description of brutality unbearable—the murder, arson, and rape by the pirates is told with an air of understatement that borders on bravado— most of its readers were thoroughly impressed. Yet Lion was correct in his statement that this robust novella did not fully foreshadow Brecht's development. While the nihilism and anarchism, the gangster milieu and the preoccupation with the great criminal, have many parallels in his later works, his psychological rather than social treatment of his material do not. One regrets, in fact, that Brecht did not write more often in this vein.

Analogously, the poem "Vom Schwimmen in Seen und Flüssen" gives no hint of Brecht's subsequent radical experiments in lyrical poetry. While the factual tone is characteristic of Brecht at all stages of his development, the choice of a subject, man's integration into cosmic love, birth, and death was no doubt suggested to Brecht by Rimbaud and the Expressionists. The poem appealed at the time not only to the Expressionists (which was scarcely surprising), but also to the traditionalists. Felix Braun, on 14 December 1921, wrote Frisch spontaneously that the poem by Brecht, whose name he had not previously known, was curiously mixed, both strong and tender, very strangely beautiful. In the interview forty years later, when Felix Braun of course knew of Brecht's later development as a lyricist, he again praised this poem, but by implication devalued his later ones: That was his most beautiful poem; these pure lyrics were his greatest creations. Hugo von Hofmannsthal had told him at the time that he esteemed Brecht very highly. There was only one occurrence to mar Brecht's successful debut as a lyricist in the pages of the *Merkur*. The lengthiest review of the special literature issue, that of the *Süddeutsche Presse* of 16 December 1921, praised two heavy-handed poems by Friedrich Sieburg and ignored Brecht's.

In one final respect this poem, or rather its submittal, was atypical of Brecht as we have come to know him. In his October 1921 letter, Brecht introduced it with uncommon modesty: He did not know whether Frisch thought it wise to print something by Brecht so soon after "Bargan," but at any rate he wanted Frisch to have the enclosed poems for possible publication of a selection of them.

Frisch's acquaintance with and admiration for Robert Musil antedated his editorship of the *Neue Merkur*. According to Fega Frisch the two Austrian writers met about 1907 in the circle surrounding Bruno Cassirer, the Berlin publisher, and renewed their acquaintance when Frisch, as reader for the Georg Müller Verlag, advocated and prepared the second (1911) edition of Musil's *Die Verwirrungen des Zöglings Törless* and, in the same year, the publication of his collection of novellas, *Vereinigungen* (Links).

The crushing reviews of this work and the eclipse of Musil's fame in consequence[42] did not diminish Frisch's esteem for its author. On the contrary he published, in March 1921, a defense of the maligned work in which Robert Müller, a Viennese Activist, berates the critics and praises the simultaneity of events [*Simultangestaltung*] and the new concept of spatiality: "It is the eery element in these novellas, that they take place in absolute space, hence spacelessly, so to speak."[43] Musil, in a letter of 30 March 1921, took no exception to this analysis: He was very happy about the little essay which the *Neue Merkur* published about *Links*; not only had it given him some pleasant satisfaction, but even aside from the subject matter it was a valuable piece of criticism.

The appearance of this favorable and sensitive review was not chance. Frisch, before commissioning it, was fully informed of its tenor by a letter of inquiry from the reviewer which must have had for him the added appeal of unintentional flattery: it vindicated his selection of the much maligned *Vereinigungen*. Robert Müller addressed the *Neue Merkur* in a letter of 8 June 1920. He asked whether a gloss on Robert Musil would be of interest to the magazine. Author of one of the strongest and most curious collections of novellas entitled *Vereinigungen (Links)*, Musil had been assessed much too low and was scarcely known, and it would be a meritorious act if the *Merkur* were to publish something about him, especially since Musil was a personal friend of Frisch and even a collaborator of the magazine, Müller wrote.

By commissioning a review by an obvious admirer of Musil, Frisch, of course, sought Musil's vindication, if not his own. But even earlier Frisch had indicated his undiminished admiration for Musil. When he solicited contributors for the reborn *Neue Merkur* in 1919, Musil was among the first to be sought, as is apparent in Frisch's letter of October 1919. Their conversation in the train had convinced him that Musil belonged, on principle, to the imaginary circle of the *Merkur*'s contributors. In consideration of the very small number of people who fell into this category he understandably set great value in soon seeing Musil work with the magazine. Musil's contributions, in response to this invitation, ran to one novella and seven articles. When writing for the *Merkur* Musil imparted even to book reviews the length and depth of aesthetic or philosophical essays.

Obviously Musil valued his position in this "imaginary circle of contributors." He repeatedly expressed his approbation of the *Merkur* in his conversations with Oscar Maurus Fontana, who told me on 21 December 1961 that Musil was very reticent; one of the few to whom he extended an unvarying esteem was Frisch, whose editorial achievements he appreciated as exemplary. In 1921, when they both worked in the same office (Austrian Secretariat of the Army), Musil once said to Fontana: "I am contributing to the *Merkur* because it applies the right standards of value, keeps up with the genuine contemporary phenomena without trying to be fashionable."

Musil's belletristic contribution, the novella "Grigia," has of late often been unjustly dismissed—with some notable exceptions—as "one of the minor works . . . in the course of his development."[44] But Musil, in "Grigia," did for the novella what later, in *Mann ohne Eigenschaften* (Man Without Qualities), he was to do for the novel: he extended its boundaries. "Grigia" is, on one level, the unravelling of the tension-filled relationship between Man and Woman; even lovers are separated by unfathomable abysses. "Sie war ihm entrückt oder er ihr," Musil speculates at one point. ("She had removed herself from him or he from her.") The two lovers act out a prototypal situation of Eros and Thanatos; significantly the hero is named Homo, and the elemental, somewhat bovine, heroine is Grigia, or "The Grey One," a name borrowed from her willful cow.

Beyond his interest in psychological and prototypal relationships, however, Musil, as the most recent scholarship has pointed out,[45] applied to his novella a new concept of narrative time, a skillful adaptation of the theory of relativity. From the opening sentence onward, ("There is a period in life, where it runs conspicuously more slowly"), till the very last sentence which announces the hero's death and the frustration of his plans at the "same hour," Musil experiments with the time perspective in his novella: a fateful friendship is formed in a few days; overnight an "inseparable" marriage falls apart. The reminiscence of a pleasant walk with the beloved person merges into a horribly changed presence. At the beginning the hero tries to kill time; at the end, time, hours and days of immolation, kill him.

When submitting the novella, Musil supplied no comment; his covering letter of 23 November 1921 was brevity itself. (Did you receive Grigia? Does it suit you? When will it appear?) Nonetheless it seems likely that Frisch recognized the originality of its structure. When, in April 1933, he reviewed the second volume of *Mann ohne Eigenschaften*, he became one of the first to recognize the complexity of the "field of force of time" in Musil's prose: "Musil's [epic] breadth and slow pace has the internal speed of genuine thought, which may take its own good time. . . . Sometimes one also thinks of events in slow motion. . . . The strange abridgments and distortions, in which man and animal present themselves at given moments, make them appear comical in their scarcely perceived animated suspension."[46]

Frisch esteemed none of his contributors more highly than Musil; in later years, in his letters to the DVA, he fought harder for maximal rates for Musil than for his own salary. It is likely that he championed Musil so consistently, long before literary scholarship so belatedly recognized his merits, because he recognized in a novella such as "Grigia" what he later admired in Musil's *magnum opus*: a new form of fiction.

Oskar Loerke's collaboration was likewise one of the valuable legacies of Frisch's years in Berlin. They had been introduced through their mutual friend, Moritz Heimann, well-known essayist, aphorist, and, as chief editor of the S. Fischer Verlag, "the conscience of German literature," to paraphrase Gerhart Hauptmann. His name, news and opinions of him, were to dominate the correspondence between Frisch and Loerke until Heimann's untimely death in 1925. Loerke's first post-war letter of 9 January 1919, for example, evoked their days in Berlin: He was most happy about Frisch's kind request to become a contributor, but quite particularly, to be reminded so nicely of old times. And fittingly his first contribution to the *Merkur* was an appreciation of Moritz Heimann.

The immediate occasion which prompted Frisch to solicit the article was the appearance of the three-volume collection of Heimann's essays and aphorisms in 1918, *Prosaische Schriften*. Loerke, despite the considerable pressure of previous commitments, accepted the assignment. His letter of acceptance on 27 June 1919 is summarized extensively here because it adds to our knowledge of Loerke and circumscribes his relationship to Frisch, S. Fischer, and Heimann, his friend and discoverer. Loerke

was at the time taking care of all the literary aspects of editorial supervision for the S. Fischer Verlag, since Heimann had been taken seriously
ill. Working nights he was also finishing two novels that had been on his
mind for a long time. For this reason, one month before he had been
forced to discontinue his collaboration with the *Neue Rundschau*, e.g., his
essays on the survey of modern literature. Regretfully declining, for the
time being, the offer to contribute regularly to the *Merkur*, he nonetheless
was happy to submit an article on Heimann's works in the near future.

Loerke's Heimann essay appeared in the issue of August 1919. The title,
"Ein Laie,"[47] was, according to a letter from Frisch to Loerke on 10 October 1919, an idea of Frisch's, who wrote that it seemed fitting since the
essay was appearing in the main part of the issue and also covered the
most essential point of Loerke's disquisition. It was inspired by one of
Loerke's chief insights into Heimann's essayistic style, which combined
the knowledge of an expert with the emotional involvement and naiveté
of a dilettante. For this unusual synthesis Loerke, following a self-
characterization of Heimann, used the term "layman." He concluded his
appreciative review by urging further interpretations. The objectivity of
the essays [*Anonymität*], which made them timeless and inexhaustible, he
felt ought to attract further critical attention.

In Loerke's aforementioned letter of 27 June 1919, he mentioned the
sudden popularity of his poetry, though, typically modest, he attributed
it to a general resurgence of interest in the lyric. About a year later, on
24 July 1920, he submitted a collection of four poems, along with a covering letter which pleasantly combined modesty and self-assurance: this
time he was approaching the *Merkur* as a poet and not as an essayist,
confident that through his true vocation he was able to make a major
contribution.

Similar remarks appeared in a letter of 2 October 1921: The poems not
included in the issue appearing that week had already been accepted elsewhere for publication. Together, these attestations to the popularity of
Loerke's poems also transmit his subtle endorsement of the *Neue Merkur*:
despite the sudden demand for his poetry and his close affinity to the *Neue
Rundschau* as chief editor for S. Fischer, its publisher, he chose to submit
to the *Merkur* some of his best poems. Frisch, of course, accepted all of
his offerings in this category.[48]

In reading Loerke's poems, one is immediately struck by their thematic
unity. It seems hard to believe, and it bears further testimony of his abundant good will towards the *Merkur*, that he consented to their piecemeal
publication. The four poems, "Das Schaufenster," "Dächermond," "Sehnsüchtig," and "Zeitlied," though quite different in form and content, are

rounded into a thematic cycle. All four sustain a mood of anxiety and sadness which Loerke both draws from and infuses into a variety of progressively unfolding images. The first one, an astonishing collage of street scenes mirrored and superimposed on the objects in a shop-window—boxes, stuffed fish, etc.—expresses, through a series of metaphors, a fusion of the light of the dawning sun and of an inner glow. But even this powerful and sweet harmony cannot banish for long an overwhelming sadness, expressed in the plaintive lines: "Den Menschen zu klagen bin ich zu stolz. / Und zögernd zu den Fischen, die in Gnaden schienen, / Tat ich mein Klagendes ins weiße Kistenholz." (To complain to men I am too proud. / And hesitatingly to the fish, who seemed to be in grace, I placed my plaints into the white wood of the boxes.) In the second poem, "Dächermond," an abstraction, the longing for distance, has divorced itself from the poet's imagination, like a "ghost grown out of me," and transverses the roofs, the stars, and the moon. The absence of life and emotion is, in the final stanza, dispelled by one of the cosmic shadows and it, a symbol of anxiety, returns to its point of origin, the mind of the poet: "Nur einer bringt den Tau der Bängnis. / Wie bricht sein Quell aus meiner Stirn?" (Just one [shadow] brings anxiety's dew-drops. / How does its source break forth from my forehead?) The same night scene, if slightly more benign, emerges in the poem "Sehnsüchtig" and again in the last poem, "Zeitlied," ascending to a crescendo of despair and sadness. Here Loerke invokes, with baroque inventiveness, a plethora of melancholic images: "Die Sterne fallen in den Schnee"; "Aus Bein und Blut und müdem Fleisch / Ein Treiben in der Leere"; "Die frischen Gruben heulen." (The stars fall on the snow; From bone and blood and tired flesh / [come] aimless doings in the void; the new-dug ditches howl.) In the final stanza, however, the poet shows that this eternal human condition has become exacerbated in modern times. With all values shattered, even sadness is bereft of its philosophical or theological foundation: "Nun ist es spät, nun ist es schwer, / Von Herzen traurig werden, / Denn keine Säulen tragen mehr / Die Traurigkeit auf Erden." (Now it is late, now it is hard / to grow sad from the heart, / For no pillars carry still / Sadness here on earth.) This poem, born out of the travail of the years after the first World War, foreshadows Loerke's poetic cries of desperation during the Hitler years.

The originality of these poems carries over into the two works of fiction which Loerke published in the *Neue Merkur*. The first narrative, excerpts from his novel *Der Oger*, was entitled "Der Fischzug."[49] Hermann Kasack, who later, in 1926, was to adapt the excerpt for a radio broadcast, told me on 17 April 1962 of its genesis. "The Fishing Expedition" was an

experience from before the first World War. Loerke took a two-week
voyage on a fishing boat as sole passenger. Everything was based upon
personal observation.

Loerke first informed Frisch of completing the novel in a letter of
31 December 1919: Until Christmas he had worked exclusively on the
novel, which had finally been completed. Now it was the turn of the *Journey Into the Desert*. In his letter of 24 July 1920, he discussed for the first
time the possibility of a partial advance publication in the *Neue Merkur*.
The prose manuscript he was sending was the beginning of his novel *The
Ogre*. Reassured by the favorable judgment of Heimann, he considered
the piece well suitable for advance publication, admitting, too, the selfish
motive of wanting to present something from the book, the publication of
which had to wait, since it would cost too much per copy to find a wide
reading public. If desirable he would add a prologue and an epilogue.

Loerke subsequently altered this plan. Rather than adding a prologue
and epilogue, he complemented and rounded out the first chapter by adding two further episodes from the novel. They show how the hero, Martin
Wendenich, confronted with the brutality of a fishing trawler, learns to
accept the ruthlessness and suffering of life without turning callous:
"Only now did he love the ship with everything on it." Loerke wrote to
Frisch on 13 October 1920, providing his own commentary to the parts
printed in the *Merkur*: he had selected that part which could be said to
compare the soul of Man to water. As a piece of art, the selection was an
entity in itself, but since it was not a novella in the strictest sense, he
would appreciate it if Frisch would mention the novel as its origin. When
Loerke finally read the galleys, he was pleased at the unity of the selected
parts of the novel. He had succeeded in cutting out of the novel something
clear in itself, he wrote. Frisch must have concurred. He did not accept
lapidary fragments.

One year later Frisch accepted, probably out of identical considerations, another fragment by Loerke, the narrative "Fahrt in die Wüste,"[50]
taken from Loerke's never completed novel of the same name. This time
Frisch published it in one of the "show-piece" issues of the magazine, the
Sonderheft Dichtung of 1921. Again the editorial correspondence takes
us into the mind and work of the poet. He wrote on 27 June 1919, that he
had planned a story of some 120–150 pages called "Journey into the
Desert" or "Journey to the Tuareg," (Loerke had traveled to the Sahara
Desert in 1914), to trace life back through the rubble of culture to the
untouched, pristine center of Man. Should Frisch be interested in publishing something of this kind, he would finish this novel first and put aside
the completion of his other book *The Ogre*.

As we know, Loerke did not postpone the completion of *Der Oger* in

favor of his "Sahara" book, as he suggested. In fact, despite several optimistic progress reports, it took Loerke almost two years to ready a manuscript for pre-book publication. In letters on 2 October 1921 and an undated one of the same month, he explained the delay and gave instructions
for publication: he would have a part of the "Journey Into the Desert"
ready and had selected a narrative that could stand by itself, and, as he
hoped, an impressive one. In the second letter he added that he had chosen
two chapters from the novel, which alluded to but few of the epic conflicts.
So far he was not sure of the over-all title, but asked for the addition of
the subtitle, from the novel "Journey Into the Desert."

In this narrative Loerke again succeeded in fashioning parts into a
whole; the story can well stand on its own. It also conveys Loerke's intention to present "a road to cognition" or self-recognition: the hero, An-
selm, finds harmony and freedom through the experience of the elemental
forces of nature as they reveal themselves in a sandstorm, the peace of an
oasis, or their proud and rebellious inhabitants. In addition, as I have
indicated elsewhere, this story provides a fascinating insight into Loerke's
workshop. The second part, "Die Grundwasser," draws heavily, in certain
key passages, upon Loerke's diary of his African journey; the identical
mementos are later utilized in a poem entitled "Nächtlicher Kamelritt."
Through careful analysis of the three different renditions of the same
experience, one can almost intuit Loerke's method of creation: a simple
observation, for example, of the camel's trepidation instilled by the gurg-
ling trickle of ground water, is transformed in the story into poetic prose;
in the poem, on the other hand, the terrestrial sounds are accompanied by
celestial music: "Der Kaskadensturz des Milchstroms / steil vom Himmel
singt dasselbe." (The cascading stream of the Milky Way's run / sings
the same thing steeply from Heaven.)

By comparing Loerke's diary notes, his novel, and his poems of the
period, we can frequently observe the creative metamorphosis of a single
experience. Recently, when this story was reprinted, several reviewers
praised it for its enduring merit. In so doing they were also, if more indirectly, paying tribute to Frisch's acumen, because he published Loerke's
prose at a time when only his poetry seemed to be in demand.[51]

Frisch displayed, for the most part, equal acumen in selecting foreign
literature in translation for the volumes 1919 to 1923. Or, it might be
said, he displayed uncommonly good judgment in selecting experts who
not only wrote superb articles on foreign literature but also recommended
works for publication in translation. Ernst Robert Curtius made recommendations about French literature, Tommaso Gallarati Scotti about Italian, Waldo Frank about American, Arnold Ulitz and (above all others)
Fega and Efraim Frisch themselves about Russian literature.[52] In addi-

tion, Frisch received the advice of the various editors and contributors of the *Auslandspost*, a digest of important political and cultural news from abroad which Frisch had founded in 1919.

One of the French contributions was primarily selected for its topicality. In a long (and somewhat polemic) foreword Kurt Hiller, the translator of the poem "Prière" by Georges Chennevière,[53] gave a few biographical facts about the author, deplored the drift towards communism of his group, the Clarté, and lauded the conciliatory and pacifistic tone of the poem. He also intended to add a pointed interpretation by identifying (correctly) the people apostrophied by the author as the Jews. On 13 April 1920 he wrote to Frisch that if he did not think it too provocative, Hiller would very much favor paraphrasing more precisely the avowal and fighting spirit of the poem by means of the words: "to the memory of the murdered Jewish revolutionaries in Germany." Frisch disregarded the suggestion, for the poem, translated by Hiller in an idiom indistinguishable from that of his contributions to *Ziel*, his own yearbook, carried its own message.

Outside of an essay by Romain Rolland,[54] a timely appeal to dissolve the clannish student organizations and to breach the rift between workers and intellectuals, the other samples from French literature were picked on belletristic interest alone. Alfred Wolfenstein provided a moving translation of several poems by Paul Verlaine,[55] but also proved that a poet, in translating another, cannot always divest himself of his own personality as a writer: in Wolfenstein's rendition, Verlaine's poems take on Expressionistic traits. Alfred Vagts translated Paul Morand's "Nacht der Sechs Tage";[56] he recalled when interviewed in January 1963 that this story, the first that captured the excitement of indoor bicycling, had tremendous resonance among readers. Not until Uwe Johnson's *Das Dritte Buch über Achim* was the sport to have again as vivid a chronicler as Morand. In later years Frisch translated a novel by Morand;[57] he could not know, in 1930, that the author he esteemed and tried to popularize in Germany was to become a Vichy collaborator.

Curtius' remarkable essay "Marcel Proust"[58] begins: "The quick rise of Marcel Proust was the first surprise of the post-war period brought to lovers of French literature." He now wanted to secure for Proust a similar reception in Germany: "It is the intention [of my remarks] to prepare one for the reading of Proust." It is scarcely an exaggeration to say that Curtius did indeed prepare the German reader for an intelligent appreciation of Proust's works and thus paved the way for his subsequent popularity in the German-speaking countries.

It was also Curtius who suggested to Frisch the pre-book publication of André Gide's essay on Stendhal and helped in securing Gide's permission.[59] In so doing he not only helped launch the Stendhal revival in Germany, but he also gained for the *Merkur* a brilliant essay and one more recognition of the excellence of its translations. On 5 December 1921, Gide wrote a letter of thanks for publication in the *Merkur* and for Hausenstein's translation. This praise of the translation weighed heavily, since Gide had expressed some concern before publication. Curtius wrote to Frisch on 30 July 1921, quoting Gide's injunction that he counted upon Curtius to watch that it was well translated.

The excursions into Italian literature all had the identical point of departure, the Dante Celebration of 1921 commemorating the six-hundredth anniversary of his death. Hans Deinhardt, whose translation of Dante was considered standard for many years, contributed renditions of three sonnets from the *Vita Nuova* and two excerpts from the *Paradiso*.[60] Scotti used Dante to berate the mediocre writers of his own time and Hausenstein contributed a perceptive article,[61] in which he concluded: "One retrospective glance suffices—the magnificent consistence is obvious: Saint Thomas Aquinas, Dante, and Giotto are the theological, the poetic, and pictorial formulation of the identical thought [i.e., of practicing Empiricism]."

English and American literature received rather short shrift in these years. The only English author to draw critical notice was Arnold Bennett; Emma Bonn, a frequent contributor to sophisticated German journals, praised him as "a novelist of great stature."[62] She also, in passing, commented favorably upon Joseph Conrad, John Masefield, Thomas Hardy, John Galsworthy, George Moore, G. B. Shaw, Compton Mackenzie, and H. G. Wells.

Felix Braun repeated popular misconceptions about American literature and culture in reviewing Hans Reisiger's translation of Walt Whitman and Clare Goll's *Die neue Welt*, an anthology of modern American poetry in translation. With few exceptions (Grace Hazard Conkling, Max Eastman, Vachel Lindsay, Amy Lowell, and a few Negro and Indian poems), Braun was little impressed. Even Whitman appealed to him more as "a personality than as a poet": "As such he convinces us but rarely." And speaking of American culture, he repeated the old cliché that it had been omitted in America's jump from barbarism to civilization.[63]

The only American writer to be published was the poet and novelist Waldo Frank, but he is represented, significantly, by excerpts from his historical study *Our America* rather than by any creative work.[64] (Frank himself would have disagreed with such an assessment. In a letter of 14 April 1922 he stated that he looked on *Our America* as a creative rather than a critical work.) But the fault for this dearth of publications by American writers in general and of Waldo Frank in particular may not have been Frisch's alone. The appearance of further, already accepted, works by Frank was thwarted by the interruption of publication of the *Neue Merkur* in 1923. As a discoverer of other American fiction, Waldo Frank proved unproductive. Both the submittal of his own fiction and his failure to find meritorious works of other Americans are documented in a letter of 11 April 1922, which does, however, contain a very sound suggestion: he hoped that *Rahab* and *City Block* (of which he was sending proofs shortly) would create a greater interest than *Our America* had, with both the magazine and the German public. He identified both works as the beginning of his definitive *oeuvre*. If Frisch wanted to publish a couple of the stories from *City Block*, he was at full liberty to do so. But, regretfully, Frank was unable to oblige with good stories by Americans, which Frisch had requested, and suggested instead examining two American magazines published in Italy, *Dial* and *Broom*, which might yield the best short stories available. He also offered to obtain the formal permission from the authors, in case publication was planned for any one of the narratives. The printing of one of his stories in *Broom* and the positive reaction by German writers, had reinforced Frank's conviction that his books would find a steady audience in Germany, perhaps the one country where there were more than scattered individuals genuinely interested in literary expression.

Frank might have made more of his opportunity to recommend the works of compatriots to a leading European journal. The year was 1922, when (among others) Sherwood Anderson, Willa Cather, John Dos Passos, and Theodore Dreiser were eminent in fiction; Eugene O'Neill in the drama; and Hart Crane, Robert Frost, Vachel Lindsay, Amy Lowell, Edna St. Vincent Millay, Edwin Arlington Robinson, and Elinor Wylie in poetry.

Russian authors and discussions of Russian literature occupied more space in the *Merkur* than all the other foreign literatures combined. In this instance the literary fashion, the vogue of Tolstoy and Dostoevski, and the curiosity about Russia's revolutionary and post-revolutionary literature coincided with Frisch's own predilections. He himself wrote the memorial article about Dostoevski and several introductory glosses to Russian works; his wife contributed numerous translations.[66]

Tolstoy's ninety-fifth and Dostoevski's hundredth birthday provided convenient springboards for a concerted revival of the two great Russians. Tolstoy himself was represented by a few aperçus on literature, contained in an otherwise undistinguished collection of memoirs of Tolstoy's secretary, which appeared in the *Merkur* prior to their more extensive publication in book form. Far more important was the appearance of a brief but highly revelatory and obviously autobiographical essay in dialogue form by Tolstoy, a preface to his short story *Wandelt im Licht* (1888).[67] The prologue may be read as a post-facto self-analysis of his return to orthodoxy. Frisch coupled this publication with two secondary works, a review of Tolstoy's early diaries by Lou Andreas-Salomé (which tried to find in Tolstoy's youth the causes for his later conversion) and two biographical articles, one by Maxim Gorky, the other by V. Bulgahov.[68] In his article "Erinnerungen an Tolstoi," Gorky also took Tolstoy's surprising change as his point of departure. While conceding Tolstoy's greatness as a writer, he saw in his latter-day martyrdom nothing but the inversion of an essentially despotic character. He went so far as to equate Tolstoy's character with that of his people: passive, not inclined to fight evil—and anti-Western. In later years Frisch was to say of this article that it revealed as much of Gorky (whom he knew personally) as it did of Tolstoy.[69] And though he did not, he might with equal justice have said of Gorky's second contribution, "Die russische Grausamkeit,"[70] that it revealed Gorky's sadism more convincingly than that of his compatriots.

Dostoevski, more than any other foreign author, dominated the literary pages of the *Neue Merkur*. Its editorial correspondence also contains items which tend to show that this preference was common in post-war Germany. On 7 October 1921, for example, Alfons Paquet sent Frisch a mimeographed appeal of the "Künstlerhilfe für die Hungernden in Russland" which, significantly, ended: "Don't leave any means untried and no road untrod which leads to the large, mighty highway which is being built from Europe to the land of Dostoevski." Obviously the drafters and signers of the appeal, among them such opposite personalities as Martin Buber and Erwin Piscator, Maximilian Harden and Kurt Wolff, were united in the belief that the evocation of Dostoevski's name would produce a strong and favorable emotional reaction.[71]

Frisch (or rather his wife) was able to secure the rights for the first German translation of Dostoevski's "Aus dem Tagebuch eines Schriftstellers," a feuilleton of the year 1876 which, as a footnote pointed out, was both unknown and significant: "The following unknown piece is very characteristic of the free-lance writer and journalist Dostoevski."[72] The essay veers over a great variety of subjects—from Goethe to the raising of children—and concludes with the charming observation that a fiction writer, even when posing as a journalist, ends up writing fiction.

Frisch's memorial article on Dostoevski revealed him at his best as an essayist and made the rarity of his own contributions to the *Neue Merkur* all the more regrettable. Even the Russian-language journal, *Golos Rossii*, published in Berlin and highly critical of "foreigners" writing on Russian literature, praised the article and the "gifted German essayist and critic Ephraim [sic] Frisch."[73] In later years, when Frisch reviewed

Julius Meier-Graefe's Dostoevski biography in the *Frankfurter Zeitung*, he
had occasion to summarize the content and intent of his memorial article.
Obviously he had intended it as a refutation of the then fashionable and
often propagandistic interpretation of Dostoevski.[74]

In taking as his point of departure contemporary events—the Russian
revolution and the Communists' exploitation of Dostoevski—Frisch exemplified the style of the *Neue Merkur*. In trying to engage Dostoevski, in
a subsequent passage, as a co-combatant in the battle for a more harmonious future, Frisch characterized himself.[75] He wrote of Dostoevski:
"He prophesied misfortune to Europe, because he longed for everyone's
fortune; in an ever-erupting passion he warns his people whom he wishes
to preserve from misfortune."[76]

Two final publications by Russian Classicists also were carefully
edited with a view towards the readers of post-war Germany. The first,
entitled "Aus Anton Tchechows Taschenbuch (1892–1904),"[77] chose,
for the most part, those aphorisms which had a timely appeal. As one example for many: In a period which was blessed (or cursed) with dozens
of serious tracts on national characteristics, Chekhov's aphorism "I hate
a playful Jew, a radical Ukrainian, and a drunk German" leavened the
deadly serious pseudo-scientific tracts with levity.

The intent and content of the second one, Mikhail Saltykov—Shchedrin's
"Aus vergangenen Tagen,"[78] is revealed in Frisch's preface. After giving
a brief biographical sketch of the writer, Frisch praised him as a social
critic and satirist comparable to Swift in his artistry and impact on contemporaries. By publishing excerpts from Saltykov's satirical writings,
first as segments in the *Merkur* and then in book form in his *Neue Merkur*
publishing house, Frisch was pursuing one of his most noble aims: to
free the viable parts of a dead author's work from the inevitable process
of petrifaction that threatened the rest of it.

As evident in both the magazine and the editorial correspondence,
Frisch's interest in Russian literature was by no means confined to the
works of the nineteenth century. His attempts to secure the latest Russian
works reveal, in fact, the zealousness of a discoverer. On 15 January 1925,
he wrote to the translator Dmitrij Umansky to send him something new
very soon and he would likewise publish it very soon, for he had not used
something Russian for a long time. And another letter, of 30 January
1920, addressed to the poet and translator Arnold Ulitz, reveals the ad-
venturous method by which Frisch secured his greatest "scoop," the first
translation anywhere of Alexander Block's famous revolutionary ballad,
"Die Ballade der Zwölf."[79] Frisch wrote: Nothing of the entire revolutionary Russian literature was crossing the border and in so far as one
heard anything about the matter, not a single book was said to have been

printed in the past two years. Through the good offices of a member of the Ukrainian Red Cross his wife had received an original hand-written ms. of the poem "The Twelve" by Alex. Block, which was often mentioned but remained unknown.

Ulitz provided a true and poetic translation of the poem, which is now a classic of revolutionary literature. On 4 March 1920 Frisch congratulated Ulitz on his "treffliche Übersetzung" (splendid translation) and added the following revelatory remarks: the passages which he had characterized as not perfectly clear had been captured quite accurately. "Without wine" could mean nothing else than the literal meaning of the words and hence was explained by the prohibition against alcohol. He hoped that they would have great success with it.

Frisch took measures to assure this effect. He wrote a preface which praised both author and translator, and, in a rare note of self-congratulation, the *Merkur* for securing and publishing the poem. And when Block died, muted by the Revolution he had served as herald, Frisch marked the occasion with an unusual step. With the dramatic postscript "translated from the Russian Ms. by Fega Frisch," the *Neue Merkur* printed the unpublished and very moving personal tribute, couched in a letter to the deceased, by Aleksei Remizov, a prominent author in exile, who had been equally misunderstood by Russia's new masters.[80]

With further good editorial judgment, Frisch followed Remizov's elegaic tribute to Block with a sample of creative work, his narrative "Jugend,"[81] an excerpt from his new novel *Im blauen Felde*. In its subtle delineation of a young student's road to suicide because of thwarted love, it also proved, as had the publication of Saltykov, that the tradition of the Russian Classicists, in this case going back to Chekhov, continued unbroken even among the young revolutionary writers.

The final example of recent Russian literature to appear in the "independent" *Merkur* also included a prefatory note of the translator, Sawiel Tartakower. It stressed the traditional in the new work: "Serjej Jessenin is a *peasant poet* who has become famous in Russia within a very brief span. He has achieved great originality of content and novelty of expression through the strange animistic mythology of old-Russian sectarians. Cf., for example, the picture of God's calving or of the New Savior, who rides to the world on a mare."[82] Frisch, happy to have been the first to introduce Jessenin to German readers, kept abreast of his development as a writer. On 7 December 1922 he reported another "discovery" to Ulitz: Among the works of Russian writers *Pugatschew* by Jessenin was referred to as the most interesting work of recent literature. He had just been able to secure a copy, and his wife was also of the opinion that the work was extraordinary. As it happened, however, the planned appearance of *Pugatschew* fell victim to the enforced interruption in the *Merkur*'s publication. By the time the magazine resumed publication, it had long been "scooped."

The Lyre
of Mercury: III

1923-1925

Two general observations can be made about the literature published in
the *Neue Merkur* while it appeared under the aegis of the Deutsche Verlags Anstalt. Frisch's decision to allocate more space to factual articles
and less to purely literary ones resulted, more than anything else, in a
reduction of the German literature appearing in the journal. Perhaps
Frisch sensed, too, that a trough was setting in after German literature
had reached a crest in the first two decades of the twentieth century.
Whatever the reason, the effect was plain. As Fritz Schlawe put it, "Politics [in the *Neue Merkur*] gradually gained ground at the expense of literary contributions."[1]

Though German literature decreased in quantity, there was no diminution of quality. In fact the *Merkur*, with some exceptions, e.g. Thomas
Mann, retained its old contributors, despite the fact that it was "consistently outbid" by other magazines. In his article "Spiegel der Zeit,"[2]
Friedrich Burschell deplored that in Germany "you can get anything for
money." Many of the old-time contributors of the *Neue Merkur*—he
among them—who placed loyalty above money, proved that such venality was not universal.

Using, once more, the *Neue Merkur* as an index of the literary market
place, it becomes clear that Expressionism, if not completely defunct, was
on the wane. It had dominated, though not monopolized, the literary por-
tion of the *Neue Merkur* from 1919 to 1923. Now few purely Expressionistic works or those with vestiges of Expressionism were accepted. In an
article printed in the *Merkur* in April 1924, Max Krell wrote of "the
days of the boom of Expressionism."[3] He sounded as though he were
writing ancient history.

Several of the Expressionistic or crypto-Expressionistic works of this period, among them the novellas of Fontana and Ulitz, have previously been discussed, together with their transcendence of the movement, but none of these revert to pre-war Expressionism. Actually only two works of the years 1923–25 do so. They are Alfred Wolfenstein's "Unter den Sternen" and the poems of Armin Wegner.[4] From Wolfenstein's opening lines, "Der Schatten des Waldes bewegte sich in Geburt der Nacht" (The shades of the forest moved during the birth of night) to the last line, "Ein Flammenmeer badete ihn und er fühlte, wie er hinausstieg und nun in die Weite ging" (An ocean of flames bathed him and he felt how he now climbed out and made for the distance), the work is an Expressionistic crescendo. Eschewing names, in the fashion of the Expressionists, the novella tells of a man's reaction to a betrayal by his wife and his friend. It culminates in his experience of death after a knife wound, the result of a barroom fight.

It is easy to see why Frisch accepted Wolfenstein's Expressionistic work though the movement itself had already passed its prime. With this author, the style and the man were identical. Even as a young writer he deliberately falsified his age(he subtracted five years) in order to be a part of the Expressionistic generation.[5] As an older writer, he reached spontaneously for the style most germane to him when telling a story, which to him also meant a catharsis. The events in the story were largely biographical; the emotions in it reflected his own reaction to a personal catastrophe. Wolfenstein's former wife wrote me on 28 November 1962, that the novella reflected the urge of the young artists, engulfed by the post-war situation, to not only find a new language and original forms but also through their lives to express themselves differently and more clearly through a more passionate involvement with humanity and a vehement yet self-centered affection for their comrades and companions. Human ties were joined with holy intentions which ended bloodily torn. There was nothing secretive or underhanded about this abandon, which, in the final analysis, was directed towards the creation of human concord.

Despite the emotional content and the extravagance typical of the Expressionistic style, the story is fully controlled. As Soergel put it: "In inevitable sentences, which contain no longer any precipitous or unsteady elements, but rather the rigidity of an unavoidable fate, he [Wolfenstein] conveys into the arms of the conciliator, Death, the life [of a man], unreconciled between this and the other world, between earth and the universe."[6] Frisch, in short, secured for his magazine one of the last genuine Expressionistic novellas.

Armin Wegner, the second example of unchanged Expressionism, adhered to his Expressionistic style all of his life, perhaps because he lived his life in reverse. He once stated in an autobiography[7] that he was never older than age sixteen. Hence as late as 1963 he published "Ein Lied aus der blutigen Stadt Berlin,"[8] which but for the subject could have been written forty years earlier. It is therefore not surprising that his poems published in the *Neue Merkur* in 1924 retained the established style and themes of Expressionism, though they sound less declamatory than his earlier poetry. In "Mein Vater geht in mir" he expresses, once again, the younger generation's sense of subjugation by the world of their fathers. (To the readers of American literature, the title and metaphors will appear as startling anticipations of the poetry of Sylvia Plath.) In Wegner's poem the overpowering image of the father has not only indentured the speaker—a new note in the protest of the Expressionists— but also future generations and their chance for peace: "Einst aus den Enkeln, blühend von Waffen, hebt er sich wieder in gelber Gewitterwolke; / Zu zerstören das sanfte Gebäude des Abends, das mir der Mutter blaues Lächeln schuf." (Some day from the descendants, teeming with arms, he will rise again in a yellow thundercloud; / To destroy the gentle building that my mother's blue smile created for me.) In "Das Fieberschiff" the world is transformed to parallel the inner landscape of the poet. The fevered visions of the "I" make him the axis of an imaginary universe: "Bin ich nicht selbst die heiß gelaufene Achse, / An der die Welt wie eine Spindel tanzt?" (Am I, myself, not the overheated axis, / Upon which the world is dancing like a top?)

In "Stadt in Afrika," finally, the familiar image of (homosexual) love, coupled with death in a predatory jungle, is evoked once again. Popular with many Expressionists, it gains here genuineness and force because the African setting makes it appear logical and appropriate.

> Liebe, Henkersknecht, die blanken Zähne
> Zeigst du lockend; denn du sinnst auf Mord,
> Und gefesselt an des Tigers Mähne
> Schleifst du mich im Dampf der Wüsten fort.
> (My love, my hangman, your bared teeth
> Temptingly you show. For you're planning murder,
> And fettered to the tiger's mane
> You drag me off into the desert's steam.)

These poems, unlike so many late Expressionistic poems, are totally convincing. From the death of the movement Frisch had salvaged not only one of the few viable prose works, but also some of its genuine lyrics.

Several stories in the last two volumes of the *Merkur* recall Expressionism by utilizing, in a highly individualized manner, one or the other

of its stylistic or thematic conventions. Ernst Weiß, who was one of the
initiators of the Expressionistic revolution, employed, in his story "Daniel
und der Kaiser,"[9] some of its stylistic devices, for example its bold syntax, but his theme, subject, faith, and vocabulary are traditional. As Karl
Otten says of Weiß's earlier novella *Daniel*, to which the one in the *Merkur*
formed the sequel: "In form and content Weiß treats, contrapuntally,
the experience offered by the mysticism of the Old Testament. The attraction of *Daniel* reposes in the contrast between the modern, Expressionistic
language and the immutable law of fate and the miracle of religion."[10]

The language of Heinrich Lersch, one of the prominent German worker-
poets, is likewise reminiscent of Expressionism. Lines such as "Die Arbeit
hängt mit gierem Mund / An unserer Seele Stund um Stund / Und saugt
die roten Tropfen" (Work clings with greedy mouth / To our souls from
hour to hour / And sucks the scarlet drops) clearly testify to their Expressionistic "ancestry." But the ultimate affirmation of a technological
age and the partnership of man and machine are alien to Expressionism,
and so is the attempt to create a myth out of the working man, as illustrated by the following line: "Vater-Werkmann. . . . Der Welt Zukunft
baut sich aus deinem Leib, deinem Geist." (Father-Workman. . . . The
world's future builds up from your body, your spirit.)[11] Frisch apparently exercised particular care in selecting the poems of Lersch. The DVA
had recommended to him the pre-book publication of several poems from
Lersch's then forthcoming collection, *Mensch im Eisen*. With little enthusiasm he responded on 20 November 1924, in a letter to Kilpper:
"Likewise I have selected some poems of Lersch which, because of the
individuality of their make-up, seemed defensible [*vertretbar*]." In one
instance, at least, Frisch made the most astute choice possible. Lersch's
"Hammer, du funkelnder" (Hammer, you sparkling one)[12] has become
a classic of German *Arbeiterlyrik*.

Wilhelm Schmidtbonn's "Mondspiegel,"[13] finally, the story of a "war
of plants and flowers" upon a lunar landscape, borrows the pacifistic
stance of some Expressionists and, obviously, the device of using a utopian, symbolistic setting as an analogue to reality. The device, reminiscent of Strindberg's *Traumspiel* and Werfel's *Spiegelmensch*, is carried
here to its logical extreme: the war of flowers is at once grotesque and
eery. The story becomes all the more horrifying because it avoids the
shrill and pathetic style of the Activists. Its last sentence characterizes
its style: "Within me I bear the picture of those sleeping eternally, within
me, longing." Reminiscent of the Romantics rather than the Expressionists, Schmidtbonn's style intensifies horror through the contrast of
content and wording. This unity through disparity is all the more remarkable in view of the fact that the narrative was part of a larger work:

As an enclosure, Schmidtbonn wrote on 22 August 1923, he was sending a fragment from a novel [*The Enchanted One*], which was completely self-contained. Randall of *The Criterion*, not knowing of the fragmentary nature of the story, apparently agreed with Schmidtbonn. He found the writing "imaginative" and its form that of a "short story."[14]

The return to tradition, both German and foreign, that had been a trickle during the *Merkur*'s years of independence, became a mainstream during its last years of existence. Perhaps most significant was the simultaneous breach with two of its own publishing taboos, one implicit, the other occasionally expressed. For the first time in its history the *Neue Merkur* "revived" Goethe. It published Ernst Bertram's intelligent collection of Goethe's sayings about literature and poetry[15] as a form of homage for Thomas Mann on the occasion of his fiftieth birthday. Such tributes were usually and programmatically avoided. Though brief and quite appropriate—Goethe's aperçus about irony and nonconformity applied to Mann—the article was symptomatic of an epigonic tendency of the German literary market place. It contained a quotation from Goethe's diaries of 1830: "Observations about German art which is slowing down with a passion." The reprinting of Goethe's aperçus was uncommonly well-timed.

Why did the *Neue Merkur* conform to this retrogression? The reason is simple. Works submitted by traditionalists were often superior. Thus Georg Burckhardt's translations from Heraclitus were superb;[16] Leo Perutz' retelling of legends from East European ghettos and Georg Munk's about Irish saints appealed equally through their simple and classicistic style and through their exploration of a strange folk culture.[17] These and other contributors must have sensed the more traditional mood of the post-inflation *Merkur*; Professor Burckhardt's statement to me, in a letter of 18 May 1962, that he sent his contribution to the *Neue Merkur* because he found the magazine congenial says as much by implication.

By far the most successful of the neo-classical works was a poem by Hermann Hesse, "Media in vita." Its inclusion, together with the publication of a novella by Heinrich Mann,[18] provide an excellent index of the literary times. In a letter to Kilpper of 20 November 1924 Frisch explained his selection of these two authors: In conformance with Kilpper's frequently expressed wish to enlist names which would impress the public, in addition to the proven younger contributors, he had been able to draw upon names such as Hesse and Heinrich Mann in this instance. In short, Hesse was someone to conjure with.

Frisch's contacts with Hesse went back to 1911, when he was chief reader of the Georg Müller Verlag. Hesse's correspondence with the publisher (which I found in a forgotten attic of the Langen-Müller Verlag) attest to this early acquaintance. Then, in 1924, according to Dr. Walter Lindenthal, Frisch visited Hesse in Montagnola; in August of that year Frisch, Lindenthal, the Arthur Schnitzlers, the Samuel Fischers, and Hesse and his bride met in Lugano. It is likely that Frisch solicited Hesse's contribution during this meeting, especially since there is no letter about Hesse's poem in the editorial correspondence.

"Media in vita" is a two and one-half page poem based, as are so many of Hesse's works in this period, on Indian philosophy. Its meter and rhyme scheme are classical, as is its form: it is written as an invocation to the human heart. But the conquest of all deaths—as in many of his works Hesse posits the Hindu concept of metempsychosis—comes about only if the heart turns inward: "Und ruhig wendest du vom Außen / Dich weg und zu dir selbst nach innen." (And calmly do you turn from outward worlds / Away and to yourself, to inner ones.)

Two short stories return to one of the oldest models of the genre, to Boccaccio's *Decameron*. When Max Krell submitted his novella "Die Frangimani,"[19] a Renaissance tale of an abduction during an orgiastic feast, he was preparing a new edition of Boccaccio's works in German translation, the most inclusive till then. Not too surprisingly, his interpretation of Boccaccio's narrative art also describes Krell's own imitation:[20]

> Boccaccio bedeutet die eigentliche Lockerung der Novelle, ihre Beweglichmachung, bedeutet ebenso Kunst wie Unterhaltsamkeit . . . Er gestaltete den bürgerlichen Renaissancemenschen Italiens unheimlich greifbar . . . Er verließ den Kothurn, er schritt unter die Masse, packte ihre Instinkte, ihre Leidenschaften, ihre Sinnlichkeit ohne Verklärung. Er versank nicht in die Derbheit, er veredelte die Anekdote, gab ihr in den spitzesten, heikelsten Momenten die elegante Wendung und machte daraus eine Sache von Geist und Geschmack.

Krell's novella, which is indeed both entertaining and artistic, has weathered the times better than many far more avant-gardistic works of the period.

When the second Boccaccio-like novella, von Boetticher's "Tomasio!", was recently republished,[21] a reviewer, Karl Boegner, called it "a jewel of erotic literature, which takes place in Italy and is completely suffused by the spirit of Boccaccio."[22] The spirit of Boccaccio has indeed been captured in this tale of the seduction of a compliant Italian village girl and the deception practiced by mother and daughter to conceal its consequences nine months later.

Boetticher's story, the most daring to be published in the *Neue Merkur*, evoked a lively correspondence which illuminated the attitude of Germany's literate public. Although the novella is, by today's standards, piquant rather than outrageous, it sharply divided even the *Merkur*'s sophisticated readers. In a letter of 16 December 1924 from Klabund to Boetticher, c/o the *Neue Merkur* (which obviously was never forwarded), the former wrote that the latter had written a completely delightful novella. "Congratulations!" Burschell, on the other hand, voiced a contrary opinion in a letter of 9 January 1925: Boetticher, in his opinion, was entirely unworthy of the *Merkur*. Conversely, the editors of the *Merkur*'s rival, the *Neue Rundschau*, liked it so much that they started a concerted effort (as Frisch reported to Kilpper in a letter of 20 November 1924) to bring about its author's defection to their own journal. Finally an additional aftermath to the story offered Frisch the opportunity to state his views on the publication of erotica.

A German writer, Julius Kühn, had felt emboldened by the publication of Boetticher's novella to submit several risqué stories of his own; the title of one of them, "Langsam aus Lesbos windet sich ein Weg" (A Path Winds Slowly Out of Lesbos), best characterizes their content. Frisch returned the stories on 13 June 1925 with the following explanation: He was declining them not for reasons of subject matter, but because he found the treatment inadequate. Such stories must be composed with a spiritedness which carried the reader across the dangers of the contents. Told with a feeling of equanimity which almost ends up in bourgeois conventionality, they cause embarrassment. In our times, when erotica so frequently are dull, Frisch's yardstick seems to have lost none of its pertinence.

In a poem, "Don Juans letzte Liebe,"[23] Boetticher again, though less successfully, tried to recapture the spirit of the Renaissance. Eduard Reinacher, on the other hand, returned to the traditional form of the idyll in his "Elsässer Idyllen und Elegien."[24] His hexameters are disciplined; the mood is reminiscent of a period when faith was still whole and people, the folk, still uncorrupted. Reinacher, when asked whether the poem's genesis was induced by Germany's loss of Alsace, answered: "The problem of Alsace was of no importance for me. But angry remonstration against *all* injustice was in the air. One did not take anything from a rude policeman or official. I was a fanatical lyrist, and hence limited in my possibilities for protest." The timeliness of the subject merely intensified the pervasive note of nostalgia in these poems which, a century earlier, Adalbert von Chamisso had struck in his poems of childhood reminiscences.

Josef Ponten, more than anyone else, epitomized the *Merkur*'s retreat to tradition. His novella "Der Gletscher"[25] reverted to a theme which, through earlier treatments by E. T. A. Hoffmann, Hugo von Hofmannsthal and others, had become a standard motif in German literature: a bereaved elderly person discovers the corpse of a long-lost relative or lover, its youthful appearance preserved, while he himself has greatly aged. The only redeeming features of Ponten's story, which save it—despite its classic form and traditional plot—from being purely derivative, are the vividness of the nature descriptions and the minor variation upon the theme: this time survivor and victim are twin brothers.

Ponten's last belletristic contribution, "Anna Paulas Besuch,"[26] was saved by Frisch from being not only epigonal but banal as well. A writer, engaged in revising his first published work, a fictional homage to Womanhood, is visited by a young lady, the embodiment of his heroine. She successfully pleads with him not to revise his work. As the story ends, the reader is left in doubt as to whether the visitor is real or imaginary; as Ponten had apparently submitted the story originally, the doubt was resolved in favor of reality. Such an ending would have shorn the novella, in essence a dialogue about the relationship of an author to his work, of its one valid feature: the writer, while occupying himself once more with the material that went into the composition of his novel, comes to realize that he had but vaguely grasped the character of the model for his heroine. His soaring imagination now transforms her into a believable prototype of Modern Woman.

Ponten's successful ending compensates, in part, for his frequent lapses into triteness—even for this one: "Ihr Herz hüpfte| Man sah es dem dunkeln schweren Tuch über ihrer Brust an." (Her heart was pounding. One could see it by looking at the dark heavy cloth over her breast.) In a letter to Kilpper of 26 May 1924, Frisch summarized the substance of his person-to-person negotiations with Ponten: he had convinced Ponten to eliminate the half-formed and novelistic elements of the ending of "Anna Paula's Visit," an imaginary conversation rather than a story, which was to appear in the June issue. Even with these changes the work is ephemeral; without them it would have been sub-literary.

An anecdote of Wilhelm Schäfer's, "Der Schnürpudel und die Tabaksdose,"[27] is equally slight; it is merely surprising that Frisch (as is apparent in a letter from Schäfer to Frisch of 10 August 1923) actually solicited it. Since the anecdote implies a parallel between the liberation of the Rhineland from French occupation under Napoleon and from its modern, equally stifling and resented counterpart, Frisch may have been prompted by political considerations. Frisch, through the publication of the "Sonderheft Rheinland,"[28] it will be recalled, had entered a strong protest against the French; from Schäfer's letter of 18 September 1922 to Frisch, it becomes clear that the editor had unsuccessfully sought Schäfer's participation. Frisch possibly viewed the anecdote as a suitable substitute for the political essay.

The return to traditional literature, however nobly motivated and no matter how excellent some of its manifestations, exacted its price. It was paid in a forfeiture of some of the magazine's excitement. Ferdinand Lion, often brilliantly perceptive in his judgment, saw both the strengths and weaknesses of the retreat to tradition. In successive letters, one of 8 December 1923 and another undated one of, presumably, a few days later, he assessed Schäfer's anecdote and Ponten's "Gletscher" as follows: Schäfer was masterfully proficient, only one knew this masterful proficiency too long and too well. The October issue was editorially the best that could then be produced; but this best was, after all, only a very relative best. The novella by Ponten was good, quite good provincial art, concentrated and poetic rural art—but what did that signify? Lion's observation that not even the best was good enough served less as an indictment of the *Neue Merkur* than of a temporary low point in the entire literary spectrum.

The articles devoted to literary criticism also reflected the new accent on traditional literature. Most of those written in the *Merkur*'s final years dealt with past centuries. Two lengthy chapters of Burschell's study of Jean Paul appeared first in the *Neue Merkur*; also no less than three articles on Hölderlin by Conrad Wandrey, Johannes Alt, and Hermann Hesse; furthermore there was one on Stifter by Heinrich Ehl, and two on Voltaire.[29] Most of them were "Rettungen" or apologias. The one by Hesse best typifies their tenor. First he deplored the fact that Hölderlin had, in the past, attracted only a few, even if the most desirable, readers; on the other hand, he did not wish the poet to fall into the hands of the uninitiated: "Indeed there was even a Hölderlin fashion and the poet, by no means easily accessible, is lying today on the tables of some ladies, next to the speeches of Buddha and the feuilletons of Tagore." Finally Hesse called attention to the timeliness of Hölderlin who, in the prevailing crisis, provided ecstatic manifestoes for the revolutions of his and the reviewer's times: "Thus it was by no means an accident, that people remembered him [Hölderlin] right now, during that agitated eschatological mood of defeated Germany."

Similarly the *Neue Merkur* featured critical articles on contemporary authors who no longer were or had never been in the van of German literature. Felix Braun, for example, wrote a laudation of Hans Carossa's war-time diary, excerpts of which had appeared in the *Merkur* some years before; Poeschel, an appreciation of Eduard Reinacher to accompany the appearance of Reinacher's poems; and Wandrey, a Spitteler obituary.[30] Significantly, Frisch had never published an obituary of an author before.

A further article, Max Mell's review of Hugo von Hofmannsthal's collected works,[31] is equally significant. For Frisch had planned it, originally, and against all his previous convictions, as a commemoration of Hofmannsthal's fiftieth birthday. On 20 January 1924, Mell replied that Hofmannsthal was asking all major newspapers and magazines to refrain from any mentioning of his fiftieth birthday, which he considered a private matter. Advising Frisch to oblige, Mell suggested that he could write an article for the *Merkur* on the collected works of the poet as soon as they had appeared. As Mell told me on 20 December 1961: "Frisch, fine person that he was, respected Hofmannsthal's wishes." On 18 February 1922 Frisch wrote Mell rather sadly that most newspapers and journals had not respected Hofmannsthal's wishes. And although he, too, was not overly fond of commemorative articles, he would appreciate a belated article upon the appearance of the collected works. The exchange between Mell and Frisch confirmed a new and deplorable tendency in the *Neue Merkur*. It was becoming, if only occasionally, what it had never been before: it was turning antiquarian.

The works by and about authors who transcended both tradition and Expressionism were, therefore, all the more exciting and refreshing. Disparate as they were, they had one unifying thematic feature that lent the magazine, on the eve of its demise, a new profile. No doubt if the *Merkur* had been given a chance, Frisch would have found means to gain further contributions from these authors, made this new profile dominant, and would thus have succeeded in endowing his magazine with a new vigor.

What united such authors as Brecht, Kafka, Heinrich Mann, Alfred Neumann, W. E. Süskind, and Regina Ullmann was their pursuit of a deeper understanding of their characters, particularly their sexual behavior, possibly as a consequence of the advances of the science of psychology.

It is often forgotten, because of his later interests in the forms of drama and poetry, and in political and didactic writing, that Brecht, in his early plays and short stories, displayed superb insight into pathology. "Bargan läßt es sein,"[32] the story with which Brecht made his debut in the *Neue Merkur*, depicted most convincingly a case of compulsion and homosexual aberration; its theme is closely paralleled in his "Leben Eduard des Zweiten von England," a free adaptation of a play by Marlowe. Parts of the drama, connected by a short synopsis, appeared in the *Neue Merkur*.[33] Here, too, a ruler jeopardizes his realm because of a compulsive love for

a man: "Eh mir mein Gaveston genommen wird. / lasse ich die Insel."
(Rather than have my Gaveston taken from me, / I shall leave this isle.)
The king himself characterizes his love as madness: "Mein Herz / klopft
in dem schwarzen Loch der Brust armselig / und macht mich toll um
meinen Gaveston." (My heart / beats poorly in that black hole of my
chest / and drives me mad about my Gaveston.) As Marianne Kesting
points out, the theme of homosexual dependency was no doubt one of the
elements that caused Brecht to write "Bargan," the poem "Ballade von
der Freundschaft," and the adaptation of Marlowe's drama.[34] In the first
and last-named works, Brecht's understanding of the hero's compulsion,
subtle despite the drastic language, might best be described as psychological realism.

The publication of Brecht's "Edward" also provides us with a close
reading of his rising stock in the literary market place. Two years earlier
he had, most deferentially, entreated for publication; now editors were
knocking at *his* door. As early as 17 May 1922, Frisch asked the intercession of Lion Feuchtwanger, Brecht's collaborator in those years, for
the rights to a one-act play by Brecht; news of Brecht's early dramas,
some still unpublished today, must have reached Frisch. On 22 October
1923 he repeated his request: he would very much like to publish something by Brecht again, indeed, quite soon, since he could make room for
it, and asked the author to either reply promptly or, best of all, to pay him
a visit.

Apparently Brecht chose for reply the second option in Frisch's letter,
a visit. He must have suggested a pre-book publication of *Eduard*, because
some months later, on 29 January 1924, Frisch asked the Kiepenheuer
Verlag for pre-book publication rights. He and Brecht then "collabo-
rated" on the shortened version for the *Merkur*. On 5 February 1924
he wrote Brecht that he had sent the piece they had agreed upon to the
typesetters and had asked that the galleys be sent to Feuchtwanger.
Brecht was to inform him in good time of the changes he still wished to
make. Brecht and Frisch seemingly had agreed on additional deletions.
Frisch wrote to the DVA on 19 February 1924: By means of additional
deletions, which he had carried out with Brecht, the issue would run to
approximately eighty-eight pages.

The reactions to the publication are likewise illuminating. Frisch, who
had recognized Brecht's talents at a very early stage in his career, wrote
to Kilpper on 11 February 1924 that he considered Brecht's contribution very important. *The Criterion*, which had praised Wilhelm Schmidtbonn, also brushed Brecht with its praise: "Imaginative writing by native
writers is contributed . . . a play in the February number by Bertolt
Brecht . . . based on the story of Piers Gaveston."[35] A reader, on the other

hand, Dr. Otto Pietsch, whose letter of 6 March 1924 sounded by no means unintelligent or ill-willed, surmised that probably more than half the readers would leave it unread. From the start of his career, Brecht's works invited controversy.

Though totally different in style, composition, and genre, Regina Ullmann's novella, "Die Streckenwärterin,"[36] shares with Brecht the exploration of characters in depth. Here she delves into the psyche of two seemingly very simple people who by chance have drifted into marriage. But she shows beneath the simplicity of a girl devoid of "the least bit of education" the same complexity of character, the same ambivalence, which one ordinarily associates with far more sophisticated persons. When the heroine arrogates too much power and too many rights and becomes, in effect, a domestic tyrant, the author says of her: "This type also exists in a small [setting]." In this story the sexual theme, which recurs in the aforementioned works, takes the form of a power struggle between a man and a woman, low in intelligence, low on the social scale. It corrodes their love and bars communication. When wisdom finally and instinctively prevails, it has become too late to avert tragedy. Without being derivative, Regina Ullmann's story closely parallels Gerhard Hauptmann's novella *Bahnwärter Thiel*. But the conflict is told here from a woman's perspective.

The designation of psychological realism also fits the contribution by Alfred Neumann, the narrative "Marthe Munk."[37] Neumann, who unravelled in virtually all his works the psychological causes behind a demonic drive for power, here turns to the demonism of an ugly woman's quest for sexual love. Ignored by her employer, an amatory owner of a fruit and vegetable store, she has a brief affair with his son. Jilted by him, she revenges herself by having his father drive him from the house on evidence manufactured by her. When she finally succeeds in blackmailing the grocer into an affair and a promise of marriage, she becomes stricken with self-disgust and attempts murder and suicide. She fails in the former, but succeeds in killing herself.

What lends the story its power is Neumann's complete understanding of the motivations behind his heroine's actions. Her sexual frustration is drawn with unsparing verisimilitude: "She heard Carapezzi at the door; from the noise made by unlocking it, she knew that he was sober. She pressed herself against the posts; she felt as if the wood were beaten by a strange and still more abandoned pulse than her own. He is not drunk, oh God, then he probably won't want to. But she will now whisper: Kasper, Kasper! and stretch out her arms, so that he can seize them. Oh, how strong he is."

The publication of Neumann's story gave Frisch a great deal of personal satisfaction. As Neumann's widow (daughter of the publisher Georg Müller) told me on 14 July 1962, Frisch discovered Neumann's literary gift. While chief reader of the Georg Müller Verlag, Frisch had steered Neumann from the business office to his own editorial department and there encouraged him to write fiction. By contributing "Marthe Munk," a suspense novella of consummate psychological intuition, at a time when there was a dearth of talent, Neumann repaid the favor.

W. E. Süskind, another author who acknowledges Frisch's role as his discoverer, contributed two stories also marked by their careful exploration of sexual psychology. His "Tordis"[38] was almost a historical necessity. For years the Expressionists had taken the conflict between father and son as the theme for their works. Each time it was intended as symbol or archetype; Süskind now analyzed a specific case psychologically. As father and son fall platonically in love with the same woman, the son slowly begins to appreciate his father and himself in their role as men, beyond the paternal-filial relationship. Süskind succeeded in revitalizing a literary theme, overworked by the Expressionists, by removing it from the realm of abstraction to a concrete and psychologically convincing situation.

Süskind's second contribution, a novella entitled "Das Morgenlicht," was an exploration into the mind of a young woman who rebels against convention, but loses her sense of sexual identity in the process. Disgusted with a past affair in which she felt herself reduced to a function—"he always demanded the same thing of me, as from a button"—she seeks truth and fulfillment on the stage, in the past, symbolized by a toy and old-clothes collection, and in vague dreams of sexual aberration: "I would prefer loving women, but it's so difficult, so much fuss," she says at one point. When her fiancé returns from America and realizes "that this is no woman," he shoots her, as he intimates, in psychological self-defense.[39] Klaus Mann suggests in his autobiography that Süskind, in creating his heroine Vera Martin, borrowed some traits from Klaus's sister, Erika Mann: Süskind "had a good deal of talent. The story in which he immortalized Erika, was indeed a remarkable piece of writing. Unfortunately, it could have no happy end; for Erika was impervious to his wooing. So Süskind revenged himself by having her assassinated. The conclusion of his plot was rather lurid, with Erika sitting in an armchair and looking peevish because her lover had killed her."[40] Whether biographical or not, the story combined psychological acuity with reticence and tact. It breached a shift in perspective—the first-person narrator, at first an admirer and partisan of the girl, turns detached reporter after the tragedy—through a uniform, classical style. W. E. Süskind, who was to become an expert on German style, in this instance provided a portent of his future role.

Martin Kessel, in his novella "Das Horoskop," also delved into abnormal psychology. A secretary, uprooted by the war from her genteel, aristocratic background, prides herself upon living "ahistorically" and making her own way. Yet her modernity becomes obsessive, absurd, and extreme. She spends one night with three men—"she consumed three in one gallop"—and, quoting passages from Wedekind, courts danger and death until she loses a leg in an automobile accident, thus fulfilling the prophecy of her horoscope.[41] Death-wish, superstition, and compulsive compensation for a drab life motivate the extraordinary actions of a seemingly ordinary woman.

On 2 March 1962, Kessel provided me with his interpretation of this, his first novella. Explaining why his heroine risks her life jumping on a dumb-waiter and dodging automobiles, he said: The underlying idea was the attraction of technology and a bent towards acrobatics. Man always needs a counterpart, a superstition, a faith, or a feeling of predestination. He was convinced that a novella should always counterpoint, here, for example, by setting technology against superstition. The quintessence of "The Horoscope"? Each judgment stands upon an artificial limb (a reference to the symbol of the heroine's wooden leg). One gains an experience and sacrifices a part of innocence.

Kessel, like Süskind, was to become famous as a master of German prose. When he received the Büchner Prize and, again, the Prize der Bayerischen Akademie der schönen Künste, he was praised for "exemplary exactness and perfection of language."[42] In publishing Kessel's first novella, Frisch made several emendations; in one instance, which Kessel remembers specifically, Frisch asked him to change the phrasing "einen Geruch, dem manche ihrer Verehrer unterlagen" (a smell to which some of her admirers succumbed) to "ein Aroma." Frisch's fastidiousness, observed in his reluctance to fight the Nazis, extended to his choice of words.

A decidedly lesser novella—Lion, in a letter of 8 December 1923, called it "abscheulich" ("execrable")—took sexual aberration one step further. In Martin Borrmann's "Der Zwerg und das Grammophon" desire and lust become grotesque. A circus dwarf falls in love with a voice heard on a record, but he cannot recapture "the ecstasy felt on the first evening" when he hears the singer in person or on his own, more modern record player.[43] After stealing the old gramophone, he is confined to an asylum for the criminally insane as an incurable obsessive. Borrmann told me, on 3 March 1962, that this fascination for the grotesquerie of eroticism had been a pervasive theme of his fiction before and after this novella. He also confided: "At that time I worked a great deal with index cards. If, for example, I heard a hurdy-gurdy, I immediately wrote this down and soon thereafter utilized it." The method may account for the story's jumpiness.

The new, more permissive sexual ethos of the post-war years is one of the points of departure, though not the chief substance, of a novella by Heinrich Mann, "Die roten Schuhe."[44] A young man accepts the new standards until he uncovers a liaison between his sister and his best friend. His ambivalent feelings about the new mores were meant to characterize the new code of ethics among Germany's upper-class children. Their apparent devil-may-care descent into lawlessness, crime, venality, and corruption are accompanied by scarcely admitted longings for the life they have left. At the end of the story, brother and sister sit on a garden bench reminiscing about their childhood and sharing each other's fears. The girl likens their fate to that of the heroine of the fairy tale, *The Red Shoes*. They, like the ballerina, must dance on and on, like it or not. In a letter to Kilpper of 20 November 1921, Frisch explained the inclusion of Heinrich Mann (and of Hermann Hesse) as an attempt to balance, in his special literature issue, established writers and young hopefuls. But "The Red Shoes," though written by a fifty four-year-old author, displayed as much and as thorough an understanding of the young generation as any literary work by one of its members.

The *Neue Merkur*'s last venture into new literary directions was a fitting close to its eight years of publishing experimental writings. Immediately following the death of Kafka it unveiled eighteen aphorisms from his literary legacy.[45] They have become too well known to require commentary; their appearance in the *Merkur*, however, provides a rare glimpse of Kafka's emergence as a major figure upon the literary scene. This emergence has its particular fascination, because (as Hans Henneke correctly points out) this sudden posthumous fame of a relatively obscure author is virtually without parallel in literary history.[46]

To the cognoscenti of literature in Munich, Kafka was no stranger. The introduction had taken place in 1916, when Kafka appeared in Munich to read his then unpublished novella *Die Strafkolonie*. In an unpublished autobiographical essay, the writer and Rilke-biographer Eugen Mondt describes this event as follows:[47] Kafka's reading was arresting and without constraint, not as if he were reciting but as though he were speaking from one person to another. The listeners found the story so gruesome that several women were unable to endure it to the end. But he and his friends Gottfried Kölwel and Max Pulver were overwhelmed by it.

In short, Kafka greatly impressed a select few in Munich, but his initial fame scarcely transcended the fifty-odd listeners which the Gallerie Goltz could accommodate. The public learned next to nothing of Kafka's reading of a just completed novella which has since become world literature. The *Münchner Post*, for example, ignored the evening completely. Worse still, the *Münchner Neuesten Nachrichten* of 11 November 1916 gave a misleading and entirely negative account of the event. It condemned not only the story as a whole ("the artistic impressions . . . were not very salutary"), but also virtually each component part ("the story should not have petered out so infinitely slowly"). Yet by reading the correspondence of the people who, in the loosest possible sense, formed the circle around the *Neue Merkur*, one can trace how a kind of subterranean fame of Kafka was spreading. Gottfried Kölwel, for example, sent an enthusiastic report to Alfred Wolfenstein;[48] W. E. Süskind recalled on 1 November 1961 that Kafka was the subject of numerous discussions at receptions in the house of Thomas Mann.

Though in the army at that time, Frisch heard of Kafka's reading from Kölwel while on furlough (Mrs. Kölwel reported this fact to me on 26 November 1962). After resuming publication in 1919, Frisch repeatedly solicited contributions from Kafka. When Kafka died in 1924, Frisch immediately published Süskind's obituary[49] and obtained for the special literary issue the aforementioned set of aphorisms, selected by Max Brod. Their publication, in turn, gave rise to further discussions. Willy Haas, subsequently the influential editor of the *Literarische Welt*, urged Frisch in an undated letter to read Kafka's posthumous novel, *The Trial*. He considered it the greatest genius of narrative writing in decades, and had not read anything like it since Dostoevski. Kafka's fame, as the *Merkur* and its editorial correspondence illustrate, had quietly been in the making for a long time.

The volume of foreign literature decreased less during the *Merkur*'s last two years than that of German literature. This practice, probably the result of chance more than of editorial policy, tended to lend a still greater cosmopolitan flavor to the magazine's belletristic part. More important, the quality of foreign literature published towards the end rivalled that of the magazine's best years. From 1923 to 1925 the *Merkur* published the first German translations of important works by Valéry, Pirandello, D. H. Lawrence, Isaak Babel and others; it helped popularize these authors in Germany where they were, until then, relatively unknown.

Ernst Robert Curtius was the mediator for Paul Valéry. As Curtius explained, Valéry's early writings had gained some popularity in Germany; the new writings which had begun to pour from his pen after a twenty-year, self-imposed silence, the period of gestation of a new style, were, however, virtually unknown in Germany. Curtius not only provided a close exegesis of some of Valéry's poetry as an introduction to his new lyric style, but he also attempted to fix his place within the tradition of European letters: "Not only Mallarmé's symbolism, but also the French Parnassian and Classical literature are among the postulates of Valéry's art. It unites these three literary movements, as Thibaudet puts it, 'in a common spirit.' "[50] Curtius supplied his own translations of two lengthy poems by Valéry to prove his own interpretations. In acquiring the rights to their publication, Curtius entered into competition with no less a translator than Rainer Maria Rilke,[51] as he was to learn from Valéry himself.

The letter from Valéry to Curtius, in which he also provides some interesting views on multiple translations of the same poem into the same language, was preserved as a "stowaway" in a letter of 22 March 1924: Valéry had agreed to a publication in a German magazine, even though Rilke, too, had just sent him translations of the same poems. The poet considered the parallel treatment of his work by two German writers of such high standard a most interesting undertaking and encouraged the publication of both translations. The translations of "Le Serpent" did indeed supplement each other by providing different perspectives upon their originals.

The story of the translation of "Le Serpent" was to have a humorous sequel. Apparently Valéry gave translation rights to this poem to yet a third German writer, W. Petry. As Curtius (correctly) reported to Frisch in a letter of 10 December 1924, Petry completely falsified its style: In the Rowohlt journal *Vers und Prosa*, he had rendered it into "Expressionese."

Curtius contributed yet another article, an analysis of Valéry Larbaud, to my knowledge the first scholarly article in German on this true-to-life portraitist of adolescents.[52] If today Larbaud is still widely read in Germany—several of his novels are available in pocketbook editions—Curtius and the *Neue Merkur* may be credited with having begun the vogue more than forty years ago. (Frisch's contact with Curtius and Larbaud probably had an additional consequence. His crusade in behalf of James Joyce, which culminated in his perceptive and influential feuilleton in the *Frankfurter Zeitung* of 11 January 1928, in all likelihood was inspired by these two acquaintances who were among Joyce's warmest advocates on the continent.)

Curtius' final contribution, a gloss about French literary journals, Franz Schoenberner's tribute to Anatole France upon his eightieth birthday, Iwan Goll's study of the French literary scene, and Heinrich Mann's biographical essay on Victor Hugo exhaust the *Merkur*'s exploration of French writings from 1923 to 1924.[53] If one takes into account how many important French writers were just then publishing their most important works (Péguy, Suarez, Barrès, and Daudet), it seems a rather sparse accounting.

Italy was even more sketchily represented. Only one Italian work appeared in the dying days of the *Merkur*, but, if one looks at the subsequent development of literature, its choice could not have been more felicitous. It was a drama by Pirandello, "Das Diplom" (By Judgment of Court).[54] Its publication crowned a two-year effort by Frisch to secure the rights to a work by the Italian author. As early as 12 December 1923 Frisch had asked Lion, then in Italy, to start negotiations with Pirandello's agent, Giuseppi Prezzolini, an occasional contributor to the *Merkur*.

This one-act drama, at first glance an uncomplicated farce, portrays the revenge of a man ostracized and thrown out of work by his fellow townspeople, who have accused him of having the "evil eye." He plans to exploit their superstitions through blackmail. To lend greater verisimilitude to his role as sorcerer, he has launched a court action for slander against two prominent citizens. If he can manage to *lose* this trial, as he takes great pains to do, he will have established the authenticity of his magic powers by a "diploma" from the court, a document as weighty as the judge's doctoral degree.

In publishing "Das Diplom," the *Neue Merkur* introduced its readers to the ambivalent world of Pirandello which was to have such a profound effect on the European stage. Much in the manner of *Right You Are, If You Think You Are*, reality and justice bear a multiple face. We are left to wonder which is to be credited. The irrational assumptions of society about a man assume a reality of their own. A harmless nobody becomes so envenomed by his senseless persecution that he begins to conform to the image his fellows hold of him; his looks *can* kill. And what of justice? At one point the judge maintains that human justice is the most cruel game imaginable. The end of the drama exemplifies this lament. We are left to assume that justice will be done, i.e., the prominent citizens will be exculpated, but Justice (with a capital "J") will be perverted, because the hero's reputation as a caster of spells will be firmly established and will serve him in his effort to terrorize and exploit the townspeople through blackmail.

English literature was represented by two very dissimilar authors, each, however, by means of thoroughly characteristic works. May Sinclair, a feminist, an adherent of philosophical idealism, and a believer in spiritualism, as well as one of the early practitioners of stream-of-consciousness writing, granted permission and waived all fees for the translation rights to her story "Jones' Karma," which had originally appeared in *The Criterion*. Its republication in the *Merkur* was yet another symptom of the fashionableness of Indian philosophy in Europe.[55] What lends this story added interest for Western readers is the fact that the Indian beliefs affect the life (or rather, lives) of a European protagonist. Given the chance to relive his existence, he is unable to escape his karma because of his inability to reach an inner regeneration.

The publication of three works by D. H. Lawrence in German translation—excerpts from two novels, *Kangaroo* and *The Boy in the Bush*, and the travel picture, *The Dance of the Sprouting Corn*—mark one of the high points in the history of the *Neue Merkur*.[56] If the magazine had accomplished nothing more than the introduction of Lawrence to the German reading public, it would have been assured, at the least, of a footnote in literary history, since Lawrence was to become a potent influence on German novelists. His introduction to Germany via the *Merkur*, both through his work and the short but accurate prefatory notes of his German translator, was a curious—and typical—blend of design and chance, as well as the story of an editor's initial misgivings and ultimate astuteness.

Two interviews, one with Else Jaffé-Richthofen on 17 July 1962 and another with Rudolf Nutt on 11 December 1961, both paraphrased here *in extenso*, will provide the background against which the works of D. H. Lawrence entered the German literary mainstream. Else Jaffé-Richthofen was Lawrence's sister-in-law, the sister of his wife, Frieda von Richthofen. She was also the widow of an early contributor to the *Merkur*, the Finance Minister of the short-lived Bavarian Soviet Republic, Edgar Jaffé. Mrs. Jaffé's memory of the 1920's appeared unimpaired despite her eighty odd years and the passage of nearly forty years: she had started to do some translations of D. H. Lawrence's work at his suggestion, and since she had met Fega Frisch in Berlin and later again in Munich, where a group of friends including Ponten, Carossa, Frisch and Lion met frequently, a tie to the *Merkur* was established. She negotiated the publication of his stories, selected by Lawrence himself, who wanted to be represented in a journal of high literary quality.

The superb translations gathered plaudits from several readers, e.g., from Kurt Tucholsky (a magazine editor) in a letter of 21 November 1924. Some time ago he had written an ardent love letter for her wonderful translation to the woman interpreter of a contribution by an Australian-American writer. The letter reveals that Lawrence, identified by Tucholsky as an "Australian-American," was little known even among the well-informed in Germany.

At first, however, the arrival of the translations raised some serious misgivings in the *Merkur*'s editorial offices. As Rudolf Nutt, one of Frisch's editorial assistants, recalled it, Frisch disliked the sex in D. H. Lawrence's novels. Nutt, Frisch, and Schoenberner debated this point of view. It was

Schoenberger, who convinced Frisch that Sex, in contrast to Eros, was being suppressed in the literature of that time and therefore *Lady Chatterley's Lover* meant a breakthrough. Frisch replied that a passage such as the one of the wreathed genitals was "impossible." To Nutt's reply that Lawrence was able, in a wonderful manner, to represent these matters tremendously subtly, Frisch answered that the monomaniacal emphasis on sex was repugnant to him. What finally changed Frisch's mind were the arguments of Schoenberger, whose judgment he esteemed. At the end of the discussion he praised Lawrence's subtle depiction of the feminine psyche.

The information supplied by Mrs. Jaffé-Richthofen and by Rudolf Nutt provides an illuminating footnote to Lawrence's conquest of the German literary market. It also gives a measure of Frisch's greatness as an editor: he recognized and accepted merit and innovations even if he was repelled by some of their aspects. Consistent to the end, Frisch lauded the psychological understanding of Lawrence and criticized his (as he thought) obsessive preoccupation with sex when he wrote, several years later, a feuilleton, "D. H. Lawrence," for the *Frankfurter Zeitung* of 6 January 1926.

American literature was described but not represented in the last two volumes of the *Merkur*. Even the descriptions were, for the most part, cursory. Beyond a mere mention of Eugene O'Neill, Theodore Dreiser, H. L. Mencken, and James Branch Cabell in an article by H. V. Velton, the only American writers to be discussed in the *Neue Merkur* were the Muckrakers.[57] In a cohesive review of three novels and two autobiographies (Sinclair Lewis' *Babbitt*, Samuel Ornitz' *Haunch, Paunch, and Jowl*, Ludwig Lewisohn's *Up Stream*, and Upton Sinclair's *Jimmy Higgins* and *Love's Pilgrimage*), all of which had just appeared in German translation—Franz Schoenberner presented a remarkable, if brief, study in comparative cultural history and literature. Consistently using German conditions and literature as a point of departure, e.g., the anti-Philistine attitude of Friedrich Hebbel, he analyzed these American works as literary counterparts to German Naturalism and a welcome contrast to the sociological ineffectiveness of German writers. The title of his article, "Amerikanische Antitoxine," expressed his view of their functions in America. To his chagrin he found no antitoxins in current German literature. Twenty years later, from the vantage point of the United States, Schoenberner had the opportunity to comment upon this early assessment of his new homeland: "I still remember the somewhat highbrow title, 'American Antitoxins,' which was to express that the modern American writers . . . by their social criticism reacted against the disintegrating poison of a purely money-minded society. The whole essay was some-

what complicated but, just for this reason, it fitted perfectly with the
intellectual and sometimes academic style of a review written for an
élite of German and European intelligentsia."[58]

The years after the Russian revolution brought a revival of interest
in the Russian classicists, especially outside the Soviet Union. German
publishers, sensing the mood of their public, brought out the first translations of the collected works of Dostoevski, Tolstoy, Pushkin, and others.
These ventures were not solely inspired by intellectual needs; probably,
to an equal extent, they resulted from the conditions of the literary market place. The Soviet Government had neglected to renew copyrights on
the older authors or to obtain them for the contemporary ones.[59] Hence
printing translations without payment of royalties or publisher's fees provided German publishers a financial margin of safety during a bleak
period in the German economy.

In the case of Frisch, a life-long interest in Russian literature rather
than financial considerations explains the continued preponderance of
primary and secondary works of the Russians in the pages of the *Neue
Merkur*. Nonetheless, managing a magazine recurrently beset by financial
difficulties, he must have welcomed these free acquisitions as an additional
boon. For example, when his wife was translating the collected works of
Pushkin for Buchenau and Reinhart, a Munich publishing house, Frisch
had access to hitherto untranslated works of Pushkin. He capitalized
upon this opportunity by acquiring the rights to the pre-book publication
of passages from an incomplete prose narrative.[60] Also, when a now
famous letter from Dostoevski to Pauline Suslova was first printed, together with a commentary by Leonid Großmann elucidating Dostoevski's
amorous relationship to this enigmatic and cruel woman, Frisch reprinted both.[61] But with the original unavailable to him because of the
chaotic state of communications with Russia, Frisch simply asked for
(and received)—free of charge—the rights to the *English* translation.
He acknowledged the latter in full, but the Russian source only in
passing.

Far more dramatic, however, and in fact a publishing coup of the first
magnitude, was the discovery of hitherto unpublished letters of Dostoevski through Dmitri Umansky, the Russian "correspondent" of the *Neue
Merkur*. Written at the apex of Dostoevski's career, the Pushkin celebration of 1880, these letters were introduced by Frisch with unusual fan-
fare.[62] To emphasize the importance of the discovery, he had the article
copyrighted and, for the only time in his magazine's history, placed the
copyright line immediately below the title. Also Frisch wrote an editorial
foreword, an event "joyously welcomed" by Director Kilpper in a letter
of 10 June 1924.

In content, the letters are curiously disappointing. Written by one of the literary giants of his time, at a moment when his sway over contemporaries in Russia was complete, they shed little light on Dostoevski the writer, on his colleagues, or on the occasion—and they illuminated the personality of the writer rather unfavorably. Dostoevski's gratuitous denigration of Turgenev, his lingering over trifles (would he be reimbursed for the wreaths to be deposited on Pushkin's grave?) his unemotional reception of unprecedented homage: all verify Frisch's introductory statement that the letters reveal new aspects of a strangely ambivalent personality. Franz Schoenberner recalled having a similar reaction at the time of publication of these letters: "These letters exhale the sulky atmosphere of a badly aired petit bourgeois soul; a soul foreign to all natural greatness but slain with a genius as with a disease, possessed like a medium by a spirit who spoke through his mouth without changing the substance."[63]

The *Neue Merkur*, though few realized it at the time, made publishing history with yet another Russian work, the first German translation of a masterly short story by Isaak Babel, then little known outside Russia. The *Merkur* thus helped prepare his renown in the Western world.[64] Ernst Bloch, for example, recalled, on 17 April 1962, how much of an impact the reading of "Pan Apolek" made upon him at the time.

Babel, the poet in the uniform of Budenny's Red Cavalry, here presents one of his sensitive genre pictures of Russian village life. It is the story of a hoboesque yet saintly painter who immortalizes the lowly by using them as models for his religious paintings. By so doing, he gives artistic expression to his heresies. He believes in a more worldly, sensuous Christ who, according to apocryphal writings, was married to a young girl, Deborah. It is fascinating to contemplate that at approximately the same time, but worlds apart, D. H. Lawrence was writing his *The Escaped Cock* (*The Man Who Died*), which was based on the same heresy.

"Pan Apolek" was published in the last issue of the *Neue Merkur*. It appeared together with yet another "discovery" of the magazine, a short story by Jordan Jofkoff. The translation of his "Lied der Räder" ("Song of the Wheels")[65] was accompanied by a translator's brief commentary. Theodor Blank hailed the Bulgarian writer as one of the most profound and consistent figures of Bulgarian literature. The story supports this accolade. Steeped in the rural lore and customs of Bulgaria, it nonetheless has a universal theme. A man, even if he be a simple artisan, as is the hero, a cartwright, can find satisfaction and meaning only in his work.

Babel and Jofkoff were the last literary works to appear in the *Neue Merkur*. In short, the belletristic part of the magazine closed upon the same high note with which it had begun. Frisch could take pride in the fact that the *Neue Merkur* died with the luster of its literature undiminished and with its dedication to European letters, both from within and beyond Germany's borders, nobly demonstrated to the last.

Epilogue

If this book, the history of the triumphs and travails of a journal, has a
hero, it is its editor-publisher, Efraim Frisch. It seems therefore appropriate to trace his career beyond the years of his editorship. When Frisch
decided to leave Munich for a vacation in Italy even before the last issue
of the *Neue Merkur* had appeared, he took with him a new, if temporary,
appointment from the Deutsche Verlags-Anstalt. He was to be a consulting editor for foreign literature, which meant sifting new foreign
books for possible publication in German translation. But in this he
failed. As Director Kilpper wrote me on 2 April 1962: Although they
punctually forwarded his salary to Italy for a long time, they never heard
from Frisch again. This behavior, so markedly opposed to Frisch's usual
punctiliousness, probably has a simple psychological explanation. To
work again for the DVA would have perpetuated the very memories that
his trip to Italy was designed to blunt.

Frisch returned to Munich for an additional four years, until 1929.
Into this period fall his numerous translations from the French, especially
of Luc Durtain, Jean Giraudoux, and Jean Cocteau, his first memorable
feuilletons in the *Frankfurter Zeitung*, and his novel, *Zenobi*.[1] His feuilletons were, in a way, a partial continuation of his work for the *Neue
Merkur*. He addressed himself to an astounding variety of topics and
wrote with considerable authority. The subject matter ranged from literature to politics, from education to music, from art and theater to
Judaism.

Nonetheless a change of mood is discernible in the essays Frisch wrote
after the demise of the *Neue Merkur*. Their style is more intense; his
perspective, which was never superficial, became even more profound. He
was more reflective and less polemic; his often brilliant aperçus of for-

mer years frequently gave way to telling examples. Frisch appeared more persuasive and less sparkling. Obviously, earnestness of intent had given way to the joy of creativity.

No doubt the times, to which Frisch was so intensely attuned, had something to do with this change. Frisch saw the intellectual at bay and the European order threatened. It gave him little satisfaction, for example, when his prophecies, expressed in "Die Zukunft der deutschen Juden,"[2] became terrifying reality.

Frisch had always been serious, but now this tendency deepened. His editorial correspondence had been completely devoid of humor—in complete contrast, for example, to that of his fellow-editor and close friend, Franz Blei.[3] In later years even an occasional humorous leavening disappeared from Frisch's letters and essays. Instead—and perhaps by way of compensation—his novel of that period, *Zenobi*, proved the most scintillating and roguish creative work of his lifetime.

In *Zenobi*, Frisch returned to the world of his childhood, but was reconciled to it through time and distance. In his first novel, *Das Verlöbnis* (The Engagement),[4] which also has an autobiographical setting, Frisch had introduced a Kafkaesque father largely responsible for the despair and suicide of his son. The hero in *Zenobi*, however, prevails by being able to change his environment by means of his powerfully volatile imagination. Apparently Frisch no longer felt that his early surroundings were immutable.

Zenobi was, at the same time, Frisch's way of taking leave of his brother Phillip, sixteen years his junior, who had been reported missing on the Russian front during World War I. Frisch's letter of 15 January 1925 to the translator and writer Dmitrij Umansky, a collaborator of the *Neue Merkur*, makes this assumption a virtual certainty: His younger brother, who served with the Austrian Army, had been taken prisoner at Kowel in 1915 during a Russian attack. Until the end of 1918 the family had received either direct or indirect news of him, but since then nothing reliable. Finally, about three years previously, a rumor had reached Frisch, via all sorts of detours, that the brother was at Krassnojarsk, Siberia, in some official capacity. That is all he knew.

The parallels to the end of his novel *Zenobi* are conspicuous. The hero, a confidence man or, rather, a lovable pretender, has disappeared; a friend tries to trace him: "[Meerengel] spread out official answers, letters, newspaper clippings before her. . . . A man such as he cannot have perished. I cannot believe it! . . . Our times need him. A returnee from Russia told me of a brigadier general of the Red Army under whom he served. Some details are striking. It might be he." The rumors about Philipp Frisch appear to have been the germinating cell of the novel.

Although not a best-seller, *Zenobi* was a popular and critical success. Karl Otten, in his epilogue to the new edition, provides a most sensitive and appreciative commentary,[5] and even when it was first published, prominent critics such as Ludwig Marcuse paid it high tribute. Marcuse, in a lengthy review, likened the protagonist to a later-day Don Quixote who always plays a role without being an actor, who is a confidence man without being a criminal, and a knight without being a hero. "It is completely logical that this man ultimately decides to fight a duel with some idiot (whom he does not know) for the sake of a young girl (whom he also does not know)." Marcuse rightly contended that Frisch had created a new type of fictional character: . . . Zenobi is a discovery of Frisch, a conquest in the realm of the Unborn, a figure which no one has as yet seen, although each one encounters him daily."[6] The originality of the novel and its artistic success make it seem all the more regrettable that Frisch's activities as editor and translator did not leave more time for Frisch, the creative writer.

The extent of Frisch's work as translator during his last years in Munich (1925–29) is indicated in my bibliography; his later translations, by the entry in Sternfeld-Tiedemann's *Deutsche Exil-Literatur*.[7] While still in Munich, Frisch translated three lengthy novels and numerous articles; he also theorized upon the art of translation in an essay-type letter to a magazine.

Frisch's preoccupation with foreign literature often provided him with topics for his feuilletons for the *Frankfurter Zeitung*, then one of Germany's most prestigious newspapers. He wrote on James Joyce and D. H. Lawrence, Dostoevski and Gorky, Giraudoux and Valéry, Upton Sinclair and Selma Lagerlöf.[8] Frisch's familiarity with foreign literature was, in fact, one of the qualities that facilitated his appointment as a major contributor to the paper. Of course his access to this post was also smoothed by close personal and professional acquaintance with some of the paper's chief editors. Bernhard Diebold, editor of the feuilleton section, had occasionally negotiated for advance releases or reprints of short stories and articles appearing in the *Neue Merkur*. He, as well as Benno Reifenberg and the paper's publisher, Heinrich Simon, had been sporadic contributors to Frisch's magazine.

Frisch's reputation among the *Frankfurter Zeitung*'s staff was excellent. Dr. Siegfried Kracauer, then a writer for the paper, interviewed one of its surviving editors on my behalf and reported on 23 August 1961: Dr. Max Gubler who often had dealings with Frisch as editor of the feuilleton from 1930–33 had told him that Frisch had something of Lessing in his character. He was not a journalist in the common meaning of the term. Categories gave directions to his arguments. "He always requested an extension of the deadline for his articles." It speaks for Frisch's consistency as a writer that as late as the 1930's someone thought of him as a spiritual relative of Lessing, since one of his first ventures as a free-lance writer had been writing columns and reviews for Christian Morgenstern's *Das Theater*,[9] which had modeled itself upon Lessing's *Hamburgische Dramaturgie*.

The Frisches left Munich in the fall of 1929. The momentous years from 1909 until then had seen Frisch proceed from *Lektor* of a major publishing house to editor-in-chief and publisher of a literary journal and, finally, to free-lance writer. A letter from Professor Leo Matthias of 17 October 1962 indicates Frisch's role in the intellectual life of Munich during that period. Matthias, a well-known German sociologist now living in Switzerland, had been a steady contributor to the *Merkur* and an occasional guest of the Frisches in Munich. He therefore should be particularly qualified to render such a verdict: Frisch to him had been one of the best editor-publishers he had encountered. A modest man, the editor sometimes printed something he disliked of authors he approved of, granting them the right to say unwelcome things. Never did he sacrifice an author because of differences of opinion. It was not his nature to let correspondence or conversations come to the point of no return. He was soft-spoken, quiet, and aristocratic. His country's indebtedness to Efraim Frisch grew largest during his years in Munich.

After two decades in Munich, Frisch returned to Berlin to take up an appointment as editor of literature for the *Europäische Revue*. This distinguished and cosmopolitan journal was similar to the *Neue Merkur* in its make-up and publishing aims. Its editor-publisher, Fürst Karl Anton Rohan, announced Frisch's editorship in the July 1930 issue, page 552, adding: "[Frisch], the former publisher of the *Neue Merkur*, is known as a journalist and writer of high rank. The readers of the *Europäische Revue* will undoubtedly and gratefully welcome the fact that he has decided to perpetuate here, at a new site, the excellent intellectual and literary tradition of his former periodical."

This new outlet for Frisch's editorial abilities, though it inspired some of his best essays and literary reviews (e.g., his superb analysis of Musil's *Mann ohne Eigenschaften* (Man Without Qualities) in the January 1931 issue), proved to be temporary. The task was simply too narrow and restricted for the former editor of the *Neue Merkur*. In the October 1931 number, Rohan regretfully announced Frisch's resignation. During Frisch's tenure the *Revue*, living up to the promise of its title, published stories, novels, and aphorisms by Kafka, Gide, Hemingway, Malraux, Aldous Huxley, Paul Morand (a novel in Frisch's translation) and numerous other foreign authors of similar stature. As one might have expected, the selections once more gave testimony to Frisch's discriminating taste. Upon comparing his choices, however, with those of his predecessors and successors, one can scarcely maintain that Frisch impressed upon the magazine the imprint of his personality.

In general it can be said of Frisch's second stay in Berlin that his outward effectiveness receded proportionately to his growing maturity as a writer—which was to reach its apogee with his unfinished novel, *Gog und Magog.* Occasionally, to be sure, Frisch still reached the general public, for example through a series of three radio broadcasts on literature[10] which culminated in a concise, highly informative sketch of the development of the English novel. He also still wrote, sporadically, a review for the *Berliner Börsenkurier.* He did not regain, however, during those waning years of an era he had helped shape, the influence he had wielded in Berlin as Reinhardt's dramaturgist, or from distant Munich as editor of the *Neue Merkur.*

In part this loss of influence was a symptom of the times: liberal intellectualism was dying in Germany. Even Berlin had changed. Its sparkle and effervescence of the first three decades of the century was nearing extinction; the accomplishments of the liberals were already being partially forgotten or consigned by many, even the intellectuals, to complete oblivion. Ferdinand Lion recalled in the 1961 interview that Frisch, a former columnist of *Das Theater* and assistant director under Reinhardt as we know, had to identify himself laboriously when he requested free review tickets to a premiere.

Frisch's loss of influence came partially through his own choice. When, for example, Herbert Guenther, a rising Berlin author, invited Frisch to contribute to his ambitious anthology, *Hier schreibt Berlin,*[11] Frisch declined out of hand. Yet he must have sensed that this anthology, with its evocation of the city's recent great past, would have a wide resonance and that Guenther, who came to him through the auspices of his old friend, the actor Friedrich Kayssler, could secure contributions from the most renowned Berlin writers.

Frisch and his wife left their quarters in Berlin's artist colony in Wilmersdorf immediately after Hitler's accession to power. After a hurried leave-taking of many new friends, literary and otherwise, the Frisches moved to Ascona, a town frequented by them on several vacations, located in the Tessin area of Switzerland. As citizens of Austria, the Frisches had no visible troubles in emigrating, but the mental anguish was something else. During Frisch's last years in Berlin, as Martin Kessel (a neighbor and friend in Wilmersdorf) told me on 2 March 1962, Frisch refused to talk about the fascist barbarians. They were, as he put it in one of his

numerous clever puns, too *sublaterne*. ("Beneath the lantern," a pun on
the word *subaltern* meaning "beneath contempt.")

This predilection for the black humor accompanied Frisch to Switzerland. In conversations with two friends, the lawyer Fritz Fischer and the
former German civil servant Walther Lindenthal (also an acquaintance
of Christian Morgenstern),[12] Frisch, speaking of the formation of the
Italian-German Axis, paraphrased an old German proverb, "eine Hand
beschmutzt die andere" (one hand soils the other). In commenting on
the news he would intensify a saying of Goethe's, "Für jede Lichtseite
gibt es zwei Schattenseiten" (Each bright side has two dark sides). And
the philosopher Max Picard recalled, on 25 September 1961 that before
1933 he argued with Frisch because he championed Germany so very
much; after 1933, because he rejected it so strongly. There is no doubt
that Frisch's attitude towards Germany underwent a complete change.
During his stay there he became completely immersed in its cultural life,
gaining from it and contributing to it in equal measure. When confronted
with a choice of nationality, open to all natives of territories ceded by
the Central Powers, he wrote the Austrian ambassador to Germany on
12 May 1919: As he had been engaged in literary activities in Berlin and
Munich for twenty-five years and had belonged, since youth, to the German linguistic and cultural realm, it appeared senseless to him to move
about in the world as a Pole or Ukrainian. In short, Frisch, without thinking twice, had decided to remain an Austrian national. His abhorrence
for the "new" Germany and Austria can best be understood through his
love for the old.

Frisch continued his collaboration with the *Frankfurter Zeitung* for a
period while in Switzerland. He wrote in a *curriculum vitae* of 1933 that
he was able to continue his journalistic and creative work, since he was
still writing contributions for the *Frankfurter Zeitung* and other journals
outside Switzerland. In fact, reviews by Frisch, under the pseudonyms of
E. Lach and E. H. Gast, continued to appear until 1934.[13] He owed this
vital means of support during the first years of his immigration to the
courageous attitude of the *Frankfurter Zeitung*'s management, which
resisted, as long as possible, Goebbels' "Gleichschaltung," and to the
circumstance that his old friend and collaborator, Wilhelm Hausenstein,
was at that time editor of the newspaper's literary section.

Then the long silence, or rather the process of being silenced, began
for Frisch as it already had for countless political or "racial" refugees.
Occasionally he gave public lectures in Ascona; the Mss. of four talks on
Judaism are extant among his papers. Sporadically he still found outlets
for his essays and reviews, for example in the emigrant journal *Maß und*

Wert, edited by Ferdinand Lion and Thomas Mann, in *Die Sammlung*, a similar magazine edited by Klaus Mann,[14] in various Zürich newspapers, in an English-Jewish monthly, and, in an obvious attempt to gain a mere livelihood, in the *Arosaer Fremdenblatt*. Many of these articles appeared under a pseudonym: it was rare that an immigrant received a work permit in Switzerland.

Despite these handicaps, the end of Frisch's career had not yet come. To the last, even during the illness of two years which led to his death, Frisch worked on his most important and ambitious work, the novel *Gog und Magog*. Lion, who had a chance to read the Ms. after Frisch's death, adjudged it as follows in the 1961 interview: Their friendship had always been troubled by the fact that Lion, as Frisch saw it, did not sufficiently appreciate his creative works. Lion admitted he was wrong. If Frisch had been able to finish *Gog und Magog*, he concluded, it would have become *the* German-Jewish novel of our times.

The prologue of the novel is "Die Legende von Kuty," recently published in Karl Otten's anthology, *Schofar*.[15] Its haunting last sentence is meant as a motto for the novel: " 'Woe unto us, woe unto us!' called [Rabbi Mosche], 'that this generation is too weak to receive Your Savior.' " The novel proper sets in towards the end of World War I and, if the subtitle *Das Ende einer Zeit* is any indication, was probably intended to close with the destruction of German and Austrian Jewry. The novel is told from the perspective of an Austrian-Jewish lieutenant, Samuel Wolf Brandes, a native of Eastern Galicia and, before the war, a law student in Vienna.

As the novel opens, Brandes, a war hero with a high Austrian decoration, is awaiting the judgment of a court-martial. He has shot a mutinous soldier who—but on this crucial point Brandes' memory is hazy—may have resisted the command to attack by pointing his rifle at his superior officer. As expected, the esteemed war hero is found not guilty. But Samuel is unable to forget, henceforth, the image of the mutineer's widow, a Ruthenian peasant woman. And he is haunted by the words of his defender, a humanist in the uniform of a reservist: "Responsibility—we will have to pay a heavy price for it, depend on that. We will have to atone for it with all we have and all we are. And, more's the pity, not only we, the guilty, [will pay] but all the more the innocent—that is the greatest horror."

At the end of the war Brandes is swept up by the turmoil of the times, the warring ideologies and feuds between and about nationalities. When a stroke of the pen places him, the Austrian officer, at the head of a unit of the newly created Polish National Army, he reflects that the ideals about national self-determination, coming full-blown from America, the

handsome language of the new constitutions, are already being compromised by caprice, martial law, pragmatism, force and violence. And unlike the ones of the past, the new abuses are not softened, he ponders, by
the wisdom of experience.

A precursor of Serenus Zeitblom and a more intelligent and active
successor to Hans Castorp, Samuel Wolf Brandes encounters all types of
post-war Europe, but he becomes most closely involved with representatives of the various ideological camps of Judaism. He talks, debates, and
argues with religious and irreligious Zionists; with advocates of assimilation and outright apostates; with ambitious politicians affecting piety;
with the fashionably devout "who on Friday evening and on Saturday go
to the large prayerhall [Schul] because now they want the image again
of being part of the people"; with cabalists and nihilists; with militant
fighters and quiet, steadfast endurers; with the cunning who can adjust
to every situation; and, finally, with the one person who does not analyze
his Judaism but practices it as a matter of course.

When Samuel returns to his home town he again becomes part of its
Jewish community; he finds his way back to the faith of his childhood as
he is saying his prayers for his deceased grandfather. In this section of
the novel, dozens of superb genre pictures give a vivid account of life in
a Jewish community in Poland. Jewish volunteer defenders battle Polish
pogromists; on the other hand, Jewish horse-thieves beat up a Jewish
watchman. A disdained Jewish prostitute behaves more decently during
a crisis than her detractors. The starving and despoiled Jews greet
Princess Sabbath in their threadbare holiday clothes.

These descriptions, despite their virtuosity, are rarely an end in
themselves. Everyday details usually have a symbolic meaning. The
changes in the life of the community which shocked Samuel upon his return symbolize the fate and mood of the returned veteran of all ages
and countries. Yet the selection and depiction of details make it appear
as if this world is that of the author, and the people who populate it his
friends and neighbors. This was, of course, precisely the case.

The "outsiders" appearing at the periphery of the novel are delineated
with equal acumen. The hero encounters a super-patriotic Polish officer,
then Kurt, a Junker and member of the *Freikorps* (an illegal border
guard on Germany's Eastern frontier). Kurt is a convinced anti-Semite,
but is willing, out of a crusty sense of *noblesse oblige*, to stay with, perhaps even to marry, a Jewish girl who is expecting his child: "I will, of
course, honor my word as a man, come hell or high water," he declares
pompously. Ideological convictions are transformed into action; they
become the plausible basis for the dramatic situations in the lives of
ordinary people.

The chapters of the unfinished novel become more disjointed towards the end, because of Frisch's fatal illness. He continued working on *Gog und Magog* even after 1940, when a partial paralysis confined him to a wheelchair. The inelegance of this posture and the atrophy of his sense of smell and taste were, to him, particularly harsh blows. He had been, before his illness, a connoisseur of wines, a gourmet, and a fastidious, elegant dresser who could even wax enthusiastic about a handsome tie. During his illness he met, for the last time, many contributors to the *Neue Merkur* who also had found refuge in Switzerland. Among them were Wolfgang Heine, Arthur Holitscher, Ferdinand Lion, Walter Strich, and his friend and philosophical confederate, Erich von Kahler. In addition, he was visited by newly acquired friends such as Curt Glaser, the former director of the Berlin art library, and Fritz Strich.

Yet another circle formed around Frisch in these last years. As Dr. Fischer told me in Ascona on 21 September 1961, young Swiss students visited Frisch during the increasingly more frequent enforced interruptions in his work. The revival of interest (and occasional idealization) of the 1920's started in Switzerland long before it began in Germany; the students wished to hear of this era from someone who had helped shape it. Frisch's personal magnetism, a major factor which had gained him friends and contributors for decades, stayed with him to the end.

Frisch tried to stay abreast of the younger generation. His friendship in his old age with the late Kurt Hirschfeld, the long-time director of the Zürich Schauspielhaus, is the best testimony to his continued responsiveness to new things. A deep understanding united the innovators of the Twenties and of the Forties, the champion of Brecht and the champion of Dürrenmatt and Max Frisch, not related, incidentally, to Efraim. In fact, had Efraim Frisch lived to see *Andorra*, one of Max Frisch's best dramas, launched by Hirschfeld, he would surely have approved. Long before, he had promulgated the same thesis through the hero of *Gog und Magog*: "But that, exactly, is part of our [Jewish] situation, that the opinion of the others about us, no matter how false, determines our behavior, precisely because this opinion has such incisive consequences."

It was Kurt Hirschfeld who, shortly after Frisch's death, delivered a memorial address during a ceremony sponsored by a Jewish cultural organization. The speech did Frisch justice; it mentioned not only his solid achievements but it also tried to assess something equally important but less tangible—the impact of his personality upon his times.

Frisch, then, to one who has "lived with" him these past nine years, was not only a German writer and editor but a cultural force in Germany as well, a link between the like-minded. Felix Braun, to choose but one example from many, viewed Frisch, in a letter of 20 September 1961,

as a strict but kind and helpful critic of literature; W. E. Süskind wrote
of him on 18 October in that same year, as a patron and paternal coun-
cillor. Hirschfeld summarized these qualities in his tribute:

> The figure of Efraim Frisch . . . contained two elements. In his
> attitude, in his human make-up, he was a Jew, . . . in the fullest,
> most serious, and most profound meaning of the word . . . by
> tradition [with a] knowledge of Jewish literature both religious
> and secular. But beyond that he was a European, an expert in
> German, French, Russian, and Polish literature who through his
> intellectual stature took a productive and mediative part [in
> contemporary culture] and, through his important position, a
> decisive one. [He was] one of the few people who felt—and was
> known for this—that our spiritual mission is an obligation.

Efraim Frisch had tried, always, to discharge this obligation to the best
of his ability.

Notes
Bibliography
Index

Notes

Introduction

1. Lina Morino, *"La Nouvelle Revue Française" dans l'histoire des lettres* (Paris, 1939); Thomas William Beach, *The Story of the "Spectator,"* 1828–1928 (London, 1928); Hans Wahl, *Geschichte des "Teutschen Merkur"* (Berlin, 1914); Wilmont Haacke, *Julius Rodenberg und die "Deutsche Rundschau"* (Heidelberg, 1950); Nicholas Joost, *Years of Transition: "The Dial,"* 1912–20 (Barre, Mass., 1967); Dale Kramer, *Ross and the "New Yorker"* (Garden City, 1951.)

2. Robert Müller, activist author and political essayist, committed suicide on 28 Aug., 1924, after the failure of his publishing venture, the Atlantische Verlag. His articles were highly esteemed by readers of the *Neue Merkur*; Thomas Mann, for example, in a letter to Frisch of 17 Feb., 1922, lauded an essay by Müller, even though it took issue with him: Robert Müller's essay is decent and intelligent, he wrote.

3. Ferdinand Lion was one of the steady contributors to the *Neue Merkur* whom the *Neue Rundschau* successfully recruited. In a letter of 6 Apr., 1921, Frisch wrote him that in the table of contents of the last number of the *Neue Rundschau* he had noticed Lion's contribution about the Alsatian problem. It was not for reasons of professional envy that this rather saddened Frisch –aside from the fact that he would very much have liked to publish the article himself. But the people at the *Neue Rundschau* had the unpleasant habit of hitching each new contributor, who appeared in the *Merkur*, to their own wagon. He could prove this by quite a number of his collaborators who never before wrote for the *Rundschau*. Now it wouldn't matter, if Frisch's collaborators were also active on other journals of their choice, but why the *Neue Rundschau* of all things, which on its own showed so little initiative towards innovation but always seized upon those who by character and direction least fit in with it. Several reviews, e.g., the *Telegraaf* of Amsterdam of 16 Jan., 1922, also maintained that the *Neue Rundschau* imitated the Merkur.

4. Frisch quotes Hofmannsthal's praise in a letter of 4 Feb., 1924, to Gustav Kilpper, director of the Deutsche Verlags-Anstalt. Rudolf Kayser's comment appears in a letter to Frisch of 26 March, 1920.

5. As Frisch reminded Gustav Kilpper, in a letter of 12 Oct., 1923, the German Foreign Office had ordered reprints the previous year of the issue of November 1922, the so-called "Sonderheft Rheinland."

6. See André Gide, "Vorrede zu Stendhal's 'Armance'," *Neue Merkur* (subsequently abbreviated *NM*), V² (1921/22), 498–510, and Thomas Mann, "Das Problem der deutsch-französischen Beziehungen," *NM*, V² (1921/22), 649–66.

7. Haacke, p. 185.

8. A few letters of the collection were sold, prior to the donation, at an auction in Zürich in 1943. In a letter of 16 Oct., 1962, Mr. Gerhart Heinimann of Schumann and Heinimann, Schweizerisches Antiquariat, informed me that the mss. sold very badly; such items were returned or acquired by the auctioneer. Several mss. I subsequently found at the Schiller-Nationalmuseum in Marbach. Excerpts of others appear in the catalogue of the above auction and in a catalogue "Auktion 41; Autographen, Zeichnungen, Graphik," advertising a sale of 6 June, 1966 in Basel by the firms L'Art Ancien, Zürich, and Haus der Bücher, Basel.

9. See, respectively, Kurt Hiller, "An die Partei des deutschen Geistes," *NM*, I²

(1914/15), 650, and August Oehler, "Stimmen aus Österreich," *NM*, II² (1915/16), 280.

10. See Max Hildebert Boehm, "Die Bewährung des kriegerischen Menschen," *NM*, II² (1915/16), 306.

11. Rather strikingly so when he refused to follow the advice of Professor Kurt Singer, an economist at Hamburg University, to publish their criticism of Rathenau's intellectual pretensions and his "prophetic" attitudes; the article expressly excluded Rathenau's political activity as Minister of Foreign Affairs. On 14 June, 1922, two weeks before Rathenau's assassination, Singer informed Frisch that the opposition of the radicals of the right (who engineered the murder) had virtually stopped; therefore the liberals should voice their criticism. Frisch rejected the article and ignored Singer's protest. Shortly after Rathenau's assassination (on 3 July, 1922), he returned the ms. with the characteristic understatement: "I think you will now be pleased that we did not print your essay." As early as 1 May, 1922, Frisch informed his Berlin correspondent, Friedrich Sternthal (pseud. Dr. Usch) that he was deleting or mitigating his criticism of Rathenau. Singer, who had conceived his article as a disputation with the living Rathenau, published it two years later without any change in his collection of essays: *Staat und Wirtschaft seit dem Waffenstillstand* (Jena, 1924), pp. 144–152.

12. In his "Vorbemerkung" to Robert Walser and Peter O. Chotjewitz, "Sebastian— und eine Variation," *Merkur*, XXI (1967), 248 Paeschke speaks of the "von Ephraim [sic] Frisch herausgegebenen Zeitschrift 'Der Neue Merkur', mit der uns nicht nur der Name, sondern auch gemeinsame Tradition im Geiste des Wieland'schen 'Teutschen Mekur' sowie eine noch in Vielem analoge Zielsetzung (auch der 'Neue Merkur' sprach vom 'europäischen Denken') verbindet."

13. One of the contributors recently had reason to recall the successful cooperation between German Jews and Christians in the publishing of the Neue Merkur. Rudolf Pannwitz, in a letter published in "From the Records of Der Neue Merkur" (Arnold Paucker, ed.), *Yearbook of the Leo Baeck Institute*, VI (1961), 150, writes, in the style of the George circle: "That time of working together with Jews has never stopped for me and was also never interrupted, but those years were a more fortunate era for all things spiritual and intellectual as well as all human concerns relating to them, possibly the most hopeful we experienced. It is good that you, beyond political and propagandist purposes, call its fertility back to mind."

14. *Literatur und Politik* (Olten und Freiburg i Br.), p. 79.

Chapter 1

1. August Mayer (1881–1920) was an Austrian poet, scholar, and translator and (under the pseudonym of August Oehler) a contributor to Stefan George's *Blätter für die Kunst*. His numerous articles in the *Neue Merkur* appeared, variously, under his name and his pseudonym.

2. Rumors of the impending suspension of publication must have preceded the event. In a letter of 28 June 1916 to Georg Heinrich Meyer of the Kurt Wolff Verlag, Kasimir Edschmidt writes: "Despite assurances to the contrary the N.M. seems to be on the verge of going into hibernation for the duration of the war and to think of rising again only in peacetime." See *Kurt Wolff: Briefwechsel eines Verlegers 1911–63*, eds. Bernhard Zeller and Ellen Otten (Darmstadt, 1966).

3. The tenor and content of Frisch's negotiations with Georg Müller were reported to me by Fega Frisch and Kitty Neumann, Müller's daughter, in interviews of 17 Sept., 1961 and 14 July, 1962.

4. "Geleitwort des Verlegers" in *1903–1908 Georg Müller Verlag* (München, 1908), p. 5.

5. *Volksstimme* (Chemnitz), 22 July, 1915, p. 12.

6. This opinion appears in an altogether favorable review by Paul Klobuscar in the *Tagesbote aus Mähren und Schlesien* of 11 Apr., 1914.

7. The advertisement spreads over nine (unpaginated) pages which appear immediately before the lead editorial. It is omitted, like all advertising matter, from the bound volumes of the magazine.

8. As the editorial correspondence shows, Frisch and Hausenstein recurrently solicited contributions from Rilke. Unfortunately Rilke's replies were among the few items sold at the previously mentioned auction. One of his letters of refusal can be reconstructed through this notice in the auction catalogue: "Schöner Brief an den Redaktor des *Neuen Merkur*, in dem Rilke davon spricht, daß es ihm nicht zum besten geht. U.a. schreibt er: 'die Scheunen sind leer—wie leer, das sagt Ihnen schon mein Nichtbeteiligtsein am Insel-Almanach auf das Jahr 1922.'"

9. See his *Mein Weg als Deutscher und Jude* (Berlin, 1921), p. 137.

10. As related to me by Fega Frisch.

11. See Michael Bauer, *Christian Morgenstern: Leben und Werk*, 4th ed. (München, 1948), *passim* (see index), which describes the friendship between the poet and Fega and Efraim Frisch. Morgenstern, who had enjoyed a holiday with his two friends in the Swiss village of Wolfenschiessen, dedicated his poem "Erinnerung an Wolfenschiessen" to them. See *Melancholie: Gedichte von Christian Morgenstern* (Berlin, 1921), p. 7.

12. Frost, "Die neue weibliche Generation," *NM*, I[1] (1914), 134–39 and Schmitz, "Hetärentum und Frauenemanzipation," *NM* I[2] (1914/15), 193–202.

13. Anon., "Der Papst und die Bischöfe," *NM*, I[1] (1914), 615.

14. Theodor Elsner, "Politische Vorschule," *NM*, I[1] (1914), 401–4.

15. The remark appears as an author's prefatory note to Franz Oppenheimer, "Lloyd George und der englische Grossgrundbesitz," *NM*, I[1] (1914), 178.

16. Arthur Holitscher, "Die Stirn Monte Carlos," I[1] (1914), 119–25, 375–86.

17. In his "Der Kaisergedanke," *NM*, I[1] (1914), 61.

18. "Grundzüge einer-neuen Idealität," *NM*, I[1] (1914), 130. See also Frisch's "Anmerkung des Herausgebers" which follows on pp. 132f.

19. "Leistung und Dasein," *NM*, I[1] (1914), 132.

20. See his "Aktivistische Erziehung," *NM*, I[2] (1914/15), 555.

21. His letter appeared in the *Vorwärts* of 19 August, 1960, p. 6. After thanking the editor for a feature article about himself upon the occasion of his impending 75th birthday he continues: "Mein Blick fiel auch auf die Spalten rechts von 'meinem.' Da fand ich, der Ausdruck 'Aktivist' sei eine Erfindung der Kommunisten, so ähnlich wie 'volkseigner Betrieb' und 'Volkspolizei.' Bitte sagen Sie doch Herrn Bodo Scheurig, daß er sich in dem Punkte ganz gewaltig irrt. Für die Gesinnung, die Beutin in seinem gut unterrichteten Essay schildert, habe ich zu einer Zeit, als es kommunistische Parteien überhaupt noch nicht gab (selbst die Bolschewiki nannten sich noch Sozialdemokraten), nämlich Ende 1914, die Vokabel 'Aktivismus' geprägt und habe sie öffentlich 1915 zum erstenmal angewandt, in einem Beitrag zu der (längst verschollenen) Münchener Monatszeitschrift 'Der Neue Merkur'—das läßt sich nachweisen."

22. See his "Unwesentliches Denken," *NM*, I[2] (1914), 319.

23. "Das Erwachen der Ästhetik," *NM*, I[1] (1914), 391f.

24. "Die leblose Gegenwart," *NM*, I[1] (1914), 442.

25. See Ernst Hierl, "Gespräch aus der pädagogischen Provinz," *NM*, I¹ (1914), 266–72.

26. See Alexander Berrsche, "Zur Alpensymphonie von Richard Strauss," *NM*, II² (1916), 420–23, and "Richard Strauss; Gedanken zu seinem fünfzigsten Geburtstag," *NM*, I¹ (1914), 652–56; René Beeh, "Anmerkungen zur Neuauflage von Meier-Gräfes 'Entwicklungsgeschichte'," *NM*, I¹ (1914), 392–97.

27. Haecker's critical essays appeared subsequently in book form. See his *Satire und Polemik, 1914–1922* (Innsbruck, 1922), pp. 51f.

28. "Das Judentum als wissenschaftliches Problem," *NM*, II² (1915/16), 407–20.

29. Frost, 136.

30. "Gedanken über Europa," *NM*, II² (1915/16), 222.

31. "Der Kaisergedanke," *NM*, I¹ (1914), 62.

32. "Die Welt der alten Burschenschaften," *NM*, II¹ (1915), 402.

33. "Der Krieg; Soziologische Betrachtungen," *NM*, I² (1914/15), 49.

34. See Johann Geffken, "Friedensidee und Weltmonarchie," *NM*, II² (1915/16), 137–161.

35. E.g., in Erich Unger, "Der Krieg; Erstes Gespräch zwischen einem Feldgrauen und einem dauernd Untauglichen," *NM*, II¹ (1915), 582–84.

36. "Auslandsbrief," *NM*, II¹ (1915), 268.

37. "Der Krieg und die Literatur," *NM*, I² (1914/15), 114, 115.

38. "Die Politisierung der Unpolitischen," *NM*, II¹ (1915), 188.

39. See Hagemann, "Aus den Kämpfen in den Karpathen," *NM*, II¹ (1915), 279–96; Schulz, Österreichische Kämpfe auf dem nördlichen Kriegsschauplatz," *NM*, II¹ (1915), 151–64; Heymann, *NM*, II¹ (1915), 67–88.

40. *NM*, II¹ (1915), 165.

41. P[aul] A[dler], "Vorwort" in Charles Péguy, "Französisch und 'Volksvertreterisch,'" *NM*, I² (1914/15), 665.

42. See note 35.

43. *NM*, I² (1914/15), 578.

44. See note 33; also his "Russland," *NM*, II² (1915/16), 144–61.

45. E.g. Kurt Eisner, "Völkerrecht," *NM*, I² (1914/15), 225f.

46. Paul Adler, "Anmerkung," in Miguel de Unamuno, "Das geistige Spanien und Deutschland," *NM*, II¹ (1915), 220.

47. *NM*, II² (1915/16), 302.

48. Scheler, "Zur Psychologie des englischen Ethos und des Cant," *NM*, I² (1914/15), 252–277; Wolff, *NM*, II² (1915/16), 512–541; Hausenstein, "Das System Napoleon," *NM*, I² (1914/15), 50–74.

49. Cf. Bernstein, "Die Klassiker des Sozialismus und der Krieg," *NM*, II¹ (1915), 654–72; Braun, "Die Gewerkschaften und der Weltkrieg," *NM*, II¹ (1915), 474–81; Boehm, "Militarisierung des geistigen Menschen," *NM*, II² (1915/16), 549–57.

50. *NM*, I² (1914/15), 645–53, esp. 650.

51. *NM*, II² (1915/16), 250.

52. See Jacques, "Wir . . . sie . . . die Welt," *NM*, I² (1914/15), 437–52; Mayer, "Kriegsbetrachtung II," *NM*, II² (1915/16), 577–91; Mendelssohn-Bartholdy, "Fremdwörter et cetera," *NM*, II¹ (1915), 737–44; Hartmann, "Friedensarbeit im Kriege," *NM*, II¹ (1915), 600–602. For the articles on Italy cf. Dalmo Carnevalli, "Italien und

der Dreibund." *NM*, I² (1914/15), 469–78 and August Mayer, "Abrechnung mit Italien," *NM*, II¹ (1915), 332–39.

53. *NM*, I² (1914/15), 489.

54. *NM*, I² (1914/15), 353–99.

55. Cf. Friedrich Soergel, *Dichtung und Dichter der Zeit*, 7th ed. (Leipzig, 1925), I, 863 and Thomas Mann, "Vorwort," p. 12, in *Altes und Neues* (Frankfurt a.M., 1953). Mann's pronouncement reads in the original: "Ehrlich gestanden: Ich habe auch heute noch etwas übrig für dies kleine historische Machwerk in seiner sonderbaren Mischung aus kritischer Besonnenheit und hitzig patriotischer Allusion. Zeit und Geschichte sind mit verdienter Geringschätzung darüber hinweggegangen,— nicht ebenso die literarische Ästhetik."

Chapter 2

1. "Rettung der Kultur," *NM*, VI (1922), 479.

2. "Politisches Tagebuch," *NM*, III (1919), 6.

3. The historical background is based on Helmut Hüttig, *Die politischen Zeitschriften der Nachkriegszeit in Deutschland 1918–1925* (Leipzig, 1928), pp. 9–14.

4. This correspondence is in the possession of Miss Miriam Beer-Hoffmann.

5. The *Auslandspost*, also founded by Frisch, was a journal that reprinted articles culled from foreign newspapers and magazines. It was edited in its first years by Paul Marc, brother of the painter Franz Marc, and later by Franz Schoenberner. See Franz Schoenberner, *Bekenntnisse eines europaischen Intellektuellen: Erinnerungen* (München, 1964), Ch. XV

6. Johannes von Günther's spurious judgment may be found in Walter Koch, "Die Ausgewogenheit von Qualität und Quantität als verlegerische Aufgabe (demonstriert am Beispiel des Verlegers Georg Müller)" (diss. München, 1950), p. 41.

7. Knowledge about Wilhelm Hausenstein is derived from his autobiographical novel *Lux perpetua* (Freiburg and Munich, 1947 and 1952), and from numerous passages in my correspondence and interviews with his wife and daughter. See also W. E. Süskind, "Wilhelm Hausenstein," in Hermann Kunisch, ed., *Handbuch der Gegenwartsliteratur* (München, 1965), pp. 255f.

8. Dates of the respective issues: *Crifalco*, March 1922; *Nouvelle Revue Française*, 1 July 1922; *Journal du Peuple*, 17 Sept. 1921; *Telegraaf*, 21 March 1922; *Leipziger Tageblatt*, 4 Sept. 1921; *Süddeutsche Presse*, 16 Dec. 1921.

9. "Mit sechzig Jahren . . . Ein Selbstporträt," *Welt und Wort* (June 1961), p. 180.

10. *NM*, V¹ (1921), 72.

11. Undated letter to Frisch at the end of 1919 from Irene Heberle, Klabund's fianceé.

12. "Erinnerung an Eisner," *NM*, III (1919), 56–58.

13. Karl Gareis emerged politically after the November-revolution and in 1920 was a leading member of the Independent Socialist delegation to the Bavarian Parliament.

14. Letters from Paquet to Frisch, 28 Dec. 1918; Paintner to Frisch, 30 July 1919; Blei to Hausenstein, 5 Dec. 1919; Frisch to Bloch, 6 June 1922; Walter F. to the editors, 10 Feb. 1923.

15. *NM*, V¹ (1921), 145–220.

16. *Ibid.*, 297–368.

17. *NM*, V^2, 521–716.

18. In a letter to Paul Graf Thun-Hohenstein of 29 April 1925, Frisch deplored this limitation of literary journals.

19. *NM*, VI (1922), 385–480.

20. *Ibid.*, 456–62.

21. *Ibid.*, 402–19.

22. See Robert Müller, "Thomas Mann, Frankreich, Aktivismus," *NM*, V^2 (1921), 717–25.

23. In a letter of 17 Feb. 1922 to Frisch, Thomas Mann responded to Müller's demurrer: The article was respectable and intelligent, he wrote. He would have liked to have written the author a few lines on the fundamentals, but it was now too late.

24. "Zur Philosophie der Technik," *NM*, VI (1922), 581.

25. Rudolf Pannwitz, "Europäische Politik, nicht Weltpolitik." *NM*, III (1919), 297; Robert Müller, "Territorialpolitik–Zivilisationspolitik," *ibid.*, 505.

26. Alfred Döblin, "Reform des Romans," *NM*, III (1919), 189–202; Otto Flake, "Über 'Die Stadt des Hirns.' Erwiderung auf Döblins Reforms des Romans," *ibid.*, 353–57.

27. Friedrich Burschell, "Geschichte und Legende (zu Döblins Wallenstein)," *NM*, IV^2 (1920/21), 787–90; Alfred Döblin, "Der Epiker, sein Stoff und die Kritik," *NM*, V^1 (1921/22), 56.

28. See letters from Döblin to Frisch of 28 Jan. 1921 and 11 Feb. 1921, and from Frisch to Döblin of 9 Feb. 1921.

29. "Zur Krisis abendländischen Denkens," *NM*, VI (1922), 317–20.

30. The honest intentions of the publisher are apparent from a letter of Joachim Friedenthal to Frisch dated 3 March 1923.

31. *NM*, VI (1922), fourth last page, unnumbered.

Chapter 3

1. "Politisches Tagebuch," *NM*, III (1919), 6.

2. This view, consistently held by Coudenhove-Kalergi, has more recently been expressed in his *From War to Peace* (London, 1959), pp. 223–24: "The study of philosophy and history shows no grounds for optimism. . . . In the midst of such dangers and in the shadow of the atomic bomb, it is now more than ever worth fighting for the conclusion of the Great Peace."

3. "Einladung zum Abonnement," special issue entitled *Vorläufer*, *NM*, III (1919), unnumbered page following p. 76.

4. Bröger, "Wilson und Lenin," *NM*, III (1919), 707; Diebold, "Kritik zur Literatur," *NM*, V^2 (1921), 642–43.

5. " 'Preussentum und Sozialismus,' " *NM*, III (1919), 573–76.

6. "Was ist Militarismus?" *NM*, V^1 (1921/22), 429.

7. Döblin, "Die Vertreibung der Gespenster," *Vorläufer*, *NM*, III (1919), 13; Holitscher, "Pranger und Gericht," *ibid.*, 66.

8. "Barbaren und Klassiker," *NM*, VI (1922), 126.

9. Dr. Usch (pseud. for Friedrich Sternthal), "Zwischenspiel," *ibid.*, 118.

10. *NM*, III (1919), 24, 92–93.

11. "E. D. Morel," *NM*, V¹ (1921/22), 442.

12. Xenos, "Ordnung," *NM*, III (1919), 211. The articles published under the pseudonym of Xenos were written by Erich von Kahler, as related by him in an interview on 28 January 1963 at Princeton, New Jersey.

13. Von Wedderkop. "Holland," *NM*, V¹ (1921/22), 199; Dr. Usch, "Von Washington über London—Cannes nach Genua," *NM*, V² (1921), 764–65.

14. "Zur Mechanik der Revolution," *NM*, III (1919), 222.

15. "Ideal und Wirklichkeit," *ibid.*, 480.

16. "Die Untergangssituation und Europa," *NM*, IV¹ (1920), 270.

17. " 'Preussentum und Sozialismus,' " *NM*, III (1919), 575.

18. "Anteil des Geistes," *ibid.*, 78. In a letter to Frisch of 25 Sept. 1921, Max Picard scores yet another German inconsistency: Only those who wanted more than what had just been revolutionized, the Liebknechts and Luxemburgs, were confronted by guns. Of course (and not curiously) by those who had most recently been legitimatized.

19. "Deutschland," *NM*, VI (1922), 489.

20. "Rundschau," *NM*, IV² (1920/21), 554.

21. Xenos [i.e., Erich von Kahler], "Ordnung," *NM*, III (1919/20), 210–13.

22. "Entthronung der Presse," *NM*, III (1919), 160.

23. "Leopold Ziegler's 'Gestaltwandel der Götter'," *NM*, IV² (1920/21), 407.

24. "Siebenbürgisch-rumänisches Tagebuch," *NM*, VI (1922), 557–58.

25. *Vorläufer, NM*, III (1919), 44–64.

26. "Wilson und Lenin," *NM*, III (1919), 707.

27. "Mazedonischer Krieg (1916–17)," *NM*, IV¹ (1920), 232.

28. *NM*, V² (1921–22), 567: How easy does all now become. It is as if dying lifted / the bodies gently upwards from the arms of the earth: / as one takes a child from its mother.— / The voices of longing fell silent. / Stilled for ever was the desire for far-away places. / Consciousness was slowly carried off / like a light. Only the eye / once more turned / eternally upward to the extinguishing heavens.— / Then came death, which makes everything simple.

29. "Rechenschaft," *Vorläufer, NM*, III (1919), 5.

30. "Der junge Hertling," *NM*, III (1919), 684–92. Willy Andreas repeated this accusation of Hertling in an interview of 20 Sept. 1961.

31. "Schatten," *NM*, IV¹ (1920), 339.

32. "Reise in die Zeit," *ibid.*, 358.

33. "Gesang von Kindchen. Ein Idyll," *NM*, III (1919), 92.

34. Th. G. Masaryk, "Für die religiöse Freiheit," *NM*, IV¹ (1920), 1–7.

35. Dr. Usch, "Von Genua zum Haag," *NM*, VI (1922), 178.

36. *NM*, IV¹ (1920), 339–40; "Die geistigen Strömungen des heutigen Italien," *NM*, V² (1921), 699–707.

37. Mendelssohn-Bartholdy, 'Großmacht und Menschlichkeit," *NM*, III (1919),

454; Otto Flake, "Fünf Romane," *NM*, IV[1] (1920), 191–192; Rob Rab, "Die englische Presse während des Krieges und nachher," *NM*, IV[2] (1920/21), 725.

38. "Ein idealistischer Irregänger: Der englische Premierminister und seine Politik," *NM*, V[1] (1921/22), 208, 213.

39. "Der Turmbau zu Babel und der Runde Tisch," *NM*, V[1] (1921/22), 13; "Sir Edward Fry," *NM*, V[2] (1921), 820–25.

40. "Deutsche und Slawen," *NM*, VI (1922), 137, 134.

41. Flake, "Zwischen Idee und Tat," *NM*, V[1] (1921/22), 67; Hiller, "Eudämonie und Evolution," *NM*, IV[1] (1920), 105; Gorki, *NM*, VI (1922), 214–20.

42. Efraim Frisch, "Dostojewskij," *NM*, V[2] (1921), 445–59; letter from Frisch to Arthur Kaufmann of 19 Feb. 1921. Fega Frisch's dislike was even more intense. According to Ernst Bloch (interview of 17 April 1962), Fega sympathized with the white guard.

43. "Deutsch-französische Kulturprobleme," *NM*, V[1] (1921/22), 147.

44. Karl Bröger, "Wilson und Lenin," *NM*, III (1919), 709, 713.

45. Braun, "Amerikanische Gedichte," *NM*, VI (1922), 189; Paquet, "Ballade von Chicago," *NM*, IV[2] (1920/21), 802–3; Müller, "Brooklyn-Bridge," *NM*, III (1919), 529–34; Frank, "Amerika," *NM*, VI (1922), 265.

46. "Berlin," *NM*, IV[2] (1920/21), 800.

47. "Dialektik der Entwicklung," *ibid.*, 579.

48. Lion, "Deutschland und Frankreich," *NM*, III (1919), 582–83; "Grundlagen der französischen Politik von 1870–1914," *NM*, IV[2] (1920/21), 653–68; "Verstandespolitik (Die französische äußere Politik von 1870–1914)," *NM*, VI (1922), 545–56.

49. Lion, "Deutschland und Frankreich," *NM*, III (1919), 582, 586; Frisch, *NM*, VI (1922), 545.

50. F. [Frisch], "Französische Stimmen," *NM*, VI (1922), 253–55.

51. Bloch, "Die Bodenständigkeit," *NM*, IV[2] (1920/21), 704; Burschell, "Die Hoffnung auf Frankreich," *NM*, V[2] (1921), 667; Flake, "Politische Ferienbetrachtung," *NM*, VI (1922), 315.

52. *NM*, V[1] (1921/22), 145–55.

53. André Gide, "Les Rapports Intellectuels entre La France et L'Allemagne," *La Nouvelle Revue Française*, XVII (1921), 513–21.

54. See letter from Frisch to Curtius, 21 Dec. 1921.

55. *NM*, V[2] (1921), 649–66.

56. Müller, "Thomas Mann, Frankreich, Aktivismus," *ibid.*, 717–25.

57. Frisch was not entirely happy about Thomas Mann's sometimes gratuitous attacks on the Activists. This is apparent in a letter of 12 September 1922 to Leo Matthias: As far as Thomas Mann's attacks upon Activism was concerned, Frisch had already explained how little he identified himself with Mann's analogy from French to German conditions. And the answer of Robert Müller surely was intended to show to what extent the bourgeois spirit and point of view needed correcting.

58. "Pontigny," *NM*, VI (1922), 419–25.

59. Dr. Usch, "Kugelpolitik und Flächenpolitik," *ibid.*, 604.

60. "Politik gegen Wirtschaft," *ibid.*, 468.

61. *Ibid.*, 315. Perhaps it might be argued that it was not in vain after all. Wilhelm Hausenstein, as Germany's first ambassador to France after World War II, fulfilled

his dreams and visions of those early years more than a quarter of a century later. To paraphrase Heinrich Lübke, former President of the Federal Republic of Germany, he created the foundation for this development "of a German-French reconciliation." See Wilhelm Hausenstein, *Pariser Erinnerungen* (München, 1961).

62. See letter from Frisch to Sternthal of 8 June 1922.

63. Kayser, "Der Geist der russischen Revolution," *NM*, III (1919), 435–36; von Moellendorff, "Das politische Wesen des Sozialismus," *NM*, VI (1922), 1–4; Flake. "Die großen Worte," *NM*, IV¹ (1920), 68–72.

64. Dr. Usch, "Zwischenspiel," *NM*, VI (1922), 117.

65. Otto Flake, "Politik in der Alten Welt," *NM*, V² (1921), 833.

66. "Die großen Worte," *NM*, IV¹ (1920), 69.

67. "Dante und Italien," *NM*, V¹ (1921/22), 385–386.

68. "Italienischer Herbst: Notizen aus einem Tagebuch," *NM*, V² (1921), 793.

69. "Zur Philosophie der Technik," *NM*, VI (1922), 587.

70. Dr. Usch, "Europa nach acht Jahren," *ibid.*, 311–12.

71. "Europas technische Weltmission," *ibid.*, 341.

72. Dr. Usch, "Politik in der alten Welt," *NM*, V² (1921), 828.

73. Mendelssohn-Bartholdy, "Großmacht und Menschlichkeit," *NM*, III (1919), 444; Pannwitz, "Europäische Politik, nicht Weltpolitik," *ibid.*, 305–6.

74. "Schuld, Völkerbund und Anderes," *ibid.*, 154. Frisch's authorship can be deduced from a handwritten original among his literary papers.

75. *NM*, III (1919), 297.

76. "Reise in die Zeit," *NM*, IV¹ (1920), 364.

77. This letter also identifies the author of the gloss "Die Genfer Tagung" as Friedrich Sternthal: *NM*, IV² (1920/21), 719.

78. "Das Gespenst," *NM*, III (1919), 128.

79. "Was ist Militarismus," *NM*, V¹ (1921/22), 427.

80. Braun, "Münchner Theatersommer," *NM*, III (1919), 361; Flake, "Reise in die Zeit," *NM*, IV¹ (1920), 361; Hiller, "Eudämonie und Evolution," *ibid.*, 105; Loerke, "Ein Laie," *NM*, III (1919), 338.

81. Grossmann, "Entthronung der Presse," *NM*, III (1919), 159; Burschell, "Die Hoffnung auf Frankreich," *NM*, V² (1921), 670; Polgar, "Prater-Botanik," *NM*, VI (1922), 100.

82. Frisch, "'Preussentum und Sozialismus,'" *NM*, III (1919), 574; Dr. Usch, "Zwischenspiel," *NM*, VI (1922), 119; Hausenstein, "Adolf Hildebrand," *NM*, IV² (1920/21), 859, and "'Vereinheitlichung,'" *NM*, III (1919), 517. Hausenstein's authorship was established with the aid of his archives, now administered by his daughter, Mrs. Renée-Marie Parry-Hausenstein.

83. "Rathenau's Ermordung," *NM*, VI (1922), 195.

84. Dr. Usch, "Europa nach acht Jahren," *ibid.*, 308–10.

85. "Die Vertreibung der Gespenster," *Vorläufer*, *NM*, III (1919).

86. See undated letter from Picard to Frisch (1920).

87. Burschell, "Deutschland" (roughly, "No State could be built on it; with nothing could a State be built." But the idiom also means, "It was nothing to brag about."), *NM*, VI (1922), 490; Müller, Aus Deutschösterreich," *NM*, III (1919), 240; Braun,

"Ideal und Wirklichkeit," *ibid.*, 481; Gareis, "Zur Mechanik der Revolution," *ibid.*, 222.

88. "Die Bodenständigkeit," *NM*, IV[2] (1920/21), 704.

89. "Verbotene Schüleraufsätze: Elementarbeispiele für eine Schule der Verantwortung," *NM*, III (1919), 33.

90. "Erinnerung as Eisner," *ibid.*, 68.

91. See undated letter, postmarked 3 June 1919.

92. Hausenstein, "Naumann in seiner Zeit," *NM*, III (1919), 430; Döblin, "Die Vertreibung der Gespenster," *ibid.*, 11–20; Esswein. "Die Majoritätenwirtschaft im Kunstleben," IV[1] (1920), 409–11, Wendel, "Der italienische Imperialismus und die Südslawen," III (1919), 522–28.

93. In Housman's poem, "Be still my soul, be still."

94. Xenos, "Ordnung," *NM*, III (1919), 211.

95. A. Hales (i.e., Arthur Salz), "Zwei Wege," *NM*, III (1919), 456. In a letter to Frisch of 2 Dec. 1919, Salz states that he must use a pseudonym because he had had to pledge to the Bavarian government that he would not indulge in any form of political activity.

96. "Staat und Freiheit," *NM*, VI (1922), 540.

97. Mendelssohn-Bartholdy, "Der Bund," *Vorläufer, NM*, III (1919), 35; Von einem Süddeutschen (i.e., Hausenstein), " 'Vereinheitlichung,' " *NM*, III (1919), 522, and "Föderalismus," *NM*, IV[2] (1920/21), 561.

98. Cf. W. E. Süskind, "Vorwort," to Wilhelm Hausenstein, *Licht unter dem Horizont; Tagebücher von 1942 bis 1946* (München, 1962), p. 19: Hausenstein demanded of his colleagues that they write in such a way that they could justify it later, with all candor short of putting oneself and one's charges to the knife.

99. "Republik Deutschland," NM, IV[2] (1920/21), 494; Fl. (identified as Flake in table of contents), "Rundschau," *ibid.*, 552–53, 557.

100. "Zarastro," *ibid.*, 864.

101. *Die Zerstörung der deutschen Politik: Dokumente 1871–1933* (Frankfurt am Main, 1959), pp. 317, 19.

102. "Nachruf an Weininger," *NM*, IV[1] (1920), 327, 333–34.

103. "Politische Ferienbetrachtung," *NM*, VI (1922), 313.

104. "Eudämonie und Evolution," *NM*, IV[1] (1920), 104.

105. Dr. Usch, "Europa nach acht Jahren," *NM*, VI (1922), 309.

106. Fl., "Rundschau," *NM*, IV[2] (1920/21), 553.

107. Lion, "Deutschland, Frankreich, Schickele," *NM*, VI (1922), 80; Müller, "Das moderne Ich," *NM*, IV[2] (1920/21), 646–47; Esswein, "Von der Kunststadt zur Kaffernsiedlung," *NM*, III (1919), 573; Paquet, "Rom," *NM*, V[1] (1921/22), 376.

108. *NM*, IV[1] (1920), 68–72, 358.

109. "Die großen Worte," *ibid.*, 69.

110. "Rechenschaft," *Vorläufer, NM*, III (1919), 10.

111. Bergmann, "München," *NM*, IV[1] (1920), 64; Mittler, "Zöllner und Pharisäer," *NM*, IV[2] (1920/21), 723; Ewald, "Nachruf an Weininger," *NM*, IV[1] (1920), 331.

112. Dr. Usch, "Europa nach acht Jahren," *NM*, VI (1922), 311; Kannitverstan (pseud. for Hausenstein), "Briefe aus Holland," *NM*, VII[1] (1923/24), 293.

113. "Republik und Kaisergedanke," *NM*, VII² (1924), 522.

114. Sternthal, "Über eine Apologie der römischen Kirche," *NM*, VII² (1924), 766; Poeschel, "Zeit- und Reisebücher," *ibid.*, 768; Prinzhorn, "Geltungsbedürfnis—Geltungspflicht: Eine Studie zur Gemeinschaftsbildung," *ibid.*, 912; Haas, "Stimmen zur Erneuerung des deutschen Menschen: Eine Diskussion," *NM*, VIII¹ (1924/25), 56, 60–61; Dr. Usch, "Weltpolitische Chronik," *NM*, VIII² (1925), 1001.

115. "Die politischen Parteien," *NM*, VIII¹ (1924/25), 83–89.

116. Flake, "Republik Deutschland," *NM*, IV² (1920/21), 494; Kayser, "Der Geist der russischen Revolution," *NM*, III (1919), 436.

117. Poeschel, *NM*, VI (1922), 126–27; Siemsen, *ibid.*, 494–515; Flake, *NM*, V¹ (1921/22), 83–98, and "Zu Theodor Fontanes hundertstem Geburtstag," *NM*, III (1919), 473–479.

118. Coudenhove-Kalergi, "Europas technische Weltmission," *NM*, VI (1922), 342; Braun, "Ideal und Wirklichkeit," *NM*, III (1919), 484.

119. Flake, "Reise in die Zeit," *NM*, IV¹ (1920), 358; Pannwitz, "Anteil des Geistes," *NM*, III (1919), 76.

120. "Zarastro," *NM*, IV² (1920/21), 864.

121. Flake, "Zur deutschen Krise," *NM*, VI (1922), 397, and "Reise in die Zeit," *NM*, IV¹ (1920), 363.

122. "Freistudententum und neue Zeit," *NM*, III (1919), 274.

123. "Reise in die Zeit," *NM*, IV¹ (1920), 363–64.

124. A case in point is Flake's article "Zum jüdischen Problem," *NM*, V¹ (1921/22), 318–28, which, despite the author's attempt to give rein to his emotions, is a rather sober disquisition. Flake had written Frisch on 17 March 1921: "I wrote my essay at least three times until I noticed that an 'objective' treatment is endless, and that it is wrong to treat an irrational subject [i.e., anti-Semitism] reasonably."

125. *NM*, V¹ (1921/22), 297.

126. Three examples are symptomatic of Frisch's desire to underplay the Jewish issue or rather the difference between German Jews and gentiles. In articles about Albert Ballin (Eduard Rosenbaum, "Albert Ballin," *NM*, VI [1922], 111–16) and about Carlo Schanzer (Dr. Usch, "Von Genua zum Haag," *ibid.*, 172) no mention is made of their Jewish faith. Sternthal protested in a letter of 12 June 1922 that Frisch had deleted his reference to Schanzer's Jewish origin: "I suppose that you did [the deleting] in order to prevent anti-Semitic attacks. But you can't make a secret of the fact that he is a Jew." Also Frisch rejected an article by Max Krell, otherwise a valued contributor, which offered in a letter of 1 June 1921 a polemic against anti-Semitic histories of literature.

127. "Jüdische Aufzeichnungen," *NM*, V¹ (1921/22), 297–317.

128. "Die Krisis des jüdischen Volkes," *NM*, III (1919), 644.

129. *NM*, V¹ (1921/22), 221–35.

130. Mendelssohn-Bartholdy, "Großmacht und Menschlichkeit,' *NM*, III (1919), 455; Masaryk, "Für die religiöse Freiheit," *NM*, IV¹ (1920), 1; Dr. Usch, "Europa nach acht Jahren," *NM*, VI (1922), 308; Flake, "Fünf Romane," *NM*, IV¹ (1920), 191; Martens, "Erinnerungen an Frank Wedekind," *NM*, IV² (1920/21), 539; von Wedderkop, "Holland," *NM*, V¹ (1921/22), 200; Braun, "Das Religiöse und die jüngste Dichtung," *NM*, III (1919), 609.

131. E.g. Judah L. Magnes, "Das Judentum am Ende des Krieges," *NM*, V¹ (1921/22), an article translated from the *Nation*, brings a wealth of facts and statistics to combat the concept of Jews as Mephisto figures.

132. Esswein, "Von der Kunststadt zur Kaffernsiedlung," *NM*, III (1919), 572; Rauecker, "Die Arbeitsteilung als eine Ursache des Zusammenbruchs," *ibid.*, 560; Flake, "Zum jüdischen Problem," *NM*, V¹ (1921/22), 324; Coudenhove-Kalergi, "Adel," *ibid.*, 75.

133. Esswein, "Die Majoritätenwirtschaft im Kunstleben," *NM*, IV¹ (1920), 409; Mendelssohn-Bartholdy, Macht, Großmacht und Menschlichkeit," *NM*, III (1919), 372; Bergmann, "München," *NM*, IV¹ (1920), 63; Hierl, "Erlebtes von der Reichsschulkonferenz," *NM*, IV² (1920/21), 482; Döblin, "Zion und Europa," *NM*, V¹ (1921/22), 338.

134. Blüher's letter is quoted in Matthias, "Antwort an Blüher," *NM*, VI (1922), 120, and "Hans Blüher und das Christentum," *NM*, V² (1921), 775–78.

135. See *NM*, V² (1921), 648.

136. "Die englische Presse während des Krieges und nachher," *NM*, IV² (1920/21), 733.

137. This error was pointed out to Frisch, in scarcely printable language, by Kurt Hiller in a letter of 26 Oct. 1919. Frisch apologized on 5 Nov. 1919.

138. Kranold, "Sozialistischer Außenhandel," *NM*, IV¹ (1920), 182; Dr. Usch, "Politik in der alten Welt," *NM*, V² (1921), 828, and "Europa nach acht Jahren," *NM*, VI (1922), 310; Flake, "Zum jüdischen Problem," *NM*, V¹ (1921/22), 320; Döblin, "Zion und Europa," *ibid.*, 342; Paquet, "Die metaphysiche Wolke," *ibid.*, 343; Magnes, "Das Judentum am Ende des Krieges," *ibid.*, 362.

139. *NM*, V¹ (1921/22), 348–60.

140. See Curt Tillmann (book dealer, bibliophile, and former business manager of the *NM*), *Sammlerglück mit Zeitschriften und Buchumschlägen*, 2nd ed. (München, 1954), p. 21. Mr. Tillmann reaffirmed his opinion, after the publication of my article, in a letter to the editor of the *Frankfurter Zeitung* of 9 March 1966, reprinted in Kurt Loewenstein, "Thomas Mann zur jüdischen Frage." *Bulletin des Leo Baeck Instituts*, X (1967), no. 37, 3f.

141. See my "A Case for Oral Literary History: Conversations with or about Lehmann, Reinacher and Thomas Mann," *GQ*, XXXVII (1964), 487–97. The first authorized publication of Mann's article was in the *Frankfurter Allgemeine Zeitung* of 15 Jan. 1966; it was reprinted in Loewenstein, *ibid.*, 11–19 and in *AGR*, XXXIV (1967/68), no. 1, 36–40.

142. Dr. Usch, "Zivilcourage," *NM*, V¹ (1921/22), 290.

143. Harald Landry, "Freistudententum und neue Zeit," *NM*, III (1919), 274; Hugo Horwitz, "Wyneken und Foerster," *Werden*, *NM*, III (1919), 83–95; Kurt Hiller, "Zum Fall Wyneken," *NM*, V¹ (1921/22), 442–44.

144. "Zur religiösen Frage," *Werden*, *NM*, III (1919), 12–36.

145. "Erlebtes von der Reichsschulkonferenz," *NM*, IV² (1920/21), 480; Rolland, "Die Intellektuellen: ihr Versagen—ihre Möglichkeiten," *NM*, III (1919), 438.

146. "Reise in die Zeit," *NM*, IV¹ (1920), 355.

147. "Geistige Bewegung in Österreich," *NM*, V¹ (1921/22), 438.

148. "Freistundentum und neue Zeit," *NM*, III (1919), 272.

149. "Anmerkung," *ibid.*, 276.

150. See, for example, Efraim Frisch, "Rechenschaft," *Vorläufer*, *NM*, III (1919), 10.

151. *NM*, IV¹ (1920), 1.

152. Frisch, "Werden," *Werden*, NM, III (1919), 1; von Kahler, "Die Krisis in der Wissenschaft," *NM*, III (1919), 119.

153. "Die Vertreibung der Gespenster," *Vorläufer*, NM, III (1919), 20.

154. "Gnade und Freiheit," *Werden*, NM, III (1919), 96–114.

155. "Die Katastrophe der Vernunft," *NM*, VI (1922), 143.

156. "Bemerkungen zu Spenglers Untergang des Abendlandes," *NM*, IV[1] (1920), 208–22.

157. "Geist und Erfahrung: Anmerkungen für Leser, welche dem Untergang des Abendlandes entronnen sind," *NM*, IV[2] (1920/21), 841–58.

158. Kayser, "Das Ende des Expressionismus," *NM*, IV[1] (1920), 248–58; Plessner, "Die Untergangsvision und Europa," *ibid.*, 265–79.

159. "Anteil des Geistes," *NM*, III (1919), 73–86.

160. "Geisteswissenschaft," *ibid.*, 98–106.

161. Kassner, "Der größte Mensch: Ein imaginäres Gespräch," *NM*, IV[1] (1920), 247. Braun, "Ideal und Wirklichkeit," *NM*, III (1919), 483; Massaryk, "Für die religiöse Freiheit," *NM*, IV[1] (1920), 1.

162. Paquet, "Deutsche und Slawen," *NM*, VI (1922), 136; Hierl, "Zur religiösen Frage," *Werden*, NM, III (1919), 27; Ziegler, "Buddha," *NM*, IV[1] (1920), 60; Horwitz, "Bemächtigung," *NM*, IV[2] (1920/21), 473–78.

163. Strich, "Der Fluch des objektiven Geistes," *NM*, III (1919), 493–504; Hiller, "Eudämonie und Evolution," *NM*, IV[1] (1920), 104; Flake, "Zwischen Idee und Tat," *NM*, V[1] (1921/22), 68; Coudenhove-Kalergi, "Krise des Adels," *ibid.*, 221–35.

164. Meier-Graefe, "Galeriepolitik," *NM*, III (1919), 289; Braun, "Münchner Theatersommer," *ibid.*, 361; Delnhardt, "Zur Krisis in der Musik," *ibid.*, 410–11.

165. *Ibid.*, 143.

166. Von einem Süddeutschen (Wilhelm Hausenstein), "Föderalismus," *NM*, IV[2] (1920/21), 489.

167. "Dostojewski," *NM*, V[2] (1921), 445.

168. "Das Religiöse und die jüngste Dichtung," *NM*, III (1919), 610.

169. *Das Land, das ich verlassen muße* (Hamburg, 1961), p. 75.

170. "Mythos des Zusammenbruchs," *NM*, III (1919), 461.

171. "Kritik zur Literatur," *NM*, V[2] (1921) 643.

172. *NM*, IV[1] (1920), 354–64.

173. Felix Braun, "Amerikanische Gedichte," *NM*, VI (1922), 189.

174. The rather recherché preoccupation with the beauty of the Samoan women occurs in a review by Hans Poeschel, "Ein neuer Südseeroman," *NM*, V[1] (1921/22), 294–96.

175. Josef Ponten, "Bericht von Lesefreuden," *NM*, V[2] (1921), 518.

176. "Nachruf an Weininger," *NM*, IV[1] (1920), 327.

177. Wandrey, "Hölderlins deutsche Sendung," *NM*, VI (1922), 221; Poeschel, "Stifters 'Naschsommer,' " *NM*, V[1] (1921), 69; Jenisch, "Buddhistische Plastik: eine fremd-verwandte Kunst," *NM*, IV[1] (1920), 416; Meier-Graefe, "Galeriepolitik," *NM*, III (1919), 289.

178. Erich Jenisch, "Indojavanische Kunst," *NM*, V[1] (1921/22), 72; Hans Kauders,

"Mittelalterliche Holzfiguren," *ibid.*, 69; Ponten, "Bericht von Lesefreuden," *NM*, V² (1921), 518.

179. "Schreiben an ein Mädchen," *NM*, IV¹ (1920), 142.

180. "Vorbemerkung," *NM*, I¹ (1914), 1–5, and in a house ad following p. 76 of *Vorläufer*, *NM*, III (1919), entitled "Einladung zum Abonnement."

181. "Richard Seewald," *NM*, III (1919), 139.

182. Hartlaub, in an interview on 9 June 1962 in Bayrisch-Zell, said that he first used this term in the catalog of an exhibit of the Mannheimer Kunsthalle. The catalog is now unavailable, but Professor Kurt Martin, interviewed on 12 June 1962, then director of the Bayrische Gemäldegalerien, confirmed this account.

183. "Hodlerlegende," *NM*, IV² (1920/21), 714–18, also 795–96. Also see letter from Hausenstein to Werner von der Schulenburg of 27 Jan. 1921.

184. "Exotik und Gegenwart," *NM*, V¹ (1921/22), 273–74.

185. Hausenstein, "Die Kunst in diesem Augenblick," *Werden*, *NM*, III (1919), 116; von Wedderkop, "Holland," *NM*, V¹ (1921/22), 207; Höver, "Zur Eigenart deutscher Raumphantasie," *ibid.*, 43.

186. Jenisch, "Buddhistische Plastik: Eine fremd-verwandte Kunst," *NM*, IV¹ (1920), 413–16; Musil, "Wege zur Kunstbetrachtung," *NM*, V² (1921), 713–16.

187. Hausenstein, "Grünewald und das Lamm," *NM*, III (1919), 131–36, and "Renoir," *ibid.*, 570–71; Kauders, "Mittelalterliche Holzfiguren," *NM*, V¹ (1921/22), 68–69.

188. F. (Frisch), "Werden," *Werden*, *NM*, III (1919), 4; Braun, "Das Religiöse und die jüngste Dichtung," *NM*, III (1919), 108.

189. Paquet, "Deutsche und Slawen," *NM*, VI (1922), 136.

190. See Kauders, *NM*, V¹ (1921/22), 68–69.

191. von Wedderkop, *NM*, V¹ (1921/22), 203, 207.

192. "Vincent und Theo," *Werden*, *NM*, III (1919), 39.

193. *NM*, IV¹ (1920), 248.

194. *NM*, VI (1922), 519–24.

195. Professor Kurt Martin, formerly director of the Bayrische Gemäldegalerien and an uncommonly reliable source, invited my attention to Wölfflin's crushing review of Zoff's *Michelangelos Zeichnungen* (Berlin, 1923). I was unable to locate this review, but Professor Martin is positive in his recollection (letter to me of Aug. 1968). While reading proof I located the review with the help of the Wölfflin scholar Joseph Santner. See *Der Bücherwurm*, IX (1924), 15.

196. Deinhardt, "Musik des Lebens: Aphorismus zum Beethoventag," *NM*, IV² (1920/21), 522; Mendelssohn-Bartholdy, "1820: Erinnerungen an den Großvater," *ibid.*, 429; Kolb, "Busoni," *NM*, III (1919), 398–400.

197. See Deinhardt as cited above, and "Zur Krisis in der Musik," *NM*, III (1919), 412, 418.

198. "Theaterstadt München 1920," *NM*, IV² (1920/21), 792, 791.

199. "Theater in Berlin," *NM*, VI (1922), 302–7.

200. "Symptomen-Theater I," *ibid.*, 186.

201. See Sternthal, *NM*, VI (1922), 307. Frisch, in a letter of 4 Aug. 1922, demurred at the blanket criticism of the "humanity poets" (*Menschheitsdichter*).

202. von Wedderkop, "Bühnenexpressionismus," *NM*, VI (1922), 105; Musil, "Symptomen-Theater I," *ibid.*, 182 n.

203. "Münchner Theatersommer," *NM*, III (1919), 361.

204. See Musil, *NM*, VI (1922), 183; Sternthal, *ibid.*, 306.

205. See *NM*, VI (1922), 306.

206. "Blendwerk, Feuer und Pharaonen; 'Haus Herzenstod' und die Säkularisation der Kirchengüter," *NM*, IV² (1920/21), 645–46.

207. A., "Der Weg zur Macht," *ibid.*, 647–49. I tried to penetrate this pseudonym during every interview, but was unable to do so.

208. "Theater in München," *NM*, VI (1922), 607.

209. Baumgarten, "Theater und Zirkus," *NM*, IV¹ (1920), 318; Musil, "Symptomen-Theater II," *NM*, VI (1922), 587; von Scholz, "Die Eroberung der Bühne durch die bildende Kunst," *ibid.*, 60; von Wedderkop, "Bühnenexpressionismus," *ibid.*, 103.

210. "Theater in München," *NM*, VI (1922), 605.

211. "Die Theaterkunst: Für Schauspieler, Regisseure, Dekorateure, Theaterdichter und verwandte Berufe," *NM*, III (1919), 539–50.

212. "Max Reinhardt," *NM*, IV² (1920/21), 819.

213. *Ibid.*, 817.

214. "Von der Kunststadt zur Kaffernsiedlung," *NM*, III (1919), 572.

Chapter 4

1. This information was given to me in part by Mrs. Hausenstein in an interview on 13 Oct. 1961. The paraphrase of the conversation between Benno Reifenberg and Hausenstein was reported in the former's letter of 23 Apr. 1923.

2. See letter from Paul Lenneberg to Frisch of 29 Aug. 1923.

3. In a letter to H. von Wedderkop of 16 Apr. 1924, Frisch wrote that he had good reasons for being satisfied with Kilpper.

4. See letters from Frisch to DVA of 12 Sept., 18 June and 20 Nov. 1924; from Frisch to Hausenstein of 15 June 1925; from Kilpper to Frisch of 22 May 1925 (regarding Heinrich Mann: "To pay 400 Marks for 7 pages is absolutely impossible").

5. See letters from Kilpper to Frisch of 19 Jan. and 21 June 1924.

6. See Frisch's "Abrechnung der Redaktionskasse für August 1924," which is preserved in the editorial correspondence.

7. Letter from Kilpper to Frisch of 7 May 1924.

8. Letter from Kilpper to Frisch of 9 Feb. 1924.

9. Kilpper, though he never said so, had one very legitimate reason to be angry about one review. In one of the few reviews of a DVA book (Josef Ponten's *Architektur die nicht gebaut wurde*, *NM*, VIII (1924/25), 438–40, by Hermann Esswein), both the reviewer and Frisch himself failed to indicate the publisher, something Frisch forgot neither before nor after.

10. See letters from Kilpper to Frisch of 9 Feb., and 7 and 27 May, 1924.

11. "Medaillen der italienischen Renaissance," *NM*, VII¹ (1923/24), 431–32.

12. Kilpper's bitterness about the special literature issue's virtual exclusion of DVA authors becomes apparent through this mollifying letter from Frisch to Kilpper.

13. Frisch wrote about his difficulties in a letter to Kilpper of 20 Nov. 1924. In an undated letter to the DVA of either Nov. or Dec. 1924, Frisch also intimated that

the controversy became so severe because the owner of the publishing house, Auerbach, had had a falling-out with Feist. Croce's article appeared under the title "Die politischen Parteien" in *NM*, VIII[1] (Nov. 1924), 83–89. Frisch gave the rightful source in the Dec. issue of the same year, cf. *NM*, VIII, 282.

14. See 1923 letters from Frisch to Arthur Holitscher of 22 Oct. and to Franz Blei of 26 Nov. Holitscher answered Frisch in a letter of 26 Oct. and pointed out that a formal disclaimer by Kilpper might be necessary.

15. *Deutsche Verlags-Anstalt, 1848–1923: zweiundneunzig Handschriften von Autoren des Verlags mit einer geschichtlichen Einleitung und einem Bücherverzeichnis* (Stuttgart, Berlin, Leipzig: DVA, 1923), p. 18.

16. "German Periodicals," *The Criterion*, II (Feb. 1924), 223–24.

17. Letter of 26 Mar. 1924. In an interview of 10 Oct. 1962, Max Rychner attributed Frisch's ability to revive the *Merkur* to his life-long sense for quality.

18. About the founding of the *Falke* see Felix Berner, "Zur Geschichte der Deutschen Verlags-Anstalt," in *Im 110. Jahr: Almanach der Deutschen Verlags-Anstalt Stuttgart im Jahre der Wiedererrichtung ihres Verlagshauses* (Stuttgart, 1958), p. 40.

19. See also letters from Frisch to Klabund, 17 Dec. 1923; from Kilpper to Frisch, 4 July 1924; from Mörike to Frisch, 17 Dec. 1924; and from Frisch to Kilpper, 9 Jan. 1924.

20. Gustav Mayer, ed., "Aus dem Briefwechsel Hans von Bülows und Ferdinand Lasalle," *NM*, VII[2] (1924), 433–56; Lersch, "Hammer, du funkelnder . . . ," *NM*, VIII[2] (1925), 569–71; Weber, "Die neue Situation," *NM*, VIII[2] (1925), 443–59.

21. James Joyce's *Ulysses* is recommended to Kilpper's attention in letters from Frisch, 26 May and 18 June 1924. On 20 Nov. 1924 Frisch wrote to Kilpper of the special talents of Süskind. The latter mentions the "wonderful . . . Efraim Frisch" who had helped him become a member of the DVA. See his "Damals in der Neckarstraße," *Im 110. Jahr . . . ,* p. 143. Karl Pagel describes his becoming a DVA editorial assistant in the same commemorative almanac (*Im 110. Jahr . . .*), in "Erinnerungen an die Neckarstraße, 1924–1945," p. 146. Rudolf Nutt, a staff member of the *Auslandspost*, was suggested as a translator in several letters, e.g., one dated 18 June 1924. Kilpper expressed his appreciation of Frisch's assessments of prospective publications in letters dated 14 Jan. and 4 July 1924, and asked for an additional judgment in a letter of 17 Dec. 1924.

22. Dr. Otto Pietsch, a subscriber to the *Neue Merkur*, wrote Frisch on 6 March 1924 that if the small typeface were not discontinued, he would have to drop his subscription.

23. See letter from Vagts to Frisch, 11 Jan. 1924. Paul Marc's widow, Helene, told me that Paul subsequently joined the staff of the *Hamburgische Monatshefte für auswärtige Politik*. Franz Schoenberner wrote in his book *Bekenntnisse eines europäischen Intellektuellen* (München, 1964), p. 197, that Marc edited the *Auslandspost* under "the more or less symbolic supervision of Frisch."

24. Introductory note to F. M. Dostojewskij, "Briefe an seine Frau von der Puschkin-Feier," *NM*, VII[2] (1924), 701; E. F[risch]., "Symptome der Umkehr," *ibid.*, 848–55; F[risch], "Die Diktatur in Spanien," *NM*, VII (1923/24), 252–56.

25. Paquet wrote Frisch on 6 Apr. 1925 that he did not particularly like to deal with scholarly topics. He would rather submit something creative. If he felt like writing an essay, he would once more write about a topic relating to the Rhine. On 9 Jan. 1924, Frisch wrote to Kilpper that he had entrusted a review of a book by Trützschler to Wilhelm Michel. This review was never submitted.

26. Georg Burckhardt, "Heraklit; Deutsche Nachdichtungen," *NM*, VII² (1924), 990–97. Ernst Robert Curtius, "Der Dichter Paul Valery." *ibid.*, 641–55.

27. The following page numbers all refer to the special issue *Literatur*, NM, VIII² (Oct./Nov. 1924): Fechter, 163–82; H. Mann, 186–92; Kafka, 197–98; Munk, 220–27; Lersch, 227–30; Perutz, 247–56; Lübbe, 199–219; Ulitz, 257–71; Weiß, 271–82; Boetticher, 193–96; Hesse, 183–85; Süskind, 231–47.

28. See letter to Klaus Pinkus of 21 Oct. 1933, in Musil, *Prosa, Dramen, späte Briefe*. Herausgeben von Adolf Frisé (Hamburg, 1957), p. 729.

29. Even A. W. G. R[andall] was misled, when he wrote in *The Criterion*, IV¹ (Jan. 1926), 218: "Like the *Merkur* the *Rundschau* . . . is the organ of a particular firm of publishers, a fact to be remembered but not unduly emphasized. If . . . Fischer's authors are put forward rather prominently in each number it is a fair retort that they are in the front rank, including Thomas Mann . . . , Gerhart Hauptmann, Hermann Hesse, and, among foreign writers, Bernard Shaw."

30. Frisch to Curtius on 18 Sept. 1924: He liked for him to write about his latest impressions in Pontigny and Paris in the *Neue Merkur* (and not in the *Neue Rundschau*). As early as 14 Dec. 1921, Frisch wrote to Lion that he would really be offended if he finally had to realise that Lion preferred to cooperate with Mr. Kayser, editor-in-chief of the *Neue Rundschau*.

31. Letter to me from Dr. Kilpper of 2 Apr. 1962.

32. A. W. G. R[andall]., "German Periodicals," *The Criterion*, IV¹ (Jan. 1926), 217.

Chapter 5

1. "Vögel in der Luft," *NM*, VII¹ (1923/24), 113.

2. Dr. Usch (pseud. for Friedrich Sternthal), "Weltchronik," *ibid.*, 331.

3. Mendelssohn-Bartholdy, "Italien und der Dreibund: Anläßlich der neuesten Publikationen des Auswärtigen Amtes," *ibid.*, 236. The whole series was published by the Deutsche Verlagsgesellschaft für Politik und Geschichte, Berlin.

4. "Die Aktenpublikation des Auswärtigen Amtes ('Die große Politik der europäischen Kabinette'): Gesichtspunkte zu ihrer Wertung," *NM*, VIII² (1925), 914.

5. "Brief aus U. S. Amerika," *ibid.*, 679.

6. "Brief an einen zehn Jahre Jüngeren," *ibid.*, 696.

7. Dr. Usch, "Weltpolitische Chronik," *ibid.*, 838.

8. Defense of the Austrian Army: Robert Müller, "Die Politisierung Österreichs," *NM*, VII¹ (1923–24), 188. Pacifistic passages, Lübbe, "Ein Richter," *NM*, VIII¹ (1924/25), 199–219; Braun, "Hans Carossas 'Rumänisches Tagebuch,'" *NM*, VIII² (1925), 602–4; Dr. Usch, "Weltpolitische Chronik," *NM*, VII² (1924), 677–80.

9. Adolf Fischer, "Fahrten im Orient," *NM*, VII¹ (1923/24,) 92–113.

10. *NM*, VIII¹ (1924/25), 443–59.

11. See letter of 5 Feb. 1925 from Frisch to Weber.

12. Burschell, "Spiegel der Zeit," *NM*, VII¹ (1923/24), 157; Michel, "Republik und Kaisergedanke," *NM*, VII² (1924), 522. One of Frisch's attacks against the Kahr government did not find its way into print. He suggested the following bracketed words to be added to a sentence in Michel's article: "From Henry the Lion to Kahr [his opposite], we have a single chain of puberty." Michel did not include the bracketed addition. See letter from Frisch to Michel of 24 March 1924.

13. *NM*, VIII² (1925), 601.

14. Von einem Süddeutschen (Wilhelm Hausenstein), "Zur deutschen Situation," *NM*, VII¹ (1923/24), 70.

15. Robert Müller, "Die Politisierung Österreichs," *ibid.*, 184.

16. Dr. Usch, "Weltpolitische Chronik," *NM*, VIII¹ (1924/25), 71.

17. *NM*, VII¹ (1923/24), 51–74.

18. See undated letter from Hausenstein to Frisch of 1924.

19. See letter from Mutius to Frisch of Oct. 1923.

20. A. W. G. R[andall], "German Periodicals" in *The Criterion*, II⁶ (Feb. 1924), 223.

21. "Fragmente über Europa," *NM*, VII¹ (1923/24), 1–14.

22. "Aus englischen und amerikanischen Zeitschriften," *ibid.*, 83.

23. Brailsford, "Was die englische Arbeiterregierung tun wird," *ibid.*, 345–51; Wells, "Prophezeiungen," *NM*, VII (1924), 941–53.

24. Franz Arens, "Ein Gerechter," *NM*, VII¹ (1923/24), 340–43.

25. "Angelsächsischer Eros," *NM*, VII² (1924), 589–98.

26. "Englische Eindrücke," *NM*, VIII² (1925), 943–58.

27. "Politik und Moral," *NM*, VII² (1924), 608–21, 685–701.

28. Dr. Usch, "Weltpolitische Chronik," *NM*, VIII¹ (1924/25), 71.

29. Grabowsky, "Der neue russische Mensch," *NM*, VIII² (1925), 849–60 (this article was recommended by *The Criterion*, IV¹ [Jan. 1926], 218); Wilhelm, "China und die Mächte," *NM*, VIII² (1925), 780; Mendelssohn-Bartholdy, "Pakt und Protokoll: Vortrag in der Rigaischen Universität," *ibid.*, 605.

30. "Brief aus U. S. Amerika," *ibid.*, *679*.

31. "Aus englischen und amerikanischen Zeitschriften," *NM*, VII¹ (1923/24), 80; "Loeb und Leopold," *ibid.*, 151–54.

32. "Mexiko und die Staaten," *NM*, VIII¹ (1924/25), 375–94.

33. "Amerikanische Antitoxine," *NM*, VIII² (1925), 847.

34. Von einem Süddeutschen, "Zur deutschen Situation," *NM*, VII¹ (1923/24), 69; Curtius, "Aus französischen Zeitschriften," *ibid.*, 162.

35. Thun-Hohenstein, "Sommergespräche in Burgund," *NM*, VIII¹ (1924/25), 141–50; Schoenberner, "Anatole France," *NM*, VII² (1924), 681–84; Dr. Usch, "Weltpolitische Chronik," *ibid.*, 847; Heinrich Mann, "Briefe ins ferne Ausland: I," *NM*, VIII² (1925), 770.

36. "Zwischen Paris und Berlin," *NM*, VII¹ (1923/24), 426–29.

37. E. F[risch]., "Symptome der Umkehr," *NM*, VII² (1924), 848–855; Thun-Hohenstein, *NM*, VIII¹ (1924/25), 147.

38. Pannwitz, "Pan-Europa," *NM*, VIII¹ (1924/25), 78–80; Müller, "Europa," *NM*, VII¹ (1923/24), 515–516; Thun-Hohenstein, *NM*, VIII¹ (1924/25), 141–50.

39. "System eines Staatenbundes," *NM*, VIII¹ (1924/25), 933.

40. Lion, "Fragmente über Europa," *NM*, VII¹ (1923/24), 1–14; Burschell, "Spiegel der Zeit," *ibid.*, 155–56; Paquet, "Brief an einen zehn Jahre Jüngeren," *NM*, VIII² (1925), 692.

41. Burschell, "Spiegel der Zeit," *NM*, VII¹ (1923/24), 157; Von einem Süddeutschen, "Zur deutschen Situation," *ibid.*, 70–71.

42. "Briefe ins ferne Ausland. I," *NM*, VIII² (1925), 770.

43. *Ibid.*, p. 772; Dr. Usch, "Weltpolitische Chronik," *ibid.*, 1000; Weber, "Oswald Spengler der Politiker," *NM*, VII² (1924), 777; Poeschel, "Die Schule am Meer," *NM*, VIII² (1925), 687.

44. "Über Demokratie: An die Gebildeten unter ihren Verächtern," *NM*, VII² (1924), 601.

45. Weber, *NM*, VII² (1924), 780.

46. Von einem Süddeutschen, "Zur deutschen Situation," *NM*, VII¹ (1923/24), 70; Hellpach, badischer Staatspräsident und Minister des Kultus und Unterrichts, "Die katholische Kulturoffensive und der politische Katholizismus," *NM*, VIII¹ (1924/25), 374, 368.

47. Heinrich Mann, "Briefe ins ferne Ausland. I," *NM*, VIII² (1925), 772; Dr. Usch, *ibid.*, pp. 602, 999.

48. Burschell, "Spiegel der Zeit," *NM*, VII¹ (1923/24), 155; Flake, "Filmbrief aus Berlin," *ibid.*, 238.

49. "Briefe ins ferne Ausland, I," *NM*, VIII² (1925), 770–71.

50. *NM*, VII² (1924), 962.

51. Editorial notes to Franz Angermann's "Das Volkshochschulheim Dreissigacker," *NM*, VII (1923/24), 486, and Eugen Rosenstock's "Das Versiegen der Wissenschaft und der Ursprung der Sprache," *NM*, VIII² (1925), 814.

52. "System eines Staatenbundes," *NM*, VII² (1925), 942.

53. Burschell, "Spiegel der Zeit," *NM*, VII¹ (1923/24), 420; Flake, *ibid.*, 237; Lion, "Relativität der Macht," *NM*, VIII² (1925), 539.

54. *NM*, VII² (1924), 517–22.

55. "Brief an einen zehn Jahre Jüngeren," *NM*, VIII² (1925), 691.

56. A. W. G. R[andall], "German Periodicals," *The Criterion*, VII² (July 1924), 495.

57. *NM*, VIII² (1925), 693.

58. Dr. Usch, "Weltpolitische Chronik," *NM*, VIII² (1925), 1000.

59. "Stimmen zur Erneuerung des deutschen Menschen," *NM*, VIII¹ (1924/25), 56, 66.

60. "Die neue Situation," *ibid.*, 443–59.

61. Kannitverstan (Wilhelm Hausenstein), "Briefe aus Holland: Herbstliche Reise eines Melancholikers," *NM*, VII¹ (1923/24), 297; Müller, "Die Politisierung Österreichs," *ibid.*, 179, 185, 187; Schoenberner, "Amerikanische Antitoxine," *NM*, VIII² (1925), 845.

62. Gerhard Schoenberner (nephew to Franz S.), *Der gelbe Stern: Die Judenverfolgung in Europa 1933–1945*, 2d ed. (Hamburg, 1961; 1st ed. 1960).

63. "Stimmen zur Erneuerung des deutschen Menschen," *NM*, VIII¹ (1924/25), 55–68.

64. Adolf Fischer, "Fahrten im Orient," *NM*, VII¹ (1924/25), 111.

65. "Die Diktatur in Spanien," *ibid.*, 253.

66. *NM*, VIII¹ (1924/25), 368.

67. Lion, "Politik und Moral," *NM*, VII² (1924), 608–21; Braun, "Geistige Führung," *NM*, VIII¹ (1924/25), 326–36.

68. "Politik des unendlichen Staates," *NM*, VII² (1924), 915–25.

69. See letter from Thomas Mann to Frisch of 22 Feb. 1925.

70. "Urwelt, Sage und Menschheit: Bemerkungen zur naturhistorisch-metaphysischen Lehre Edgar Dacqués," *NM*, VIII² (1925), 551–63.

71. *Ibid.*, 971–78.

72. "Der Kampf Heinrich Friedrich Jacobis," *NM*, VII¹ (1923/24), 128–44.

73. "Nietzsche und das Wertproblem," *NM*, VII² (1924), 823; "Kant in Südamerika," *ibid.*, 1014–19.

74. "Hegel und unser Geschlecht," *NM*, VII¹ (1924/25), 360–62.

75. "Kierkegaard," *NM*, VII² (1924), 536–44.

76. Utzinger, *NM*, VII¹ (1923/24), 245–47; Burschell, "Spiegel der Zeit," *ibid.*, 157.

77. "Tradition und Revolution in Deutschland und Frankreich," *ibid.*, 357.

78. "German Reviews," *The Criterion*, VII² (April 1924), 368.

79. *NM*, VIII² (1925), 571–586.

80. "Philosophie der Tragödie (Zu Leo Schestow's Werk)," *ibid.*, 757.

81. *NM* VII¹ (1923/24), 157.

82. Editor's note, *NM*, VIII² (1925), 814.

83. "Voltaire," *NM*, VII¹ (1923/24), 241–43.

84. Flake, "Der Mythos von morgen," *ibid.*, 77; Mittenzwey, "Generationswechsel in der Wissenschaft," *NM*, VIII² (1925), 671.

85. "Mythos . . . ," 75.

86. "Neuer Umkreis der George-Bewegung," *NM*, VII¹ (1923/24), 149.

87. *NM*, VIII² (1925), 760.

88. "Briefe aus Holland: Herbstliche Reise eines Melancholikers," *NM*, VII¹ (1923/24), 294. Bertha von Suttner's book had appeared in Vienna two years earlier.

89. "Zwischen Paris und Berlin," *NM*, VII¹ (1923/24), 427.

90. "Aktualität und Utopie: Zu Lukács Philosophie des Marxismus," *ibid.*, 459.

91. "Oswald Spengler der Politiker," *NM*, VII² (1924), 773–77.

92. "Das Volkshochschulheim Dreissigacker," *NM*, VII¹ (1923/24), 493.

93. "Angelsächsischer Eros," *NM*, VII² (1924), 589.

94. Musil, "Der 'Untergang' des Theaters," *ibid.*, 826–42; Rosenstock, "Unternehmer und Volksordnung," *ibid.*, 1001.

95. Kassner, "Der Sinn und die Eigenschaft," *NM*, VIII¹ (1924/25), 303–17; "Gesichter," *NM*, VII¹ (1923/24), 411.

96. F[risch]., "Das Menschengesicht," *Europäische Revue*, VI² (Oct. 1930), 791–92 (review of Max Picard, *Das Menschengesicht*).

97. "Über Graphologie und Physiognomik," *NM*, VIII¹ (1924/25), 161.

98. "Vom Axiom der Astrologie: Eine Einführung," *NM*, VIII² (1925), 979, 984, 987.

99. "Die tänzerische Generation," *ibid.*, 586–97.

100. *Der Wendepunkt* (Frankfurt a.M., 1952), p. 139.

101. "Ein Wort über Hölderlin," *NM*, VIII¹ (1924/25), 360.

102. "Dreispaltung oder Dreieinigkeit in der Psychoanalyse," *ibid.*, 346–54.

103. Brinkmann, *ibid.*, 437.

104. *NM*, VIII¹ (1924/25), 358.

105. "Die Schule am Meer," *NM*, VIII² (1925), 688.

106. *NM*, VII¹ (1923/24), 165. Musil begins with a review of Leopold v. Wiese, ed., *Soziologie des Volksbildungswesens* (München, 1923).

107. Willy Hellpach, in his article "Die katholische Kulturoffensive und der politische Katholizismus," *NM*, VIII¹ (1924/25), 369, made a similar charge. He also noted the inconsistency of the Catholic clergy in advocating *separate* elementary schools and *joint* high schools for Catholic and Protestant pupils.

108. "Der 'Untergang' des Theaters," *NM*, VII² (1924), 835.

109. "Das Volkshochschulheim Dreissigacker," *NM*, VII¹ (1923/24), 486–98.

110. Editorial note in *NM*, VII (1923), 486.

111. "Generationswechsel in der Wissenschaft," *NM*, VIII² (1925), 669–78.

112. Kannitverstan, "Briefe aus Holland," *NM*, VII¹ (1923/24), 307. Hausenstein's earlier attack entitled "Die Welt der alten Burschenschaft," had appeared in *NM*, II¹ (1915), 307.

113. "Englische Eindrücke," *NM*, VIII² (1925), 955.

114. A. W. G. R[andall]., "German Periodicals," *The Criterion*, IV¹ (Jan. 1926), 218.

115. "Cäsar und die neuere Geschichtsschreibung," *NM*, VIII² (1925), 923–27.

116. *NM*, VII¹ (1923/24), 169–76.

117. "Aktivität und Passivität in der Politik," *NM*, VIII¹ (1924/25), 89–103.

118. *NM*, VII¹ (1923/24), 257–70.

119. *NM*, VII² (1924), 777–93.

120. "Unternehmer und Volksordnung," *ibid.*, 997–1004.

121. "Europäer, Amerikaner und Indianer," *NM*, VIII¹ (1924–25), 1–14; Matthias "Mexiko und die Staaten," *ibid.*, 374–94, which revealed a thorough bias against the U. S., was reprinted in the most important journal in economics, printed by the *Deutsche Wirtschaftsverband*, crediting the *Neue Merkur* (letter from Matthias to Frisch of 28 Apr. 1925).

122. "Ifé: Ein Kulturproblem," *NM*, VIII² (1925), 745–56.

123. Borrmann, "Bilder aus Sumatra," *NM*, VIII¹ (1924/25), 479–87; Fischer, "Fahrten im Orient," *NM*, VII¹ (1923/24), 92–113; Wilhelm, "China und die Mächte," *NM*, VIII² (1925), 774–80.

124. "Die Mitte: Gedanken zu Leopold Zieglers [Buch]," *NM*, VIII¹ (1924/25), 460–67.

125. "Urwelt, Sage und Menschheit: Bemerkungen zur naturhistorisch-metaphysischen Lehre Edgar Dacqués," *NM*, VIII² (1925), 551–63.

126. Turel, "Dreispaltung der Dreieinigkeit in der Psychoanalyse," *NM*, VIII¹ (1924/25), 346–54; Bloch, "Das Bild bedeutender Menschen und die Identität," *NM*, VII² (1924), 926–32.

127. "Prophezeiungen," *NM*, VII² (1924), 941–53.

128. Hobgoblin, "Medaillen der italienischen Renaissance," *NM*, VII¹ (1923/24), 431–32.

129. Adolf Grabowsky, "Der neue russische Mensch," *NM*, VIII² (1925), 856.

130. "Über die Dualität künstlerischer Gestaltung," *NM*, VII¹ (1923/24), 31–39.

131. "Aktualität und Utopie: Zu Lukács Philosophie des Marxismus," *ibid.*, 457–58.

132. "Zwischen Paris und Berlin," *ibid.*, 427–28.

133. "Zur deutschen Situation," *ibid.*, 54.

134. "Deutsche Malerei in den letzten fünfzig Jahren," *NM*, VII² (1924), 1005–9.

135. "Max Beckmann," *NM*, VII¹ (1923/24), 329.

136. "Corinth," *NM*, VIII² (1925), 997.

137. *NM*, VII¹ (1923/24), 328.

138. *NM*, VII¹ (1923/24), 31–39.

139. *NM*, VII¹ (1923/24), 427.

140. "Jakobs Segen," *NM*, VIII¹ (1924/25), 337–45.

141. Esswein, "Carpaccio," *ibid.*, 518–21; Braun, "Phydias," *NM*, VIII² (1925), 915–19; Hausenstein, "Michelangelo als Zeichner," *ibid.*, 920–23, and "Rembrandt als Zeichner," *ibid.*, 1002–8; for Goll on cubism and French art, see *NM*, VII¹ (1923/24), 426–29.

142. Musil, "Ansätze zu neuer Ästhetik: Bemerkungen über eine Dramaturgie des Films," *NM*, VIII¹ (1924/25), 488.

143. Preetorius calls himself a "creative artist" in "Über die Dualität künstlerischer Gestaltung," *NM*, VII¹ (1923/24), 31; on Romantic and Germanic art: *ibid.*, 33.

144. *NM*, VII¹ (1923/24), 51–74.

145. *NM*, VII² (1924), 869–83.

146. "Neue Hölderlin-Bücher," *NM*, VIII¹ (1924/25), 76–78.

147. *NM*, VII² (1924), 673.

148. Fifth ed. (München, 1918); new ed., München. 1959.

149. Walter Dahms, "Giacomo Puccini," *NM*, VIII¹ (1924/25), 440–42.

150. "Symptomen-Theater I" and "Symptomen-Theater II," *NM*, VI (1919), 179–86 and 587–94 respectively.

151. *NM*, VII² (1924), 826–42.

152. *NM*, VIII¹ (1924–25), 488–506.

Chapter 6

1. Rheinhardt, "Ferien," *NM*, II² (1915/16), 496–510, "Orphische Besinnung," *NM*, IV² (1920/21), 533–36; Fontana, "Das Abenteuer," *NM*, V² (1921), 480–97, "Himmel und Hölle," *NM*, VI (1922), 200–213, "Die Nacht in Mantua," *NM*, VII² (1924), 794–815; Lehmann, *NM*, II¹ (1915), 744–68.

2. Brecht's story "Bargan läßt es sein," appeared originally in *NM*, V (1921), 394–407.

3. See his *Failures of Criticism* (Ithaca, 1967), p. 33.

4. "Geleitwort des Verlages," *1903–1908, Georg Müller Verlag München* (München, 1908).

5. "Vorbemerkung," *NM*, I¹ (1914), 4.

6. Letters from Curtius to Frisch of Feb. and 15 Dec. 1921; letter from Thomas Mann to Frisch of 22 May 1925, and interview with Lion on 25 Sept. 1961.

7. *Confessions of a European Intellectual* (New York, 1946), p. 199.

8. The "house-ad" is retained only in the unbound first issue. See *NM*, I¹ (1914), v–xiii. Frisch's 1914 correspondence with the author and editor Siegfried von Vegesack recounts his difficulties with Emil Schering.

9. August Strindberg, "Ungedruckte Briefe über fünf Werke," trans. Emil Schering, *NM*, I¹ (1914), 76–97, quote from 83.

10. Editorial note, *NM*, II² (1915/16), 465; the prologue extends to p. 484.

11. "Gebet," *NM*, I¹ (1914), 217; "Gedichte aus dem Nachlaß," *NM*, II² (1915/16), 189–93. See letters between Frisch and Margareta Morgenstern.

12. "Das Gänsemännchen: Roman," *NM*, I¹ (1914), 6, 145, 273, 405, 534, 657; *NM*, I² (1914/15), 7, 203, 321, 493, 671. Cf. interview with Fega Frisch on 16 Sept. 1961.

13. Krell, *NM*, VIII² (1925), 635–44; Schreiber, *NM*, I¹ (1914), 504–17, *NM*, II² (1915/16), 167–74; Kehlmann, *NM*, III (1919), 668–683; von Boetticher, *NM*, VIII¹ (1924/25), 193–98.

14. *NM*, I¹ (1914), 558.

15. August Oehler (pseud. for August Mayer), "Aus der griechischen Anthologie," *NM*, II¹ (1915), 572–77.

16. *NM*, II² (1915/16), 604–21.

17. *NM*, I¹ (1914), 325–50.

18. See *Konstellationen*, ed. Stern (Stuttgart: Deutsche Verlags-Anstalt, 1964).

19. Boognor, "Konstellationen," *Die Bücher-Kommentare* (Berlin, 15 June 1964), p. 6.

20. Döblin, *NM*, I¹ (1914), 63–76; Ulitz, *NM*, I² (1914/15), 604–15; Edschmid, *NM*, II¹ (1915), 436–48; von Gütersloh (pseud. for Albert Conrad Kiehtreiber), *ibid.*, 704–12. Edschmid had also submitted the novella "Der Bezwinger," to the *NM*, but withdrew it when he heard rumors of the impending suspension of publication in 1916 (see *Kurt Wolff; Briefwechsel eines Verlegers 1911–1963*, hrsg. Bernhard Zeller and Ellen Otten [Darmstadt, 1966]), p. 173.

21. See letters from Frisch to Flake of 18 Aug. 1919 and to Döblin of 29 Nov. 1921.

22. Döblin submitted *Die drei Sprünge des Wang-Lun* on 17 June 1919, *Klein Nolte* on 30 Apr. 1924, and the film script on 29 Nov. 1921.

23. In a letter of 21 Aug. 1921 to Wilhelm Hausenstein.

24. "Das Bekenntnis und die Dichtung," *NM*, VIII¹ (1924/25), 163–82.

25. See letter from Frisch to Döblin of 9 Feb. 1921, and Döblin's answer in an undated letter.

26. *NM*, V¹ (1921/22), 56–64.

27. "Das Werk Alfred Döblins," *NM*, VI (1922), 368–82.

28. See headings to Part I and Part II of Walter Sokel, *The Writers in Extremis: Expressionism in Twentieth-Century German Literature* (Stanford, 1959), pp. 7, 226.

29. *NM*, VI (1922), 347–364.

30. Krell, "Zur Prosa der Gegenwart: Bemerkungen aus einem historischen Abriß," *NM*, VII² (1924), 576.

31. *NM*, I¹ (1914), 499–503, and "Gedichte," *NM*, V² (1921), 549–51.

32. München, 1920.

33. *NM*, I² (1915), 604–35.

34. *NM*, II² (1915/16), 655–96.

35. *NM*, VII² (1924), 884–907 and 464–90.

36. *NM*, VIII¹ (1924/25), 257–71.

37. *Deutsche Literatur der Gegenwart*, rev. by Max Wieser (Berlin, 1932), p. 397.

38. *NM*, VIII¹ (1924/25), 72–76.

39. Sokel, *Writers in Extremis*, p. 231.

40. In June 1919 Frisch sent a form letter to a selected list of past and future contributors which began: "The *Neue Merkur* is asking for your collaboration." One of these went to Johannes R. Becher.

41. Lersch's "Hammer, du funkelnder . . ." appeared in *NM*, VIII² (1925), 569–71.

42. Sokel, p. 3.

43. "Prosa, Dramen, Verse" in *Werke*, III (München and Wien, 1964), 10.

44. Ernst Alker, "Gottfried Kölwel," *ibid.*, 398.

45. See letter from Buber to Kölwel of 12 Feb. 1917, owned by Rosa Kölwel, the poet's widow.

46. *NM*, II² (1915/16), 566.

47. *NM*, III (1919), 113.

48. Alker, p. 397.

49. Quoted in full in this writer's *Konstellationen*, pp. 75–76.

50. *NM*, II¹ (1915), 298–301.

51. "Die deutsche Epik des 20. Jahrhunderts." *Deutsche Literatur im 20. Jahrhundert: Strukturen und Gestalten, Zwanzig Darstellungen*, eds. Hermann Friedemann and Otto Mann, 3rd ed. (Heidelberg, 1959), p. 60.

52. See Ehrenstein's *Gedichte und Prosa*, ed. Karl Otten (Neuwied am Rhein, 1961), p. 417.

53. See *Der Sturm, ein Erinnerungsbuch an Herwarth Walden*, eds. Nell Walden and Lothar Schreyer (Baden-Baden, 1954).

54. *NM*, I¹ (1914). 98–99.

55. *Ibid.*, 517–20.

56. "Erlebnis und Flucht in Werk Albert Ehrensteins" (diss. University of Cincinnati, 1966): "The theory cannot be rejected out of hand that Ehrenstein, who never was a literary success in Vienna, displayed, however, in his relationship with book and magazine publishers no inconsiderable adroitness and used the new literary movement [Expressionism], if one can call it that, only for the purpose of establishing himself and gaining literary success, which he needed for his livelihood. He never did have a money-making job. . . . Ehrenstein was, after all, never concerned with aesthetic principles, but only with communicating his own life situation; the form in his works played only a subordinate, secondary role."

57. See Franz Lennartz' *Deutsche Dichter und Schriftsteller unserer Zeit*, 8th ed. (Stuttgart, 1959), p. 790.

58. *NM*, I¹ (1914), 217–24.

59. "Robert Walser," *Jahresring, Beiträge zur deutschen Literatur und Kunst der Gegenwart* (Stuttgart, 1957/58), pp. 323–28.

60. "Sebastian," *NM*, I² (1914/15), 400–410; "Reisebeschreibung," *NM*, II¹ (1915), 317–32.

61. Chtojewitz in *Merkur* XXI (1967), 247, says of Walser's narrative: "Obviously by consciously exploiting the linguistic peculiarities of the Biel [region] and of Switzerland and by going as far as the borderline of triviality, Walser saw the last possibility of presenting the small bourgeois drama [of the story of a triangle] through its ironic treatment. He could not possibly take it seriously any more."

62. Mell, "Die Brille," *NM*, II² (1915/16), 380–97; Heinrich Mann, "Die große Liebe," *ibid.*, 1–126; Wedekind, "Bismarck: Bilder aus der deutschen Geschichte," *NM*, II (1915), 1–12, 129–37, 257–65, 385–96, 641–54; Thomas Mann, "Gesang vom Kindchen: Ein Idyll," *NM*, III (1919), 16–32, 87–97.

63. Albert Soergel, *Dichtung und Dichter der Zeit, Dichter aus deutschem Volkstum*, 3rd ed. (Leipzig, 1934), pp. 100–110.

64. *NM*, II² (1915/16), 1–126. Heinrich Mann's self-assessment appears in Ulrich Weisstein, *Heinrich Mann* (Tübingen, 1962), p. 251.

65. Weisstein, p. 236.

66. *NM*, II¹ (1915), 1–12, 129–37, 257–65, 385–96, 641–54.

67. Frank Wedekind, *Gesammelte Werke* (München, 1920), VII, 84.

68. Mann, "Über Frank Wedekind," *NM*, I¹ (1914), 520–25; Frank, "Modernität und Bekenntnis," *ibid.*, 525–28; Martens, "Erinnerungen an Wedekind (1897–1900)," *NM*, IV² (1920/21), 537–49.

69. "Typen des neuen Frankreich," *NM*, I² (1914/15), 92–104.

70. Claudel, "Goldhaupt: Ein Trauerspiel in drei Teilen," *NM*, I¹ (1914), 449–86, 567–608, 686–728; Rung, "Fadl Paschas Schicksal," *NM*, I² (1914/15), 124–43; bin-Gorion, "Zwei alte Erzählungen," *ibid.*, 280–84; Prischwin, "Bilder von der Steppe," *NM*, I¹ (1914), 224–43.

71. Klabund, "Li-tai-pe. Nachdichtungen," *NM*, II¹ (1915), 202–4; Perutz, "Der Tod des Meisters der Materie," *NM*, I² (1914/15), 104–12; Jacques, "Jangtse-Tagebuch," *ibid.*, 162–79, 277–307.

72. "Vom Übersetzen," in "Briefe an das Tage-Buch," *Tage-Buch*, VIII (29 Oct. 1927), 1767.

73. Mrs. Frisch was nominated by W. E. Süskind, who shared this information with me. Eliasberg translated Prischwin, *NM*, I¹ (1914), 224–43; Ulitz translated Alexander Block, "Die Ballade der Zwölf," *NM*, III (1919), 693–706; Fega Frisch translated Aleksei Remisov, "Aus dem flammenden Russland zu den Sternen: Alexander Block zum Gedächtnis," *NM*, V² (1921), 686–98.

74. *NM*, I² (1914/15), 308–16. See also Mann ["Hans Reisigers Whitman Werk"] in *Gesammelte Werke* (Frankfurt, 1960), X, 626–27 and ["Hans Reisiger,"] 539–43, especially 540: "Ich darf mich einer der ersten Bewunderer und Lobpreiser nennen von Reisigers Whitman-Übersetzung und dem prachtvollen Einführungsessay, den er ihr beigab, und halte mich überzeugt, daß diese Verdeutschung bleiben und unübertroffen, unüberholbar bestehen wird gleich dem Tieck-Schlegel' schen Shakespeare." See Allen, *Whitman Handbook* (Chicago, 1946), p. 519: "Despite the great critical excitement over Whitman, however, no really good translation of his poems existed in Germany, until the gifted Munich poet, Hans Reisiger, undertook the task. . . . This work is now regarded as a classic."

75. *Dichtung und Dichter der Zeit*, II (Düsseldorf, 1963), 664.

76. "Känguru," trans. Else Jaffé-Richthofen, *NM*, VII² (1924), 522–36.

77. *NM*, II¹ (1915), 165–74. Cf. his *Ausgewählte Werke* in Einzelausgaben, XI (Vol. I of *Novellen*) (Ost-Berlin, 1961).

Chapter 7

1. Bloch, *NM*, V² (1921), 806–20; Mann, *NM*, III (1919), 16–32, 87–97. Discriminating critics apparently realized the limitation of Thomas Mann's work even then. Stefan Grossmann wrote to Frisch on 2 June 1919 that he was no little upset about Thomas Mann's "Little Child." Though some reviewers were favorable—the *Berliner Tageblatt* of 27 Dec. 1919 called it, together with Mann's *Herr und Hund*, "erlesene kleine Kunstwerke" (rare little art-works)—Frisch refused to have the work reviewed when it appeared in book form. When a Munich writer offered on 6 March 1920 a favorable review which defended Thomas Mann and opposed all the other criticisms, Frisch rejected the Ms. On 11 March 1920 he wrote Dr. W. Mathiesen that within the frame of reference of the magazine it would look too much like an argument pro domo.

2. *Ahnung und Aufbruch: Expressionistische Prosa*, ed. Karl Otten (Darmstadt, 1957), pp. 32–33.

3. *NM*, VI (1922), 51–53.

4. "Neue Gedichte," *NM*, V² (1921), 541–44.

5. *Literatur-Revolution 1910–1925: Dokumente, Manifeste, Programme*, I (Darmstadt, 1960), 9.

6. Flake, "Prognose des Dadismus," *NM*, IV¹ (1920), 408; Gide, *NM*, IV² (1920/21), 558.

7. *Kritisches Lesebuch* (Hamburg, 1962), pp. 42–43.

8. *NM*, VI (1922), 274–283.

9. Mann, *NM*, V² (1921), 521–40; Reisiger, *NM*, III (1919), 469–72; Wegner, *NM*, IV² (1921), 669–84; Weiß, *NM*, IV¹ (1920), 119–39.

10. In a letter of 15 Feb. 1922 to Frisch, Weiß not only offered his appreciative review of Vischer but also suggested that Frisch publish Vischer's future works.

11. Lennartz, p. 202.

12. *NM*, IV¹ (1920), 386–96.

13. *NM*, VII² (1924), 794–815.

14. "Das Abenteuer," *NM*, V² (1921), 480–97; "Himmel und Hölle," *NM*, VI (1922), 200–213.

15. Benn, *NM*, VI (1922), 51–53; Becher, *ibid.*, 364–67; Klabund, *NM*, III (1919), 114.

16. *NM*, VI (1922), 345–47.

17. *NM*, III (1919), 167–87. See also *Konstellationen*, ed. Stern, pp. 133–34.

18. *NM*, III, Heft *Werden* (1919), 117. "But the objective contents of Expressionism took shape according to its own laws. It became what it could become. Our enthusiasm, subjectivism, alone did not create it. Today we stop, resting, and ask what it produced. Today—for today it has run its course."

19. "Die Krippe," *NM*, V² (1921), 545–49; "Die Forelle," *NM*, V¹ (1921/22), 329–37.

20. *NM*, VI (1922), 557–72.

21. *NM*, VI (1922), 14–41.

22. This anonymous review appeared in *Münchner Neueste Nachrichten*, 2 June 1922.

23. Felix Braun, "Der Dichter Hans Carossa," *NM*, V¹ (1921/22), 366–68. In a letter to Dora Brandenburg of 7 Dec. 1921 (now in the Handschriftenabteilung der Stadtbibliothek München) Carossa refers to Braun's review with little enthusiasm: He thought lyrics, *"especially,"* should be discussed more *"soberly."*

24. *NM*, IV¹ (1920), 296–306.

25. *NM*, V² (1921), 726–33.

26. *NM*, V² (1921), 556–69; "All the people drift towards one end. / One sun only courses above all / people. There everything flowers and dies in a like frame of mind. And, in the eternal, / Goodness is / like evil / good."

27. *NM*, III (1919), 314–34.

28. *Von Richard Wagner zu Bertolt Brecht: Eine Geschichte der neueren deutschen Literatur* (Frankfurt a.M. and Hamburg, 1959), pp. 267–68. See also Klein, *Geschichte der deutschen Novelle:Von Goethe bis zur Gegenwart*, 4th ed. (Wiesbaden, 1960), pp. 519–32.

29. *NM*, V² (1921), 618–25.

30. *Geschichte der deutschen Novelle* (Bern, 1963), p. 460.

31. Sieburg, *NM*, V¹ (1921/22), 15–36; Flake, *Vorläufer*, *NM*, III (1919), 44–64, and *NM*, V¹ (1921/22), 83–98.

32. *NM*, VI (1922), 494–515.

33. T. F., "German Periodicals," *The Criterion*, I³ (April 1923), 310–11.

34. Boegner, [Review of] "Konstellationen," *Bücher-Kommentare*, II (1964), 6.

35. Hatzfeld, *NM*, III (1919), 213–15; Harich, *NM*, VI (1922), 187–89; Picard, *NM*, IV¹ (1920), 262–64; Poeschel, *NM*, V¹ (1921/22), 69–71; Wandrey, *NM*, VI (1922), 221–35.

36. Wandrey, "Klassik und Romantik," *NM*, VI (1922), 540–42.

37. Jean Paul, "Elf Zeit-Polymeter auf den letzten Tag von 1807," *NM*, III (1919), 368; Neumann, *NM*, VI (1922), 515–18.

38. I³ (April 1923), 310–11.

39. *NM*, III (1919/20), 509–512. "[The story is] something classical, exceedingly restrained, something that perfects the most noble tradition." "The times thought that Hofmannsthal had stood still; in reality he has advanced, but no one advanced with him."

40. An excerpt from Brecht's letter appears in the catalog "Auktion 41," 6 June 1966, p. 15, of the firms L'Art Ancien, Zürich, and Haus der Bücher, Basel. Also see Ferdinand Lion, "Der Neue Merkur," *Akzente*, X (Feb. 1963), 35.

41. "Bargan läßt es sein, Eine Flibustiergeschichte," *NM*, V¹ (1921/22), 394–407; "Vom Schwimmen in Seen und Flüssen," *NM*, V² (1922), 637.

42. The decline of Musil's fame after *Vereinigungen* is described by Adolf Frisé in his introduction to Robert Musil's *Prosa, Dramen, späte Briefe* (Hamburg, 1957), p. 11.

43. "Ein Beginner (Robert Musil)," *NM*, IV² (1920/21), 860–62.

44. *NM*, V² (1921), 587–607. This rather negative assessment of "Grigia" appears in Wilfried Berghahn's *Robert Musil in Selbstzeugnissen und Bilddokumenten* (Reinbek bei Hamburg, 1963), p. 89.

45. Ulrich Karthaus, *Der andere Zustand: Zeitstrukturen im Werke Robert Musils* (Berlin, Bielefeld, München, Philologische Studien und Quellen 25; diss. Köln, 1964).

46. Efraim Frisch, *Zum Verständnis des Geistigen*, ed. Guy Stern (Heidelberg, 1963), pp. 133–34. Originally this review appeared in the *Frankfurter Zeitung* of 6 April 1933, p. 7.

47. *NM*, III (1919), 335–40.

48. Oskar Loerke, "Gedichte," *NM*, IV¹ (1920), 323–25.

49. *NM*, IV² (1920/21), 505–23.

50. *NM*, V² (1921), 552–65.

51. *Konstellationen*, ed. Stern, pp. 235–36. The review appeared in *Die Welt der Literatur*, IV (30 Apr. 1964), 7. Two such distinguished poets as Hermann Hesse and Wilhelm Lehmann have pointed out, within the past ten years, how neglected Loerke has been as a writer of fiction. See, respectively, *Die Weltwoche*, March 1956, and Oskar Loerke, *Gedichte und Prosa* (Frankfurt a.M., 1958), inside cover. The parallel descriptions appear in Loerke, *Reisetagebücher*, ed. Heinrich Ringleb, "Veröffentlichungen der deutschen Akademie für Sprache und Dichtung," XXXVII (Heidelberg, 1960), 259, and in "Nächtlicher Kamelritt" in *Gedichte und Prosa*, I, 227–28.

52. See, for example, Curtius, "Marcel Proust," *NM*, V² (1921), 745–61; Scotti, "Dante und Italien," *NM*, V¹ (1921/22), 381–90; Frank, "Amerika," *NM*, VI (1922), 257–74; Ulitz and Fega Frisch, see Fn 73 to Ch. VI; Frisch, "Dostojewskij," *NM*, V² (1921), 445–59.

53. "Gebet," *NM*, IV¹ (1920), 27–30.

54. "Die Intellektuellen: ihr Versagen—ihre Möglichkeiten," *NM*, III (1919), 438–39.

55. Verlaine's "Gedichte aus einer neuen Übertragung," trans. Wolfenstein, *NM*, IV² (1920/21), 617–21.

56. *NM*, VI (1922), 160–71, trans. of "La Nuit des six Jours."

57. Frisch's trans. of Morand's *Champions du monde* entitled *Weltmeister* appeared in 1930 in successive issues of the *Europäische Revue*, VI, 348–64, 424–48, 516–34, 595–614.

58. *NM*, V² (1921), 745–61.

59. Gide, "Über Stendhal (Vorrede zur 'Armance')," *NM*, V² (1921), 498–510. The negotiations are described in a letter from Curtius to Frisch of 23 July 1921.

60. "Drei Sonette aus Dantes Vita Nouva," *NM*, IV¹ (1920), 170–72; "Neue Dante-Übertragungen," *NM*, V¹ (1921/22), 391–93. In order to justify his new translation, Deinhardt submitted his own translation together with a copy of that by Stefan George. While conceding the beauty of George's translation, he felt that it contained errors in the formulation ("Prägungsfehler"). See letter from Deinhardt to Frisch of 7 Jan. 1920.

61. *NM*, V¹ (1921/22), 381–90; Hausenstein, "Dante und Giotto," *NM*, VI (1922), 573–79.

62. Emma Bonn, "Arnold Bennett," *NM*, V¹ (1921/22), 216–20.

63. Braun, "Amerikanische Gedichte," *NM*, VI (1922), 189–92.

64. Frank, "Amerika," *ibid.*, 257–74.

65. Frisch had written Frank of his plan to publish *Our America* in German translation as a book of the *"Neue Merkur* Verlag."

66. Frisch, see Fn 52; Frisch's introductory notes, *NM*, III (1919), 693 (Alexander

Blok); *NM*, ibid., 244 (Mikhail Saltykov-Shchedrin); *NM*, IV¹ (1920), 279 (Maxim Gorky); trans. Fega Frisch, *NM*, V² (1921), 460 (F. M. Dostoevski) and (Aleksei Remizov).

67. Tolstoi, "Unterhaltung müßiger Menschen," *NM*, III (1919), 78–82.

68. Salomé, "Tolstois Jugendtagebuch," *ibid.*, 137–139; Gorki, "Erinnerungen an Tolstoi," *NM*, IV¹ (1920), 279–95; Buldakov, "Korolenko's Besuch bei Tolstoi," *NM*, VI (1922), 84–87.

69. Frisch, *Zum Verständnis des Geistigen*, ed. Guy Stern (Heidelberg/Darmstadt, 1963), p. 165.

70. *NM*, VI (1922), 214–20.

71. The following were listed as members of the Society: Käte Kollwitz, Alfons Paquet, George Grosz, Tilla Durieux, Professor [Paul] Eltzbacher, Hans Baluschek, Heinrich Vogler, Ines Wetzel, Arthur Holitscher, Maximilian Harden, Dr. Kurt Pinthus, Gertrud Eysold, Karlheinz Martin, Max Barthel, Paul Zech, Martin Buber, Kurt Wolff, Lu Marten, Erwin Piscator, Wieland Herzfelde.

72. *NM*, V² (1921), 460.

73. The original of this review could not be located. An excerpt, apparently written by a translator whom Frisch employed, is among the papers of the *Neue Merkur*.

74. "Meier-Graefes Dostojewskij-Buch," 24 June 1926: "I myself have tried to show in a summarizing study how the unity of idea and personality developed out of [his] experience and how much further the idea of Dostoevski aimed than can be gleaned from his close ties to his contemporary ideological allies. Also that there is no figure in Dostoevski's work, which because of its character or convictions could be used in justification of the political and social condition in Russia."

75. Frisch's attitude towards the new Russia emerges in his letter to Arthur Kaufmann of 19 Feb. 1921: No reasonable person would doubt that a transference of equal or similar conditions into a sphere with different conditions is virtually impossible.

76. Frisch, "Dostojewskij," *NM*, V² (1921), 445.

77. *NM*, V¹ (1921/22), 264–71.

78. *NM*, III (1919), 244–65.

79. Block, *ibid.*, 693–706.

80. Remizov, "Aus dem flammenden Russland zu den Sternen: Alexander Block zum Gedächtnis," *NM*, V² (1921), 686–98.

87. Remizov, "Jugend," *NM*, VI (1922), 90–99.

82. Jessenin's "Anmerkung des Übersetzers," precedes "Russische Bauernpoesie," *NM*, V² (1921), 476–79.

Chapter 8

1. *Literarische Zeitschriften* (Stuttgart, 1962), II, 53.

2. *NM*, VII¹ (1923/24), 154–59.

3. "Zur Prosa der Gegenwart: Bemerkungen aus einem historischen Abriß," *NM*, VII² (1924), 568–77.

4. Wolfenstein, *ibid.*, 545, 553; Wegner, "Gedichte," *NM*, VII¹ (1923/24), 499–501.

5. See *Konstellationen*, ed. Stern, note on p. 340.

6. Albert Soergel, *Dichtung und Dichter der Zeit* (Leipzig, 1926), II, 584.

7. Quoted in Albert Soergel and Curt Hohoff, *Dichtung und Dichter der Zeit: Vom Naturalismus bis zur Gegenwart* (Düsseldorf, 1963), II, 209.

8. *Aufbau* (New York, 8 Mar. 1963), p. 62.

9. *NM*, VIII¹ (1924/25), 271–82.

10. *Das leere Haus: Prosa jüdischer Dichter*, ed. Karl Otten (Stuttgart, 1959), p. 614.

11. Lersch, "Dichtungen aus 'Mensch in Eisen,'" *NM*, VIII¹ (1924/25), 227–30.

12. *NM*, VIII² (1925), 569–71.

13. *NM*, VII¹ (1923/24), 189–99.

14. "German Reviews," *The Criterion*, VII² (April 1924), 368.

15. "Goethe über Schrifttum und Dichtung," *NM*, VIII² (1925), 766–67.

16. Burckhardt, *NM*, VII² (1924), 990–997. In a letter to me of 18 May 1962, Prof. Burckhardt wrote that he had sent his adaptations of Heraclitus to Frisch at that time because he was hoping for a publication in the *Neue Merkur* with which he felt very much in accord. After Burckhardt's first enthusiasm, which expressed itself in that poetry, he translated the Heraclitus-fragments precisely and once again.

17. Perutz, "Legende aus dem Ghetto," *NM*, VIII¹ (1924/25), 247–56; Munk (pseud. for Mrs. Martin Buber), "Irisches Heiligenleben," *ibid.*, 220–27.

18. Hesse, *ibid.*, 183–85; Mann, "Die roten Schuhe," *ibid.*, 186–92.

19. *NM*, VIII² (1925), 635–44.

20. "Einleitung" in *Boccaccios Werke*, ed. Max Krell (München, 1924), I, 9. Boccaccio signifies the actual liberation of the novella, its becoming flexible; he signifies art as well as entertainment. . . . He created the middle-class people of the Italian Renaissance with uncanny plasticity. . . . He left the cothurnus, he walked amongst the crowd, grasped its instincts, its passions, its sensuality without idealization. He did not submerge himself in coarseness; he ennobled the anecdote; he gave to it, at the most critical and titillating moments, an elegant turn, and made it something of wit and good taste.

21. *NM*, VIII¹ (1924/25), 15–37—republished in *Konstellationen*, ed. Stern, pp. 387–406.

22. *Bücher-Kommentare*, II (1964), 6. Since no reference work provides information about Boetticher past 1925, the following data is pertinent: While in Italy in 1925, he had a nervous breakdown and was confined in the Michaelis-Kloster, a sanatorium in Hildesheim. He was subsequently discharged, but had a relapse on a second journey to Italy, which, unlike the first breakdown, made all further work impossible. After his transfer to a sanatorium in Sonnenstein, Saxony, in 1941, he died a few months later, on 8 May 1941. (Based on a letter to me from Deaconess Elisabeth von Boetticher, the poet's sister, of 30 Oct. 1962.)

23. *NM*, VIII¹ (1924/25), 193–96.

24. *NM*, VII¹ (1923/24), 478–86.

25. Ponten, *ibid.*, 14–31. Elisabet Albert also rates Ponten's later novellas as "classical." She attributes his successful nature descriptions to his ascent of the Watzmann mountain, an experience that inspired the novella. See her "Nachwort" in Josef Ponten, *Der Gletscher* (Stuttgart, 1952), pp. 63–64.

26. *NM*, VII² (1924), 731–52.

27. *NM*, VII¹ (1923/24), 144–48.

28. *NM*, VI (Oct. 1922), 385–480.

29. Burschell, "Schwarzenbach: Ein Kapitel aus Jean Pauls Jugend," *NM*, VIII[1] (1924/25), 408–20, and "Jean Paul: Sein Leben im Umriß," *NM*, VIII (1925), 781–92; Wandrey, "Hölderlins Rhein-Hymne: Eine Exegese," *NM*, VII[2] (1924), 553–68; Alt, "Neue Hölderlin-Bücher," *NM*, VIII[1] (1924/25), 76–78; Hesse, "Ein Wort über Hölderlin," *ibid.*, 358–60; Ehl, "Stifter oder die Form," *NM*, VII[2] (1924), 753–63; Poeschel, "Voltaire," *NM*, VII[1] (1923/24), 241–43; Turel, "Gegen Voltaire," *NM*, VIII[2] (1925), 761–63.

30. Braun, "Hans Carossas 'Rumänisches Tagebuch,'" *NM*, VIII[2] (1925), 602–4; Poeschel, "Todes-Tanz," *NM*, VII[1] (1923–24), 429–31; Wandrey, "Zum Gedächtnis Carl Spittelers," *NM*, VIII[1] (1924–25), 515–18.

31. "Hofmannsthal und das Theater," *NM*, VII[2] (1924), 598–600.

32. *NM*, V[1] (1921/22), 394–407.

33. *NM*, VII[1] (1923/24), 362–92, this version is also discussed in "The First Version of Brecht / Feuchtwanger's *Leben Eduard des Zweiten von England* and its Relation to the Standard Text," by Ulrich Weisstein, *The Journal of English and Germanic Philology*, LXIX[2] (April 1970) 193–210.

34. Marianne Kesting, *Bertolt Brecht in Selbstzeugnissen und Bilddokumenten* (Reinbek bei Hamburg, 1959), p. 28.

35. A. W. G. R. [andall], "German Reviews," *The Criterion*, VII[2] (1924), 368.

36. *NM*, VII[1] (1923/24), 270–92.

37. *NM*, VII[2] (1924), 622–41.

38. W. E. Süskind, "Tordis," *NM*, VIII[1] (1924/25), 231–47. Klaus Mann, in his *Kind unserer Zeit*, supplies the biographical facts that led to the writing of "Tordis": "Ella [the girl from Norway] squatting on her couch between squashed hats and pillows, all of them the color of parrots, singing her ribald-melancholic ditties to the accompaniment of a lute: a snapshot that I preserve for myself as symbol for a certain, the most harmless and most endearing side of this whole period. [Of all writers] W. E. Süskind has captured her most charmingly and vividly. The Nordic and capricious girl twice grew into his most beautiful and vital women characters, first in 'Tordis' then in his novel *Jugend*."

39. *NM*, VIII[2] (1925), 870–901; quotes from pp. 893, 887, and 891, respectively.

40. Klaus Mann, *The Turning Point* (New York, 1942), p. 92. A similar description appears in his *Der Wendepunkt* (Frankfurt, 1952), p. 139.

41. *NM*, VIII[1] (1924/25), 130–41; quote from p. 136.

42. Quoted in Franz Lennartz, *Deutsche Dichter und Schriftsteller unserer Zeit*, 9th ed. (Stuttgart, 1963), p. 356.

43. *NM*, VII[1] (1923/24), 119–28; quote from 121.

44. *NM*, VIII[1] (1924/25), 186–92.

45. "Aphorismen; aus dem Nachlaß von Franz Kafka," *ibid.*, 197–198.

46. See his *Kritik* (Gütersloh, 1938), p. 215.

47. Mondt's "Literarisches Erinnerungsbüchlein" is the property of the Handschriftenabteilung der Stadtbibliothek München.

48. The correspondence between Kölwel and Wolfenstein is part of a private collection of the poet's widow, Mrs. Rosa Kölwel, Munich.

49. See W. E. Süskind, "Der Dichter Franz Kafka," *NM*, VII[2] (1924), 1010–14. Max Brod, in a conversation after his lecture on Leoš Janáček in Munich on 2 Oct. 1961, told me that he had selected the aphorisms for the *NM*.

50. Curtius, "Der Dichter Paul Valéry," *NM, ibid.*, 641–55; quote from 655. See also Paul Valéry, "Dichtungen," trans. Curtius, *ibid.*, 656–69.

51. For Rilke's translation, see his "Entwurf einer Schlange" and "Der Friedhof am Meer" in *Gesammelte Werke* (Leipzig, 1930), VI, 316, 288, which are translaions of Valéry's "Le Serpent" and "Le Cimetière Marin."

52. "Valéry Larbaud," *NM*, VIII¹ (1924/25), 38–55.

53. Curtius, "Aus französischen Zeitschriften," *NM*, VII¹ (1923/24), 160–65; Schoenberner, "Anatole France," *NM*, VII² (1925), 681–84; Goll, "Zwischen Paris und London," *NM*, VII¹ (1923/24), 926–29; Mann, "Victor Hugo and '1793'," *NM*, VIII² (1925), 861–70.

54. *NM*, VIII² (1925), 698–709, trans. Else Hadwiger.

55. *NM*, VII¹ (1923/24), 312–24, trans. Rudolf Nutt.

56. *NM*, VII² (1924), 522–36; VIII² (1925), 793–813; VIII¹ (1924/25), 104–10 respectively, all trans. Else Jaffé-Richthofen. The translation of *The Boy in the Bush* identifies only Lawrence as the author; the work is, of course, an adaptation of a Ms. by Mollie Skinner.

57. Velton, "Brief aus Amerika," *NM*, VIII² (1925), 679–84; Schoenberner, "Amerikanische Antitoxine," *ibid.*, 841–48.

58. Schoenberner's *Confessions of a European Intellectual* (New York, 1946), p. 176.

59. For fuller information on this "windfall," see John N. Hazard, *Law and Social Change in the U.S.S.R.* (London, 1953), which paraphrases a statute enacted as late as 1928: "works existing abroad, whether of Soviet citizens or foreigners, were not protected unless a treaty had been negotiated with the foreign State concerned."

60. Alexander Pushkin, "Epische Fragmente," trans. Fega Frisch; poem in text trans. Arnold Ulitz, *NM*, VII¹ (1923/24), 218–31.

61. "Dostojewskij und Pauline Susslow (Neues zu einer Dostojewskij-Biographie)," *NM*, VIII² (1925), 645–54.

62. F. M. Dostojewskij, "Briefe an seine Frau von der Puschkin-Feier," trans. Dmitri Umansky, *NM*, VII² (1924), 701–31.

63. Schoenberner, *Confessions*, p. 200.

64. "Pan Apolek," *NM*, VIII² (1925), 971–78.

65. *Ibid.*, 959.

Epilogue

1. (Berlin, 1927). Reprinted in *Das leere Haus*, ed. Karl Otten (Neuwied am Rhein, 1960), pp. 451–599.

2. E. Lach (pseud. for Frisch). Date and place of publication of this printed essay, found among Frisch's papers, is not ascertainable. From its location in Frisch's files, however, it apparently appeared in an Austro-Jewish journal in 1934.

3. Parts of Blei's editorial correspondence of the journal *März* are extant. I found them in a storage room of the Langen-Müller Verlag. Several significant letters have since been purchased by the Leo Baeck Institute, New York.

4. (Berlin, 1902). Pre-book publication in *Vossische Zeitung*, 1901.

5. Otten, "Nachwort," and "Biographische und Bibliographische Hinweise," *Das leere Haus*, pp. 608–10, 635–37.

6. L[udwig] M[arcuse], "Efraim Frisch: *Zenobi*," *Das Tagebuch*, 10 Dec. 1927, p. 2031.

7. Veröffentlichung der Deutschen Akademie für Sprache und Dichtung, XXIX (Heidelberg/Darmstadt, 1962), 98.

8. Reprinted in *Efraim Frisch; Zum Verständnis des Geistigen*, ed. Guy Stern, pp. 281–86.

9. *Das Theater: illustrierte Halbmonatsschrift*, ed. Christian Morgenstern (Berlin, 1904–5).

10. The scripts for these broadcasts are part of Frisch's literary legacy, now in the possession of the Leo Baeck Institute.

11. (Berlin, 1929).

12. The following note by Margareta Morgenstern appears in *Alles um des Menschen Willen: Briefe, Christian Morgenstern* (München, 1962), p. 437: "Walter Lindenthal, a friend of the Frisches, held a position as a jurist in the Berlin Municipal Council when Morgenstern met him. Before, he had belonged to the circle around Stefan George. He immigrated to Sweden and worked for the Bermann-Fischer publishing house."

13. Sternfeld-Tiedemann, *Deutsche Exil-Literatur*, p. 98.

14. Both review articles appeared under the pseudonym of E. H. Gast: "Zum Briefwechsel zwischen George und Hofmannsthal," *Mass und Wert*, II (March/April 1939), 544–49; "Die Geschichten Jaakobs," *Sammlung* I (1934), 245–49. The latter, a review of the first part of Thomas Mann's Joseph tetralogy, was received by Mann with rather mixed feelings: "Ephraim Frisch has written a very intelligent article about it [the book]; but since he still has concerns in Germany, his contribution can be published only under a pseudonym, and that cuts the joy in half." Letter of 30 Dec. 1933 to A. M. Frey in Thomas Mann, *Briefe, 1889–1936*, ed. Erika Mann (Frankfurt a.M., 1961), p. 342.

15. *Schofar: Lieder und Legenden jüdischer Dichter*, ed. Karl Otten (Neuwied am Rhein, 1962), pp. 56–63; quote from p. 63.

Selected Bibliography

Primary Sources

Correspondence with contributors to the *Neue Merkur* and their relatives and acquaintances, as well as records of supplementary interviews, all in my possession.

Frisch, Efraim. Nachlaß. In the archives of the Leo Baeck Institute, New York.

Georg Müller Verlag. Verlagskorrespondenz. In 1965 scattered items were in the possession of the Langen-Müller Verlag, but have since been sold, in part, to the Leo Baeck Institute, New York. I hold photostats.

Hausenstein, Wilhelm. Nachlaß. In the possession of Margot Hausenstein, München, and Reneé-Marie Hausenstein, London.

Kölwel, Gottfried. Nachlaß. In the possession of Kuratorium zur Pflege des dichterischen Werkes Gottfried Kölwel, z. Hd. Frau Rose Kölwel, or at the Handschriftenabteilung der Stadtbibliothek München.

Mann, Thomas. "Zur jüdischen Frage," reprinted in *AGR*, XXXIV (1967/68), No. 1, 36–40.

Morgenstern, Christian. *Alles um des Menschen willen*: *Briefe*. München, 1962. Additional letters to Efraim Frisch not in this collection are at the Leo Baeck Institute.

Müller, Georg. "Geleitwort des Verlegers," *1903–1908 Georg Müller Verlag* (München, 1908).

Der Neue Merkur: *Monatsschrift für geistiges Leben*. Published by Georg Müller, 1914–16; Verlag der Neue Merkur, 1919–Sept. 1922; O. C. Recht Verlag, Oct. 1922–Jan. 1923; Deutsche Verlags-Anstalt, Oct. 1923–25.

Der Neue Merkur. Redaktionskorrespondenz. With few exceptions in the archives of the Leo Baeck Institute, New York; scattered items at the Schiller-Museum, Marbach. Excerpts from additional letters quoted in Schumann und Heinimann, Zürich [Auktion 1943] *Katalog*, pp. 8–16; L'Art Ancien, Zürich and Haus der Bücher, Basel, "Auktion 41; Autographen, Zeichnungen, Graphik" (catalogue of an exhibit and auction in June 1966). A letter by Thomas Mann printed in Loewenstein (see Secondary Sources).

Secondary Sources

Anon. *Deutsche Verlagsanstalt, 1848–1923*: *Zweiundneunzig Handschriften von Autoren des Verlags mit einer geschichtlichen Einleitung*. Stuttgart and Berlin, 1923.

Anon. "Efraim Frisch," *Deutsche Exil-Literatur*, Wilhelm Sternfeld and Eva Tiedemann, Veröffentlichung der deutschen Akademie für Sprache und Dichtung, Darmstadt, XXIX. Heidelberg and Darmstadt, 1962.

Bauer, Michael. *Christian Morgenstern*: *Leben und Werk*, 4th ed. München, 1948.

Geiger, Hanns Ludwig. *Es war um die Jahrhundertwende*. München, 1953 (esp. pp. 114–24).

Hausenstein, Wilhelm (Pseud. Johann Armbruster). *Lux Perpetua: Summe eines Lebens aus dieser Zeit.* München, 1947.

Hüttig, Helmut. *Die politischen Zeitschriften der Nachkriegszeit in Deutschland: von der ersten Milderung der Pressezensur bis zum Locarnovertrag*, Diss. Leipzig. Magdeburg, 1928.

Koch, Walter. "Die Ausgewogenheit von Qualität und Quantität als verlegerische Aufgabe (demonstriert am Beispiel des Verlegers Georg Müller)," Unpublished diss. Müchen, 1950.

Lehmann, Wilhelm. "Mühe des Anfangs," in his *Sämtliche Werke*, II, 385–452. Gütersloh, 1962.

Lion, Ferdinand. "Der Neue Merkur" in "Symposion, Zeitschriften unserer Zeit," *Akzente*, Sonderheft 10 (1963), pp. 34–36.

Loewenstein, Kurt. "Thomas Mann zur jüdischen Frage," *Bulletin des Leo Baeck Instituts*, XXXVIII (1967), No. 37, pp. 1–59.

Mann, Klaus. *Kind dieser Zeit.* München, 1932.

———. *The Turning Point: Thirty-Five Years in This Century.* New York, 1942.

———. *Der Wendepunkt.* Frankfurt a.M., 1953.

Morgenstern, Margareta, "Nachwort" and "Anmerkungen," pp. 409–41, in *Alles um des Menschen Willen: Briefe, Christian Morgenstern.* München, 1962.

Nagle, Johann and Jakob Zeidler. *Deutsch-Österreichische Literaturgeschichte*, IV, 1393. Wien, 1931–37.

Otten, Karl. "Nachwort" and "Efraim Frisch," pp. 602–21, 635–37, in Otten's anthology *Das leere Haus: Prosa jüdischer Dichter.* Stuttgart, 1959.

———. "Einführung" and "Efraim Frisch," pp. 6–25, 549–59, in Otten's anthology *Schofar: Lieder und Legenden jüdischer Dichter.* Neuwied a.R., 1962.

Paeschke, Hans. "Vorbemerkung," in "Sebastian und eine Variation" by Robert Walser and Peter O. Chotjewitz, *Merkur*, XXI (1967), 247.

Pross, Harry. *Literatur und Politik; Geschichte und Programme der politisch-literarischen Zeitschriften im deutschen Sprachgebiet seit 1870.* Olten und Freiburg i.Br., 1963.

Schlawe, Fritz. "Der Neue Merkur," pp. 52–53, in his *Literarische Zeitschriften: Teil II 1910–1933.* Sammlung Metzler No. 24. Stuttgart, 1962.

Schmidtbonn, Wilhelm. *Die unerschrockene Insel* (esp. p. 121). München, 1925.

Schoenberner, Franz. *Confessions of a European Intellectual.* New York, 1946. Revised and enlarged German version: *Bekenntnisse eines europäischen Intellektuellen.* Icking and München, 1964.

Stern, Guy. "A Case for Oral Literary History: Conversations with or about Morgenstern, Lehmann, Reinacher and Thomas Mann," *GQ*, XXXVII (1964), 487–97.

———. "Efraim Frisch and the *Neue Merkur*," *Yearbook of the Leo Baeck Institute*, VI (1961), 121–51.

——— "Efraim Frisch: Leben und Werk," pp. 13–38, in Stern's anthology *Efraim Frisch: Zum Verständnis des Geistigen.* Veröffentlichungen der deutschen Akademie für Sprache und Literatur, Darmstadt, XXXI. Heidelberg and Darmstadt, 1961.

———. "Einleitung" and "Efraim Frisch," pp. 7–9, 133–34, in Stern's anthology *Konstellationen: Die besten Erzählungen aus dem "Neuen Merkur" 1914–1925.* Stuttgart, 1964.

————. "Hanns Braun, Kritiker der zwanziger Jahre," in "Festschrift für Hanns Braun," *Publizistik*, VIII (1963), 572–75.

Süskind, W[ilhelm] E[manuel]. "Damals in der Neckarstrasse," pp. 135–144, *Im 110. Jahr: Deutsche Verlags-Anstalt Almanach*. Stuttgart, 1958.

————. "Mit sechzig Jahren . . . Ein Selbstportrait," *Welt und Wort*, XVI (June 1961), 179–80.

————. "Vorwort," pp. 7–24, in Wilhelm Hausenstein, *Licht unter dem Horizont: Tagebücher von 1942 bis 1946*. München, 1967.

————. "Wilhelm Hausenstein," *Handbuch der deutschen Gegenwartsliteratur*, ed. Herman Kunish and Hans Hennecke. München, 1965.

Ude, Karl. "Rückblick auf den Neuen Merkur," *Welt und Wort*, XVIII (January 1963), 30.

Weigand, Wilhelm. *Welt und Weg: Aus meinem Leben*. Bonn, 1940.

Wolff, Kurt. *Briefwechsel eines Verlegers*, pp. 173, 552, 556. ed. Bernhard Zeller and Ellen Otten. Darmstadt, 1966.

Index